Midland Railway Locomotives

by
Stephen Summerson

Volume 1

A Comprehensive Primary Account
General Survey 1844-1922,
Growth and Development,
Boilers, Tenders, Fittings and Details

Acknowledgements

My early researches in official records were carried out at the British Railways Board archives at 66 Porchester Road London in a typically severe 'stool and desk' railway Clerks' environment. Nevertheless every assistance was given to the researcher and the excellent service is hereby acknowledged. At this distance in time, a little story concerning this somewhat austere establishment may now be given. There were no refreshment facilities available on the premises and the consumption of food and drink in the Reading Room was of course not allowed. The staff understood the requirements of the day visitor, and one day, the duty staff were feeling the weight of their responsibilities somewhat and I was advised that as the consumption of food was not permitted in the Reading Room I 'could go out there' pointing to a door at the end of the room. 'Out there' was in fact a platform on the open metal fire escape, cantilevered off the side of the building, two floors up! It was a bit breezy. The subsequent opening of the Public Record Office at Kew, to which the Porchester Road Archive was transferred and the National Railway Museum at York, provided the superior facilities and improved access to the Company records which has greatly facilitated the study of our railway heritage. The MR records at Kew come principally in the RAIL 491 series with the relevant LMS archive at the RAIL 418 and 422.

The great part of official MR records are now in the care of these two august establishments and thanks are due to the staff at both, for their unfailing courtesy and help in the search for information. At York the more personal attention possible has been especially appreciated, in particular from Jane Elliott and Lynne Thurston in the Reading Room and Philip Atkins the Librarian. The formal permission of the British Railways Board, the Public Record Office and the National Railway Museum to use the material in their care is hereby gratefully acknowledged.

The ready help and advice from many like-minded historians has contributed significantly to this account, from the loan of official documents in private collections to the chance remark on a particular matter and to all, my thanks are due, in particular to: the late David Bayes, Andrew Biwandi, the late G. Harry Daventry, John Edgington, Bob Essery, Roger Farrant of the GER Society, the late Vic Forster, Dr John Gough, Geoff Goslin, Mark Higginson, D. Ibbotson, Brian Radford, Peter Rowledge, David Tee, John True, Hugh Ware, the late Geoffrey Webb and Geoff Woodward. Their contributions to the 'jigsaw' have been invaluable.

Thanks are also due to the Institution of Mechanical Engineers for permission to quote from Charles Markham's paper of 1860 to that Institution, on coal burning in locomotives.

In a work of this nature the original script has to be transcribed into a form acceptable to the printer and my thanks and appreciation are due to Chris Missenden whose ability to read my manuscript has been a constant source of amazement as the narrative has progressed.

Finally to my wife Maureen, my thanks for putting up with it over all these years. When we married in 1960, she thought that steam engines and my interest in them were *both* on the way out!

Front cover upper. **A resplendent rebuilt Kirtley 800 class 2-4-0. No.822 was photographed shortly after renumbering to 822A in May 1903.**

Front cover lower. **The essence of Midland power in 1922. Compound No.1024, superheated in March 1922 stands in Kentish Town Yard with the familiar 'Read Brothers Bottling Stores' behind.**

First published in the United Kingdom in 2000
by Irwell Press
59A, High Street, Clophill,
Bedfordshire MK45 4BF

Printed in Malta by Interprint Limited

Contents

In Preparation

Volume 2   *The Kirtley Classes*
Volume 3   *Johnson Classes Part I :*
    The Slim Boiler Passenger Tender Engines
    Passenger and Goods Tank Engines
Volume 4   *Johnson Classes Part II:*
    The Goods and later Passenger Tender Engines
    Deeley, Fowler and LTSR Classes

Frontispiece: Johnson's Masterpiece. Compound No.2634 of September 1903

Preface

For as long as I can remember, I have been fascinated by railways and steam locomotives. The nearest lineside vantage spot when I was a child, was a field near Limbury Sidings, a coal yard between Luton and Leagrave on the main line to St Pancras and here I used to persuade my mother to take me to watch the trains. Now Limbury Road signal box, which controlled the goods lines only and access to the sidings, was normally closed, being opened by a porter-signalman when entry was required for traffic. Thus its signals were usually 'off'. With child-like logic I insisted to my mother that if the signal was at 'go', there must be a train coming and in due time it always did. Mother of course was unaware of the niceties of boxes switched out and was in no position to argue! The 'long time train' was an institution in our house for many years. Later on, when old enough to go on my own, I went in the evenings to watch the daily shunting ritual.

At about 5pm an 0-6-0 arrived, usually 3F No.3245, which then set about noisily segregating the empty wagons from the rest. About two and a half hours later another 0-6-0 arrived on the down goods line with some half dozen empty wagons and a brake van. This was the 7pm St Albans-Wellingborough. The engine, usually No.3801, left its train on the main line and went inside to collect the empty coal wagons from Limbury. After a decent interval it emerged, with much black smoke, hauling a batch of twenty or so rattling empties to attach to the rump of its train. Its departure was impressive, regulator well open and in full gear, but then the driver shut off, heaved on a lever and opened the regulator again. Now the puffs were quieter, as it slowly went up to Leagrave and away to the north. But what was going on? Why did the driver heave on a lever? What *were* Nos.3245 and 3801? How old were they? How many of them were there and what did that little plate with 14C on it fitted to the smokebox mean? This youthful curiosity started a lifetime of interest in the locomotives of the Midland Railway, the fruits which are now presented in this History.

The engine which started it all. Class 3F No.3245 in the shed yard at St. Albans 14 March 1936. 'If there's work to be done, give me a class 3 any day.' R.C. Jarvis/Mid Rail Photographs.

'Authority to proceed' – Lines clear at Derby North Junction spring 1957. S. Summerson collection.

V

'Built in the Company's shops at Derby' – No.1044, the last of the famous Compounds in the erecting shop for a 'service repair', on 8 November 1931. S. Summerson collection.

The Midland power classification system was retained by the LMS and BR. No.500 is seen here displaying the 2in numeral '2' on the cabside soon after 'rebuilding' to 483 class in October 1912. Note also the bogie brakes, bye-pass valve cover and bogie splash plates.

Chapter 1 - Introduction

The locomotive history of the Midland Railway is a very substantial and complex subject and one is very conscious of these factors when describing the evolution and development of the various engine classes. Apart from the stock inherited from the constituent companies of the 1840s*, the Midland owned a total of some 4,131 engines at one time or another, purchased, absorbed, or built in the Company's shops at Derby, over a span of nearly eighty years from 1844 to 1922. Many engines were extensively rebuilt, this term covering a wide variety of alterations from cylinders to an engine new in virtually every respect, but shown as rebuilt for accountancy purposes. The precise figure of new engines depends on where the line is drawn between a rebuild and a new engine and for clarity Table 1A has been included to show the construction of the figure quoted. Engines affected by the complex changes of wheel arrangement in the Kirtley era are regarded as rebuilds and are excluded, but included in the total are all five of the Kirtley 156 class 2-4-0s of 1873/4 (three renewals and two rebuilds), the twenty six well tanks (all except four extensive transformations of various earlier engines) and 142 of the Fowler 483 class superheater rebuilds of Johnson 4-4-0s (fifteen more were completed by the LMS). Rebuilding in these cases was so extensive that they were virtually new engines of different classes and this status assists description of the

historical narrative. Unravelling the history has proved a fascinating and sometimes frustrating task.

*That is, the Midland Counties, Birmingham & Derby Junction, North Midland, Bristol & Gloucester, Leicester & Swannington, Sheffield & Rotherham and Leeds & Bradford Railways.

Sources

So far as is practical, Official Records have been used, supplemented by other information and observations which may be regarded as authentic. The Kirtley period is primarily covered with information from Board minutes, the Committee of Management 1844-49 and Locomotive Committee from 1849 onwards. F.H. Clarke made a copy of the 1849 locomotive list and an official 1860 list has also survived. Other official records surviving from the Kirtley period 1844-73 are sparse. Many were destroyed in the periodic clear out of old material which occurred from time to time, particularly during Deeley's period of office, 1904-09, and again during the 1939-45 war. Thus, the further back towards 1844 that researches are directed, the less evidence there is remaining. However, a great deal can be gleaned about this period from subsequent records which have been retained and it is also fortunate indeed that F.H. Clarke who worked at Derby from the early 1850s kept meticulous records of his own which eventually passed into the Dewhurst collection.

A study of these reveals *inter alia*, a knowledge of Locomotive Committee decisions which, when compared to the actual minutes indicates that Clarke had access to official material. This adds standing to his records, thereby filling gaps in the formal records. These sources provide a sound base for study and are supplemented by the results of research undertaken many years ago by B Baxter, L Wilson, E Craven and W Beckerlegge. Much of this was published by Stephenson Locomotive Society in their journal and subsequently by D Baxter. G H Daventry was most helpful in a lengthy correspondence in clarifying detail and providing additional information. Therefore, a reasonable outline of pre-1873 history can be given. Johnson produced a numerical classification of the Kirtley engines and this additionally provides a good deal of boiler information not found elsewhere. Importantly, it enables the change from Kirtley to Johnson boilers in the reboilering of the double framed 0-6-0s to be pinpointed.

From the Johnson period onward it is fortunate that retained official records are more plentiful. The Locomotive Committee minutes, both Midland and LMS, Registers of 1888, 1901 and 1908 together with the Derby Order books from 1874 provided a substantial primary source of material upon which to build. The 1908 Register is of particular value in that it was clearly constructed from records going back to the Kirtley era

Midland Royalty. 483 class superheater rebuild No.502 of May 1912, prepared for Royal Train duties on 11 July 1912 with Royal Cypher in place of the Midland Crest. Note the carriage warming gauge on the tender. National Railway Museum.

No.1570 of the 1562 class on the traverser at Kentish Town in the six months between renumbering to 336 in June and rebuilding to Class 2 with an H boiler in December 1907. National Railway Museum.

which were not shown in the earlier Registers and which are now lost to us, so adding more useful data from that period. A comment is appropriate here on one point regarding these Registers. This relates to the fitting of large cylinders which occurred in many instances. It was shown in several ways.

1 When an engine was reboilered.
2 With a specific date between reboilerings.
3 Without a specific date between reboilerings.

In the class tabulations, case 3 above is shown as 'by date', the date being that of the next reboilering or 'by 1901' if the

1888 Register shows the undated change, which is shown as effected in the 1901 Register. The value of these principal sources is vastly enhanced by numerous other pieces in both public and private collections and these are summarised below.

Costs of Engines, repairs, train mileage, machinery, stores, running expenses

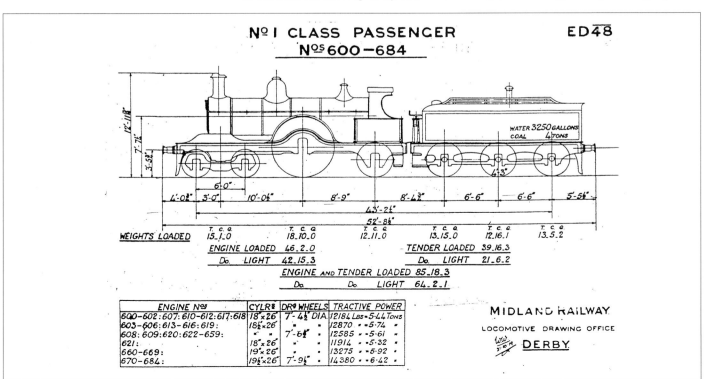

The perils of Engine Diagrams. ED48 of 1919 covers all the 4-2-2s but shows the dimensions for Nos. 660-669 only!

The fascination of detail. No.69A of the rebuilt Kirtley 890 class at South Lynn. Note the new crest on the *leading* splasher dating the photograph to 1906-7, pre-1907 duplicate number on Johnson smokebox door (107 in December 1907), new frames (convex curve on top at front) one piece chimney and, 10 (Leicester) shed plate on the spectacle plate. National Railway Museum.

etc. is a remarkable volume which despite its title, contains information principally relating to the years 1871-83, regarding engines broken up, miscellaneous engine purchase, boilers, engines renewed and rebuilt, charged to revenue, work in progress covering orders from 1874-82 and some lists of tenders broken up.

S.W. Johnson notebooks - new work in progress 1880-88 and Patent Brakes contain much of importance. The latter is an invaluable record of the various brakes fitted to different engines which sheds much light on the statistics quoted in the Locomotive Committee minutes in the saga of continuous brakes set out in Chapter 5. Locomotive Specifications, Drawing Registers and Drawing Schedules and Sketch Registers have been invaluable regarding fittings and details, the Registers also revealing drawing numbers for several interesting 'might have beens' which clearly proceeded no further.

A particularly interesting file, containing circulars and letters received at Sheffield in the years 1900-05, covers the routines of locomotive maintenance in correspondence from the Divisional Locomotive Superintendent at Derby. The tensions between the locomotive and traffic departments are well seen in a missive of 4 October 1900 ... 'If you have the least doubt about the safety of any boiler in your charge, do not hesitate to stop the engine at once, no matter *how hard* [author's emphasis] you may be pressed for power by the Traffic Department...' There is much else of interest besides, which is noted in the narrative. Engine diagrams of 1903, 1905 and 1919 are useful statistical items, the former especially, as it is more comprehensive and includes details of a few of the remaining miscellaneous absorbed tank engines not found elsewhere.

The Loading Tables covering the period 1896-1910 for Main Line Passenger engines reveal the ever increasing complexity involved in classifying engines for power, which eventually resulted in the system adopted by the LMS and BR to the end of steam.

The Working Timetables with their Appendices may be thought to be an unlikely source of locomotive information, but a great deal has been gleaned from this source relating to headlamps, motor carriage and motor train operations and even surprisingly, the allocation of new large boiler 0-6-0s in 1904, amongst a host of minor items. Loading gauge restrictions for trains to Poplar and the Great Eastern line provided an entertaining pursuit which led to the proceedings of the GER Way and Works Committee before it was solved! Similarly the loan of several 4-4-0Ts from the Midland and Great Northern Joint Committee in 1906 led to the minutes of that body and

of the Officers Conference in order to complete the picture.

The record of tenders is much enhanced by the 1910 tender diagram book and the three files on Reports and Experiments covering the years 1907-22, whilst concerned with problems and details, were a mine of background information on such matters as safety valves on the larger boilers. A contemporary file 'Classification of various Engine Details' provides much statistical information between 1909 and 1931 and the Reports on Indicator and Coal consumption Tests do just that between 1910-1919. A precious survival is very dog-eared and much thumbed book of records kept in the Erecting Shop. A careful assessment of the information recorded therein and the handwriting of the entries over the years suggests that the original entries were made about the end of the 1913 or early 1914, with information included back to about 1906, as details of the Kirtley 0-6-0s sold to Italy in that year are included. It is a mine of building, rebuilding, cutting up dates and, amongst other things revealed the elusive identity of all the engines which were fitted with vacuum controlled regulators for motor train working in 1908-9.

Allocations are derived from various sources. F.H. Clarke kept records over a long period. His 1880 list agrees precisely with that of Walter Laidlaw and Ahrons

LMS ENGINE HISTORY CARD. CR.204

(CME)

DIVISION ___MIDLAND___   NUMBER ___1854___

~~PASSENGER TENDER SHUNTING SUPERHEATER~~   CLASS (MP) __1__   NAME OR No OF TYPE

GOODS TANK NON SUPERHEATER   WHEEL TYPE __0-6-0__   WHEEL BASE (E & T) __15'-6"__

EMPTY WEIGHT __36-18¹⁹__ WORKING WEIGHT __45-9__ DIA OF DRIVING WHEELS __4'-7"__

CYLINDERS No. __2__   DIA __17"__   STROKE __24"__   OVERALL LENGTH OVER BUFFERS (E & T) __30'-1⅝"__

CLASS OF BOILER __A__   TUBES No __194__   COPPER   BOILER PRESSURE __140__ LBS

FIREBOX GRATE AREA __14·5 SQ.FT.__   TRACTIVE POWER AT 85% __15,007 LBS.__

BRAKES VACUUM (Pump EJECTOR)   VALVES SLIDE   MOTION (TYPE) STEPHENSON   CARRIAGE WARMING WITH/WITHOUT
STEAM __E__

BUILT BY __M.R. Co.__   DATE BUILT __JULY, 1895__

COST £ _____ CHARGED TO _____ DATE "IMPROVED" 1/12/28. # 29/4/36

COST OF "IMPROVEMENT" £33-10-8 CHARGED TO Q+J Suspense a/c #Capital a/c   TOTAL COST OF "IMPROVED" ENGINE £
#16.2.2

DATE REPLACED & TRANSFERRED TO DUPLICATE STOCK _____ REPLACED BY No.

AMOUNT TRANSFERRED £ _____ FROM _____ A/c TO _____ A/c

DATE TAKEN OUT OF TRAFFIC _____ DATE BROKEN UP _____ SCRAP VALUE

CREDITED TO _____ A/c.   MILEAGE UP TO DEC. 31ST. 1926 __562·217__

BOILER CHANGES 729593

DATE	PARTICULARS OF BOILERS FITTED							PARTICULARS OF BOILERS TAKEN OUT				
	VALUE £	FROM	DATE NEW	MILEAGE	Belpaire or Round Top	Belpaire or Round Top	HOW DISPOSED OF	RECOVERED VALUE		MILEAGE	COST OF REPR
13-6-30	B 128 / F 127 / 19 11	1777	May 1916 Aug 1913 June 1927	210,667 524,820 73,242	R.T. R.T (r.4)	R.T. RT(M4)	Reusable Scrap	B 74 11 33		589,300 77,498 310,799	
15.4.36		1919									

*Impt. Fitting Carriage Warming Apparatus (Serial No.2230).
NWO 3138 Flg water desanding app. #16.2.2

RENEWAL PROVISIONS.

YEAR	COST PER TON	REPLACEMENT COSTS							LIFE		RENEWAL PROVISION		R.P. No.
		ENGINE INCLUDING BOILER			BOILER			ENGINE EXCLDG. BOILER					
		GROSS COST	NETT RESIDL. VALUE	NETT COST	GROSS COST	NETT RESIDL. VALUE	NETT COST	ENGINE R. REPLACEMENT COST	ENGINE EXCLDG BOILER	BOILER	ENGINE EXCLDG BOILER	BOILER	
	£	£	£	£	£	£	£	£	YRS.	YRS.	£	£	
1929	80.23	2960	323	2637	592	192	400	2237	46	19	49	21	
1930	80.23	2960	323	2637	592	192	400	2237	46	19	49	21	
1932	67.12	2480	153	2327	537	127	410	1917	46	19	42	22	17
1933	66.81	2469	173	2296	589	128	466	1830	46	19	40	25	
1934	66.16	2445	161	2284	525	112	413	1841	46	19	41	22	
1935	66.84	2470	186	2284	548	114	434	1850	60	20	31	22	

ENGINE NUMBER

The Engine History Cards provide a wealth of detail; No.1854 had carriage warming apparatus added on 1 December 1928.

has left us a record written out on 23 June 1892 which includes engines built up to March 1892 and is presumed to refer to that date. The MR list of 1914 and amendments to 1920 covers the late Midland period and increasingly through the LMS and BR periods, official records are available. Dates for rebuilding, withdrawal and so on in the Midland period were recorded as the month and year but, some time in 1923, the LMS introduced the 4-weekly method of recording. This produced thirteen such periods, per year and every 5-7 years an odd 'filler' week to balance the calendar. This was not brought fully into use in the 1908 Register until the third quarter of 1924. The class tabulations reflect this, individual dates being shown as 'P9/24' and so on,

and it does throw up some peculiarities. The period ending 13/33 for instance ended on 30/12/33 while the year before, the same 13 period ended precisely, on 31/12/32. Other times through the year showed 'P7/33' for instance, ending on 15/7/33. A full tabulation of the dates will be given in a subsequent volume.

In its efficiency drive of the 1920s, the LMS determined upon keeping records for each engine. The company produced individual History Cards, and their use commenced in January 1927. For those engines which lasted into the late 1950s, the records necessitated the use of three successive cards. As the need for a second and then a third card arose, so the opportunity was taken to redesign the layout. This produced some odd results,

particularly in regard to boilers. The first card showed the origin of a replacement boiler, the second also showed the boiler number, but the third only showed the number! This last card design also had space to show the works where repairs were carried out which is of added interest in the BR era. LMS policy was to discard the records when an engine was withdrawn and those that remain, are the results of a 'dustbin rescue exercise' in the 1960s. So far as is known, no cards remain, apart from those for 2-4-0 No.12, for engines withdrawn before the end of 1948; the first card only survives for engines withdrawn in 1949, whilst all cards are present for MR withdrawals from 1950 to the end. Incomplete as they are, they form a valuable resource. At the same time as the Engine History card came the Tender History card and the issue of tender numbers for the Midland tenders and these have materially assisted in recording the tender allocations.

Classification of alterations, modifications and experiments by the LMS was introduced under two main headings - New Work Orders and Displaced Work Orders. Thus for example NWO2446 related to Exhaust Steam Injectors and DWO 5864 related to steel instead of copper boiler tubes. The Derby Order book system was continued by the LMS and in 1938 the Job Number system was introduced. This was a Company wide system of issuing instructions relating to Additions, Alterations and Improvements to Rolling Stock and was backdated regarding some works in progress as noted in the memo of 28 March 1940 opposite.

Job numbers were issued to the works concerned, the works in turn then issuing its own Order Number for executing the instructions. The fitting of Continuous Blowdown apparatus for example, illustrates the way the system worked. Authority was given by Mechanical and Electrical Committee Minute No.924 of

Memorandum relating to Job Numbers

To Messrs. Lemon
Rankin
Williamson
Bond
Pugson
Peters
& Anthony
Copy to Mr. Stanier.

K.8504
T.28/2/12

Ext.693

28th March   40.

Additions, Alterations and Improvements
to Locomotives and Rolling Stock.

As you are aware a system of issuing
instructions, relating to Additions, Alterations and
Improvements to Rolling Stock, under Job Numbers was
instituted some two years ago.

I am sending herewith a copy of a
complete list of all Job Numbers allocated to date and which
you will no doubt find very useful for reference purposes.

As further Job Numbers are allocated,
these will be supplied in a convenient form for inserting in
the enclosed book, and as only one copy of this is available
for each workshop, I shall be glad if you will arrange for
it to be issued to the person most concerned with the
issuing of instructions relative to these jobs.

Detailed instructions in the standard
form have been or will be issued for all jobs subsequent to
No.5030, but it has been found necessary to allocate Nos.
4866 to 5019 inclusive to works which were already in progress
and which are not covered by the standard form of instruction.

Please acknowledge receipt.

26 February 1936. Instructions were issued on 20 March 1936 and Job Number 5016 was allocated. Several series of Derby Works Orders were then issued, the first for various MR classes having Order Numbers between 9545 and 9558, on 21 April 1936 under NWO3098. This system was used latterly for several minor jobs. One of the last to affect MR engines was Job Number 5739 of 11 January 1955, for spark arresters to a pair of class 1F 0-6-0Ts.

LMS test reports and Instructions for Rail Motor Trains provide much background information whilst the Derby Works Shopping lists - the weekly list of engines to be admitted and the proposed repair - covering the post war years 1947-62 provides a fascinating insight on how the system worked. Engines of classes being withdrawn were sometimes proposed for 'Special Examination' and there was much rejoicing by enthusiasts in the know if the next weekly list included the same engine - 'now to have General Repair'; 'Now to be cut up' was the more common entry. 'Even up to 1962 engines survived. Class 4F No.43949 was submitted for breaking up on 25 April 1962, but in week ending 5 May 1962 was agreed for General Repair. The preserved Compound No.1000 was ready for departure to Clapham Museum on 30 November 1962 and the last Midland engine to receive any class of repair was 0-4-0T No.41535 noted ex works on Derby shed on 29 September 1963.

In all these records, it is salutary to remember that because authority was given for a certain purpose, it does not necessarily mean that it was carried out.

41748 near Cam on the Dursley branch in June 1957 passing fields which had suffered fires as a result of the efforts of the branch engines. This was before the fitting of spark arresters (to job No. 5739) in 1955. S. Summerson collection.

'Big Emma' No.2290 nears completion in the Erecting shop on 3 November 1919. Note the second axle cranked to provide clearance to the inside connecting rods.

TABLE 1A MR ENGINE SUMMARY 1844-1922

CLASSES	NUMBER	NOTES
KIRTLEY		
2-2-2 1844-9	61	
2-2-2 1850-66	110	
2-4-0 1844-9	40	
2-4-0 1856-75	240	Includes 2 'rebuilt' 1873/4 to 156 class from large 70 and 150 classes
4-2-0	2	
2-4-0T	10	
4-4-0T	6	
0-4-4T	26	
0-6-0WT large	4	
0-6-0WT large	10	'rebuilt' from various 0-6-0s
0-6-0WT small	12	'rebuilt' from 2-2-2s
0-6-0T	10	
0-6-0 1844-9	55	includes 4 delivered Jan 1850
0-6-0 inside frames 1851/57	9	
0-6-0 straight framed double frames	260	
0-6-0 480 class double frames	225	
0-6-0 700 class double frames	321	
ABSORBED ENGINES		
Miscellaneous 1851-84	65	
Severn & Wye 1895	6	
LTSR 1912	94	
JOHNSON		
2-4-0	135	
4-4-0	30	Not rebuilt with larger boilers
4-4-0	235	Rebuilt with larger boilers.
4-4-0 Belpaire	80	Includes modified engines by Deeley
4-4-0 Compound	5	
4-2-2	95	
0-4-4T	205	
0-4-0ST	30	
0-6-0T small	280	
0-6-0T large	60	
2-6-0	40	
0-6-0 small	865	
0-6-0 large	70	Includes modified engines by Deeley
DEELEY		
4-4-0	10	
4-4-0 Compound	40	
0-4-0T	10	Includes 5 'rebuilds' of Johnson 0-4-0STs
0-6-4T	40	
FOWLER		
4-4-0 483 class	142	15 more completed by LMS
0-10-0	1	
0-6-0	192	
Total	**4131**	

Conversely, where no formal authority was issued, it does not necessarily mean that a certain job was not done. Authority was sometimes changed during the course of a job which resulted in figures 'not adding up'. The rebuilding of tenders from inside to outside springs below the platform was a case in point in this last case. Here, it appears that formal orders were deemed necessary after the work had commenced. The fitting of double cabs to tank engines was sometimes as a result of a formal order and sometimes not. Occasionally, orders were cancelled and sometimes work was not completed. Where these departures occurred, appropriate reference is made in the narrative. In a work of this nature, accuracy is paramount and study of the various archive records, many hand-written, reminds one of the old adage - to be good is easy; to be excellent is difficult and to be error free is a counsel of perfection. The official records usually show a good correlation but some significant differences have been noted in a few cases and several minor ones also. It only needs a slip of the pen or an entry on the wrong line to produce an error.

Firstly, the 1849 locomotive list shows building dates to the day and the 1860 list shows, in respect of engines surviving at that date, building dates which in most cases agree. But in some twenty cases the dates are different with discrepancies varying up to twelve months. The reasons may be related to completion dates, hand-over date or dates to traffic, but the inconsistency gives no pointers and no conclusions may be drawn. The 1860 list was clearly used subsequently as a reference, as an official list of MR locomotive stock dated 7 June 1918 which shows the number of engines and their year of build included a solitary tank engine of 1847. This could only refer to well tank No.1600, the origins of which was a Crampton 4-2-0 of October 1848 (1849 list) or December 1847 (1860 list).

In the subsequent narrative regarding pre-1849 engines remaining in 1860, the 1849 dates have been preferred. A further source of difference again involving the 1860 list, arises from the fact that the building date of engines built at Derby from June 1856 to December 1864 was shown both here and in later official listings in six month periods ending June and December, with occasional odd exceptions. Daventry/Baxter quote dates to the month which generally, but not always, fall within the appropriate Derby period. Here the inconsistency is consistent, in that where Daventry differs, the dates are always into the next six month period by up to three months. This therefore suggests dates to traffic rather than dates of completion. Again relating to withdrawal dates there are a few inconsistencies with official records. The conclusion to be drawn from all this seems to be that it is preferable not to favour absolutely one source or the other, as much appears to hinge on the question of the interpretation of events in distant years past, rather than a view that this date or that is incorrect. However, where an official date is available that is used, with comments as appropriate. Other odd cases of inconsistency in later records are referred to in the appropriate class chapters.

The value of each of the records which have survived is significant, but they are of course immensely enhanced when considered together. Each may be likened to the pieces of a jigsaw, which, when combined provide a picture of the whole. I hope that the results of researching the pieces and assembling the jigsaw, however imperfect gives as much pleasure to the reader as its compilation has to me.

The whole has been carefully checked in pursuit of the said 'counsel of perfection' but if errors remain, the responsibility is mine alone. The stage is therefore now set to survey in the following chapters, the development, high noon and demise of the Midland Railway locomotive fleet.

Official Sources
MR
Board Minutes 1844 *et seq*
Committee of Management 1846-9
Way and Works Committee 1849 *et seq*
Traffic Committee 1849 *et seq*
Locomotive and Stores Committee 1849 *et seq*
Carriage and Wagon Committee 1873 *et seq*
General Purposes Committee 1870 *et seq*
Locomotive Registers 1860, 1888, 1901, 1908
Order numbers which concern locomotive Drawing Office 1874-1939
Derby Works Order books 1889-1922
S.W. Johnson – Locomotive notes 1880-88
S.W. Johnson – Patent Brakes 1879-83
Orders for locomotive Boilers
List of Engines built by Contractors
Drawing Register 1873-1905
Drawing Register 1905-1932
Drawing Schedules
Locomotive Specifications
Sketch lists
Classification in detail of Engines (Johnson classification 1874-82)
Classification of Passenger Engines 1889/93
Loads for main line passenger engines and classification of passenger engines 1896-1910
Book of Costs of engines, repairs, train mileage, machinery, stores, running etc. 1873-83
Leading Particulars of MR locomotive engines 1908
Circulars and letters received at Sheffield 1904-5
Derby Works Erecting Shop record
New and rebuilt engines from 1.1.04
Classification of various engine details
Reports and Experiments
Reports on Indicator and coal consumption tests
Locomotive engine performances - working of bank engines
Lickey Incline
Engine Diagrams 1903, 1905, 1919
Diagrams of locomotive boilers
Tender diagrams 1910
Route availability 1914

Locomotive allocation 1914
Locomotive allocation 1920-2
Shed list 1911
Working Timetables and Appendices 1855-1922
Weekly notices
Public Timetables

LMS
Rolling Stock Committee
Locomotive and Electrical Committee
Mechanical and Electrical Committee
Register of renumbering of Locomotive stock
Engine History Cards 1927 et seq
Tender History Cards 1927 et seq
Distinctive numbers for tenders 1927
Derby Order books
Job number records relating to alterations and improvements 1933-56
Proposed standardisation of boilers
Instructions respecting the working of Rail Motor and Motor trains 1935
Diesel Hydraulic shunting locomotive - Minutes, Memoranda etc. relating to conversion of 0-6-0 tank engine
Locomotive Test Reports
        Dabeg pump v Injector
        Langer combustion control apparatus
        M&GN 4-4-0T and MR 0-4-4T – Comparative Tests
        2000 type passenger tank engines
Locomotive Allocation - various details
Derby Works shopping lists 1947-62
Working Timetables - Midland division

GER
Way and Works Committee

M&GN
Minutes of Officers Conferences
Joint Committee Minutes

Board of Trade
Accident Reports

Bibliography

Several contemporary newspapers have yielded vital information, including *The Derby Mercury, Harpenden Mail, Hemel Hempstead Gazette* and the *Morecambe and Heysham Times. The Railway Gazette,* the *Journal* of the Stephenson Locomotive Society and the *Railway Observer* of the Railway Correspondence and Travel Society have all proved fruitful sources of information. Other principal publications consulted are as follows

Midland Style - HMRS
Midland Locomotives - Essery & Jenkinson
Midland Railway Carriages - Lacy & Dow
S W Johnson MR Locomotive Engineer and Artist - J Braithwaite
Locomotive and Train working in the Nineteenth Century Vol 2 - E L Ahrons
The Midland Railway - C Hamilton Ellis
British Locomotive Catalogue Vol 3A - B Baxter
Derby Works and Midland Locomotives - J B Radford

The 2-2-2 remained the principal express passenger engine until the end of the 1860s. No. 29 with 6ft 8in driving wheels was built in June 1865 as a member of Kirtley's final 2-2-2 design, the 30 class built between 1863 and 1866. It is seen here with Johnson chimney after fitting with vacuum brakes in the 1880s and before renumbering to 29A in June 1887. It was one of the last two to be withdrawn in 1904 after further rebuilding with a Johnson boiler in April 1888.

Whilst singles were preferred for express work, 2-4-0s with smaller driving wheels were used on goods and slow passenger duties. The double plate frame was introduced in the 1860s and was used on the celebrated 156 class. This is No. 158 in Johnson's time before 1882 when it was first rebuilt. This engine remained in service until 1947 and is now preserved as part of the National Collection, currently resident at the Midland Railway Centre, Butterley as No. 158A. Its history will be covered in Volume 2. S Summerson collection.

Chapter 2 Growth and Development 1844-1922 - An Outline

'A considerable number of the older goods engines are out of date and in consequence of the call on the locomotive shops for repairs, the replacement of these engines by modern ones cannot be wholly dealt with at Derby.'

Introduction

The expansion of the railway system in the middle of the 19th century coincided with the prodigious growth of the coal industry to serve the rapidly growing industrial towns of the country. Such growth made for colossal strains on the railways, moving coal and people on a scale never seen before.

The Midland Railway, sitting astride the East Midlands and Yorkshire coalfields, was particularly affected; increasingly so in the light of its expansion to Hitchin and Kings Cross in the 1850s, St Pancras and Manchester in the 1860s and Carlisle in the 1870s. A maze of secondary lines and branches grew to serve adjacent areas, giving access to collieries and in the process providing alternative routes to ease the inevitable congestion which arose. In the field of locomotive development, as will be seen time and again, progress was often only achieved after long and drawn out consideration of factors which might adversely affect an issue. This was particularly in evidence in the sagas of continuous brakes, carriage warming, superheating and even in fittings such as safety valves, where in August 1918 it was declared 'the Construction of the Ross (pop) valves is such that they could not be expected to last anything like as long as the Midland (Ramsbottom)'. One assumes design improved later!

Advance came slowly, but there was also the major factor of cost. In all commercial and industrial undertakings, there is a natural reluctance to incur expenditure where it does not result in a reasonable financial return, which can be quantified accordingly. Add to this the problems of financing a rapidly expanding organisation, as the Midland Railway Company was during the latter part of the nineteenth century, and it is easy to appreciate a reluctance to move forward into untried technology.

Whilst the Minutes faithfully record the progress of the various schemes authorised, what they do not give is any hint of the attitude of the Directors, whether it was encouragement to their officers in the advancement of a scheme, or the reverse. The tenor of a report emphasising difficulties may merely be the result of a lukewarm attitude of the Directors, otherwise conveyed to the Chief Officers, or the result of real and genuine uncertainty or difficulty. These factors must be borne in mind when appraising the course of some of the major projects, which may seem to have been unduly hamstrung.

The first two Locomotive Superintendents, Kirtley and Johnson, therefore faced a considerable task in providing suitable engine power for such a rapidly expanding system. Their reports to the Board and Locomotive Committee over the years betray a very genuine concern for the locomotive stock. The conditions faced by Deeley and Fowler were very different.

The Whyte notation of wheel arrangement is used throughout this narrative but it must be remembered that it was not introduced until 1900, originally in America. The Midland records continued to refer to '4 wheels coupled' and so on, until the second decade of the century. Even then, the Whyte system was used only sparingly. Table(s) 2A at the end of the Chapter gives a summary of the engines built up to 1922.

The Locomotive Stock in Brief

The earliest engines built for the new company were principally 2-2-2s for passenger work and 2-4-0s, and then 0-6-0s, for goods traffic. The latter soon predominated for goods and 2-4-0s began to supersede 2-2-2s for passenger duties. Right hand drive was adopted and retained as standard until the Amalgamation of 1923.

After an initial flush of new construction in 1847/48 when 125 engines were added to stock, construction of passenger engines settled down to a modest pace until 1866, when the last Kirtley 2-2-2 was built. They did not exceed fifteen in any one year, which allowed for additional requirements as well as the replacement of withdrawn engines. The first of the celebrated 156 class 2-4-0s appeared in that year and from 1870, engines of this wheel arrangement appeared in greater numbers, forty-two in that year with peaks of forty in 1874, fifty in 1876 and forty in 1881, the last year of their construction, reflecting the expansion of the line and services. Johnson's first thirty 4-4-0s of 1876-77 were a tentative move towards using a leading bogie on engines having the same general boiler and cylinder dimensions as the 2-4-0s. The re-

By the late 1860s with the main line to London completed, the singles were no longer adequate to handle the best trains, so in 1870 Kirtley introduced the express passenger 2-4-0 800 class with 6ft 8in wheels. This is No. 813 as built in October 1870 by Neilsons. Note the engine has no brakes; only a tender handbrake was provided and efficient braking systems were still in the future. It was renumbered 46 in 1907 and withdrawn in 1924.

Enginemen's comfort was not a primary concern and a proper 'cab' was not introduced on the Midland until 1872. This Kirtley 890 class 2-4-0 was the first passenger design so equipped. No. 78 was built in October 1874 after Johnson's arrival and has standard smokebox door and chimney fitted sometime before 1883. It was rebuilt in April 1889, became 115 in 1907 and 20115 in 1935 before withdrawal in February 1937.

placement of the 2-4-0 by the 4-4-0 did not come until 1882 and engines of this wheel arrangement were added to stock each year (except 1887, 1889 and 1890) until 1909. The rate of building averaged ten per year until 1898, but from 1899 to 1906 the rate was more than doubled to nearly twenty-two per year, to cope with demand. To these must be added the ninety-five 4-2-2s which Johnson introduced from 1887-1900 following the invention of a satisfactory method of steam sanding by Francis Holt, Works Manager at Derby, in the 1880s.

From 1851 when the first entirely new engines were built at Derby Works, the flow of new goods engines was considerable and continuous. An average of thirty 0-6-0s per year was maintained up to 1859, rising to almost forty over the following seven years to 1867. But it was the next ten years, spanning the Kirtley/Johnson transition in 1873, which saw the greatest expansion, to meet all the growth factors. During that period, the annual rate of delivery was a remarkable ninety-four, to give 943 new 0-6-0s put into traffic. In the peak years of 1870 and 1876, the figures were 133 and 149 engines respectively. Then followed a relatively quiet period through the 1880s, when the average was sixteen per year. In the early and late 1890s came further vast increases in new construction, in this case to compensate in part for the withdrawal of a few older Kirtley goods. Between 1890 and 1892, two hundred and thirty 0-6-0s appeared and then another 289 in the five years 1897-1901, to which must be added the forty Schenectady and Baldwin 2-6-0s purchased from American in 1899. A further 101 0-6-0s were put into stock between

1902 and 1908 and then no more until 1917 apart from the two pioneer superheated 0-6-0s in 1911. There was an eventual total of 192 engines in this class, and to some degree these were replacements of withdrawn Kirtley goods engines.

For shunting purposes, Kirtley was generally content to use tender engines, but Johnson immediately introduced the 0-6-0T in 1874 and a total of 340 were built up to 1902. This brief survey provides bare figures to the background which follows, taken largely from Minutes of the Company.

The Kirtley Era 1844-73

The first meeting of the Board of Directors took place on 24 May 1844. At that first meeting a small sub-Committee was set up to appoint a Locomotive and Carriage & Wagon Superintendent. They duly reported on 13 June 1844, with the recommendation that Mr Matthew Kirtley be appointed at a salary of £250 per year. He had previously been Locomotive foreman of the Birmingham and Derby Junction Railway, from May 1839 to June 1842, and Locomotive Superintendent from then until his appointment by the Midland. His salary was raised to £400 backdated to the date of his appointment and raised again to £500 from 1 July 1845. It was an auspicious start.

The principal business of the Company was conducted by the Board for some five years with the assistance of a Committee of Management but the increasing workload resulted in the creation of standing Committees. On 12 September 1849, it was 'resolved that a Committee be appointed to manage the Locomotive arrangements, Carriage and Wagon

building and Stores Department to be called 'The Locomotive and Stores Committee'. Three other Committees were also created on the same day – Traffic, Way & Works and Finance with the Chairman and Deputy Chairman to be ex-Officio members of each.

The reports to the Board and Locomotive Committee by the successive Locomotive Superintendents, which are considered below, can only hint at the perpetual struggle to obtain authority for additional engine power. On 20 December 1844 Kirtley was requested to present a summary of the engines at work, under repair and out of work, to each meeting of the Board. This, it was clear, was in order to maintain the necessary control over a rapidly changing and expanding railway. On 2 December 1845 Kirtley gave to the Board a comprehensive report 'in reference to locomotive power for present traffic on the Midland Railway.' At that time the stock of engines was noted as 'sixty-seven engines, passenger class and twenty-seven engines goods class exclusive of those light engines laid up for sale'; the number of the latter was not given. The number of engines in daily work were forty-seven passenger and twenty-two goods: 'As there are frequent demands for extra power, we sometimes are without any spare engines at Leeds, Birmingham, Rugby etc., which it is desirable to supply. The new stock ordered are four passenger and twelve goods engines, which will only come up to our present wants for existing traffic. I will therefore recommend a further supply of engine power to be contracted to meet the requirements of the line and for new branches now making. Ordered, that Mr Kirtley report to he *next Board the number of new engines he recommends to be ordered and how he proposes to obtain them.'*

Tenders were considered on 6 January 1846 for forty-eight engines to be delivered in the next three years. Forward planning! At the end of that year, Kirtley reported the locomotive stock at 31 December 1846 as 122 including the new engines received in the previous half year. Ninety-five were in working order, twenty-three awaiting repairs with four to be sold. Being dependent on contractors for all new engines, as well as some repair work, brought problems of availability. As early as 10 September 1844, the Board resolved *'that unless one of the engines now building by Messrs Hick & Son (ordered by the Midland Counties Railway) be delivered during the present month, that the penalty incurred for not having delivered in the month of May last according to contract, be enforced'*. On 5 March 1845 five engines were agreed for repair by Messrs. Tayleur & Co. at a cost of about £1,092; until the works at Derby were developed in the early 1850s engines were constantly sent to contractors for repair. In this regard Wilsons were pre-eminent and a close relationship developed between the firm and the Midland .

The considerable building programme to both Capital and Revenue accounts resulted in 125 new engines added to stock in 1847/48 and on 18 December 1849 Kirtley reported to the newly formed Locomotive & Stores Committee on the number of 'engines employed' i.e. those *in use* for the month of September in 1848 and 1849 as follows:

	1848	1849
Passenger engines	75	77
Goods or mineral engines	50	55
Shunting and pilot engines	24	28
Total	149	160

This was a considerable advance on the sixty-nine at work in late 1845, though shortages of power were not unknown and on 5 November 1850, Kirtley was authorised to accept the offer of H Wright of Saltley Works Birmingham, to provide on hire ten or twelve engines to work trains between Derby and Birmingham. Through him, five second-hand ex-North Staffordshire engines, were also purchased, following approval given on 31 December 1850.

In his report to the Locomotive Committee on rolling stock on 3 February 1852 relating to 'the six months ending last December' Kirtley gave statistics on new construction, commenting again on the need for new engines: *'The greatly extended traffic in goods and minerals which will be apparent by the return appended, of mileage of trains and tonnage of Goods and Minerals for 1850 and 1851 makes it necessary that I should direct your attention to the necessity for providing additional engines, as it is impossible to maintain efficiency with an overworked stock. To maintain an efficient working stock at moderate cost, the average duties of each engine must not exceed 18,000 miles per annum. You will observe the mileage of trains last year was 1,500,000 to which must be added for pilot, bank shunting and ballast engine service 650,000. This service will require 320 engines. On 31st December last, the number of engines including the old light stock laid up was 300 engines'*.

Recommendations then followed for more new engines, with a table showing the number in steam in 1850/51:

Date*	Passenger Engines		Total
	For trains	For pilots	
30/6/1850	69	16	85
31/12/1850	70	17	87
30/6/1851	72	19	91
31/12/1851	76	20	96

date is 'six months ending'

Date*	Goods Engines		Total
	For trains	Forshunting and banking	
30/6/1850	69	14	83
31/12/1850	68	14	82
30/6/1851	77	14	91
31/12/1851	80	14	94

date is 'six months ending'

The figures shown here indicate how equally balanced the passenger and goods requirements were at that time and also the fact that only about two thirds of the stock required was in steam. How many of the 'old light stock' were laid up of course, is not known.

In 1856, the service required seventy passenger, 116 goods (including four bank engines), ten for pilot and twenty for 'shunting and forming trains at stations', out of a stock which had risen to 379. Reporting on 5 February 1856, Kirtley recorded that average traffic had increased by 300,000 miles per annum over the last five years: *'A further increase of stock is necessary to work the Leicester-Hitchin line (under construction) and the ordinary increase on other lines.'* And so it went on, with requests for authority to order additional stock to cover requirements. Derby Works took an increasing share of new construction and the detail

To handle the rapidly developing goods and coal traffic, four coupled engines were displaced early on and a vast series of 0-6-0s were built with double frames. The first had outside sandwich frames and then double plate frames until over 800 had been built, the last orders being completed in 1874. No. 324 was a straightframed engine built at Derby in the second half of 1860 and seen here with an 1869 boiler and Johnson chimney. The builder's plate has been moved from the centre splasher to the cab panel. No. 324 became 2361 in 1907 and was broken up in June 1920.

Six Metropolitan type 4-4-0Ts were acquired in a hurry in 1868 for working to Moorgate after MR 2-4-0Ts had been rejected by the Metropolitan, a saga described in Vol 2. They were, however, cherished by the Midland and had new boilers fitted in 1887-1888 as on No. 208, still with no overall cab. As No. 208A it was broken up in May 1905.

is presented in the class chapters. The invention of the injector in 1859 and the classic work of Charles Markham at Derby in that decade which resulted in a satisfactory method to burn coal in fireboxes, advanced the steam locomotive to a basic form which remained unchanged to the end. The provision of tank engines to work local services over the widened lines of the Metropolitan Railway, once the London Extension was completed in 1867, got Kirtley into a spot of hot water, when the Metropolitan decreed that the fixed wheelbase of the new 2-4-0Ts was too long, *after* they had been delivered. In this way, some Metropolitan type 4-4-0Ts were acquired.

Relationships with contractors were not always cordial either. On 5 October 1869 Kirtley reported on the question of inspecting engines being built under contract, clearly in order to check on standards and compliance with specifications. It was *'ordered that Mr Kirtley be requested to visit the builders of the engines from time to time'*.

Relationships with the Great Western appear to have been cordial but on 19 January 1864, in the course of a report on engines ordered from Stephenson, it was revealed that the GWR asked if it could have some of the engines on order for itself. As replacements could not be provided for over twelve months, the Midland refused. It indicates the growing pressure of work on the manufacturers; the firms' rates were always paramount, with the lowest tender generally the one accepted. Company costs also came under scrutiny, and, presumably as a result of a request, Kirtley presented a statement to the Locomotive Committee on 16 July 1872 showing the detailed cost of a GW goods engine. As a result of this Kirtley was

requested to visit the GW Works at Swindon and to submit a further report. Unfortunately there are no further references on the matter but the implication of required cost savings is clear.

The spate of new construction in the early 1870s took the total engine stock to over 1,000, a Kirtley 0-6-0 of November 1872 bearing that number in the Capital stock series. Thus when Johnson presented a general report on engine condition to the Locomotive Committee on 17 February 1874 he was able to quote the figure as at 30 June 1873, at the close of Kirtley's tenure of office, as 1,058 engines of which forty-six were Duplicate stock. This was a considerable achievement; Kirtley had taken up office on 13 June 1844 with just 110 engines from the constituent companies.

By the early 1870s the expansion of the Locomotive Department, both in respect of locomotives, carriages and wagons, made it desirable to divide the Locomotive Committee and create separate Locomotive and Carriage & Wagon Committees. At the same time a separate Carriage & Wagon Superintendent was to be appointed with that side of the work being relinquished by the Locomotive Superintendent.

The Locomotive Committee recommended to the Board on 4 March 1873, after consulting with Kirtley (who, it was reported, concurred with the arrangement) that the Carriage & Wagon department be placed under a separate Superintendent. Thomas Clayton of the GWR was appointed on 20 May 1873 and took up his duties on the following 1st July. The first meeting of the Carriage & Wagon Committee took place on 15 July 1873. To provide the necessary increase in manufacturing and maintenance capacity, the Locomotive Committee ordered on 17 June 1873 that Mr Sanders (the Company Architect) *'be requested to proceed with the erection of the new fitting shops at Derby with all speed'*. This work was completed early in 1877.

Meanwhile, Kirtley had fallen ill. At the 4 March 1873 meeting referred to above, it was reported that 'In consequence of the continued illness of Mr Kirtley since 3rd February last, it was suggested that a Commission be appointed to deal with all questions arising during his absence.' Messrs. W Kirtley, C H Jones and W Adams were duly appointed. W Kirtley was subsequently appointed Locomotive Superintendent of the London Chatham & Dover Railway and resigned in March 1874, but the other two rose to senior positions on the Midland and are referred to later. Kirtley died on 24 May 1873, four days after Clayton had been appointed C & W Superintendent.

The Johnson Era 1873-1903
No time was lost in appointing a successor to Kirtley. On 2 July 1873 the Chairman of the Locomotive Committee recommended to the Board that, of twenty-six applicants, S W Johnson of the Great Eastern Railway be appointed Locomotive Superintendent. This was confirmed at a salary of no less than £2,000 per annum (Clayton was paid £700) with the Locomotive Department arranging for him to enter upon his duties as soon as possible. The actual date was not recorded but he was present at the Committee meeting of 15 July. Johnson and Clayton developed a close working relationship, especially in regard to brakes and carriage warming.

Having just been appointed, one of his first actions was to recommend in a report of 5 August 1873 the desirability of

The celebrated Johnson singles were introduced in 1887, and were justly famed for their attractive appearance. A total of ninety-five were built, the last in 1900. They became a practical proposition after twenty years of coupled designs following the invention of steam sanding. The sanding pipes are clearly visible each side of the driving wheel in this view of No. 173 at St Pancras. Built in March 1893, it was renumbered 654 in 1907 and withdrawn in April 1925. S Summerson collection.

having an Inspector of Engines to ascertain the condition of the Companys' stock and to inspect engines under contract. As a result it was agreed to appoint Mr J Lane of the GER at £250 per annum. Johnson clearly favoured a man from his old company whom he probably knew. From 16 February 1893, Lane became Works Manager, a post he held until 31 December 1901.

Johnson immediately pressed on with current requirements after delivery of outstanding orders, and at the meeting 17 February 1874 announced that 'looking to probable progressive growth' it was necessary to order 150 additional engines 'to commence in September next, spread over two years'. He further reported on 20 April 1875, demonstrating the provision desirable in view of the opening of

the Settle and Carlisle line, recording the stock position at 31 December 1874 as 110 engines and estimating figures for the year ends of 1875/76, showing a rise to 1,375 engines. A subsequent slackening of the building programme is reflected in the report on the engine stock as at 30 June 1879, as requested by the Board on 4 June. On that date, the Capital stock comprised 1400, and the Duplicate stock

Johnson's final inside cylinder 4-4-0 was provided with a much larger boiler with belpaire firebox and was introduced in September 1900, having 6ft 9in driving wheels and 19½in x 26in cylinders. Deeley continued to build further examples with modifications until eighty engines had been put into service by September 1905. No. 2784 was built in January 1902 and was photographed on 9 July 1904 at Kettering. It was renumbered 713 in 1907, superheated in October 1919 and withdrawn in October 1935. H L Hopwood.

The first of Johnson's lengthy series of 0-6-0s was authorised on 19 May 1874. Known as Class B or 1142 class, a total of 120 was built. They entered traffic between February 1875 and December 1876, having 4ft 10½in wheels and 17½ x 26in cylinders. No. 1182 was built in June 1875 and given a major rebuild in August 1924. It became successively 2950 in 1907, 22950 in November 1934 and 58139 in 1951 and was withdrawn in November 1956.

sixty engines. Their condition was reported as 'Good 973, Moderate 209, under repairs 278, total 1,460'. 'Duplicate' stock engines were those which though replaced by new engines, still had some useful life left before withdrawal.

Later that year, on 18 November 1879, Johnson returned to the theme of additional stock. *'Next year'* he declared, *'the Nottingham and Melton and Manton and Kettering lines will open and there will probably be an increased demand for engine power for the Walsall and Wolver-* *hampton and Swinton and Knottingly lines, also for working, traffic from the Chatburn and Hellifield line. The work is equal to sixty-two engines.'* Details of requirements then follow...

The annual mileage run per engine was quoted for the years 1877-79, remaining pretty static at (for 1879) 19,124 train miles per engine and 24,931 engine miles. It was to rise. Kirtley had begun to address the problem of providing a satisfactory braking system early in 1873 after an initial trial with a form of coun- ter pressure brake in 1870, but main line goods and passenger engines continued to be turned out with no brakes - only a handbrake on the tender - until 1878. The next five years saw the development and widespread introduction of the automatic vacuum brake, so that by the close of 1883 all passenger engines had been fitted.

On 2 August 1882 the Board resolved that a statement of engines and carriages be prepared... *'and a monthly statement with numbers of engines ready for work*

Johnson's second series of 0-6-0s built from 1878 were known as the 'Express Goods' and had larger wheels of 5ft 2½in diameter. Thereafter, the majority of the Midland goods engines had wheels of this size. Many were fitted with vacuum brakes after 1883 as on No. 1623, built in February 1884. It became 3121 in 1907, was rebuilt in February 1925 and withdrawn August 1946. S Summerson collection.

For the many and varied local and branch line services Johnson built a total of 205 0-4-4 tanks between 1875 and 1900. No. 1824 was a typical example built in May 1889 and after 1892 displayed the company initials on the side tank. No. 1824 was renumbered 1332 in 1907, given a belpaire boiler in August 1928 but withdrawn only three years later, in September 1931. S Summerson collection.

compared to what is requisite, the object being that the Company always have a sufficient supply of engines and carriages ready for service.' Clearly, the Board was in a position to provide what was required. By 1 June 1883 the stock was 1,666 with a net deficiency, allowing for those on order, of 114.

A significant development of the mid-1880s was the introduction of steam sanding, though in one sense it held back the development of passenger engines, by making practical the reintroduction of engines with a single pair of driving wheels. On the other hand, problems with bent coupling rods were far from solved, and steam sanding provided an efficient system for preventing slipping, itself the cause of damaged rods. By the later 1880s the pressure of traffic was increasing again, Johnson reporting on 17 March 1887 the proposed new services over the Lancashire & Yorkshire Railway between Hellifield, Manchester and Liverpool and between Manchester Victoria and Marple.

On 17 April 1889 the deficiency in goods engines was reported as 182. There had been a large increase in goods train mileage in 1888, to 1,240,565 compared to 1887 and although the number of goods engines of all classes in stock, including duplicates, had risen to 1,291, it was necessary to have 86.75% in steam, whereas there should not be more than 75%. By December 1889 it was recorded as 'about 93%' and in the following October the figure for passenger engines was 81.2%. The resulting building programmes can be seen in Table 2A. The tone of Johnson's report on 17 September 1891 says it all. 'Many complaints have been received from the traffic department be-

ing short of engine power to deal with the large and increasing goods and mineral traffic. When I drew attention to this matter in October 1890, I estimated the increase in goods and mineral engine mileage would be to 2,061,007 for 1890. It was in fact 2,352,332. The engine deficiency on the basis of 75% in steam was 226 engines.'

He went on to draw attention to the further increase in goods mileage in the first half year of 1891 and to report that the percentage in steam for August was 91%. He next sought approval for further goods and tank engines, which was agreed. Increases in passenger, goods and coal traffic over the Metropolitan line in the south, the opening of the Dore and Chinley and the Tottenham and Forest Gate lines in the first half of the 1890s all contributed to the need for additional goods, passenger and tank engines. Johnson returned to the theme of 'engines not available for trains' on 13 November 1895: 'as the number in stock is quite inadequate'. There was also a need to keep men's hours below twelve per day, he declared. Serious delays on the road contributed to the shortage, 'though since December 1891 we have received 167 goods engines.' Approval was sought and given for a hundred more engines. Less than two years later, on 15 July 1897, the report was the same - 'Since 1895 there has been a large growth in all classes of traffic. The additional duty to be performed equals the work of 123 engines, apart from the opening of the Chapeltown and Barnsley branch from 1 July... I recommend purchase of thirty additional main line goods and thirty goods tank engines. Our stock of passenger engines is 791, but out of this, forty-four are at

present required to work goods and mineral trains in the Metropolitan District.'

The remarkable fact was, that whilst the Metropolitan widened lines had been open for thirty years, conveying an ever increasing volume of traffic, particularly coal for south London and the counties beyond, no condensing 0-6-0Ts had been built to haul this traffic over the steeply graded lines involved. In consequence, loads for the 0-4-4Ts were strictly limited. Johnson continued - 'there is not sufficient margin to admit of engines being thoroughly repaired, cleaned and washed out and where this is the case, it results in a shorter boiler life. Boilers have had to be broken up at 7-10 years old.'

The total stock of engines by this time was well over 2,000 and one hundred additional engines were then approved, thirty goods, thirty goods tank, twenty main line express passenger together with twenty heavy goods tanks for the Metropolitan line. In three weeks of March 1898, no fewer than 820 cases of trains starting late were recorded and in July, serious delays in working goods and mineral trains were reported. 'The bad effect of overworking the existing stock has led to the condemnation in the half year to 30 June 1898 of eighty-one boilers, compared to fifty-seven in the corresponding period of 1897, and forty-five in 1896.' Matters were getting serious.

The other aspect of train working that was giving rise to concern by 1898 was the increasing weight of passenger trains consequent on the introduction of heavy corridor carriages from the previous year. Johnson requested a report on loads for passengers trains on 5 August 1898 from his two Divisional Superintendents in

No. 2755 of the final series of 0-6-0Ts built in April 1902. These carried the same C1 boiler as the last 0-4-4Ts and many were fitted with condensing apparatus for working in London. Non-condenser No. 2755 was photographed at Kentish Town on 6 June 1903. It was renumbered 7234 in 1907 and became one of the regular Lickey banking engines. BR 47234, it was withdrawn in February 1958.

the Locomotive Department, C H Jones and W H Adams. They responded on 27 October 1898: *'we recognise the fact that, in proposing to augment the loads on some sections of one line, with the ever increasing weight of trains, we are lessening the already narrow margin in which, under favourable circumstances, drivers are able to make up a little time... We have emphasised the importance of drivers avoiding taking pilot engines except where absolutely necessary by altering the instructions at the head of the new list. If the pilot mileage is to be reduced and the trains run to time, the weight of the trains must be kept down.' The new stock is 23%* *heavier than the old without extra seating accommodation, so the tendency will be to increase the weight of the trains, unless a strong effort is made by the traffic department to prevent the running of unnecessary vehicles.'* The classification of engines was amended (see Chapter 3) to incorporate the recommendations made.

Up to this time, Johnson continued to build his classic slim boilered (4ft 1in diameter) 4-4-0s. From 1887 boilers had been given greater steaming capacity by having longer fireboxes fitted, the 5ft 11in of the original 4-4-0s becoming 6ft 6in (D boilers of 1887) and then 7ft 0 in. (E boilers of 1896). The last of these en-

gines was delivered in 1901. However, it is clear that Johnson decided, around the end of the 1898, to design an altogether larger 4-4-0 in order to provide adequate power for the principal express trains. Despite their proven use on the continent, belpaire fireboxes had been slow to receive widespread acceptance in this country. The Great Central introduced them on some 4-4-0s in 1896, but Johnson cautious as ever, waited a little longer before incorporating a belpaire box in the boilers of this new design.

These engines were a considerable advance on their predecessors, with 4ft 8in diameter Belpaire boilers, which for

The unfamiliar lines of the thirty Baldwin 2-6-0s, bought as a result of demand for new engines at a time of strikes in the English locomotive industry. With Derby works unable to produce additional orders, this caused much comment at the time of their introduction in 1899. No. 2501, the first of them, became 2200 in 1907 and was broken up in June 1911. S Summerson collection.

Although Johnson introduced the 3-cylinder Compound design in 1902, it was the Deeley version built from 1905 which became so well known. No. 1008 at Holbeck carrying the first crest on the cabside was one of the first ten with deep front end frames. Becoming 1013 in 1907 and superheated in 1925 it was withdrawn in June 1949.

ever after gave the class their nickname of 'Belpaires'. The first of them were ordered at Derby on 3 February 1899, ultimately reaching a total of eighty.

Meanwhile, in November 1898, Johnson's reports continued the familiar theme of increased traffic, and this time it was new railways in the Bradford district, the New Mills and Heaton Mersey lines and the Heysham dock lines which demanded additional power. Increased excursion traffic and the growth of ordinary and excursion traffic over the Tilbury line also contributed. A further seventy goods, ten goods tank and twenty passenger engines were authorised. The engineering strikes which continued from the summer of 1897 to about January 1898 resulted in excessive delays to the already large order books of commercial and locomotive building firms, and in common with the GN and GC railways, the Midland ordered 2-6-0s from American firms. A special meeting of the Locomotive Committee was called for 16 December 1898, at which tenders were received for the forty engines required. After further negotiation tenders were accepted in February and March 1899. In August 1900, an official booklet was published entitled *Plan of and other information relating to the Locomotive Department*. This contained a table of statistics for 1899 which showed that the number of locomotives had risen to 2,676 and the train mileage to 47,259,450.

Traffic growth continued and on 20 September 1900 Johnson gave some further revealing statistics... '*Due to increased delays on the road, the average miles run per engine for each twelve hours in steam has fallen from ninety-three in 1888 to seventy-eight in 1899, a reduction of 16%. The growth of traffic is still going on so as to require the immediate ordering of additional engines ... the additional mileage warrants 210. This contains no*

provision for allowing for detentions on the road. If the increased time engines are in steam is taken into account, it would require the purchase of 518 engines to meet satisfactorily the existing conditions of working'. After hearing further arguments in favour of more engines, the Committee duly acquiesced to 140 main line goods, forty heavy goods tank engines and thirty express passenger engines.

Now the extraordinary thing about all these reports from Johnson is the complete lack of any suggestion for larger goods engines, to speed up or lengthen goods trains in order to economise on motive power and ease the chronic congestion which was occurring. It eventually fell to the Midland Chairman to make the suggestion, as revealed by Minute 6717 of the Locomotive Committee on 2 November 1900: '*Mr Johnson reported that, as desired by the Chairman of the Company, he had gone into the question of length and weight of trains which could be worked by main line goods engines of a larger capacity than those hitherto constructed and he was prepared to make goods engines capable of taking at the present ordinary booked speeds, loads 20% greater than now handled. The following statement gives the estimated greater length of train and increased tonnage taken in comparison with present maximum loads. At present the maximum train is 41 twelve ton wagons between Wigston and London and 50 twelve ton wagons between Toton and Leicester. Mr Johnson had sent this information to the General Manager and Engineer to enable them to report whether benefit or inconvenience is likely to result from taking such increased loads, having regard to length of sidings and also indicating that the brake power required should be taken into account.*'

This episode demonstrates clearly the

Length and weight of mineral trains, both engines				
	Existing Engine		Proposed Engine	
	length	weight	length	weight
Wigston –London	864ft	587 tons	1021ft	698 tons
Toton - Leicester	1035ft	695 tons	1220ft	830 tons
Weight of existing engine and tender in working order 75 tons - length 50ft.				
Weight of proposed engine and tender in working order 90 tons - length 55ft.				

cautious nature of Johnson's approach which, as will be seen, was also reflected in other developments. The standard goods engine had remained basically the same for the past twenty-five years. Running staff, timetablers, civil engineers and all those concerned with running the railway had been conditioned to 'more of the same' when it came to additional power and the suggestion to vary it produced an inevitably negative reaction.

Authority was eventually given to the building of new, larger, goods engines, the first ten of which were built to Derby Order 2328 of 22 January 1902. These were given 4ft 8in diameter boilers, like the first of the large 4-4-0s, but they retained the round top firebox. Meanwhile, in September 1899 a 10% increase in goods and mineral train loadings was sanctioned and on 4 October 1901 Johnson agreed to an increase of 8.33% where loads were under 'the present maximum of fifty wagons'. If the 'lye-bye sidings' could be lengthened, he wrote, 'so as to admit of a modification to the restriction of fifty wagons as a maximum train, a still further increase might be made in the loads of engines.' The increase in goods and mineral traffic peaked around the beginning of 1901, Johnson reporting on 18 April 1901 that, although there had been some falling off in goods and mineral traffic during the previous few months, passenger mileage showed 'an almost continuous increase each week.'

Returning to the problem of providing

The Deeley 0-6-4Ts became synonymous with local passenger trains in the Birmingham district. No. 2031 in original condition is between Kings Norton and Northfield in 1912. It was built in November 1907, superheated in 1926 and withdrawn in April/May 1936. S Summerson collection.

adequate power for the express passenger trains, Johnson's knowledge of the 3-cylinder compound No.1619 of the North Eastern Railway and his acquaintance with W M Smith, Chief Draughtsman of the NER who was responsible for its design, clearly bore fruit in the next advance on the Midland. On 10 July 1900, only seventeen months after the first of the Belpaire 4-4-0s had been ordered, Derby order 2109 was issued for five compound engines on the Smith principle, with one inside high pressure cylinder and two outside low pressure cylinders. Thus in the space of some four years, 1899-1902, larger goods and passenger engines had been conceived and ordered, an advance not seen before and on a scale which was not to be repeated.

This brought to the fore many problems, not the least of which was axleweight. Enter the Civil Engineer. The maximum permitted as from 20 September 1897 was 18½ tons and this figure was reached by the Johnson bogie singles, whilst the first ten Belpaires had a maximum axle weight of 18 tons 5cwt. The two new Compounds weighed in with a maximum of 19tons 11cwt, and the Civil Engineer reported to the Board on 21 February 1902, a month *after* their formal delivery. The resulting rumpus can only be guessed at, but the Locomotive Committee accepted the Engineer's recommendation that to permit them to run on the main lines London-Derby and Derby-Manchester, Bristol-Carlisle, 108 underbridges required strengthening at a cost of £96,000, the Accountant to report as to how the expenditure should be dealt with. It was agreed and further resolved that, *'a report be submitted to the Board, setting forth the number of engines with their weight which put heavier weights*

on bridges than that agreed in 1897 between the Locomotive Superintendent and the Engineer'.

In the meantime, the Compounds were restricted to the Leeds-Carlisle line. The matter was resolved, but Compounds were not permitted on the Bristol line until after Grouping. The final slim-boilered 4-4-0s and 0-6-0s were delivered in June 1901 and August 1902 but Johnson's last major work was to secure authority for commencing the rebuilding of the majority of the slim boilered 4-4-0s with the larger 4ft 8in diameter H boilers and also the last 575 small 0-6-0s, built with 5ft 3in wheels. Orders for this work were issued in November 1903.

By this date, something larger than the 0-4-4T was becoming desirable for the heavier suburban passenger traffic and a 4-4-4T design was prepared. This was to have 18in x 26in cylinders, 5ft 7in driving wheels and an entirely new design of boiler, of 5ft 1in diameter. Pressure was 175lb/sq.in with a firebox 7ft 0in long. It was, in essence an H boiler with a larger diameter and shortened barrel. Order 2651 of 10 September 1903 covered five engines, but was subsequently cancelled. The same fate awaited Order 2694 of 5 December 1903 which covered a more remarkable proposal, for ten 0-8-0s with outside 20in x 26in cylinders and 4ft 7in wheels. Neither of these designs had excessive axleloads, but were intended to provide increased power for duties not covered by new engines already authorised. Doubtless changing traffic prospects were at the back of these cancellations.

The year 1903 was also significant for the final decision to adopt the Johnson and Bain system of carriage warming, after some ten years of experimentation

with different systems, and much hesitation.

So, by this date, the steam hauled Midland train had reached the form it was to retain until finally despatched by diesel and electric power from the 1950s. The 1903 diagram book records that by 1 July 1903, the locomotive stock had risen to 2,948 – the reproduced extract gives the analysis. Johnson's contribution to this development was therefore immense and his achievements in an era of rapid expansion were remarkable. The last engine to retain a Johnson design boiler and so remain virtually in original condition, was 1F 0-6-0T No.41835, as late as 1961. Johnson's influence remained in various ways almost to the end of steam, even in minor decorative matters – the design of his brass numerals for instance, was repeated on Deeley's smokebox numberplates, adopted as the LMS standard, and finally used on a few of the first BR numberplates in 1948. So it was possible to see, for example, Stanier Pacific No.46236 proudly displaying Johnson style numerals, taking part in the Locomotive Exchanges of that year.

The Deeley Era 1904-9

S W Johnson retired on 31 December 1903 and was succeeded by R M Deeley on 1 January 1904. By this date conditions in respect of motive power requirements had markedly changed. A continuing need for more large express engines was reflected in orders for thirty more modified Johnson Belpaire 4-4-0s in 1904-5 and for forty modified Compounds following on from 1905-9. An entirely new inside cylinder design, equal in power rating to the Compounds, produced nine engines in 1909, following a solitary ex-

The Deeley era was characterised by the rebuilding of many of Johnson's 4-4-0s and 0-6-0s with larger boilers. No. 1812 was a member of the 1808 class of 1888 and was rebuilt in June 1904 with this H boiler . Becoming 382 in 1907 it was further rebuilt in June 1911 and was withdrawn in October 1935.

ample built in 1907. Only thirty new 0-6-0s were ordered in the five years 1904-8, all similar to Johnson's final design, but goods traffic had fallen off to a considerable degree, allowing many of the old Kirtley 0-6-0s to be withdrawn. In 1904-6 over eighty were withdrawn and a further fifty sold to Italy, an unthinkable situation only five years earlier.

Overall, the engine stock remained static during Deeley's term of office; from 2,928 in June 1902, it had risen only slightly, to 2,962 when he reported to the Locomotive Committee on 15 July 1908. No engines had been authorised to Capital account since September 1900, all engines to Deeley's design, including the Compounds, having been to revenue account. He pursued the rebuilding policy

initiated by Johnson to fit larger H boilers to the earlier 4-4-0s and 0-6-0s. All except the first two classes of Johnson's 4-4-0s were rebuilt by 1908, whilst the 1698 class of 4ft 11in. 0-6-0s was added to the list of 0-6-0s to be rebuilt. This was still in progress when Deeley resigned in the following year.

In line with the pursuance of economical working on branch lines, Deeley ex-

Table 2B. The 1903 Diagram Book Summary 1 July 1903

GENERAL		TYPES DISTINCTIVE		VARIETIES	Nº OF ENGINES REGULAR STOCK	DUPLICATE STOCK	TOTAL
1	NON COUPLED PASSR	1	WITH BOGIE	5	95	-	95
		2	NO BOGIE	2	-	2	2
2	4 WHEELS COUPLED PASSENGER	3	INSIDE FRAMES AND BOGIE	14	302	-	302
		4	INSIDE FRAMES NO BOGIE	6	199	18	217
		5	OUTSIDE FRAMES & CRANKS NO BOGIE	4	4	72	76
		6	COMPOUND WITH BOGIE	1	2	-	2
3	G WHEELS COUPLED GOODS	7	INSIDE FRAMES	9	865	-	865
		8	OUTSIDE FRAMES AND CRANKS	1	723	-	723
		9	MOGUL OUTSIDE CYLINDERS	2	40	-	40
4	4 WHEELS COUPLED PASSR TANK	10	TRAILING BOGIE	8	205	-	205
		11	TRAILING BOGIE OUTSIDE FRAMES & CRANKS	3	16	10	26
		12	LEADING BOGIE OUTSIDE CYLINDERS	1	-	5	5
5	G WHEELS COUPLED TANKS	13	SIDE TANKS	12	322	31	353
		14	SADDLE TANKS	3	-	1	1
		15	BACK TANKS	5	-	9	9
		16	SIDE TANKS OUTSIDE CYLINDERS	2	-	2	2
6	4 WHEELS COUPLED	17	SADDLE TANKS	3	2	23	25
					2775	173	2948

ENGINES RUNNING ON JULY 1ST 1903

Fowler continued the rebuilding policy of his predecessor, initially with saturated belpaire boilers, replacing the H boilers. In many cases new frames were also provided so that the rebuilds were virtually new engines. Compare the photograph of No 384, also of the 1808 class, with that of 1812 on page 19. No. 384 was built in 1888, received an H boiler in 1904, a G7 boiler (shown here) in May 1910 and was withdrawn in September 1925.

plored the concept of Motor Carriage and Motor train working in 1904-1907. Whilst the former did not prove successful, the introduction of motor trains for branch lines, whilst limited in extent, paved the way for a much wider application by the LMS in the 1930s.

At the other end of the scale, Deeley recognised the acute need for larger passenger and goods engines, to deal more expeditiously with the enormous traffic being conveyed. In 1907 engine miles run were recorded at the very large figure of 71,231,120, so that any reduction from the use of larger engines and longer trains would have been a benefit. However, the restricted length of the lye-bye sidings and the maximum train length of fifty wagons continued to lay a dead hand on progress.

It is often said that the Midland pursued a small engine policy, but in truth it was more a case that they did *not* have any policy (so far as we understand the term today) of systematically upgrading the underbridges in order to be able to accept larger and heavier engines. Whilst the engines built under Deeley and Fowler continued to be 0-6-0s and 4-4-0s, there were nevertheless a great many

The final stage of 'rebuilding' the slim boilered Johnson 4-4-0s was to the superheated 483 class as seen here, having 7ft 0in driving wheels. Not all were so rebuilt – the complexities of the subject are considered in Volumes 3 and 4 but 157 engines were rebuilt to this form between 1912 and 1924. No. 477 was built in March 1900, given an H boiler in 1904 and rebuilt with superheater and 7ft 0in driving wheels in July 1922. It was withdrawn as BR 40477 in February 1951.

schemes in outline diagram form for larger engines, which went no further. It is fortunate that information on many of these has survived among the MR records at the National Railway Museum and a brief outline is appropriate.

Between 1904 and 1906 a number of large passenger tank designs, including 2-6-2T and 2-6-4T, were drawn up to succeed the Johnson 0-4-4Ts before the 0-6-4T arrangement was decided upon; details of these are further considered in Volume 4. In 1905 a proposal was drawn up for fitting a corrugated flue firebox boiler to a standard goods chassis. This was to sketch DS550 of 14 June 1905. The boiler was to be 6ft 0½in diameter with a very stubby appearance surmounted, of necessity, by a short chimney and dome. It contained 346 x 1¾in tubes and the firebox was 8ft 7ins long. The corrugated flue firebox was essentially the same arrangement employed on 'Cornish type' stationary boilers and had the great merit that it did not require staying to the outer firebox in the same way that conventional locomotive boilers do. The Lancashire and Yorkshire Railway had built some 0-8-0s about two years previously with boilers to this arrangement, but they proved poor steamers and had other unconventional troubles, so it is perhaps just as well that this particular idea progressed no further.

The corrugated flue proposal was followed on 2 October 1905 by an 0-8-0 having 20 x 26 in outside cylinders, a Deeley version of Johnson's proposal of two years earlier. Whereas the Johnson engine had a short cab similar to that on the first H boiler 4-4-0 rebuilds and a standard low sided tender, this version had the long

Deeley cab and his standard high sided 3,500 gallon tender. However, the dead hand of the Civil Engineer saw this idea disposed of.

Ideas began to be formulated for a large banking engine for the Lickey incline as early as July 1907 when a compound 2-8-2 tank was sketched out. This and the further ideas formulated under Fowler will be considered in Volume 4, which covers the banker actually built.

An advance on the standard 4-4-0 Compound was also actively considered. The drawings are dated 26 November 1907, and were for a four cylinder compound 4-6-0. Like the proposed 2-8-2T banker, piston valves were to be used for all four cylinders and Deeley's adaptation of inside Walschaerts valve gear (needing only the two sets of gear to operate all four valves) was to be employed. This gear was also used in the two cylinder arrangement of course, on the contemporary 990 class 4-4-0s. The maximum axle load of 18½ tons should not of itself been an insurmountable problem, but the estimated overall weight of 76 tons doubtless animated the Civil Engineer again. This proposal, with a larger boiler than the 4-4-0s, had considerable potential, so that locomotive *design* on the Midland, far from stagnating as might be implied from actual construction during this period, was making some notable advances.

In 1907-8 the 'Paget' 2-6-2 engine was built. This was constructed at Derby to the design and at the expense of Sir Cecil Paget utilising single acting cylinders with rotary valves. It was an experimental engine, which was given the Midland number 2299, although it never entered revenue service. The Erecting Shop

record shows that it was broken up on 15 April 1920. In these circumstances, it is not considered in this history but interested readers are referred to the paper by James Clayton in *The Railway Magazine* reprint of November 1945, with a note by Kenneth H Leech. The engine was provided with a standard Deeley tender, modified to suit and when the engine was broken up, this was retained and eventually fitted, with further modifications, to LMS Compound No.1055, in 1924. This tender was then unique amongst the Deeley tenders and instantly recognisable by the fact that it was the only one with the shallow panel above the top beading to have 'commode' handles (the term described vertical handrails on the side of a tender) fitted at the front end. The tender was numbered 3180 in 1927 and was withdrawn on 11 August 1951, a reminder of a remarkable experiment in locomotive engineering.

In 1909 the Board considered a major reorganisation of the Locomotive Department, which involved the Locomotive Running Department being transferred to the Traffic Department. Two new posts were to be created, Chief Mechanical Engineer and Chief Motive Power Superintendent, to head the new arrangements. This proposal was not to Deeley's liking and he tendered his resignation. The Board met on 13 August 1909 and the Chairman reported that *'owing to certain contemplated changes in the Locomotive Department, Mr Deeley had placed his resignation in his hands'. That Deeley was highly regarded is revealed in the continuation of the Minute. 'It was resolved that Mr Deeley's resignation be accepted from 30 November 1909 and that*

Superheaters were fitted to the large boiler 4-4-0s of 1900 onward. No. 760 of the 'Belpaire' 4-4-0s as modified by Deeley was built in February 1905 as No. 850. It was superheated in September 1921 and withdrawn in April 1946. S Summerson collection.

No. 998 of Deeley's ten 990 class 4-4-0s was the first Midland engine to receive a superheater in May 1910 and all were equipped by January 1914. No. 993 of June 1909 was fitted in July 1912. As a 'non standard' class in the LMS scheme of things, they were unfortunate to be all withdrawn by December 1928. S Summerson collection.

he be granted a retiring allowance of £1,200 per annum during the pleasure of the Directors. Also that Mr Deeley be requested to retain his gold pass over the Company system for life.'

The following Minute dealt with the reorganisation: *'The General Manager reported with regard to the Locomotive Department and after full discussion, it was Resolved that the control of that part of the Locomotive Department known as the Locomotive Running Department be* *transferred to the Traffic Department'*. The reorganisation was discussed further on 17 December 1909 when Henry Fowler was promoted from Works Manager to Chief Mechanical Engineer, with effect from 1 January 1910. L C Geach was made Superintendent of Motive Power from the same date.

The Fowler Era 1910-22
Henry Fowler remained CME until 31 December 1922, when the Midland be- came a part of the London Midland & Scottish Railway. Although, again, there was a lack of significant advance as revealed by the engines built during this period, there was no lack of ideas. The benefits of superheating were beginning to be appreciated and just before Fowler took office, sketch No.1484 of 29 November 1909 showed a proposed goods engine and tender with a Schmidt superheater, developed from the Belpaire 0-6-0 design to Order 3412 of 18 December 1907,

Although the advantages of superheating were apparent, permitting increased loadings to engines in the same power class and the Compounds were the top link passenger engines, only the original five Johnson engines plus No. 1040 had been superheated by the close of 1918. No. 1003, built in September 1903, was superheated in May 1915 and withdrawn as 41003 in April 1951.

Reliance on saturated rebuilt Johnson 0-6-0s was almost total until 1917. In 1911 Fowler introduced a superheated version with piston valves but utilising the same boiler, though only two were built. Quantity production commenced in 1917 and No. 3997 was built in June 1921. Becoming an LMS standard, the 192 Midland engines were extensively augmented, the last being built in 1941. No 3997 was withdrawn as BR 43997 in December 1959. S Summerson collection.

which was subsequently cancelled. On the very next day, 30 November 1909, Order 3649 was issued to fit a 990 class 4-4-0 with a superheater. The goods engine proposal was further advanced on 8 September 1910 with a sketch for a 2-6-0. This could have resembled the Caledonian and Glasgow and South Western Railway engines which were built in 1912/15, but it was not pursued and the superheated goods that finally appeared were 0-6-0s. Another 2-6-4T proposal was drawn up, with inside cylinders, to sketch DS1553 of 14 June 1910 and the acquisition of the LTS line in 1912 produced a further flurry of ideas for 2-6-2Ts for that section. These will be further examined in Volume 4.

Apart from the diagrams for a 'standard' 2-6-0 and 2-8-0 for ARLE in 1917, proposals for a 2-8-0 for the Midland were made on 12 June 1912, described as '*Proposed 2-8-0 Mineral engine, superheated (based on S.934 but superheated)*'. It appeared again on 12 August 1920, so it wasn't for the want of trying on the part of the CME that the MR failed to build the large goods engines that were so clearly needed.

After the initial experiments with a 990 class 4-4-0 in 1910, a programme of superheating the Class 3 and 4 4-4-0s was commenced in 1911. Despite the benefits, which allowed superheated engines to take 10% greater loads than saturated engines of the same class, progress was very slow and still incomplete at the end of 1922. With regard to the Class 2 4-4-0s, all had received new, larger boilers in the five years 1904-08, which brought them from Class 1 to Class 2 in haulage capacity. Deeley had commenced replacing these boilers by belpaire versions of simi-

lar size in 1909, long before it was necessary on the grounds of wear and tear. This was continued by Fowler until 1912 when this form of rebuild ceased. The event of 1912 of course, was the acquisition of the London Tilbury and Southend Railway and its stock of ninety-four engines, inclusive of those delivered that year. As with other absorbed engines before them, they were nurtured and acquired many Midland fittings and details, but generally retained their own designs of boiler. Having wheel arrangements not otherwise found on the Midland they always remained distinctive and 'different'.

The year 1912 was also notable for the introduction of an entirely new superheated Class 2 4-4-0, to replace previous engines carrying the same numbers and still, for accountancy purposes, regarded as rebuilds. (Royalties to the Superheater Co. were less than for new engines!) With Derby's usual thrift, any reusable parts were incorporated in the new engines. This rebuilding continued to the close of 1922 and beyond, but was never finished due to change of circumstances following the Grouping.

The slow pace of the rebuilding reflects the conditions of the period, covering the Great War of 1914-18 when Derby was engaged in munitions work, so reducing its capacity. One result of this was the repair of some seventy-four Midland 0-6-0s at the M&GN works at Melton Constable, as recorded in the *Melton War Album*. Two of these are known to have been Kirtley 0-6-0 No.2442 and H boiler Johnson 0-6-0 No.3625. Rebuilding Johnson 0-6-0s with small G6 or large G7 boilers commenced in 1916, but this was largely a replacement exercise for worn-

out Johnson and Deeley boilers. The preparation for service in France of eighty-one Kirtley 0-6-0s in 1917 and their rehabilitation after their return in 1920 all added to the stresses of the wartime period. Only two of the many proposed designs prepared under Fowler were actually built – the famous Lickey banker, which appeared after a long gestation in January 1920 and the superheated Class 4 0-6-0s of which the first two examples appeared in 1911. Numerous tests and trials were conducted, as with the Superheated 4-4-0s, but it was 1917 before series production began. Meantime, the vast army of Kirtley 0-6-0s were showing their age and on 15 April 1920 the Locomotive Committee was advised as follows. '*A considerable number of the older goods engines are out of date and in consequence of the call on the locomotive shops for repairs, the replacement of these engines by modern ones cannot be wholly dealt with at Derby.*' As a result, a tender was sought from Armstrong Whitworth Ltd. for fifty class 4 0-6-0s, to form part of the total of 192 eventually completed by September 1922; withdrawal of the old Kirtleys began in earnest. The building of Midland engines finally came to a close when the LMS turned out the last of the superheated class 2 4-4-0s in January 1924. As is well known, these engines, along with the Class 4 Superheated 0-6-0s and the Compounds, were adopted as standard for new construction in the early years of the LMS. But this falls outside the scope of this work. During the final years the stock reached and remained at 3,019 engines.

Table 2A New Locomotive Construction 1844-1922

TYPE	1844	1845	1846	1847	1848	1849
2-2-2		2		29	28	2
2-4-0			7	16	17	
4-2-0					2	
4-4-0						
4-2-2						
2-4-0T						
4-4-0T						
0-4-4T						
0-6-4T						
0-6-0WT						
0-6-0T						
0-4-0T						
0-6-0SF	2	3	11**	6	19	
DF					8	2*
2-6-0						
0-10-0						
TOTAL	2	5	18	51	74	4

*Replacement for two 0-6-0s of 1848 in exchange for two returned to makers.
**One additional engine ordered but sent to ECR when new and not included. Net addition to stock 1844-49: 152 engines.
SF=Single Frames
DF=Double Frames

	1850	1851	1852	1853	1854	1855	1856	1857	1858	1859	1860	1861
2-2-2	1	2	15	13	3	11	8	7	5	6	8	11
2-4-0							6	5		6		
4-2-0												
4-4-0												
4-2-2												
2-4-0T												
4-4-0T												
0-4-4T												
0-6-4T												
0-6-0WT								2			2	
0-6-0T												
0-4-0T												
0-6-0SF		2	2					5				
DF	6	21	21	29	9	18	16	13	26	25	30	30
2-6-0												
0-10-0												
TOTAL	7	25	38	42	12	29	30	32	31	37	40	41

TYPE	1862	1863	1864	1865	1866	1867	1868	1869	1870	1871	1872	1873
2-2-2		2	10	7	1							
2-4-0	13	13	4		10	42	6		42	26	6	14
4-2-0												
4-4-0												
4-2-2												
2-4-0T							10					
4-4-0T							6					
0-4-4T								6	20			
0-6-4T												
0-6-0WT	5	1			4					4	8	
0-6-0T										10		
0-4-0T												
0-6-0SF												
DF	13	28	20	29	36	37	66	57	71	62	52	62
2-6-0												
0-10-0												
TOTAL	31	44	34	36	47	83	88	63	133	102	66	76

TYPE	1874	1875	1876	1877	1878	1879	1880	1881	1882	1883	1884	1885
2-2-2												
2-4-0	40	7	50	10		10	25	40				
4-2-0												
4-4-0			6	24					11	19	10	5
4-2-2												

continued on page 25

TYPE												
2-4-0T												
4-4-0T												
0-4-4T		21	19					15	5	8	17	10
0-6-4T												
0-6-0WT												
0-6-0T	9	26	5		20	20	10		10	10	25	5
0-4-0T										5		
0-6-0SF		51	69		20		14	26	8	22	20	20
DF	33											
2-6-0												
0-10-0												
TOTAL	82	105	149	34	40	30	49	81	34	64	72	40

TYPE	1886	1887	1888	1889	1890	1891	1892	1893	1894	1895	1896	1897
2-2-2												
2-4-0												
4-2-0												
4-4-0	15		15			10	20	15	20	10	5	10
4-2-2		5	3	14	3	5	20	15			7	3
2-4-0T												
4-4-0T												
0-4-4T	10				10		30	10		20		
0-6-4T												
0-6-0WT												
0-6-0T				4	41	20	20			15		
0-4-0T				2	3			5				10
0-6-0SF	10	28	12		60	78	92	20	18	2	35	65
DF												
2-6-0												
0-10-0												
TOTAL	35	33	30	30	107	113	182	65	38	47	47	88

TYPE	1898	1899	1900	1901	1902	1903	1904	1905	1906	1907	1908	1909
2-2-2												
2-4-0												
4-2-0												
4-4-0	10	30	15	25	22	18	14	31	20	1	5	14
4-2-2		11	9									
2-4-0T												
4-4-0T												
0-4-4T	10		20									
0-6-4T										40		
0-6-0WT												
0-6-0T		41	19	10	30							
0-4-0T						5				5		
0-6-0SF		45	55	64	31	20	20		9	1	20	
DF												
2-6-0		40										
0-10-0												
TOTAL	20	167	118	99	83	43	34	31	29	47	25	14

TYPE	1910	1911	1912	1913	1914	1915	1916	1917	1918	1919	1920	1921	1922
2-2-2													
2-4-0													
4-2-0													
4-4-0			30	37	27	8	8	4	5	3	4	3	13
4-2-2													
2-4-0T													
4-4-0T													
0-4-4T													
0-6-4T													
0-6-0WT													
0-6-0T													
0-4-0T												2	3
0-6-0SF		2						15	28	22	33	57	35
DF													
2-6-0													
0-10-0										1			
TOTAL		2	30	37	27	8	8	19	33	26	37	62	51

Class H 0-6-0 No. 1597 of February 1883 was built by Beyer Peacock & Co and clearly displays its makers plates on the middle splasher and on the tender. The former reads 'Beyer Peacock & Co 1882 Manchester' and the latter ' Beyer Peacock & Co Gorton Foundry 1881 Manchester'!

The use of letters was discontinued for Derby- built engines after 1875; No. 1819 (at Trafford Park in 1904)was built to 0.734 of 25 January 1888 . The various orders became known generally as the 1808 class.

Chapter 3 - Engine and Power Classification

'Classes 1 and 2 passenger will take a third less than the loadings for classes 1 and 2 goods when working class A and B goods trains.'

1. Engine Classification

The Minutes of the Company during Kirtley's period of office from 1844-73 show no evidence of a formal engine classification despite Minute 1181 of 1 June 1852: *'Ordered. That a new classification of the Company's engines be arranged by 1st July next'*. No details of a classification are subsequently quoted, and it is probable that it referred to a mid-1852 renumbering which grouped passenger and goods engines separately, by wheel arrangement. Engines continued to be referred to in the Minutes as passenger, goods or by number depending on the circumstances.

The absence of other official Registers covering the Kirtley period leaves a considerable gap in our knowledge of what, if any formal engine classification existed during that period. This inauspicious beginning seems to have been a precursor for future years, in that no consistent, all-embracing classification scheme was ever produced for the locomotive stock.

1a. Letters and Order Numbers

During the later part of 1873, drawings were in preparation for the first of Johnson's new designs, an 0-6-0T with 17in cylinders and 4ft 6in coupled wheels. These were initially shown in the Drawing Register as '17in cyl tank engines' but the drawing for the springs,

dated 3 January 1874, has 'Class A' written additionally in the description column and all subsequent drawings for this class refer to Class A. The specification for the first ten engines has *'A class September 23 '73'* written in ink on the front cover; that for the last thirty (dated 7 December 1874) has *'Class A'* printed on the cover.

Successive new designs were allocated a letter as they were produced up to January 1875, the first 0-6-0s being designated Class B which was printed on the specification dated May 1874. The two following 0-4-4T designs were designated classes C and D. Bearing in mind that Johnson produced a numerical classification in the same period – to be discussed later – it appears that the letter classification was produced by the Drawing Office to identify the new Johnson designs, A, B and D built by contractors and C by Derby.

In 1874, Johnson introduced an Order number system for all work carried out at Derby Works which included new engines. Order number One was dated 30 December 1874 and covered the first ten 0-4-4Ts, which were also allocated Class letter C.

The letter system was then limited to cover contractor-built classes only, while Derby-built engines were henceforth referred to by their order numbers. Thus drawing 75290 of 28 January 1875, for

the driving and trailing wheels of 6ft 6in coupled passenger engines, was noted 'Class E, 0.107'. Thirty Class E were built by Dübs and ten more to the same design were built to 0.107 by Derby. This parallel system was then continued to the end of the century and official diagram sheets had columns headed Class/Order Number.

There were several inconsistencies and variations in the letter allocation which is set out in Table 3A on the next page (top). The first of these related to the thirty contractor-built 2-4-0s Nos.1502-31 which were shown as 'Like 0.232'. The previous 2-4-0s built by contractors were Class E and similar engines from Derby designated by their order number, as noted above, so that in this case a Class letter would seem to be appropriate.

The two batches of fifty 0-6-0 goods engines built by Neilsons to specifications of 1889 had no class letter but were referred to as 'Neilsons Goods' whereas in the sequence so far allocated they should have been Class I. It seems that it was not used in order to avoid confusion with the numeral 1. The non-condensing and condensing 0-4-4Ts of 1892/93 from Dübs and Neilson were given separate letters, K and P, despite being variations of the same design. When the next type of 0-4-4T appeared with larger tanks and a different boiler in 1895,

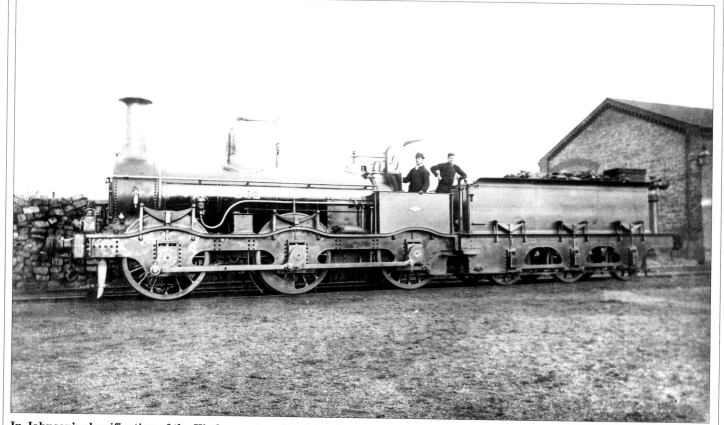

In Johnson's classification of the Kirtley engines the 0-6-0s became classes 22-26. No. 862, built in July 1871, was one of the final series having 17in cylinders and a 5ft 6in firebox boiler which placed it in class 22. Class 23 had 16½in cylinders and 5ft 6in firebox, Class 24 16½in cylinders and 5ft 0in firebox, Class 25 16in cylinders and 4ft 9in firebox and Class 26 16in cylinders and 4ft 10in firebox.

Table 3A. List of Engines built by Contractors

Class.	Maker.	Description.	Total No.	Original Engine Numbers.	Class of Boiler
A	Neilson & Co.	Tank Sh'g 6 W.C.	10	1102 to 1111.	A
A	Neilson & Co.	Tank Sh'g 6 W.C.	15	1112 to 1126.	A
A	Vulcan Fd'y.	Tank Sh'g 6 W.C.	5	1127 to 1131.	A
A	Vulcan Fd'y.	Tank Sh'g 6 W.C.	10	1132 to 1141.	A
B	Kitson & Co.	Goods, 6 W.C.	20	1142 to 1161.	B
B	Dubs & Co.	Goods, 6 W.C.	30	1162 to 1191.	B
B	Beyer, Peacock.	Goods, 6 W.C.	20	1192 to 1211.	F
B	Beyer, Peacock.	Goods, 6 W.C.	10	1212 to 1221.	E
B	Neilson & Co.	Goods, 6 W.C.	20	1222 to 1241.	B
B	Neilson & Co.	Goods, 6 W.C.	10	1242 to 1251.	B
D	Neilson & Co.	Tank, Pass'r.B.	30	1252 to 1281.	C
E	Dubs & Co.	Pass'r 4 W.C.	30	1282 to 1311	P
F	Kitson & Co.	Pass'r 4 W.C.B.	10	1312 to 1321.	B
G	Dubs & Co.	Pass'r 4 W.C.B.	20	1327 to 1346.	B
H	Dubs & Co.	Goods, 6 W.C.	20	1357 to 1376.	B
H	Stephenson & Co.	Goods, 6 W.C.	30	1432 to 1451, 1462 to 1471.	B
H	Beyer, Peacock.	Goods, 6 W.C.	50	1582 to 1631.	E
Like 0/232	Neilson & Co.	Pass'r, 4 W.C.	30	1502 to 1531.	P
-	Neilson & Co.	Goods, 6 W.C.	50	1873 to 1922.	B
-	Neilson & Co.	Goods, 6 W.C.	50	1923 to 1972.	B
J	Kitson & Co.	Goods, 6 W.C.	40	2023 to 2062.	B
J	Dubs & Co.	Goods, 6 W.C.	30	2063 to 2092.	B
K	Dubs & Co.	Tank, Pass'r B.	20	1833 to 1842, 2013 to 2022.	C
L	Sharp, Stewart.	Pass'r 4 W.C.B.	20	2183 to 2202.	D
M	Sharp, Stewart.	Goods, 6 W.C.	40	2093 to 2132.	B
N	Vulcan, Fd'y.	Tank, Sh'g 6 W.C.	20	1993 to 2012.	A
J2	Dubs & Co.	Goods, 6 W.C.	50	2133 to 2182.	B
O	Sharp, Stewart.	Pass'r 4 W.C.B.	15	2203 to 2217.	D

again in non-condensing and condensing versions, these became K2 and P2, whereas one might have expected K and K2 for the 1892/93 engines and P and P2 for the 1895 engines.

On the other hand, the variations in the 5ft 2in 0-6-0s built from 1891 which were classes J, J2 and M, were more logically noted. As built, J and J2 were fitted with steam brake only and had different tenders, whilst M were all vacuum fitted. The ten 4-4-0s, Nos.2581-2590 of 1900, were logically described as 'Like M & GN C' because they were built to the specification for that class with minor amendments. But if the system of allocating a letter to contractor-built engines had been adhered to, they should have had a letter, being dissimilar to earlier such designs.

This particular instance reinforces the view that the whole question of letter classification was merely a Drawing Office method of identifying the different classes rather than the result of any formal Company decision. The inclusion in the list of the ten 2-4-0s to Kirtley's design built after his death as Nos.1070-1089 and shown as 'Like 0.97' is further evidence. In this case, the 2-4-0s built to 0.97 were in fact the same engine design as the Kirtleys, with Johnson boilers, so the 'likeness' was the other way round!

Finally classes S, U and U2 are all variations of the same basic 0-6-0T. Class S had condensing apparatus and was vacuum brake fitted, whilst classes U and U2 were non condensing, the former with steam brake only and the latter with vacuum brakes and carriage warming apparatus.

The 2-6-0s supplied by Baldwin and Schenectady of America were erected at Derby and so the problem was resolved

The complexities of the early power classification whereby each new and more powerful design was successively class 1 is best left to the imagination. No. 207 of the 150 class built in 1897 was initially class 1, was class 2 from 1898-1902, class 4 in 1904, class 2 in 1905 and finally class 1 again in 1906.

by describing them as - 'Mogul'! Successive batches of engines built to the same design by contractors presented no problems of description as they could readily utilise the same letter. The successive 0-6-0s to class M are the principal example, but with the Derby-built engines it was different, as each batch had its own order number. This may be demonstrated by the 2-4-0s referred to above, whereby the first Derby-built batch of ten engines, Nos.1400-1409 were to 0.232. Two more lots of ten engines were built, to 0.273 and 0.279.

Thus a very good working knowledge of the order book and letter allocation was (and is!) required to identify particular classes. Of course, the Kirtley classes did not come within the system...

1b. 'The first member of the Class'

The Drawing Office clearly had the same problem to some degree and from 1877 references are made in the Drawing Register, mainly regarding Kirtley classes, to 'the first member' of a class. Thus drawing 77.775, concerning alterations to the bogie spring cradle of the Johnson 1262 class 0-4-4T and drawing 78.1037 ('Details steam brake – 690 class') referring to the Kirtley 0-4-4Ts are examples.

This method of describing the various classes had the benefit of being readily applied, applicable to all classes and easily understood. For these reasons, it has been widely used by authors and will be used here in the class chapters which follow, to provide a consistent approach.

1c. Johnson's Numerical classification

Johnson produced a numerical system for the Kirtley classes, to which were added the early Johnson classes. In view of the

Table 3A. (continued) List of Engines built by Contractors

Class.	Maker.	Description.	Total No.	Original Engine Numbers.	Class of Boiler
P	Neilson & Co.	Tank, Pass'r B..	10	2218 to 2227.	C
P2	Dubs & Co.	Tank, Pass'r B..	5	2228 to 2232.	C1
Like 0/97	Sharp & Co.	Pass'r 4 W.C.	20	1070 to 1089.	P
K2	Dubs & Co.	Tank, Pass'r B.	10	2233 to 2242.	C1
K2	Dubs & Co.	Tank, Pass'r B.	5	2243 to 2247.	C1
Q	Sharp, Stewart.	Tank, Sh'g 6 W.C.	5	2248 to 2252.	A1
M	Neilson & Co.	Goods, 6 W.C.	75	2284 to 2358.	B
M	Sharp, Stewart.	Goods, 6 W.C.	25	2259 to 2283.	B
M	Kitson & Co.	Goods, 6 W.C.	30	2391 to 2420.	B
Q	Stephenson & Co.	Tank, Sh'g 6 W.C.	30	2361 to 2390.	A1
R	Sharp, Stewart.	Pass'r, 4 W.C.B.	20	2421 to 2440.	D
S	Vulcan Fd'y.	Tank, Gds 6 W.C.	20	2441 to 2460.	C1
M	Neilson & Co.	Goods, 6 W.C.	30	2461 to 2490.	B
M	Dubs & Co.	Goods, 6 W.C.	20	2551 to 2570.	B
M	Vulcan Fd'y.	Goods, 6 W.C.	20	2491 to 2500, 2541 to 2550.	B
Mogul	Baldwin Co.	Goods, 6 W.C.	10	2501 to 2510.	
Mogul	Schenectady Co.	Goods, 6 W.C.	10	2511 to 2520.	
Mogul	Baldwin Co.	Goods, 6 W.C.	10	2521 to 2530.	
Mogul	Baldwin Co.	Goods, 6 W.C.	10	2531 to 2540.	
Q	Stephenson & Co.	Tank, Sh'g 6 W.C.	10	2571 to 2580.	A1
Like M&GN C	Beyer, Peacock.	Pass'r, 4 W.C.B.	10	2581 to 2590.	B
K2	Dubs & Co.	Tank, Pass'r B. .	10	2611 to 2630.	C1
T	Neilson & Co.	Pass'r, 4 W.C.B.	10	2591 to 2600.	E
S	Vulcan Fd'y.	Tank, Gds 6 W.C.	10	2741 to 2750.	C1
M	Kitson & Co.	Goods, 6 W.C.	20	2641 to 2660.	P
M	Neilson & Co.	Goods, 6 W.C.	55	2681 to 2735.	B
M	Sharp, Stewart.	Goods, 6 W.C.	20	2661 to 2680.	B
U	Vulcan Fd'y	Tank, Gds 6 W.C.	10	2751 to 2760.	C1
U2	Vulcan Fd'y	Tank, Gds 6 W.C.	20	2761 to 2780.	C1

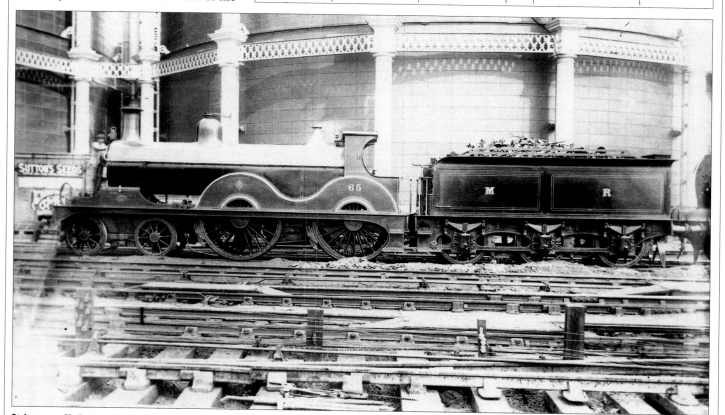

It is as well that prior to 1905/6 the power class was not displayed on the engines. No 65 of the 60 class (built in 1898) went through the same vicissitudes as No. 207 opposite, becoming successively class 1, 1B in 1902, class 2 in 1904, and class 4 in 1905. The engines then became the only slim boilered Johnson 4-4-0s to be placed in class 2 in the new system as finalised in 1906.

The Johnson 'Belpaire' 4-4-0s were the only Midland engines to be placed in Class 5 as the most powerful on the line, in 1905. This was tempered to a more realistic class 3 in 1906. No. 2788 is at Kentish Town in 1904, as class 1! S Summerson collection.

other systems just described, the reason for including the latter is not clear. It appears that it was devised early in 1874 and embraced Capital stock only, with Kirtley engines divided into twenty-six classes. New Johnson and two rebuilds of Kirtley classes up to 1882 were then added, to give a total of thirty-eight classes.

From the evidence set out below, it is apparent that the manuscript Register 'Classification in detail of Engines' (PRO RAIL491.870), was not written out until late 1875. The original list, which dates from early 1874, had been amended to take account of new construction and changes in classification between its inception and the end of 1874 and the list was set out as at January 1875. Amend-

ments between January and about October 1875 were then added/deleted as appropriate. It was subsequently further amended as a consequence of new construction, rebuilding, withdrawals or transfers to/from the Duplicate list and remained in use until July 1882, providing an interesting insight into Johnson's view of the Kirtley engines.

The classes were loosely grouped according to type, in generally descending order of size. They commenced with the engines with the largest cylinders, beginning with the larger 2-4-0s. Using the 'first member of class' to describe them. Class 1 was the 890 class in original form with 17in cylinders; the 1070, 800, 3 and 80 classes forming classes 2 to 5. The smaller 2-4-0s of the 156, 170, 230, 'large'

and 'small' 70 classes followed as classes 6 and 7. The 2-2-2s were sub divided into classes 8 to 11 and included the 1, 30, 120, 130 and 136 engine classes.

Class 12 is believed originally to have been allocated to some 2-4-0s built by Sharps in 1847-8, afterwards comprising various absorbed small tank engines.

Class 13 was the small 50 class 2-4-0s in capital stock at various periods, somehow separated from the other 2-4-0s, to which were added the three small 2-4-0s received from the Somerset and Dorset Joint Railway in 1878.

There then followed the principal tank engines as classes 14-19, including the 690 and 780 class 0-4-4Ts, the Metropolitan type 4-4-0Ts, the 'Poplar' 0-6-0Ts and various six coupled well tanks.

This view of No. 2661 at Cheltenham in 1905 clearly shows the brass '2' beneath the engine number, goods engines being unclassified before this date. S Summerson collection.

Table 3B. Loads for Main Line Passenger Engines

MIDLAND RAILWAY.

Locomotive Department,

Derby, October 20th, 1897.

Loads for Main Line Passenger Engines.

The following Table of Loads for Passenger Engines supersedes all others except such as are shewn in the Time Table or Appendix thereto, and with them drivers should, as a rule, be able to keep time without the assistance of pilot engines. It may frequently happen, however, that the Traffic Department will find it necessary to make up the trains heavier than shewn in this list, and in such cases it must, of course, be left to the discretion of drivers whether they call for the help of a pilot engine; but whether working trains alone or with an assistant engine, the speed limitations on various parts of the line must be rigidly observed, and there must be no excessive or rash running down falling gradients.

Both Up and Down Between	No. 1 Class Engines. Vehicles.	No. 2 Class Engines. Vehicles.	No. 3 Class Engines. Vehicles.	Remarks.
Carlisle and Skipton	12	11	10	
	11	10	9	Applies to 9.15 p.m. ex London.
Skipton, Bradford, Leeds, Trent, and Nottingham (via Eckington and Radford)	14	13	12	Ordinary Fast Trains.
	12	11	10	Applies to 12.25 a.m. and 12.42 p.m. ex Carlisle, and 10.30 a.m., 9.15 p.m., and 10.0 p.m. ex London.
	13	12	11	Ordinary Fast Trains.
	12	11	10	Applies to 12.23 a.m. (Mon.), 12.40 a.m., 12.50 p.m., and 4.0. p.m. ex Carlisle, and 2.10 p.m. ex London, 12.9 a.m. ex Trent (Mon.), and 1.44 a.m. ex Chesterfield.
Skipton, Bradford, Leeds, Trent, and Nottingham (via Sheffield and Radford)	11	10	9	Applies to 7.50 a.m., 10.25 a.m., 1.1 p.m., and 4.55 p.m. ex Bradford, and 7.25 a.m. ex Sheffield, and to the 9.0 a.m., 12.25 p.m., and 3.0 p.m., and 5.40 p.m., ex London.
	10	9	8	Applies to 7.58 a.m. Trent to Sheffield.
Clay Cross and Derby	14	13	12	
Swinton and York	14	13	12	
Morecambe, Carnforth, and Skipton ...	13	12	11	
Liverpool, Manchester, and Ambergate ...	12	11	10	
	9	8	7	Applies to Fast Expresses, via Chaddesden and 11.0 a.m. ex Manchester.
Dore and Chinley	11	10	9	Express Passenger Trains.
	12	11	10	Ordinary Passenger Trains.
Liverpool and Blackburn	12	11	10	

Classes 20 and 21 were other small four coupled tanks from the 'little' North Western Railway, Swansea Vale and Staveley companies.

The Kirtley engines were concluded with the various double frame goods as classes 22-26, from the 17in x 24in cylinders/5ft 6in firebox engines as class 22 down to the 16in x 24in cylinders/4ft 10in firebox engines as class 26.

The new Johnson classes then generally followed as classes 27-38 but the first 6ft 6in 4-4-0s (1312 class) were allocated class 7 as the remaining Kirtley small 70 class had previously been placed on the duplicate list. The 0-6-0STs absorbed from the Swansea Vale line were included in this group as class 30, and the rebuilds of the 800 class Kirtley 2-4-0s were classes 32 and 34. The corresponding rebuilds of the Kirtley 0-6-0s were not separately identified.

This classification will be further considered in Volume 2 – The Kirtley Classes.

The Derby Drawing Office Register, which commenced in 1873, makes a number of references to this classification system up to 1876 and three examples may be given. Drawing 76.733 for 'General arrangement of No.3 class rebuild 0.155' and referred to Johnson's rebuild of the 800 class 2-4-0s and drawing 74.195 is for 'Tender frame class 24 rebuilds' - that is, for the 2,200 gallon tenders provided for some of the early 480 class 0-6-0 rebuilds. Drawing 75.382 was headed 'General drawing (Beyers) 690 tanks class 16.' As noted earlier, the Register was maintained until July 1882, but otherwise this classification was not con-

Loads for Main Line Passenger Engines—*continued*.

Both Up and Down Between	No. 1 Class Engines. Vehicles.	No. 2 Class Engines. Vehicles.	No. 3 Class Engines. Vehicles.	Remarks.
Liverpool and Marple	12	11	10	
Manchester and Hellifield	11	10	9	
Nottingham and Lincoln	15	14	13	
Derby and Leicester	15	14	13	
Nottingham and London	11	10	9	
	12	11	10	Applies to 10 p.m. ex London.
Leicester and London	13	12	11	
	12	11	10	Applies to 11.32 a.m. ex Leicester.
	11	10	9	Applies to 5.15 a.m., 10.30 a.m., 2 p.m., and 6.45 p.m., ex London, and 5.26 p.m. and 8.49 p.m. ex Leicester.
Derby and Birmingham	15	14	13	
Birmingham and Bristol	14*	13*	12*	
	11	10	9	Applies to 9.45 a.m. ex Bristol.

*When the weather is unfavourable a pilot engine may be required between Birmingham and Blackwell, and Bristol and Mangotsfield.

Engines 115, 116, 117, 118, and 119 should, as a rule, take equivalent to two more vehicles than ordinary first class Engines.

MIDLAND RAILWAY.

Classification of Passenger Engines, October, 1897.

No. 3 CLASS.

No.	No.	No.	No.	No.	No.
69	88ᴀ	116ᴀ	153ᴀ	157ᴀ	162ᴀ
75ᴀ	89ᴀ	117ᴀ	154	160ᴀ	163ᴀ
79ᴀ	96	150ᴀ	155	161ᴀ	164ᴀ

NOTE.—The following Engines belong to No. 3 class, but owing to tender tanks being small or engines being small single-wheeled ones, &c., they are only suitable for a certain class of work in connection with the No. 3 class of engines, and the District Superintendents must apportion them to the work they are fit for.

No.	No.	No.	No.	No.	No.
4ᴀ	133ᴀ	180ᴀ	188ᴀ	196ᴀ	234ᴀ
16ᴀ	156ᴀ	181ᴀ	190ᴀ	197ᴀ	235ᴀ
17ᴀ	171ᴀ	182ᴀ	192ᴀ	230ᴀ	238ᴀ
81ᴀ	175ᴀ	184ᴀ	194ᴀ	232ᴀ	
104ᴀ	179ᴀ	187ᴀ	195ᴀ	233ᴀ	

MIDLAND RAILWAY.

Bogie Passenger Tank Engines, October, 1897,

The numbers given below, when working on the Branches, will be considered as included in No. 1 Class.

No.	No.	No.	No.	No.	No.	No.	No.	No.	No.	No.
6	692	795	1266	1325	1546	1645	1724	1828	2017	2231
15	693	796	1267	1326	1547	1646	1725	1829	2018	2232
18	694	797	1268	1428	1548	1647	1726	1830	2019	2233
137	695	798	1269	1429	1549	1648	1727	1831	2020	2234
140	780	799	1270	1430	1550	1649	1728	1832	2021	2235
141	781	1252	1271	1532	1551	1650	1729	1833	2022	2236
142	782	1253	1272	1533	1632	1651	1730	1834	2218	2237
143	783	1254	1273	1534	1633	1652	1731	1835	2219	2238
144	784	1255	1274	1535	1634	1653	1732	1836	2220	2239
147	785	1256	1275	1536	1635	1654	1733	1837	2221	2240
202	786	1257	1276	1537	1636	1655	1734	1838	2222	2241
204ᴀ	787	1258	1277	1538	1637	1656	1735	1839	2223	2242
205ᴀ	788	1259	1278	1539	1638	1697	1736	1840	2224	2243
206	789	1260	1279	1540	1639	1718	1737	1841	2225	2244
207	790	1261	1280	1541	1640	1719	1823	1842	2226	2245
208	791	1262	1281	1542	1641	1720	1824	2013	2227	2246
209	792	1263	1322	1543	1642	1721	1825	2014	2228	2247
690	793	1264	1323	1544	1643	1722	1826	2015	2229	
691	794	1265	1324	1545	1644	1723	1827	2016	2230	

S. W. JOHNSON,

LOCOMOTIVE SUPERINTENDENT.

The largest of the Johnson singles shared the distinction of being placed in class 2 in the final 1905 scheme, with the 60 class 4-4-0s, all the earlier 4-4-0s and 4-2-2s being class 1 along with the 2-4-0s. No 690 of the 'Princess of Wales' class at Kentish Town shows how incongruous the rebuilt tender appears.

tinued and no later references have come to notice.

Clearly the drawing office was aware of it, from the references made up to 1876, but other systems were in more general use and it is not clear what status this classification held or why it was so assiduously maintained up to 1882. E Craven suggested it was personal to Johnson and this is certainly a possibility.

From the later 1870s another limited numerical system appears to have been used in regard to the Kirtley goods engines. Initially there were Drawing Register entries concurrent with the previously described system. For example in 1876, drawings 76.500 and 76.522 of 2 and 8 February detail the outside crank and pin for No.1 and No.2 class goods. These references to Nos.1 and 2 class appear occasionally up to 1890, when drawing 90.3370 of 7 May was listed as 'metallic packing for old goods engines 1 and 2 class'. This is interesting because F H Clarke, in a listing of engines about 1905 which generally indicates the *power* class still shows the straight frame, 480 class and 700 class D F 0-6-0s as Classes 1, 2 and 3, so presumably this was a convenient shorthand way of describing them, still in fashion.

As noted above, the Drawing Register for 1876-77 showed examples of all the systems so far described, indicating the problems of the time and providing historians with a situation of fiendish complexity. Nor was it conclusive, for in due course, power classification produced a yet further complication...

2a. Midland Power Classification

As successive passenger engine designs became larger, and haulage capacity began to differ markedly, the need arose to define the loads each class was permitted to haul, having regard to its capacity. The earliest evidence to hand of the existence of a power classification is a manuscript list headed 'Classification of Passenger Engines January 1st 1889.' This list is incomplete for that date, but has three columns headed No.1 Class, No.2 Class and No.3 Class, with the in-

The passenger engines displayed their power class on the cabside from 1906. No.319, one of the 1877-built 7ft 0in 4-4-0s rests at Kentish Town after 1907, by now Class 1.

All the larger 4-4-0s, saturated and superheated, were placed in class 3. No. 724 a superheated 'Belpaire, in immaculate condition at Kentish Town.

dividual passenger tender engine numbers in the appropriate columns. Another manuscript list, dated October 25 1893, and again incomplete, shows only two classes but includes the passenger tank engines under the following heading 'Bogie Passenger Tank Engines, the numbers of which are given below when working on the Branches will be considered in No.1 class'.

From 1896, a series of official MR papers have survived giving Tables of Loads for Passenger Engines, which set out loads in terms of numbers of vehicles for various engine classes. The 1896 list shows Nos.1, 2 and 3 class engines. Then follow the lists of engines in each class, under the heading 'Classification of Passenger Engines'. The Engines in the three power classes as at January 1896 were as follows:

Class 1 (engines with 160lb boilers)
4-4-0s with B boilers built 1885-95 including the 'Joys' engines as reboilered except for No.1673, which reverted to a

140lb boiler for two years at this period.
2-4-0s 800 class Nos.811/817
4-2-2s All engines built 1887-95. They were regarded as Class 2 when working between Ambergate and Manchester. In subsequent variations of the scheme they were also regarded as one Class lower when working over the Peak line.

Class 2 (engines with 140lb boilers)
2-4-0s, all Kirtley and Johnson engines with P or B Boilers except 811 and 817 (Class 1), No.69 (890 class possibly with

About 1908, the 990 4-4-0s and Compounds were placed in class 4 in recognition of their superiority. The painted '4' is clearly shown on No. 991. Reasons for not using brass figures are unknown.

TABLE 3C
MR Passenger Engine Power Classification 1896-1910

CLASS	1/96	10/97	10/98	7/00	7/02	7/04	7/05	7/06	7/07	7/10	Notes
Kirtley 2-2-2	3*	3*	4*	4*	*	*	-	-	-	-	
170 and 230 2-4-0	3*	3*	4*	4*	*	-	-	-	-	-	
156 C boiler small tender	3*	3*	4*	4*	-	-	-	-	-	-	A
156 C boiler Johnson tender	3	3	4	4	*	*	*	*	-	-	
Remaining Kirtley and all Johnson 2-4-0 140lb	2	2	3	3	3	5	1	1	1	1	B
1312 and 1327 4-4-0 140lb	2	2	3	3	3	5	1	1	1	1	
1562 and1657 4-4-0 140lb	2	2	3	3	3	5	1	1	1	1	
2-4-0 160lb	1	1	2	2	2	4	2	1	1	-	
1312 and 1327 4-4-0 160lb	-	-	-	-	-	4	2	1	1	1	C
1667, 1738, 1808, 2183, 2203, 4-4-0 160lb	1	1	2	2	2	4	2	1	1	1	D
150 4-4-0 150/3/4/5, 204-9	-	1	2	2	2	4	2	1	1	-	
2421-40	-	-	-	1	1C	3	3	1	1	-	
60 4-4-0	-	-	1	1	1B	2	4	2	2	-	E
60 4-4-0	-	-	1	1	1C	3	3	2	2	-	F
All H Boiler rebuilds	-	-	-	-	-	2	4	2	2	2	
25,1853 and 179 4-2-2	1	1	2	2	2	4	2	1	1	1	
115 4-2-2	-	1	1	1	1C	3	3	1	1	1	
Princess 4-2-2	-	-	-	1	1B	2	4	2	2	2	
2606 4-4-0	-	-	-	-	1A	1	5	3	3	3	
2631 4-4-0 Compound	-	-	-	-	1A	1	5	3	3	4	
990 4-4-0	-	-	-	-	-	-	-	-	3	4	
Passenger tank	1	1	2	2	2	4	2	1	1	-	G
0-6-4 tank	-	-	-	-	-	-	-	2	2	-	G

A 198A classed as 140lb 2-4-0 1896-1903 and 238A the same 1900-05
B 890 class 69/69A was one class lower than 140lb 2-4-0 1896-1905. Possibly small tender.
C 800 class 806/11/4/5/7/25/7/8/9 and 1070 class 1085 were fitted 160lb 1889-1908
D 4-4-0 1315/28 were fitted 160lb 12/03
E Nos 60-9, 93, 805-9, 2591-2600, 2636-40
F Nos 138/9/51/2/65-9
G The tank engines 'will be considered as included' in the classes shown
* In 1902 classes 4 and 4* were abolished, the remaining engines then shown as * after class 3 and were unclassified.

small tender) and No.96 (Johnson 1 class still with 17in cylinders) in Class 3.
170 class No.198A
4-4-0s 1312, 1327, 1562 classes and No.1673 (Joy class)

Class 3 (Small engines)
2-4-0s 156 class with C boiler and large tender Nos.69 and 96 as noted above.

Class 3*
2-4-0s 156 Class with C boiler and small tender, 170 and 230 classes except No.198A
2-2-2s Twelve surviving Kirtley singles

It will be noted that the passenger tender engines were divided into three groups with the most powerful in Class 1 and the least powerful as Class 3. This latter group included the smallest engines, which were separately listed under the heading: *'The following engines belong to No.3 class but owing to tender tanks being small or engines being small single wheel ones etc., they are only suitable for a certain class of working connection with the No.3 class of engines and District Superintendents must apportion them to the work they are fit for.'* These are shown in Table 3C as 3*. The actual capacity of tenders described as 'small' is not given, but the engine lists indicate

that all Kirtley tenders up to 2,000 gallons were included. The passenger tank engines were also listed in the table dated 20 October 1897 (shown as Table 3B) under the same heading as in 1893: *'Bogie passenger tank engines. The numbers given below when working on the Branches will be considered as included in No.1 Class.'* This identical wording to the earlier manuscript lists regarding the passenger tank engines lends credence to the view that these earlier lists are from official sources. Thus, although the passenger tender engines were classified for power, the passenger tank engines continued to have more limited recognition. Goods engines were not classified.

The five new 115 Class singles added to Class 1 in the 1897 table, *'Should as a rule take equivalent to two more vehicles than ordinary first class engines'* and at the other end of the scale only four of the old Kirtley singles survived in class 3*.

In November 1898 the system was expanded to four classes, the existing three becoming 2-4 with the new 170lb engines comprising the 60 class 4-4-0s and 115 class singles (both with E boiler)

Unclassified for power but 'considered as class 1 when working on the branches'. No. 1316, condenser fitted for working main line locals to Moorgate, is in the familiar location of Kentish Town yard. S Summerson collection.

When continuing the Midland system from 1923, the LMS 'regularised' the tank engines and classified them formally but with a P or G suffix as shown in table 3D. These suffixes were not carried and often the power class wasn't shown either, but from 1928 suffixes P or F were displayed. No. 1416, newly rebuilt with a belpaire boiler in 1926 shows its painted class 1.

becoming Class 1. The July 1900 list shows the 150 class 4-4-0s Nos.2421-2440 and the new 'Princess' class singles as added to Class 1.

The introduction of the much larger belpaire and Compound 4-4-0s in 1900/2 necessitated further revisions to the system and by 1902 Class 1 was subdivided into 1A, 1B and 1C. The Compounds and Belpaires were Class 1A, the Princess singles, in recognition of their F type boilers at 180lb, became Class 1B and the 115 class singles were 1C. The 60 class 4-4-0s were divided between

Classes 1B and 1C and the 150 class 4-4-0s between Classes 1C and 2, for reasons which are not readily apparent in either case.

However, by the date of this list, 1902, No.4 class had been abolished and the engines formerly in this group (class 3 in 1896 – 2-4-0s with 17in cylinders and C boilers) and those then shown in the No.4 class supplementary list (4*, which included 2-2-2s and engines with small tender tanks and so on) were combined and shown in the supplementary list, worded as before but not now classified at all!

The revised classification was clearly deemed to be unsatisfactory and by 1904 was expanded to five classes. The subdivisions of Class 1 became classes 1, 2 and 3, the old classes 2 and 3 becoming classes 4 and 5. It must then have dawned on Authority that this type of revision would go on *ad infinitum* with the introduction of more powerful engines and so from 1905, to avoid repeated confusion, the system was reversed, with the least powerful becoming Class 1 and the most powerful class 5, thus laying the foundation of the scheme which lasted

No. 211 in the quiet of Carnforth shed has the shaded numerals and power class 1P in the 1928 scheme, the painted P fractionally out of line with the brass 1. Note also the 'LMS Built Derby' plate adorning the leading splasher. S Summerson collection.

Compound 1019 Class 4P pilots LMS Class 2 4-4-0 564 at Dore & Totley in the late 1930s. Red livery, block numberplate and Deeley tender with a riveted Fowler tank. S Summerson collection.

through the LMS to the end of steam under BR in 1968. It was simplified in 1906 to three classes, with 1 and 2 combined into a Class 1 which included all the 2-4-0s and unrebuilt 140lb and 160lb 4-4-0s. Class 2 covered the 60 class 4-4-0s, all H boiler rebuilds and the Princess singles, whilst the Belpaires and Compounds formed Class 3.

The bogie passenger tank engines suffered the same vicissitudes. In 1893, they were 'considered as' Class 1, in 1898 Class 2, in 1904 Class 4, in 1905 Class 2 and in 1906 Class 1. It is interesting to note, in view of their later LMS classification, that the 0-6-4Ts introduced in 1907 were 'considered as' Class 2 by the Midland. Until 1903, goods engines comprised for the most part the basic Kirtley and Johnson 0-6-0s carrying 140lb, 150lb or 160lb B boilers and a classification system had presumably not been found necessary. The new Johnson engines with H boilers and the rebuilt earlier Johnson 0-6-0s with H boilers changed this. In the Working Timetable they were described as 'New goods engines of more powerful type' with increased loadings compared to their predecessors.

Clearly a classification was becoming desirable, and the decision to proceed appears to have been taken at the end of 1904. This was followed by the idea of displaying the power class number on the good engines. There is, fortunately, preserved at the Public Record Office, some correspondence from Derby to (Foreman?) Rigby of Sheffield engine shed on the subject. In a letter dated 9 January 1905, reference is made under the heading 'Classification of goods engines' to 'Paget's circular of 4 January 1905'. This

The 0-6-4 tanks were 'regarded as' class 2 by the Midland but the LMS upgraded them to class 3P as displayed by No. 2012 parked out of use at Nottingham. S Summerson collection.

British Railways quickly adopted the practice of painting the power class just above the number as seen on Class 2 No. 40439, but without removing the MR brass '2' on the cabside. S Summerson collection.

unfortunately is not available but the correspondence continues: *'The question is still under consideration as to whether figures denoting the Class to which engines belong shall be painted or whether we shall use transfers. It will be necessary for all figures to be of the same size and at the same distance below engine numbers and of the same colour'*. So it is clear that the decision to denote power classifications on the goods engines was taken by January 1905, and that the position was to be beneath the engine numbers. The decision to use brass numerals instead of painted numerals was taken later the same month, as is clear from a letter dated 24 January 1905 from W H Adams, Locomotive Department Divisional Superintendent, at Derby: *'Referring to my Circular of 12th instant (not available) so soon as you receive your supply of brass figures from Derby for this work be good enough to advise me by 9am each Monday of the engines fitted the previous week.'* The goods tender engines were placed in three power classes as follows:

Class 1
All Kirtley double framed 0-6-0s with B Boilers and 140lb/sq.in. pressure. The one remaining Johnson 0-6-0 of the 1357 class no 1437(3055) with a 140lb B boiler and still retaining 17½in cylinders.

Class 2
Kirtley double framed 0-6-0s with B boilers and 150lb or 160lb/sq.in. boilers.
American 2-6-0s.
Johnson 0-6-0s with B boilers, 140lb/160lb sq in boilers 18 in cylinders.
Three Johnson 0-6-0s when rebuilt in 1906 with 6ft 0in driving wheels and H boilers.

Class 3
Six Kirtley double framed 0-6-0s with H boilers and 175lb/sq.in. pressure.
Johnson and Deeley 0-6-0s with H boilers 175lb pressure.

The H boiler Kirtley 0-6-0s were soon downgraded to class 2 and the sixteen Kirtley engines subsequently rebuilt with D or E boilers were placed in Class 2. When the 6ft 0in driving wheel 0-6-0s reverted to 5ft 3in they became class 3, like the other standard members of the class.

From 1906 the system of displaying the power class was extended to the passenger tender engines, but while the goods engines had the numeral fixed below the engine number, the two inch brass figure was now mounted on the cabside adjacent to the cut out. This position was then adopted for the goods engines as well.

The WTT Notice for December 1906 shows the loading for passenger engines working class A and B goods trains and bears a note to the effect that: *'Those worked by Classes 1 and 2 passenger will take a third less than the loadings for Classes 1 and 2 goods. No.3 class passenger will take a tenth less than for No.3 goods'*.

The October 1907 supplement which showed changes consequent upon the renumbering scheme stated that *'No further list will be issued as engines now carry the class to which they belong'*. The loading tables, however, continued to appear.

A Class 4 for passenger engines was introduced towards the end of 1908 and the 990 class 4-4-0s and Compounds were thenceforth placed in Class 4. Unusually, Nos. 990-999 and Compounds Nos.1035-1044 built between November 1908 and October 1909, initially had the power class painted on. Table 3C shows the changes which occurred during the period 1896-1910.

When the first two superheated 0-6-0s, Nos.3835 and 3836, appeared in 1911, they were placed in Class 3 and given the customary brass numerals on the cabside. A 'Classification of Engines' list issued by the Locomotive Drawing Office on 7 October 1913 shows them still as Class 3, but this was subsequently

changed and, with succeeding engines, they became the familiar Class 4 goods. Superheated engines were allowed a 10% greater loading than saturated engines in the same power class, clearly in deference to their superior abilities.

In 1921, the passenger tank engines were (in the ponderous terminology of the times) still 'considered as included' in their respective classes but the July Working Timetable omits reference to 'the Branches'. They therefore did not display any power class numeral on the cabsides and the goods tanks remained unclassified for power. The 0-4-4Ts remained 'as class 1' with the 0-6-4Ts and Tilbury 4-6-4Ts as power class 2. In respect of the LT&SR 4-4-2Ts, loads are shown also for the No.1 class Nos.2110-2145, the No.2 Class No.2158-2175 and the No.3 class Nos.2146-2157 and 2176-2179, but with no power classification.

Power Class as Engine Class
The comprehensive renumbering scheme of 1907, and the (then) recently introduced basic revision of the power class system, brought a whole new dimension to the matter of engine classification. *Power* became the principal way of describing the engine classes. Because it was not fully comprehensive, examples may be found in official correspondence and in the Working Timetables whereby a combination (as well as one or the other) of power class and 'first engine number' was used. Appendix No.24 of June 1911, for instance, produces references using both power class and engine number such as 'No.1 class 2300-2867' and 'No.2 class 2900-3469' while, used separately, '2000 class' and 'No.2 class goods' also appear. Thus in the post-renumbering period, power class and/or engine number was used to describe the various classes, as appropriate or convenient.

The LMS and British Railways Power Classification
The LMS power classification scheme

was based on that of the Midland and details were first issued in 1923. A numeral only was shown for all classes, passenger and goods, tender *and* tank engines. An oddity was that the Midland Division tank engines were shown with P or G in addition, to denote passenger or goods, and this included the ex-North Stafford Railway engines. The tank engines of the other Divisions however, were shown with numeral only.

All the details were shown in the LMS Table of Renumbering dated 14 February 1924, which showed the stock as at September 1923. The Midland Division Table is shown at Table 3D, opposite. It is of interest to note that the SDJR adopted a classification with a P or G suffix (displaying it on all engines) at about the same time.

Thus the Midland tender engines retained their previous classifications and continued to display their brass numerals. On the other hand, the tank engines, though now formally recognised, still appear (in some cases) not to have displayed the power class in the period up to 1928. A study of photographs taken of engines repainted in this period shows this to be so with several 0-4-4 passenger tanks. Examples are Nos.1274, 1283, 1321 and 1324, but in the case of the 0-6-4Ts only Nos.2011 and 2017 can be confirmed as *showing* a numeral. No suffix letter was displayed as on the SDJR engines.

The 0-6-0Ts with A boilers were in power class 1G and the sixty 0-6-0Ts Nos.1900-1959 with C, C1 or G5½ boilers were placed in class 3G, but no evidence has been uncovered to show that the power class was carried on any of the goods tanks. The 0-4-0Ts remained unclassified.

In 1928, a minor change to the system was made by adding P or F to the numeral classification and these suffixes (produced to sketch S.4344 of 2 April 1928) were painted on, adjacent to the brass numeral of the tender engines. At last the full classification was applied to the tank engines. So that they should not be left out, the 0-4-0Ts were solemnly classified OF. There were of course some inconsistencies in application and these will be considered in the class chapters.

British Railways perpetuated the LMS/MR scheme, the Midland engines remaining as before. The MR classification had thus endured, and embraced the whole of the British Railways steam fleet until the last was withdrawn in 1968.

These classification systems are set out at this point in the narrative order to facilitate the description, understanding and identification of the various engine classes and their details. Conversely, the classifications are perhaps better appreciated with a knowledge of the classes. Read on!

TABLE 3D – 'LONDON MIDLAND AND SCOTTISH RAILWAY COMPANY
Engine Re-numbering for Midland, North Stafford and Stratford-upon-Avon and Midland Junction Engines
SUMMARY OF LOCOMOTIVE STOCK'

(This LMS statement of renumbering clearly shows the designated letter suffixes for Midland Division tank engines, which did not apply to the tank engines of the other divisions as shown on the corresponding lists.)

Class.	New Engine No.	Type	Railway	Remarks
PASSENGER TENDER ENGINES				
1	1-281	2-4-0	MR	
1	290	2-4-0	SMJ	
1	300-327	4-4-0	MR	
2	328-562	4-4-0	MR	
3	595-599	4-4-0	NS	G and KT classes
1	600-683	4-2-2	MR	
3	700-779	4-4-0	MR	
4	990-999	4-4-0	MR	
4	1000-1044	4-4-0	MR	
4	1045-	4-4-0	LMS	
TANK ENGINES				
1P	1200-1430	0-4-4	MR	
3P	1431-1439	0-4-4	NS	M class
1P	1440-1451	2-4-0	NS	B class
1P	1454-1459	2-4-2	NS	A & B classes
	1500-1537	0-4-0	MR	
2G	1550-1598	0-6-0	NS	D class
1G	1600-1603	0-6-0	NS	KS class and Saddle Tanks
1G	1605-1899	0-6-0	MR	
3G	1900-1959	0-6-0		
3P	2000-2039	0-6-0	MR	
5P	2040-2047	0-6-4	NS	C class
4P	2048-2055	0-6-4	NS	F class
3P	2100-2107	4-6-4	MR	
2P	2110-2124	4-4-2	LMS	
1P	2125-2145	4-4-2	MR	
1 and 2P	2146-2179	4-4-2	MR	
3P	2180-2186	4-4-2	NS	K class
1P	2200-2214	4-4-2	MR	
3G	2220-2233	0-6-2	MR	
2G	2234-2239	0-6-2	NS	DX class
3G	2240-2273	0-6-2	NS	L class
BANKING ENGINES				
2290		0-10-0	MR	
GOODS TENDER ENGINES				
1 and 2	2300-2311	0-6-0	SMJ	
1	2320-2342	0-6-0	NS	E class
2	2343-2358	0-6-0	NS	100 and 159 classes
3	2359-2367	0-6-0	NS	2359-2366 H class
1, 2 and 3	2369-3834	0-6-0	MR	
4	3835-4026	0-6-0	MR	

In the above classification for Tank Engines, 'P' denotes that engines have been classified as 'Passenger', and 'G' that they have been classified as 'Goods'.
The 1 class Engines are the following: 2159, 2161, 2163, 2166 and 2170.
This summary and attached list refers to the stock at September 1923.

The LMS classification of the Midland engines was retained by B.R. No. 43570 ex- works at Derby has 3F on its cabside, retaining the brass '3' painted over adjacent to the cut-out.
S Summerson collection

Flush top 5ft 0in long fireboxes were introduced on 0-6-0s in 1861. No 592 was one of the second main series of double framed goods engines, built in August 1867. It is in original condition apart from Johnson chimney. Note the absence of brakes on the engine and the wooden shoes to the tender brakes. No. 592 received a Johnson boiler in 1882, became 2510 in 1907 and was broken up in 1930.

The final series of double framed 0-6-0s had the footplates 4ft 0¾in above rail level, 1¾ inches lower than their predecessors which gave a deeper hump over the driving wheel centres. The 5ft 6in flush firebox boiler was Kirtley's final standard. No. 990 was built in August 1872, received a Johnson boiler in 1884, became No. 2805 in 1907 and was broken up in February 1924.

Chapter 4 - Boilers

'The Engines of this Company are all provided with one, and most of them two, soft plugs'

Boiler Classification

Before commencing a general survey of the various MR boilers, it is appropriate to consider the means by which boiler were classified. No formal classification of Kirtley boilers is known but during Johnson's time a letter designation was developed for most of the 'standard' boilers in use. The Kirtley boilers were not included in this and it will be seen from what follows that it was a somewhat piecemeal process. It is therefore felt that some knowledge at this stage of the evolution of the system will assist in the discussion of boiler development generally.

In the volume RAIL 491.879 at the PRO Kew – *'Costs of Engines, Repairs, train mileage, machinery, stores, running expenses etc.'* – current from 1871-83, with some information to 1888, references to orders for replacement Johnson boilers are to 'goods boilers' (even when intended for 800 class 2-4-0s), 'passenger boilers' and 'C class boilers'. This last clearly refers to those latterly classed as C boilers, but almost certainly (at that date) refers to boilers 'the same as those on the C class 0-4-4Ts of 1875' (Nos.1226-35 in 1907). A new description, P, first appears on 25 April 1882 for boilers to rebuild 2-4-0s and appears to be a natural abbreviation for passenger boilers.

The order books from 1889 onwards confirm this situation and initially show C, P and goods boilers. The first Contractor-built 0-6-0Ts and 0-6-0s of 1874-75 were known as classes A and B and the first use noted of 'A class' boilers was in the Order Book for 1890, where 0.953 of 6 August 1890 was for five 'A class boil-

ers'. These were the first replacements of that type, indicating the adoption of 'A' from the A class. Goods boilers ordered up to October 1894 however, continued to be shown as such but from the next order, No.1442 of 10 April 1895, they were described as B boilers. It should be noted though, that from 0.1362 of 26 April 1894 the relevant orders were marked 'B' in pencil. It seems clear that the descriptions used up to this date in the official records for what became known as A, B,

the Singles. That they were not intended for the tanks is supported by the fact that the order which followed it, 0.1890, was for C boilers, which *were* used on the 0-4-4Ts.

It therefore appears that the system of relating boiler descriptions to particu-

Johnson 4-2-2 Singles in 1896/97. These did not refer to a letter despite the type having existed since 1887, but to boilers for 'Single type' or 'Single engine rebuilds'. In the case of these engines, there was no class letter because the engines had been built to Derby orders and so the boilers had to be related to a description of the engine class. But 0.1889 of 1 March 1899 was for D boilers. Now, the D class were Neilson-built 0-4-4Ts of 1875 which certainly didn't carry the same boilers as

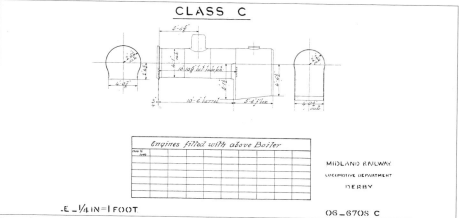

A series of boiler diagrams was produced in book form about 1906/7. This representative example includes, in the list of engines fitted, Nos. 1381-1400 which should be on the C1 diagram!

C and P boilers were shorthand for 'boilers for A class engines' or 'boilers as used on A class engines' and so on, while P, as suggested, referred to 'passenger' boilers. That a systematic boiler classification had not yet been introduced is borne out by orders for replacement boilers for

The Johnson 'A' boiler was synonymous with the 0-6-0 tank and enjoyed the privilege of being the last Johnson boiler type to remain in use. From No. 1102 (1620 in 1907) of 1874 until the rebuilding of No. 41835 (1835 in 1907) in 1961 it was a familiar part of the scene. No. 1781 was built in July 1890 and withdrawn in July 1951 and is seen here at Derby in March 1938. S Summerson collection.

No. 447 at Derby in the late 1890s. It was one of the first eight engines (all Kirtley 0-6-0s) to receive a Johnson B boiler, in the second half of 1874. No. 447 was built in 1861 at Derby. Note the one piece chimney and MR insignia carefully placed to avoid the rivet heads.The engine was broken up in November 1904.

lar classes was discontinued about 1898/99. It couldn't be consistent and a proper boiler classification was brought into use, the previous letter designation conveniently forming the basis of the new system. This also explains the oddity of a P classification retained in an otherwise consecutive letter sequence. Why this had not been adopted earlier is not clear. A 1902 order refers to E boilers and this was followed by the first orders for H boilers in 1903, which were duly shown as such. This also implies a classification for the boilers on the Princess class and the first of the belpaire 4-4-0s (confirmed later as F and G boilers) and supports the idea of a general adoption of the scheme around the turn of the century. The boilers on the Johnson 0-4-0ST of 1883/97 were classed J and J1 which indicates that they were not allocated a letter until after 1902/3. Order 2108 of 10 July 1900 for 0-4-0ST replacement boilers does not refer to a classification letter, but an official (abridged) classification list of boilers dated 4 October 1904 confirms the J and J1 classification at that date.

Subsequent Belpaire boilers, of various sizes, were generally designated by adding the firebox length in feet to the letter G, resulting in such oddities as G5½ and G8½. Some variations on original designs had a '1' added, but J1 was a different design to J and J2 was a variant of J1! Others had an A or X (occasionally both) suffix. When superheating was introduced from 1910, an S was added resulting, for example, in G8AS. Exceptions which were not given classification letters were the small, well tank replacement boilers, Metropolitan 4-4-0T replacement boilers, American 2-6-0s, and an S&W 0-6-0T replacement.

Boiler Numbering – Introduction, Stock Boilers

Evidence is very scant concerning any systematic boiler numbering scheme in the Kirtley, Johnson and Deeley periods. The practice of an engine retaining the same boiler until the engine itself wore out meant there was no difficulty in identifying a boiler, simply by the engine which carried it. The need for boilers to be changed on occasion and the developing practice of manufacturing stock boilers to facilitate repairs and replacement made it desirable to identify them more readily. The eventual outcome was the introduction of a boiler numbering scheme – certainly an identification of stock boilers was in being by about 1900, but information is sparse. Order 2621 of 22 June 1903 provided for two B boilers, describing them as 'stock boilers Nos.2087 and 2088 made to 0.2397', to be appropriated for the M&GN. The twenty boilers built to 0.2397 were allocated boiler numbers 2698-2717 in the subsequent 1912 scheme and no MR allocations (according to H.M. Ware, a noted chronicler of MR locomotive matters) have been found for boilers Nos.2714 and 2715 of the series. It would appear that stock boilers Nos.2087 and 2088 were allocated boiler numbers 2714/15.

Assuming a decision to number stock boilers from No.1, calculating backwards from these would indicate 1885 as the year of commencement, around the time of Order 587 of 12 June 1885 but the numbers, inevitably, 'do not quite fit'. There is a photograph of the firebox front of No.1000 (later 1005) with a figure of 86 on the right hand side and 0.2742 refers to boiler No.99 sent to Highbridge for stationary work. These agree with the existence of a stock list of belpaire boilers. There also appears to have been an H boiler list. 0.2622 referred to a boiler for the M&GN, 'stock boiler H.81 of 0.2646 to be used'. This appears to have been the H boiler from this order, subsequently allocated No.2930, for which no engine allocation has been found. Further information is conspicuous by its absence and unless a definitive list is found, the stock boiler numbering system must remain somewhat conjectural.

The 1912 Scheme

No *official* statement on this scheme has been found, and the following exposition attempts to explain the known facts from official MR and LMS records, supplemented by observations and the comprehensive studies of D.F. Tee, H.M. Ware and the late W.L. Good.

It appears that the system was devised in the period October-December 1911 and introduced about February 1912. The supporting evidence for this is as follows:-

1. The earliest order which gives boiler numbers is 0.4046 of 15 February 1912 for ten G7S boilers numbered 4012-4021.

2. The previous order for boilers, 0.4024 of 10 December 1911 for ten C boilers had the numbers (4002-4011) noted in pencil in the order book.

3. The first two Class 4 0-6-0s appeared in October 1911 and the boilers were numbered 4000 and 4001.

4. The LTSR boilers were included in the scheme and knowledge of these would have been available by late 1911.

The B boiler was also used on the first 115 Johnson 4-4-0s built from 1876-91 with a further ten in 1900. No. 320 was one of the twenty 7ft 0in driving wheel series of 1877 which never received larger boilers. As LMS class 1 it is at Burton on Trent on 9 May 1925; it was broken up in August/September 1928. S Summerson collection.

5. Sketch No.1755 of 1 January 1912 was for a 'Boiler number tablet'. W Leslie Good had also noted that the fitting of boiler number plates was commenced that year.

The Numerical System

The two Class 4 0-6-0s, Nos.3835 and 3836, whose boilers were numbered 4000 and 4001, were constructed to 0.4000/1 of 3 December 1910. This order number was issued in advance, out of sequence and on the same day as 0.3841, a year before the natural progression of orders reached that number. This appears to

have been a deliberate decision. Hugh Ware, moreover, considers that prior to the cancellation of twenty more Class 3 goods ordered on 18 December 1907 (which were to have been numbered 3835-3854), it was also proposed to number the *engines* 4000 and 4001. It is therefore clear that for some reason, importance was attached to the number 4000.

So it can be demonstrated that, commencing with the two Class 4 goods and from the sequence allocated to 0.4024 etc. noted above, new boiler construction was numbered from 4000 upwards at the com-

mencement of the scheme. The indications are that the numerical allocation of earlier boilers was then worked backwards from 4000. The numbers are continuous with the exception of Nos.100 and 101 which were not allocated. These earlier boilers were accounted for as follows:-

1. All boilers built to Derby Order No.3999 of 19 October 1911 back to 0.991 of 13 January 1891 for new engines and replacements, together with boilers for Contractor-built engines. These latter boilers were inserted into the sequence relative to the Locomotive Committee

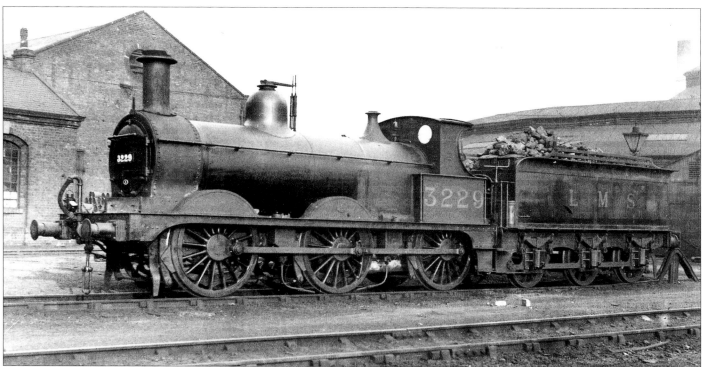

Boilerside clacks were a standard fitting until c1887 but engines built subsequently had clacks on the boiler back. One such was No. 3229 photographed at Derby in 1934. S Summerson collection

P boilers were used on Johnson 2-4-0s until 1904. B boilers then gradually superseded them as on No. 20254 which was the last to carry a P, removed in March 1927. Note clacks on the front ring. S Summerson collection.

date of authorisation. This group was allocated numbers whether broken up or still in use at the date of introduction of the scheme and were numbered 281-3999.

2. All boilers still in use from earlier Orders etc. These were numbered 102-280. In this group the surviving Contractor-built boilers authorised in 1889-91 were numbered at the end of the series instead of as in group 1.

3. LTSR boilers numbered 1-99.
It is clear that the system had to be split,

as noted above, because there were insufficient numbers available for all the earlier boilers. It was arranged in order to utilise (so far as was possible) all the available numbers back to No.1. It also seems clear that as a result of this the choice of 0.991 as the commencing point for all boilers to be allocated a number was an arbitrary one. Any earlier Order number would have resulted in too many boilers to fit the available numbers and any later Order would have left unnecessary blanks, so it is reasonable to believe that there were no boilers allocated Nos.100 and 101.

The oldest numbered boiler on an MR engine was No.102 of September 1875, originally on engine No.1644 (post-1907 number) and was put to stationary use in 1894. The oldest boilers still on engines at the date of introduction of the scheme were Nos.106 and 107 of July 1878, carried by engines Nos.1665 and 1667. Both were broken up in 1913. The LTS boilers existing at 1912 were likewise numbered in date order. The honour of being numbered MR boiler No.1 thus fell to an LTS No.1 class boiler of July 1896.

No. 58246 was the last engine to carry a B boiler. This was No. 5940, one of ten built to 0.6232 of 6 May 1924. Note the clacks on the middle ring. A number of 'passenger' boilers with clacks on the front ring and a longer pipe run were also used on 0-6-0s. No. 58246 was built as No. 1783 in October 1887, became 3175 in 1907 and 58246 in 1948. It is serving as Way & Works pilot at Derby on 14 August 1958 and was withdrawn in mid-1959. S Summerson.

Boiler Numbering - Exceptions

There is one exception to category 1, in that the boilers for 0-4-4T Nos.1341-1350 (in 1907) built to 0.981 of 28 November 1890 were all given numbers (351-60) but nine were broken up before 1912. The one surviving boiler should have been numbered earlier with a consequent revision of others.

In category 2 there are four individual exceptions where boilers were allocated numbers in error. These are:-

Boiler No	Date	Broken up	Engine No (1907)
181	5/90	1/09	1779
202	12/90	3/06	1240
204	4/91	5/04	1241
218	11/90	9/08	1799

Boilers were numbered in order of delivery, and a few minor inconsistencies arose in the strict date sequence of Orders for the boilers numbered back from 4000. As well as this, there is a lack of information on several early boilers. Nos.112, 116, 127, 222 and 246 have not been accounted for and it is probable that they were originally fitted to Kirtley double framed 0-6-0s withdrawn before 1907. These would have been put to stationary use and were still in existence when numbers were allocated, in which case they would not be traceable from the 1908 Derby Register. The number allocation of other odd boilers built later also has not been traced.

No boilers were allocated Nos.2268-72; Locomotive Committee Minute No.6696 of 18 October 1900 authorised the purchase of sixty goods engines from Neilsons but the last five were diverted to the SDJR. It is assumed therefore that in calculating the boiler numbers allowance was made for all sixty instead of the fifty five delivered to the MR. 0.2742 of 6 February 1904 was for fifteen G8 boilers for Belpaire rebuilds, but there is no trace of any G8 boilers identifiable with this Order and no replacement G8 boilers were made. However, five boilers suitable for Belpaires were built, Nos.3092-3096, for which no order number can be directly identified. Other evidence also confirms this, notwithstanding the fact that the boiler numbers are about a hundred out of sequence.

In a few cases, orders were not executed, or only in part. 0.3424 of 15 January 1908 for twenty H type boilers was apparently cancelled, as the boiler numbers do not allow for them and the second ten of twenty G7 boilers to 0.3591 of 24 June 1909 were not made, leaving numbers 3696-3705 blank.

No Orders can be found for ten C boilers Nos.3505-3514, or for five G7S boilers, Nos.4277-4282. It is believed that the order sheets are missing from the relevant loose leaf Order books.

Four LTS No.2 boilers were numbered 4235-4238 between 0.4325 and 0.4326 and it is believed (having regard to their position in the sequence) that they were ordered by the LTSR before absorption and numbered adjacent to two MR Orders for LTSR type 1A and 3 boilers, issued on 3 October 1913.

Boiler numbers were carried on a small oval plate (to sketch No.1755 of 1 January 1912) on the firebox back and were introduced at the inception of the scheme. The fitting of plates to the LTS boilers was carried out at Plaistow to Derby Order 4353 of 31 October 1913.

Some Midland boilers were ordered direct by the M&GN and SDJR; these were not numbered in the MR/LMS sequence. On the other hand, a number of boilers were sent to the joint lines from Midland/LMS stock orders - these *did* have numbers originally allocated, leaving blanks in consequence. In the case of the SDJR these assumed their allocated MR boiler numbers on absorption in 1930 – these are considered later.

A scheme of this magnitude and complexity is almost certain to contain minor discrepancies of the sort noted above but these do not detract from the validity of the scheme as now described. The *reasoning* behind the pattern it took however, is now unlikely to be determined all these years after the event. It is also a matter for conjecture as to why a simple numeration of existing boilers was not adopted as a starting point.

Boiler Numbering - LMS-built boilers

At the close of 1922, boiler numbers had reached 5490 and the Derby boiler number sequence was continued by the LMS; Orders from November 1928, commencing with No.8025, were prefixed with a D. In the early 1930s it was decided that all new boilers were to be built at Crewe and the last built at Derby were a batch of five LTS No.2 boilers, Nos.D8292-8296 to 0.8101 of 30 March 1932. The final Derby series numbers was allocated to the Kitson-built 0-4-0STs Nos.1540-1544 of 1932, as X8297-8301. Other works had their own boiler numbering systems, but some boilers built at Crewe for new MR type Class 4 0-6-0s in the 1920s were numbered in the Derby series. To avoid confusion, a directive was issued in 1928 that boilers were to be numbered in the series of the works that built them. As some of the first MR type and LTS boilers built at Crewe had Crewe numbers which were identical to some earlier Derby numbers, it was decided to introduce a new Crewe series commencing at C8400. Crewe also subsequently introduced a system of classification which indicated the allocation of new boilers. Boilers for new engines built at Derby were prefixed B1 and stock boilers intended for use at Derby were prefixed BS7.

**The C boiler was essentially the 0-4-4T boiler, the last being built to 0.6396 of 7 February 1925. No. 1327 is at Derby in August 1936.
Built in May 1886, it was less than four years from withdrawal in April 1940.**

The C boiler as fitted to a Kirtley 156 class 2-4-0. All twenty-nine of these engines were fitted between 1879 and 1891. No. 106A carried a C boiler from 1881-95 and still retains a Kirtley 1600 gallon tender. It subsequently became No. 8 in December 1907, 20008 in 1934 and was withdrawn in 1942.

A few stock boilers were built by contractors in the 1923-32 period. Twenty G9AS boilers were turned out by Beyer Peacock in 1927 and Armstrong Whitworth built twenty G7S and ten G7 boilers in the following year. Other contractors and works also built new engines.

Kirtley Boilers
General survey

Kirtley developed a progressive boiler policy, to provide the more powerful engines required for the rapidly expanding traffic of the mid-Victorian years. This was most successfully tackled with a succession of improved designs which also spanned the change from coke to coal burning, an aspect which will be discussed later in this chapter.

The earliest engines had boilers with fireboxes raised above the boiler barrel. The change to boilers with flush fireboxes was made in two stages, initially on goods engines. The first Derby-built double framed 0-6-0s of 1857/58 led the way and all subsequent goods engines followed suit, but passenger designs continued to sport raised fireboxes until 1869, when the 0-4-4 'back tanks' built for working to Moorgate appeared. These had flush fireboxes which then became standard for all new construction.

From the late 1840s the fireboxes of the smaller designs – the Jenny Lind type 2-2-2s (1847-56), the small well tanks (1871) and the 50 class 2-4-0s (1862-64) – were 4ft 3in long, with a boiler diameter of 3ft 9in. On virtually all the other designs, boiler diameter was 3ft 11in-4ft 1in, while fireboxes were lengthened over the years. This was in-variably carried out in three inch increments. The 6ft 8in singles of the 136 class (1857-58) had boilers with 4ft 6in fireboxes, but the other 2-2-2s and 2-4-0s of 1852-62 had boilers with 4ft 9in fireboxes – as did the standard straight framed double frame goods 0-6-0s of the same period. In 1861 a further lengthening of fireboxes, to 5ft 0in was made for the last thirty of the straight framed goods and this became the standard for the five 2-4-0 classes – large 70, 80, 170, 230 and 156 – as well as the celebrated 30 class 2-2-2s, all built between 1862 and 1868.

A larger increase was deemed necessary for subsequent new classes and the 5ft 6in firebox boiler was introduced in 1869. This was fitted to the last seven 480 class double frame goods and all the subsequent 700 class, while the 780 class 0-4-4 back tanks and those 800 class 2-4-0s built in 1870 also had these boilers.

Further thought was given to subsequent passenger designs and all these had boilers with a shorter 5ft 3in firebox, comprising the last six 800 class and last five 156 class 2-4-0s along with the 890 (except six) and 1070 classes; the final members of this latter class did not appear until 1875, after Kirtley's death.

Many of the earlier 2-2-2 and 2-4-0 classes which were produced in small numbers were not extensively rebuilt and were replaced rather than reboilered. As a result, few boilers were built in Kirtley's time for passenger engine replacement purposes – four 5ft 0in firebox boilers in 1870/71 for two of the 120 class singles and two of the 'large 70' class 2-4-0s. However, fifty-three more of the earlier designs were reboilered by Johnson with serviceable Kirtley boilers from the 800 and some of the 890 classes, which were given new Johnson boilers in the late 1870s and early 1880s. Additionally, six further engines – Nos.133, a Stephenson 2-2-2 of 1852, two 136 and two 1 class singles plus 156 class 2-4-0 No.75 were given *new* Kirtley boilers in 1874-79. These were flush topped 5ft 3in firebox boilers with 148 tubes. Circumstantial evidence suggests that they could in fact have been made for 890 class engines, which had received Johnson boilers from new. Having been rendered surplus, they were then utilised by Johnson for reboilering earlier engines, as was done with similar second-hand boilers. Thus the last new Kirtley boiler was not used until 1879, some six years into Johnson's superintendency.

With the goods engines, it was a different story and ninety of the earlier straight framed goods engines received new 5ft 6in firebox boilers between 1869 and 1874. As they wore out, the Kirtley boilers were replaced by Johnson designs on engines retained for further service and the last Kirtley boiler to be carried by a locomotive was a 5ft 0in firebox boiler of August 1871, on 'Poplar' tank No.885A, retained until replaced by a Johnson 'A' boiler in December 1897.

Boiler Explosions

Boiler design and an understanding of the causes of corrosion advanced considerably during Kirtley's term of office. These factors and the painstaking investigation of the Board of Trade Railway Inspectorate into boiler explosions and their causes, with resultant recommendations, came to eliminate basic weaknesses in boiler design.

The provision of fusible plugs in fireboxes was an early matter of concern. On 19 November 1850, a letter was read to the Locomotive Committee from the Commissioners of Railways regarding boiler safety. Kirtley reported *'that the engines of this Company were all provided with at least one, and most of them two, soft plugs made of composite metal which will melt at a temperature of 350 degrees'*.

Nevertheless, it took time to (virtually) eliminate the problem and there were five explosions on MR locomotives after this date which came to the formal notice of the Locomotive Committee. Whether they were barrel or firebox failures was not recorded. The first was on an 0-6-0 built by Rothwell of Bolton in May 1846 which exploded at Birmingham, on 5 March 1857 and the second concerned a small inside framed 0-6-0 built in 1851 which exploded at Finedon ballast pit in December 1864. The other three occurred in 1864-67 on straight framed double frame 0-6-0s. In the first case there was a fatality and in the second the fireman was reported as slightly injured, but in two of the three later cases no personal injuries were recorded. The engines concerned are referred to in Volume Two.

The Board of Trade report on this last episode, by Captain Tyler, is of considerable interest and significance and in view of its importance is examined below. The engine involved was straight framed 0-6-0 No.356 of January 1854. It had worked from Leeds to Colne, arriving about 2am on 5 May 1864 and was about

to commence its return journey later that night when the boiler exploded, killing the driver and seriously injuring the fireman. An elderly lady, who was in bed in a cottage about a quarter of a mile from the spot, received a leg injury from a portion which fell through the roof! The boiler 'was blown away in sixteen larger and a number of smaller pieces'.

The explosion took effect on the barrel of the boiler; of plate a little under half an inch thick, it had had its pressure increased from 120lb to 140lb sq.in. in November 1863. Extensive corrosion had taken place above a horizontal seam below the water line and also vertically, adjacent ot the smokebox ring, so much so on the horizontal seam that the boiler had been nearly eaten through in parts. Capt. Tyler continued: *'This is one of three cases of the same description which I now have under report, which occurred in the month of May on the GN, Midland and LNW Railways. It has also been my duty to report on four other cases in the last three years, two on the LNW, one upon the North Eastern and one upon the Great Western, in all of which the barrels have been similarly eaten through.*

'These seven cases represent a more serious amount of risk than would appear at first sight, that is daily incurred by the officers and servants of railway companies as well as by the public. Of the 6,500 locomotive engines and upwards which are in use on the railways of the United Kingdom, a large proportion are affected by corrosion to an extent which is more or less dangerous. For every engine that explodes there are a greater number of others which have been much weakened

from this cause, and which are constantly working with a less margin of safety than ought to be preserved between ordinary pressure and bursting pressure. There are several measures which may be adopted to remedy this state of affairs:

'1. Boiler barrels should be made more perfectly cylindrical by the use of butt joints and cover strips in place of the lap joints more commonly used.

'2. The longitudinal joints should be placed in all cases above the water line instead of below it, so as to prevent the risk of corrosion.

'3. The boiler should be firmly attached to the framing at one end only, the other end being allowed to slide backwards and forwards to allow for expansion and contraction, as is now frequently, but by no means always, done'.

'4. The barrel should be strengthened at the vertical (or transverse) joints and at intermediate intervals, either by the addition of belts or by plates rolled thicker in the middle as well as at the edges. A locomotive boiler thus reinforced would leak when the plates had been eaten through by corrosion, but could never explode.'

These last comments would have been especially noted, as many of the earlier double framed engines were constructed with the inside frames stopping at and attached to the firebox front, as in this case, giving the undesirable rigidity referred to by Captain Tyler. As noted above, there were more explosions on the MR after this episode, but a combination of vigilance and improved design eventually put an end to this hazard.

The C1 boilers on the last thirty 0-4-4Ts were pitched 4in higher than the C boilers on the earlier engines and this, coupled with a shorter 3ft 4in chimney, made the engines look appreciably larger. No. 2625 is at St Albans on 19 July 1902. Note the alarm whistle to the left of the brass safety valve casing and the two lamps over the left-hand buffer. The former was about to be dispensed with and the lamp positions changed. No. 2625 was built in August 1900, became 1425 in 1907 and 58088 in 1950 before withdrawal in March 1953.

On the 1896 series of 4-2-2s the firebox length was increased to 7ft 0in in the E boiler, as on No. 124 of February 1899. Becoming 678 in 1907 this engine was broken up in August 1926. Note the curved safety valve levers and the drumhead smokebox flush with the boiler barrel, emphasising the slim 4ft 1in diameter boiler. S Summerson collection.

Coal Burning

Fireboxes from the earliest days were designed to burn coke, legislation requiring engines to effectively 'consume their own smoke'. Kirtley's early fireboxes were thus coke burners. There were, however, considerable advantages to be had, if only a way could be found of burning coal and at the same time eliminate the problem of smoke emission. This came about through the pioneering work of Charles Markham, Assistant Locomotive Superintendent to Kirtley and his work is now considered, together with the background which led to it.

Coke has to be produced from coal in coke ovens. Some types are very friable and others extremely hard and unreactive, so only certain 'coking coals' were suitable for use in locomotives. Another important issue, whether using coal or coke, was the percentage of ash and the propensity (or otherwise) to form clinker. Now, a ton of coal produces only 12-15cwt of coke and as all the original ash remains in the coke, the result is that any given coke has a much higher ash content than the coal it was derived from. This, plus the fact that the density of coke is much less than coal, means that a ten-

der is only able to carry approximately half the tonnage that would be possible if coal was carried.

The cost of coke production was a further inhibiting factor, and could be compounded if there were difficulties in selling the coal gas given off. Distribution was also more expensive, because of the greater quantities involved; coke was a much bulkier product than coal, requiring roughly twice the number of wagons. From this very brief account, it can be seen that the incentive to find ways of burning coal in locomotive boilers was very great indeed.

The Gx boiler on the earliest Belpaires was succeeded by a variant classified G8 and fifty were built in 1902-5. The large cannister concealed both Ramsbottom and a lock up valve now considered necessary on the larger boilers. No. 827 was built in July 1903, with no alarm whistle, revised lamp positions and pick-up gear to the tender. It became No. 737 in 1907 and was the last to carry a G8 boiler when broken up in August/September 1925.

The Johnson H boiler, with lock up valve in front of Ramsbottom valves within a tall cannister, on No. 333 of the 1562 class as rebuilt in 1906. At Derby on 24 July 1920, this engine was broken up in December 1926. S Summerson collection.

Many experiments, of varying effectiveness and complexity, were carried out on a number of railways and on the Midland, Kirtley is recorded as early as 1852, mixing a small proportion of coal with the coke, with some success. The problems of regulating the mix, carrying two different fuels, differing combustion rates and so on, meant that this could not be a practical proposition, so the search went on. From 1856 the work intensified. General expansion of the railway system, with resultant demand, was outstripping the production of coke, while increasing distribution problems produced further difficulties.

In his paper to the Institution of Mechanical Engineers on 8 August 1860, Charles Markham set out the work he had done between 1853 and 1860 in the search for a method of burning coal, tabulating the evaporative power of different varieties of coal and coke. In 1853, records were taken using Tapton, Brancepeth and Peases' West cokes on double frame goods engines Nos.227 and 265 and on Stephenson single No.135. Two years later No.131 of the same class was tested with Staveley coke, as was double framed goods No.371. On 21 April 1857, the Locomotive Committee ordered that 'Mr Kirtley be instructed to use coal in some of the goods engines'. The work had begun.

In an initial experiment, extended to some twenty-six engines, a water filled 'midfeather' – a type of division – was placed across the centre of the firebox, so that it had two sections. The idea was to maintain a hot fire in the furthest section, which would burn the smoke from

fresh fuel added to the rear section. Quite how this was supposed to work in practice is not clear and no more engines were equipped. It has not been possible to identify all the engines fitted but the official MR Locomotive List of 1860 lists seven of them as 120 class 2-2-2s Nos.120-125 and 129, built by Sharpe between July 1853 and January 1854.

Using various coals, a whole series of experiments were then undertaken between 1858 and 1860. By this time coke was almost twice as expensive as coal and this work finally produced the desired result. The engines concerned are of some interest - the Stephenson single No.131 built in August 1852 was again used together with three of the small six foot 2-2-2s, Nos.4, 7 and 14, all built in 1855. The goods engines involved were straight framed double frame goods, Nos.393 of November 1856 and 419 of June 1859. Whilst the goods engines and No.131 had the largest fireboxes then in use, 4ft 9in long, the three small singles had fireboxes of only 4ft 3in length, so the work properly represented the different fireboxes then in use.

Coke has a very low volatile content and therefore very little secondary air needs to be admitted over the firebed, but the majority of coals suitable for locomotives release volatile hydrocarbons on heating. If the twin conditions of sufficient heat and turbulence with air are not met, then some of these hydrocarbons are released as smoke and pass unburned to atmosphere, causing pollution and a loss of efficiency. Therefore the initial work was directed to this facet and it was found that a great improvement

could be effected by fitting a plate to deflect air from the firedoor down onto the fire. The first experiment attached the plate to the firedoor but the maximum length that could be used, nine inches, was limited by the need to open the door. The next move was to fit a semi-cylindrical plate inside the firebox, independent of the door and some three feet long. This was very successful and Markham reported that about 240 engines with these plates were in steam daily at the time of his lecture.

Once this adaptation was proved, attention was then given to the possibility of fitting the twenty-six engines having a transverse midfeather with deflector plates. This was also successful but the problem with these engines was the difficulty of removing clinker from the front part of the firebox because of the presence of the midfeather. As this feature had not shown any particular advantage, it was desirable to remove it.

Attention was then directed to the firedoors. These have not previously been the subject of much comment, but were of considerable importance in the overall process of coal burning. To provide for sufficient secondary air over the firebed at certain periods of the firing cycle, it was considered desirable to increase the area of the firedoors. By enlarging them to 18in wide by 11 in high, an increase of 20% in area was achieved and Markham reported that engines in course of construction were fitted with the new size.

A further important trial was carried out, utilising sliding doors. The advantage was that the air opening was always at the centre and that the two doors

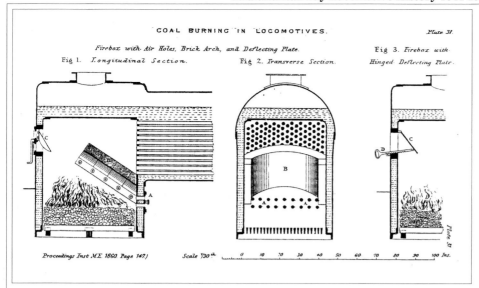

COAL BURNING IN LOCOMOTIVES.   Plate 31.

Firebox with Air Holes, Brick Arch, and Deflecting Plate.

Fig 1. Longitudinal Section.   Fig 2. Transverse Section.   Fig 3. Firebox with Hinged Deflecting Plate.

Proceedings Inst. M.E. 1860. Page 147.)   Scale 1/30th.

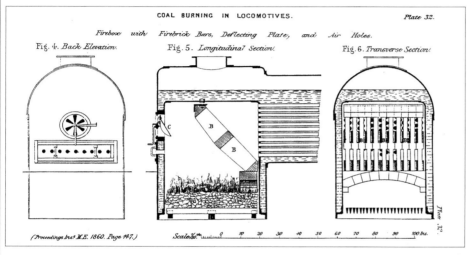

COAL BURNING IN LOCOMOTIVES.   Plate 32.

Firebox with Firebrick Bars, Deflecting Plate, and Air Holes.

Fig. 4. Back Elevation.   Fig. 5. Longitudinal Section.   Fig. 6. Transverse Section.

(Proceedings Inst. M.E. 1860. Page 147.)   Scale 1/30th.

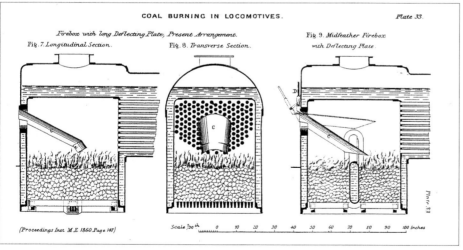

COAL BURNING IN LOCOMOTIVES.   Plate 33.

Firebox with long Deflecting Plate; Present Arrangement.

Fig. 7. Longitudinal Section.   Fig. 8. Transverse Section.   Fig. 9. Midfeather Firebox with Deflecting Plate.

(Proceedings Inst. M.E. 1860. Page 147.)   Scale 1/30th.

This page and opposite. This series of five plates accompanied Markham's paper to the Institute of Mechanical Engineers on 8 August 1860. They show the successive experiments in development of the coal burning firebox culminating in figure 10 showing the 'Present Arrangement'. Note in particular the sliding firedoor elevation shown at figure 11, the principle of which became widely used in later years, into the British Railways period.

particles through the tubes and the resultant accumulations which could occur in the smokebox.

By the date of his paper, 8 August 1860, Markham was able to report that the deflecting plate and brick arch was now adopted as standard on the Midland Railway, a simple statement resulting from acute observation, knowledge of combustion and the putting into practice the results of sound and considered experimentation. Its success was undoubted and it became the basic and universal form of locomotive firebox detail until the end of steam.

These arrangements catered primarily for the conditions prevailing when the engine was working. When the regulator was shut, the induced draught, both primary and secondary, was considerably less and this could result in smoke emission arising from insufficient combustion air. To overcome this a 'steam jet', later known as a 'blower' was fitted in the smokebox to provide some draught under these conditions. In Markham's arrangement this was operated from the footplate via a rod passing through the right-hand handrail to the smokebox. He reported that it was rare to find drivers omitting to use it when approaching stations. Figure 9 of Markham's paper shows the midfeather firebox with deflecting plate and figure 10 the final arrangements. This pioneering work of Markham was fundamental in the development of the steam locomotive and its importance seems not always to have received the recognition it deserves.

Following the adoption of coal burning it was found desirable to reduce the air spaces between the firebars, to reduce the loss of small particles into the ashpan. Further work was then undertaken on the ratio of air space to firebar area, to permit the maximum possible rate of combustion for the size of firebox. This subject was to occupy boiler designers on a pretty well permanent basis in their search for efficiency, with a wide variety of coals right into British Railways days. A final matter of detail related to the ashpan and the control of air through the fire. When burning coke, the damper was kept wide open but with coal it was found that half or slightly less open was normally sufficient. There was therefore some margin if it became necessary to increase combustion and produce more steam, to surmount a steep gradient, say.

In the year ending 30 June 1860, the proportion of coal used as locomotive fuel was 75.7% but in the last half year of the period, the figure had risen to 82% and would have been higher but for unexpired contracts for coke. This demonstrates the rapidity with which the change was ex-

moved simultaneously open or shut, whatever opening was required. This arrangement removed the difficulty of a hinged door opening across the footplate and was a considerable advance on the earlier arrangement. The extent to which this was adopted is not clear. Johnson did not use it, despite its clear advantages, but the basic design was widely used elsewhere. The LMS and the BR standard classes were all fitted with it, a remarkable tribute to the soundness of the original concept.

Having produced a satisfactory deflector plate, firehole opening and a door, attention was then given to means of fur-

ther improving combustion. The combustible gases from coal burning on the grate adjacent to the tube plate had insufficient time to mix with secondary air admitted through the firehole and burn before passing into the tubes. This meant the production of some smoke. Markham hit upon the idea of fitting a shallow firebrick arch adjacent to the tubeplate, so that the products of combustion from this area had to pass *under* it, before being drawn through the tubes. This simple expedient gave sufficient time for adequate mixing of gases and air and for combustion to take place in the firebox. It also reduced the carry-over of small

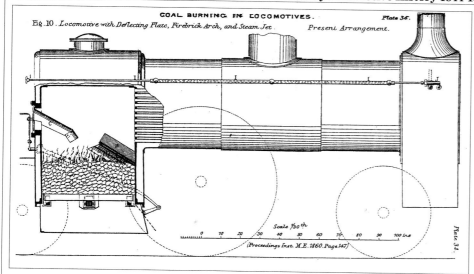

COAL BURNING IN LOCOMOTIVES.

Fig. 10. Locomotive with Deflecting Plate, Firebrick Arch, and Steam Jet. Present Arrangement. Plate 34.

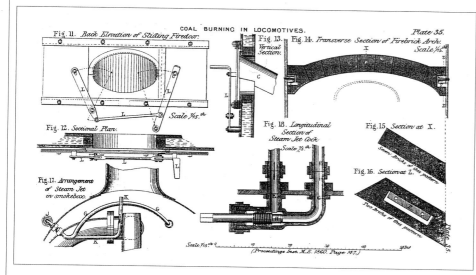

COAL BURNING IN LOCOMOTIVES.

Fig. 11. Back Elevation of Sliding Firedoor.
Fig. 12. Sectional Plan.
Fig. 13. Vertical Section.
Fig. 14. Transverse Section of Firebrick Arch.
Fig. 15. Section at X.
Fig. 16. Section at X.
Fig. 17. Arrangement of Steam Jet in smokebox.
Fig. 18. Longitudinal Section of Steam Jet Cock.

ecuted and is further evidence of its success. Markham's paper concludes with a table showing the total cost per engine to convert to coal burning:

	£	s	d
Steam jet and connexions complete	2	8	8
Sliding firedoors with levers, guides etc.	2	2	6
Deflecting plate	0	6	6
Brick arch and supporting bars	0	19	1
	£5	16	9

Annual maintenance had of course not yet been accurately determined but was not expected to exceed £3 per engine. Needless to say, all subsequent boilers conformed to the new arrangements.

The quality of the various coals available at that time was of course often unknown and in the latter half of 1861 the Locomotive Committee ordered trials of several varieties. Trial purchases were made from Dixons Green, Dudley, Churwell colliery Leeds and Whitwick colliery, Leicestershire. On 15 October some difficulties were reported: *'Read drivers reports respecting the Whitwick coal, which were unfavourable'*. Coal had arrived!

Boiler Feed
Up to about 1860, boiler feed was by means of two motion driven pumps and difficulties were experienced when locomotives were stationary in steam for any length of time. Low water levels resulted from the inability to place more water into the boiler without movement. The solution, if possible, was to run the engine to and fro until the water level was restored but clearly this was not always practical. The invention of the injector, therefore, by Henri Gifford in 1858, was a most welcome development and its use was taken up quickly. New engines were fitted with one injector and one pump and this became the norm throughout the rest of Kirtley's time with earlier engines altered to conform. The provision of two injectors had to await Johnson's designs.

In a very short space of time therefore, boiler design had progressed from what may be described as primitive to a basic satisfactory arrangement, one that has remained unchanged to the present day.

JOHNSON BOILERS
Introduction
Johnson introduced four boiler types, all in service by mid-1875, forming a standard range for all new construction and the reboilering of earlier designs for the next twelve years. The Drawing Schedules show all drawings dated 1873-74, the earliest being 10 September 1873, for what became the A boiler. The merit of these early boilers is reflected in the fact that apart from the P and A1/C1 variants, examples continued to be built for some fifty years. They are now considered in turn, using the classification subsequently adopted to distinguish the various designs. A fifth boiler was produced in 1875, an enlargement of the goods boiler, for fitting to ten of the Kirtley 800 class 2-4-0s. This had a 6ft 2in firebox, three inches longer than on the goods boiler with 264 tubes of 1⅝in diameter, giving a total heating surface of 1,333sq.ft. No more were built and they did not receive a classification letter, but were known as 'special' boilers.

The Early Designs - A Boilers
The first new locomotive design introduced by Johnson was an initial series of ten 0-6-0Ts built by Neilson and numbered 1102-1111, required primarily for work in south Wales consequent on the take-over of the Swansea Vale Railway. These had boilers with 220 x 1¾in tubes, and a firebox 5ft 0in long with 14.5sq.ft grate area. The diameter was the same as the goods and passenger boilers at 4ft 1in and the pressure of 140lb/sq.in continued as standard. These became the A class boiler. The first engine of the class entered traffic in November 1874, and was followed by thirty nine more. It was also used on the subsequent '1377' class 0-6-0Ts of 1878-1892, comprising a further 185 engines, to make a total of 225.

The next fifty-five 0-6-0Ts made up the 1121 class, and were given a slightly modified boiler classed A1, and this had a firebox 4in deeper. Only five more of this type were made (to 0.3666 of 3 January 1910) for reboilering purposes and A boilers were used otherwise. The first A boilers built for replacement purposes were ten to 0.953 of 6 August 1890. In addition to the Johnson 0-6-0Ts they were also fitted to the ten Kirtley 880 class 'Poplar' 0-6-0Ts from 1895 as well as several ex-Severn & Wye 0-6-0Ts. Before that, a number were made for the S&DJR - these are dealt with later. Further orders were issued at intervals covering 290 boilers until the last, 0.6362 of 23 December 1924, which was for five. The last to remain in service was boiler No.5669, built to 0.5992 of 4 September 1923; this stalwart was finally removed from engine No.41835 in 1961. The A boiler was thus in service for some eighty-six years.

The Early Designs - B Boilers
At the time of Johnson's appointment as Locomotive Superintendent on 2 July 1873, reboilering of the Kirtley goods engines was in full swing. This was continued at first, utilising the latest Kirtley 5ft 6in firebox boilers until his own design of goods boiler had been prepared and introduced.

This new Johnson boiler was first employed on the final eight Kirtley goods, reboilered during the second half of 1874 - Nos.273, 280, 284, 335, 343, 423, 428 and 447 and was to become the B class boiler. It carried 223 x 1¾in tubes with a 17.5sq.ft grate area in a firebox 5ft 11in long. Total heating surface was 1,233 sq.ft. This became the most prolific of all Midland boiler designs and twelve were built before Johnson's order number system was introduced in 1874. Of the

The raised firebox of the J boiler is clearly evident on No. 1501, together with the building plate recording 'Rebuilt Derby 1903'. This boiler, No. 2101, was transferred to engine No. 1502 in September 1920 and broken up in 1924. No. 1501 was 'replaced' in July 1921.

Kirtley engines, a total of 760 of the good engines were given the B boilers and to these must be added six of the large well tanks, five 2-2-2s and 145 2-4-0s - comprising three 80 class, one 170 class, one 230 class, twenty-two 156 class, forty-four 800 class, fifty-six 890 class and eighteen 1070 class.

Rebuilding the 0-6-0s ceased in 1891, but this boiler was not fitted to the smaller Kirtley 2-4-0s of the 170, 230 and 156 classes or any 2-2-2s *until* 1891 and after. Before this, C boilers were used on these engines where new boilers were

required. Similarly the B boilers were not generally used on the 890 and 1070 classes until 1904 and after. This gives a grand total of 916 Kirtley engines fitted, apart from Johnson's own designs with B boilers. These began with the B class 0-6-0s, the first of which appeared in February 1875. All the subsequent 0-6-0s built up to 1902 had them, some 865 engines, and the first 115 4-4-0s built up to 1891 plus ten more in 1900. From 1904, after P boilers ceased to be made, 122 Johnson 2-4-0s were fitted with B boilers over a long period up to 1927.

Thus a total of 2,028 Midland engines carried a B boiler at one time or anther – and the joint lines had some more!

To provide these, a constant succession of orders were issued, usually in batches of ten. So great was the need towards the end of the century, that two orders were issued for contractors to supply B boilers. 0.1832 of 28 October 1898 covered twenty from Neilson Reid and ten from George Fletcher. These were fitted to various Kirtley and Johnson 0-6-0s between June 1899 and April 1900. The second order, 0.1910 of 28 April 1899,

The Johnson version of Kirtley's boiler for the small well tanks. The boiler on No. 1601 which was 'rebuilt' from a 2-2-2 in 1872, was fitted in 1896 or 1897 – there is some doubt – and remained until it was broken up in January 1924. Note the raised firebox.

The Deeley G8A boiler reverted to the earlier pattern front tubeplate with raised smokebox as on Belpaire No. 858 of April 1905. The washout plugs are now on the top angle of the firebox. Note the rare combination of the 1906 crest and pre-1907 number. S Summerson collection.

went to the Yorkshire Engine Company for ten boilers and these were all put on Kirtley goods, between October 1900 and February 1901.

In 1903 the great reboilering scheme for the later Johnson 0-6-0s commenced. They were to be fitted with the larger H boilers, followed by a similar programme for 4-4-0s. This rendered surplus considerable numbers of serviceable B boilers which were then put into stock. Where they put them all is an interesting speculation! As a result there were no orders issued for new B boilers from November 1902 to August 1908. Further orders were then issued at intervals and despite the introduction of a Belpaire design of like dimensions in 1917, continued until 0.6766 of 12 November 1926. As a result of this, several B boilers survived into BR ownership, the last being No.5940 built to 0.6232 of 6 May 1924, on Johnson 0-6-0 No.58246 (old 3175).

One of these boilers has survived into preservation, on the Kirtley 2-4-0 No.158A. This is a genuine Midland boiler (No. 4366) and was built to 0.4601 of 9 January 1915, so it had given a good thirty years service when withdrawn in 1947.

Before leaving the B boilers, mention must be made of six boilers made to 0.626 of 11 December 1885 specifically to reboiler the Metropolitan type 4-4-0Ts. These were basically B boilers but with narrower fireboxes, to fit between the frames of this particular design. Because of their specialist allocation they were never given a classification letter.

The Early Designs - P Boilers

A passenger engine version of the B boiler was introduced at the same time, being of the same general dimensions but with a barrel 2in shorter. This resulted in a slight reduction of tube heating surface so that, with other principal dimensions the same, the total heating surface came down to 1,216 sq.ft. This boiler was first used on six of the last Kirtley 890 class 2-4-0s, turned out from Derby between December 1874 and March 1875, and fitted to all 135 Johnson 2-4-0s as built. Four of Kirtley's 800 class, all the remaining 890 class engines and all the 1070 class were reboilered with this boiler. It was also fitted to three Kirtley singles between 1888 and 1891 whilst to add interest to an already complex story, two Kirtley double framed 0-6-0s carried P

boilers for a few years from 1893. Thus 226 engines carried P boilers at one time or another. A total of 528 of this type were made but orders ceased after 0.2502 of 15 November 1902. It is interesting to note that this cessation occurred at the same time as the halt in construction of B boilers consequent on the introduction of H boilers. This had resulted in large numbers of spare B boilers being available and it is clear from the official records that it was found practicable to fit them to the 2-4-0s, rendering unnecessary the manufacture of any more P class boilers.

When engines carrying this boiler required reboilering after this date and no P boilers were available, B or (latterly) G6 boilers were substituted. The last engine to carry a P boiler was Johnson 2-4-0 No.254, its P boiler being taken off in March 1927 and a G6 fitted in its place.

The Early Designs - C Boilers

Johnson's second new locomotive design introduced a fourth boiler, of intermediate dimensions. The engines involved were the first 0-4-4 tanks with condensing apparatus built at Derby from June 1875, Nos.6, 15, 18, 137, 140-144 and 147.

The Deeley compounds carried the G9 boiler. This view shows the two washout plugs on the right-hand side. The left side had three as on No. 858 illustrated above. No. 1031 was superheated in 1922 and withdrawn without further renumbering in November 1949. S Summerson collection.

The G9A boiler on No. 992 is caught in its short existence between June 1909 and August 1912 before being fitted with a superheater. The MR buffer beam insignia are of the serif pattern, briefly used in the early years of the century.

Again, the boilers were 4ft 1in diameter pressed at 140lb/sq.in and they had 223 x 1¾in tubes but in this case with a firebox 5ft 6in long, having 16sq.ft grate area. They were built to Derby order No.1 of 30 December 1874. One hundred and forty-five subsequent 0-4-4Ts were fitted, plus all twenty-six Kirtley 0-4-4Ts when reboilered by Johnson from 1888. It was also the most appropriate boiler for some of the Kirtley 2-2-2s and his smaller 2-4-0s. Thus fifteen singles (thirteen 30 class and one each from 1 and 136 classes) and sixty-nine 2-4-0s (twenty-nine each to 170 and 156 classes plus ten 230 class and one large 70 class) carried C boilers. This gives a total of 265 engines, not including any in the section on C1 boilers which follows.

A belpaire version was introduced, in 1919 but C boilers continued to be made until 1925 when 0.6396 was issued on 7 February to make a total of 545 boilers. Again, several survived to the early years of BR and the last engine to carry a C boiler (No.6376 from the last 1925 order) was 0-4-4T No.58071 (old 1377), withdrawn in 1956.

The Early Designs - C1 Boilers
The C1 boiler was a variant of the C and like the A1 boilers, had a firebox 4in deeper. They were only fitted to the last thirty 0-4-4Ts and the sixty 2441 class 0-6-0Ts, all built in 1895-1902. No more were built and when replacement boilers were required, C or G5½ boilers were substituted. In a number of cases C class fireboxes were fitted to the original barrels. The last of these boilers in original condition was taken off 0-6-0T No.1909, in November 1931.

Later Developments - Steel boilers
The use of steel for boiler making in place

of wrought iron began very cautiously. The first recorded steel boilers were for some of the 1738 class 4-4-0s, to 0.554 of 12 January 1885, and these were followed by 0.658 of 30 July 1886 for ten goods (B) boilers, five in wrought iron and five in steel. These were fitted to five Kirtley 0-6-0s, all in December 1886. Two and a half years elapsed before any more were ordered and then 0.809 was issued on 15 January 1889 for ten 4-2-2s, five to have steel boilers and five wrought iron. The caution is evident as 0.829 of 3 May 1889 was for 'five spare wrought iron boilers to replace five in steel to 0.809 if necessary.' It wasn't necessary in the event and the spare boilers were used on the next batch, but there was still no urgency to switch permanently to steel. The MR Order summary book shows in its boiler order list that steel was not adopted generally until 1895 when the first of the series production was 0.1442 of 10 April 1895 - ten B boilers for rebuilding goods engines.

Later Developments - D Boilers
By 1887, increased boiler power was becoming imperative and a new boiler was designed for the first of the celebrated 4-2-2 'Spinners' introduced that year, later known as 'D' class. This had 240 x 1⅝in tubes with a firebox having 19.5sq.ft of grate area, which was 6ft 6in long. Total heating surface was 1,223 sq.ft. Diameter was again 4ft 1in but the pressure was increased to 160lb/sq.in. As noted above, five of them were the first steel boilers for passenger engines.

D Boilers were fitted to the first seventy of the Spinners from 1887-1896. They were also put on a hundred new Johnson 4-4-0s between 1892 and 1899 and were used to reboiler ten more (previously carrying B boilers) between 1896 and 1901. Eighty-seven additional boil-

ers for reboilering were produced, the last to 0.2587 of 20 April 1903. All these 4-4-0s were then rebuilt with the larger H type boilers between 1904 and 1908. As with the B boilers, this resulted in considerable numbers of serviceable D boilers being put into stock.

In an effort to find some use for them, it was decided in 1907 to reboiler twenty Kirtley double framed goods engines with the D boilers, but only nine were altered. Twenty-four ex-4-4-0 D boilers found stationary use in various places but a number remained in stock for several years. One served as a stationary boiler from 1906 to 1923, but was then resurrected and put on Spinner No.614! Another, from 4-4-0 No.191 (450 in 1907) was in stock for twelve years before reuse, whilst boiler No.612, taken off engine No.180 (661 in 1907) in April 1905, went into stock and was then broken up in August 1922. It was not the only one to rot away in stock. By an odd coincidence the first engine to receive a D boiler was the last to retain one. No.25 entered traffic in June 1887 and was withdrawn in July 1928 as No.600.

Later Developments - E Boilers
A further nine years were to elapse before the next new boiler design appeared. This came in 1896, for the celebrated 115 class 4-2-2 Spinners with 19½in cylinders having piston valves and driving wheels 7ft 9in diameter. These E boilers were an enlargement of the previous design, with firebox length increased to 7ft 0in and a grate area of 21.3sq.ft. Boiler diameter remained as before, at 4ft 1in, and between the tubeplates were 236 x 1?in tubes. With the firebox this gave a total heating surface of 1,233 sq.ft. Boiler pressure was increased to 170lb/sq.in. They were confined to sixty examples,

fifteen on the Spinners and forty on the 60 class 4-4-0s, all built between 1896 and 1901, plus five built for reboilering to 0.2349 of 3 March 1902. Here again the 4-4-0s were all rebuilt with H boilers, between 1906 and 1908. Two of the Es were broken up immediately but most were subsequently re-used after periods in stock. In this case twenty-five Kirtley 0-6-0s were to be equipped but only seven were rebuilt. As with the D boilers, several spent years in stock before being broken up, seven suffering this fate in 1925-1926, having been stored since the 1906-1910 period.

One has survived, boiler No.2636 built in 1902. It was fitted to engine No.673 in December 1909 and remains with that engine, displayed at the NRM as one of only two Johnson boilers preserved for us to admire in the flesh.

Later Developments - F Boilers
For the final series of Spinners in 1899, the 'Princess' class, a still larger boiler was produced, class F, very slightly greater in diameter than the earlier series, at 4ft 1⁷⁄₈in. Firebox length was increased even further to 8ft 0in long and 24.5sq.ft of grate area. The number of tubes was reduced slightly, to 228 x 1⁵⁄₈in and the total heating surface was 1,217sq ft. Boiler pressure rose to 180lb/sq.in. This series, in contrast to all the others, was simplicity itself - ten boilers for ten engines and no replacements. The boiler on No.686 was recorded in the Register as broken up in December 1916 and the engine in July 1919! Stored unserviceable, we assume.

General
So, for some twenty-five years Johnson boilers were characterised by their slim and attractive aspect; they merely got

longer as fireboxes were enlarged to provide greater steaming capacity. It is interesting to note that from the smallest to the largest distance between the tubeplates only increased by some six inches. Apart from the smallest used on the 0-6-0 tanks, the total heating surfaces only varied between the narrow limits of 1,216-1,233sq.ft. On the other hand, and this was where it mattered, firebox lengths increased from 5ft 0in to 8ft 0in and firebox heating surfaces from 90sq.ft to 147sq.ft.

The Final Phase - G Boilers
By 1899 bigger boilers of larger diameter had become necessary and belpaire boilers classed 'G' led the way in a series of 4ft 8in diameter. Appearing in September 1900, they had 272 x 1¾in tubes with a firebox 8ft 0in long, 25sq.ft grate area and 145sq.ft heating surface. These latter dimensions were similar to those of the final Spinners, but there the similarity ended. The much larger barrel gave a greater water capacity and reserve, and had a tube heating surface of 1,374sq.ft. Boiler pressure was 175lb/sq.in. This boiler was fitted to the first ten engines of the 2606 class of 4-4-0s which thereafter, despite other belpaire boilered classes being built, were known as 'the Belpaires'. Pressure was increased to 180lb/sq.in on all but two of them in 1909-11, but no more were built, being ultimately replaced by superheated G8AS boilers. The last one in service was removed from No.706 when it was superheated in February 1921. After alterations including safety valves, they were reclassified GX by 1904.

The Final Phase - G8 Boilers
A modified version of the G boiler, classified G8, was introduced in January 1902,

for the next batch of fifty Belpaire 4-4-0s. It was six inches longer between the tube plates, at 11ft 0in, but had fewer tubes, 262 x 1¾in. Pressure was 180lb/sq.in from new. Again no more were built and the last to remain in service was carried by No.737 at the time of its withdrawal in 1925. Four were rebuilt to G8A in 1914, of which more anon.

The Final Phase - G8½ Boilers
The second belpaire design was larger than the first for use on the celebrated Compound 4-4-0s. Again of 4ft 8in diameter, it had 261 x 1¾in tubes and a longer firebox (8ft 6in), 26sq.ft grate area and 150sq.ft heating surface. Boiler pressure was 200lb/sq.in. Only five were made, for Nos.2631-2635, delivered in 1902-03. The last in service was taken off No.1002 in November 1917.

The Final Phase - H Boilers
Up to 1902 all new 0-6-0 goods engines had been fitted with boilers having the same general dimensions as those of 1875. As with the passenger engines, a new 4ft 8in diameter boiler was designed for what became Johnson's last design, introduced in 1903. Unlike the passenger engines this had a round top firebox, as employed before. On this design (as with the G8 and Compound boilers) Ramsbottom safety valves were fitted, with a lock up valve in front. These new boilers were a welcome advance on what had gone before. They had 258 x 1¾in tubes, 21.1sq.ft grate area and a total heating surface of 1,428sq.ft. Boiler pressure was 175lb/sq.in. It was only fitted to fifty new engines, the ten 2736 class 0-6-0s of 1903 and the first forty of the subsequent 245 class of 1903-04. However a total of 427 were made to MR Orders, all placed by December 1905, plus

Deeley 0-4-0T No. 41533 was the last engine to run with a Midland built boiler. The J2 boiler No. 5171, on 41533 at Staveley Works on 5 March 1961 was one of five built to 0.5543 of 31 December 1920. It was fitted in 1954 and lasted until the engine was stored in October 1965 before formal withdrawal in December 1966. S Summerson collection.

The G7 boiler was almost invariably provided with an extended smokebox when used on 4-4-0s. No. 381 of May 1888 had been given on H boiler in 1904 and then a G7 with new frames in August 1910. Seen here in the 1930s, it was withdrawn in March 1936. S Summerson collection.

several more for the joint lines. They principally served to reboiler many of Johnson's 4-4-0s and 0-6-0s, then carrying B boilers – thus bringing about a sorely needed increase in power. Fifty-seven were ordered for reboilering in 1903, before Johnson's retirement, and it is interesting to note that the first 0-6-0 was rebuilt in June 1903, pre-dating the first order (of 13 November 1903) for rebuilding them by some five months! Matters were clearly urgent. The bulk of the reboilering was completed under Deeley, who introduced his own variants. The first passenger engines to carry an H boiler however, were the three S&DJR 4-4-0s, Nos.67-69 which appeared in November 1903! From 1909, G7 Belpaire boilers were used in their place but the last original H type boiler in service was carried by 0-6-0, No.3413 withdrawn in March 1928. The other variants to be described also became extinct that year. On the Somerset & Dorset however, an H type with shorter barrel survived until September 1931 on their 4-4-0 No.18, which had become LMS No.301. Johnson retired at the end of 1903 and further development was carried out by his successor, R.M. Deeley.

J and J1 Boilers

Before leaving the Johnson period, mention must be made of two small boiler types, J and J1, introduced in 1883 and 1897 respectively for the successive classes of 0-4-0ST. These replaced a number of small engines inherited from various sources in Kirtley's time, which were withdrawn. They were required for shunting on lines with sharp curvature which existed in some industrial areas and docks. The first J class, which perpetuated the raised firebox design of that earlier era, were 3ft 0ins in diameter with

113 x 1¾in tubes, an 8sq.ft firebox and 535sq.ft heating surface. The later design was larger by comparison but still diminutive. This was 3ft 8in diameter with 141 x 1¾ tubes and a firebox with 10.5sq.ft grate area and 764sq.ft heating surface. This became the J1 boiler.

The continuing need for a small fleet of 0-4-0 tanks meant new boilers were required from time to time and a few of each type were built for replacement. Thirteen Js and three J1s were built for their respective classes, the last ordered in 1918.

Non-standard Boilers

Having regard to the standardisation of boilers introduced by Johnson, it is in some ways remarkable that a series of individual boilers were made over a period of twenty years from 1875-95, in order to prolong the life of some of the absorbed non-standard tank engines. None of these were given a classification letter. The first was a boiler for one of the Staveley 0-4-0STs, No.1091, fitted in May 1875. The other five Staveley 0-4-0STs also received new boilers by June 1884. The three ex-'Little' North Western Railway engines which had been rebuilt as 0-4-2STs in 1864/65 received new boilers in 1877/78. Even the extraordinary Dursley tank was given a new boiler in 1877 and then it was the turn of the series of 0-6-0STs inherited from the Swansea Vale line. Five were reboilered between 1879 and 1888. The three little 0-6-0WTs from the Sheepbridge Company received new boilers in 1879/87 and when some of the engines belonging to the Severn and Wye and Severn Bridge Railway were taken into stock in October 1895, new boilers were made for three of them.

Most remarkable of all was Johnson's

perpetuation of a Kirtley design on the small well tanks. These engines required reboilering within three years of their conversion from ancient singles and instead of an entirely new design, Johnson produced a boiler of very similar dimensions, with raised firebox as before. This boiler was also used to renew some of the Kirtley 50 class 2-4-0s and no less than twenty-nine were produced at various dates, the last ordered in 1896. All these odd boilers are further discussed under the appropriate class headings.

DEELEY BOILERS
Introduction

The development of Johnson's larger boilers continued under R.M. Deeley who took command on 1 January 1904; the culmination was a new belpaire design with variations for the Compounds of 1905 and the 990 class 4-4-0s of 1907.

G8A Boilers

When Deeley took office, the last of the Belpaire 4-4-0s ordered by Johnson were in the course of delivery. Deeley built thirty more of the class with modifications and the first ten, Nos.840-849, continued with the G8 boiler, having a drumhead smokebox as on the Johnson engines. The remaining twenty, appearing in 1905, had a G8A boiler and reverted to the raised smokebox pattern.

As with the earlier boilers on the Belpaire 4-4-0s, these were destined to be a small group and only five more were built, to 0.3999 of 19 October 1911. Superheating superseded them; one of the five in fact was rebuilt to G8AS with superheater in 1924. Four of the earlier G8 boilers were rebuilt to G8A in 1914, as referred to previously and it was one of these, boiler No.2770, which was the last to survive, on engine No.751 withdrawn

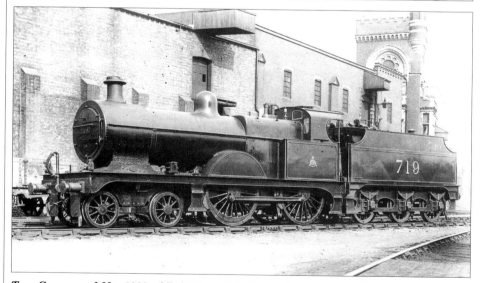

in December 1926. As mentioned earlier, 0.2742 of 6 February 1904 was for fifteen boilers, marked in pencil as G8 for belpaire rebuilds, though there is no record which can identify any G8 boilers with this order. However, five boilers *were* built, Nos.3092-3096, for which no order can be related directly. They were delivered (apparently) around the time of other types ordered in *November* 1904. Three, Nos.3093, 3094 and 3096, were shown as G8AX and fitted to belpaire 4-4-0s in 1910-11 and one (No.3092 shown as GXA) was put on engine No.707 in 1910.

Sketch No.1556 of 13 June 1910 was for alterations to a boiler (of 0.2742) to suit engine No.707 and seems to confirm the fact that these five boilers were built under the authority of this order. A further pencil note on the order records that the fifth was sent to Highbridge SDJR for stationary work, on 13 April 1907.

G9 Boilers

For his own Compound design, Deeley produced a new Belpaire boiler, of 4ft 8in diameter and pressed initially at 220lb/sq.in, having 1,458 sq.ft heating surface 216 x $1^7/8$ in tubes and a large grate 9ft 0in long of 28.4sq.ft area. This was classified G9 and appeared in 1905. It was fitted to the forty engines Nos.1005-1044 (1907 numbers). One of these, boiler No.3591, was rebuilt to G9AS to superheat engine No.1040 in July 1913. Three more G9 boilers were built to 0.3685 of 17 February 1910 before superheating became fashionable and the last of the type in service was one of this trio, boiler No.3793 from engine No.1022, the last of the class to be superheated, in January 1928.

G9A Boilers

A variation of the G9, classified G9A, was used for the ten 6ft 6in inside cylinder simple engines of the 990 class, first built in 1907 (the others followed in 1909). This had the same basic dimensions and $1^7/8$ in tubes, a size otherwise used on the Midland only on the Lickey Banker. Only the ten were built and they were all rebuilt with superheaters by January 1914 as G9AS.

Steam Railcar Boilers

Small vertical boilers for the two steam railcars were built to 0.2741 of 8 February 1904. These proved to be somewhat inadequate and two small horizontal locomotive type boilers were constructed, to 0.2741A of 5 December 1906 to replace them. These are discussed further in Chapter 7.

J2 Boilers

By 1905 some of the earlier Johnson 0-4-0STs were in need of renewal and a batch of five 0-4-0Ts to a new design was built to replace them in 1907. The boiler was designated J2 and had the same basic dimensions as the J1 fitted to the later Johnson 0-4-0STs of 1897 but with closed dome and safety valves over the flush round top firebox. The boiler had 764sq.ft total heating surface, 141 x $1^3/4$in tubes and a 4ft 0in long grate of 10.5sq.ft.

Top. Compound No. 1029 of Bristol with G9AS boiler pauses at Kings Norton on 14 April 1932 with a local passenger train. Together with No. 1002, it was the first to be withdrawn, in June 1948. S Summerson collection

Middle. A feature of the first superheated boilers was the provision of superheater dampers in the smokebox. The control cylinder is seen on the smokebox side on No. 488, rebuilt to '483 class' in March 1912 with a G7S boiler. These were fitted with a lock up valve behind the Ramsbottom valves, a practice discontinued on this boiler type from 1920. Splash plates and bogie brakes are clearly seen on No. 488, about to work an express from Manchester Central.

Bottom. No. 719 as rebuilt with a G8AS boiler in February 1921. The use of a lock up valve in addition to the Ramsbottom valves was discontinued on all engines of this class rebuilt from February 1920. Note the absence of bogie brakes. The general removal of this fitting was authorised in 1933 and quickly completed.

Five more engines were built in 1921-22, and ten additional boilers were made by the LMS and BR, the last two being built as late as 1954. This latter pair were not the last in service: that honour fell to one each of those built in 1921 and 1946, condemned in December 1966.

H1 and HX Boilers

For his new 0-6-4 tank engine of 1907, a variation of Johnson's H boiler was designed in 1906, classified H1. The tubes were arranged in vertical rows but their number was reduced, producing a lower total heating surface, though the firebox remained as before. Principal dimensions were 1,347sq.ft heating surface, 242 x 1¾in tubes, a 7ft 0in long grate with 21.1sq.ft area and boiler pressure of 175lb.

A further variation of this boiler was introduced the same year, 1906, classified HX. This was similar to the H1 but retained the Johnson pattern firedoor and single gauge glass. A total of sixty-five H1 and one hundred and fifteen HX boilers were made to orders issued between August 1906 and December 1907. The former were fitted to the last twenty of the 245 class 0-6-0s in addition to the 0-6-4T and of the remaining five boilers, two went to the SDJR. The others and all the HX boilers except one were used for reboilering. The odd HX boiler went to the M&GN.

From 1909 G7 Belpaire boilers and from 1912 G7S boilers displaced large numbers of the H type from 4-4-0s. A hundred and thirty one of these were then used to continue the rebuilding of class 2 0-6-0s, thus serving twice in the upgrading of older engines. Other 0-6-0s had previously received new H type boilers. The last H1 boiler in service was withdrawn with 1698 class 0-6-0 No.3155 in September 1928 and the last HX on 4-4-0 No.331 in March 1928.

G7 Boilers

Deeley's final boiler design was produced for a new class of 0-6-0 goods engines, which in the event were never built. Twenty were ordered, to 0.3412 of 18 December 1907 and it was intended that they should follow the previous goods engines and be numbered 3835-3854. The boiler was a belpaire version of the H family classed as G7, and had dimensions virtually the same as the H boilers they succeeded. Although the order for the goods engines was cancelled, the boilers were nevertheless built and with a further batch of twenty (ordered to 0.3463 of 15 May 1908) these served to commence reboilering the 4-4-0s then carrying H series boilers.

Very large numbers were subsequently produced, all used for reboilering purposes only. Of the initial fifty, forty-four were put on MR 4-4-0s and six went to M&GN 4-4-0s. No more were required for rebuilding additional 4-4-0s as superheated boilers were subsequently used, or for 0-6-0s whilst the displaced H type boilers all less than five years old, were still available.

After they were all used, there came a steady stream of orders for G7 boilers from Derby (commencing with 0.4721 of 28 July 1915) up to December 1931, principally for carrying on the rebuilding of 0-6-0s. A batch of ten ordered in 1917 were fitted with steel fireboxes due to the wartime shortage of copper, but these had replacement copper fireboxes fitted at the first general repair. From 1933 all new boilers were made at Crewe and the succession of G7 orders continued until April 1947 when the last fourteen, boiler Nos.12689-12703 were ordered. Again several went to the SDJR and the M&GN so that a total of 986 can be accounted for on MR/LMS orders. To complicate matters, several more were ordered direct by the M&GN. The last G7 boilers in use were three dating from the middle 1930s, on 3Fs Nos.43620, 43637 and 43669 - all withdrawn early in 1964.

FOWLER BOILERS
Superheaters

The merits of superheating were beginning to be appreciated when Fowler was appointed Chief Mechanical Engineer. Just before the resignation of Deeley on 30 November 1909 and Fowler's appointment, Locomotive Committee Minute 9793 of 18 November 1909 records: *'It was recommended that a Schmidt Superheater be fitted to an express passenger engine at an estimated cost of £256 (including Royalty of £50) for experimental purpose as it is claimed that a locomotive fitted with it will show an economy of 15-20% in coal and water'*. The outlay was agreed and the usual approval from the General Purposes Committee sought. A new G9A boiler was ordered to 0.3649 on 17 December, recording in the process that on 30 November 'a superheater had been ordered and is to be fitted to a 990 class of engine for experimental purposes'. No.998 was duly fitted in May 1910.

The next move came the following year; at a Locomotive Committee meeting of 19 January 1911 Fowler reported *'his intention of fitting up two locomotives with the Swindon type of superheater and recommended that two sets of parts for the same be purchased from the GWR at a total cost of £90 which includes the sum*

0-4-4T No. 1272 at Bedford on 3 August 1936; G5½ boiler was fitted in January 1926. The Transport Treasury.

The smaller 0-6-0Ts all came to the LMS with Johnson pattern boilers. The G5 boiler on No. 1695 was one of thirty built in 1928/9 with plug washouts on the firebox top angle instead of the usual 'hand hold' doors. Note also the flat top dome cover has replaced the Midland pattern. At Derby, the engine is chalked 'prepared' and what looks like '14/3/38'. S Summerson collection.

of £10 per engine royalty'. In fact this referred to the proposed new superheater goods engines which appeared later that year, carrying superheated G7 boilers. On 5 May 1911, in approving the fitting of thirty engines with Schmidt superheaters, a royalty payment of £45 per engine was accepted by the Committee. At the same time the tender of Thermo and Pressure Instruments Ltd to supply six 'Fournier' pyrometers for indicating the temperature of superheated steam, was accepted. This feature was fitted only to a few of the first superheated engines. The Schmidt Superheating Co had decided to reduce the royalty for old engines fitted with their superheaters and piston valves from £45 to £40 per engine and this was reported on 19 October 1911. The Schmidt piston valves were excellent when new but brought leakage of steam as they wore. It was left to the LMS to replace them with a series of orders for multiple narrow ring piston valves in the 1930s.

Fowler and Anderson (the Derby Works Manager) obtained a patent (No.12334 of 1911) relating to superheaters but the Locomotive Committee agreed on 16 May 1912 to its transfer to the Schmidt Superheating Co, on consideration 'that they supply fifty sets of superheater elements at a cost of £77 per set'. Including these, a total of 160 sets were ordered by July 1914. On 24 September 1913, a Locomotive Drawing Office note headed 'Variations in workings between Superheated and Saturated Locomotives' set out the advantages of the former - more powerful and greater economy in coal and water. This was recognised in the loadings subsequently permitted for superheated and saturated engines of the same power class as noted in Working Timetable figures of July 1921 - 'Passenger engines with superheaters will take a tenth more than the load shown for the class to which they belong.'

The benefits of superheating accepted, superheated versions of G7, G8A and G9A were designed and a total of 325 MR engines were rebuilt with superheated boilers. The programme of rebuilding the Class 2 and 3 4-4-0s was never completed and ceased in 1924 and 1925 respectively, but as the superheated Compounds were adopted as an LMS standard, their rebuilding was continued to completion, through to January 1928. To the superheated rebuilds must be added the 192 Class 4 0-6-0s and the Lickey Banker, fitted from new. Three Class 3 0-6-0s were also superheated in 1922-23 but they reverted to saturated after about five years.

G9AS Boilers

The first of these was a superheated version of the G9A boiler used on the 990 class, designated G9AS. The first one, fitted to No.998 in May 1910, had the following principal dimensions: pressure 200lb/sq.in, 148 x 1¾in small tubes, 21 x 5⅛in flue tubes for the superheater elements and firebox area of 28.4sq.ft. The heating surface was 1,170sq.ft small tubes, 360sq.ft superheater and 151sq.ft firebox - a total of 1,681sq.ft and represented a considerable advance on the saturated boiler.

As noted earlier, the ten G9A boilers on the 990 class 4-4-0s were converted to G9AS between 1910 and 1914 but the first G9AS boiler built new (later numbered 3746) in effect provided a spare while the 990 class boilers were rebuilt. Rebuilding the Compounds with these boilers proceeded very slowly; No.1040 was the first, in July 1913, and utilised its original boiler which had been superheated.

Only twenty-eight further boilers were ordered up to December 1922 and the last of the forty-five engines to be superheated was No.1022, in January 1928. The original six SDJR 2-8-0s of 1914 were fitted with this boiler and the last five, originally with larger boilers, ended their days with them. The LMS-built Compounds also had the same boiler and a total of 444 were built, the last to Crewe Order BS956 of January 1948.

The last Midland Compound proper to be withdrawn was No.41025 in January 1953, but the last G9AS boiler in service was that on 2-8-0 No.53807, withdrawn in 1964. However, three of these boilers have survived into preservation. The Compound No.1000 has No.12594 of 1947 and the two SDJR 2-8-0s Nos.13808 and 13809 have boilers Nos.10464 and 11346 from Crewe Orders of 1938/1942. By an odd quirk of fate boiler No.11346 was the last carried by No.1000, when withdrawn in 1951.

G7S Boilers

The first G7S boilers were included in 0.4000/1 of 3 December 1910, covering the building of the first two superheated 0-6-0s which appeared in October 1911. This design was closely followed by the 483 class 4-4-0 rebuilds which appeared in 1912, also utilising this boiler. After initial experiments, pressure on the

LTS 4-4-2T No. 2136 of January 1885, at Plaistow, carries the LTS 1 boiler with Ramsbottom and lock up safety valves and has acquired a Midland chimney. It became No. 2057 in 1929 and was withdrawn in December 1932.

goods engines was 175lb/sq.in and 160lb on the passenger engines. Layout was similar to the G9AS boilers, with 148 x 1¾in small tubes and 21 x 5⅛ in flue tubes, but 10ft 10?in between tubeplates as compared to 12ft 3¾in in the larger G9AS boiler. Heating surface was less at 1483sq.ft in total and the grate area 21.1sq.ft.

The first boilers for the 483 class rebuilds were to 0.3953 of 5 July 1911 and as with the G9AS boilers, a considerable number was built. In addition to the Class 4 0-6-0s it was also fitted to the 0-6-4 tanks in succession to their H1 boilers, as well as three Class 3 0-6-0s in

1922-23. The SDJR and M&GN joint lines also had several and all the LMS 2P 4-4-0s and 4F 0-6-0s carried this boiler. This resulted in a constant procession of orders from Derby, then Crewe, as well as those built by contractors for new engines. Calculations give a total of 1,787 of these boilers, the last being made to Crewe Order BS 8 10 of 1956. The last MR engine to run with a G7S boiler was 4F 0-6-0 No.43953 withdrawn late in 1965 but the last in traffic was a survivor from a batch of Class 4 0-6-0s built at St Rollox in 1925. This was No.6173 on engine No.44525, which had ended its days as a Crewe Works shunter

in 1966. Four boilers remain on preserved engines: MR 0-6-0 No.3924 and LMS 0-6-0s Nos.4027, 4123 and 4422. These date from 1937-55.

G8AS Boilers

0.4133 of 31 August 1912 referred to *G8A* boilers 'with tubeplates suitable for Schmidt superheaters'. So equipped, they were the first G8AS boilers and served to superheat the first ten Belpaire 4-4-0s, rebuilding of which had been authorised three days earlier.

No.700 appeared in rebuilt form in September 1913. These boilers were intermediate between the G7S and G9AS

LTS No. 48 of January 1899 retained its 1912 MR number 2157 as demonstrated here at Plaistow on 8 August 1925. It was rebuilt with an 'LTS 3' boiler in 1911, became LMS No. 2146 in 1929 and BR 41964 before withdrawal in February 1951. H C Casserley.

and had 25sq.ft fireboxes and a tube lay-out as before. Barrel length was 11ft 4¾in and the total heating surface came out at 1,496sq.ft. Boiler pressure was 175lb/sq.in. Their history is less complex than the preceding G7S boilers as they were only fitted to the MR 700 or Belpaire 4-4-0s and, from 1927, the Fowler 2-6-4Ts. One G8A boiler was re-built with superheater to G8AS and al-though the first two orders 0.4133 and 0.4325 were for G8A they were turned out as G8AS. A total of eighty boilers were ordered up to September 1924 but re-building the Belpaires ceased with seven engines not fitted. A total of 281 of these boilers were built, the final batch to Crewe order BS7 3568 as late as 1958. The last of the Belpaires to remain in service was No.40726 withdrawn in 1952 but the last G8AS boiler in use belonged to 2-6-4T No.42410, withdrawn in 1966. None of these boilers were preserved. A modified version was used in the post-war 2-6-4Ts built for the NCC.

G10S Boilers

The only entirely new boiler design to the be built in Fowler's period of office up to Grouping in 1923 was that for the Lickey banker. This was included in 0.4482 of 13 May 1914 and was a big boiler by any standard. Truly enormous, of 5ft 3in di-ameter, it was designated G10S. The fire-box was 31.5sq.ft and 10ft long, the boiler was 14ft 4¾in between tube plates and contained 147 x 1⅞in tubes, 27 x 5⅛in superheater flue tubes and a tube heat-ing surface of 1,560sq.ft. The firebox was 158.25sq.ft and superheater 445sq.ft, to give a grand total of 2,163.25sq.ft. One spare was built to 0.5738 of 9 June 1922 and used alternately with the original.

The Later Saturated Boilers

From 1917 Belpaire versions of the smaller Johnson boilers were introduced for fitting to 0-6-0s, 0-6-0Ts and 0-4-4Ts as appropriate and these were desig-nated G6, G5½ and G5. In addition the G7 boilers used on 4-4-0s from 1909-12 (already referred to) began to replace H boilers and some B boilers on 0-6-0s from 1916.

This rebuilding programme had ceased by 1930 but was resumed in 1939 on a limited scale in respect of the first three mentioned, initially because of the need to keep locomotives available for wartime traffic. It continued sporadically until 1961 when 0-6-0T No.41835 was given a G5 boiler.

G6 Boilers

The G6 was a Belpaire version of the B boiler and the principal dimensions were 196 x 1¾in tubes and 1,071sq.ft total heating surface, of which 104sq.ft was firebox compared to 110sq.ft on the B boiler. Grate area was 17.5sq.ft. It was introduced for the rebuilding of the origi-nal Johnson 0-6-0s of the 1142 class, which commenced in 1917. The first order, 0.4976 of 13 December 1916, was for ten boilers and these had steel inner fire-boxes, consequent on the wartime short-age of copper. As with a batch of G7 boil-ers, copper was substituted at the first

general repair. The G6 was then used on some of the later Johnson 0-6-0s built with B boilers, plus sixteen Kirtley 0-6-0s, in some cases succeeding larger H type boilers. Between 1924 and 1928, eighty-four Johnson 2-4-0s were reboilered with the G6, so that a total of 468 engines carried this boiler at one time or another. To these must be added the ten LMS 2P 0-4-4Ts Nos.6400-6409, which were given second-hand boilers from MR engines.

To service this requirement, orders followed on a regular basis up to 0.6987 of 10 October 1927. The 2-4-0s, however, soon became surplus to requirements and the majority were withdrawn in the 1930s, releasing large numbers of serv-iceable G6 boilers to stock. This, with the withdrawal of some 0-6-0s, meant no fur-ther G6 boilers ordered until mid-1939 and then only because of potential war-time traffic. Further orders followed up to August 1946, when Crewe order BS7 6029 was issued for ten boilers. This brought the total of these boilers to a re-spectable 558 and the last in service, No.12374 from that last Crewe batch, was withdrawn with engine No.58182 (old 3010) in January 1964.

G5½ Boilers

The next to appear was a successor to the C boiler and this was designated G5½ in recognition of its 5ft 6in long grate, as on the C. The first five were built to 0.5246 of 22 October 1918, specifically for rebuilding the 0-6-0Ts in the 1900-1959 series. Five more were ordered in 1920. These had 196 x 1¾in tubes, 977.5sq.ft tube heating surface and 97sq.ft fire-boxes to give 1074.5sq.ft total. (The C boilers had fireboxes with 104sq.ft heat-ing surface.) Boiler pressure was 160lb/sq.in and grate area 16sq.ft. No more were ordered until after grouping, but then, in addition to new standard 0-6-0Ts, a start was made in 1925 on fit-ting the 0-4-4Ts, which carried the C or C1 boiler. The building of large numbers of standard 0-6-0Ts and their retention more or less to the end of steam on BR produced a continuing requirement for new boilers as late as 1958. As a result a calculated 932 boilers of this type were produced up to Crewe Order BS7 3570 of March 1958 which was closed with four outstanding. The total of Midland en-gines fitted was 148. Several more were used on SDJR engines whilst two were modified for LTSR 0-6-0s Nos.2898 and 2899 in 1924. The last Midland engines to run with this boiler were 0-6-0Ts Nos.47201 and 47202, withdrawn in De-cember 1966, though the last standard 0-6-0T, No.47629, survived until 1967. Some ten of the latter engines are pre-served, so G5½ boilers are well repre-sented around the country.

G5 Boilers

The final Belpaire replacement design did not appear until after the formation of the LMS. This was the G5, to succeed the A boiler on the smaller 0-6-0Ts. 0.6124 was issued on 29 January 1924 for five boilers with a layout similar to the G5½ and G6 boilers, but with a

shorter barrel (10ft 4⅝in) between tubeplates. Heating surface was corre-spondingly less at 1017.5sq.ft with a 14.5sq.ft grate. It was used to replace A and A1 boilers on the 1377 and 1121 class 0-6-0Ts and was also put on the ten standard Dock Tank 0-6-0Ts of 1929, which became Nos.7160-7169. A total of 130 G5 boilers were made between 1924 and 1929 with a further twenty-seven turned out in the war years, 1939-45. A number were sent to the SDJR and one, No.12038 survives in preservation on 0-6-0T No.41708.

The LTS Boilers

The absorption of the LTSR in 1912 brought ninety-nine boilers which were given MR numbers, as well as four which were not, for the ninety-four engines taken into stock. The numbered boilers had the privilege of occupying Nos.1-99 in the new boiler numbering system of 1912, previously referred to. The fitting of boiler number plates was carried out at Plaistow and a specific order was is-sued to cover the work, 0.4353 of 31 Oc-tober 1913, quoted in full as follows, in view of its interest.

'Boiler numbering on LTS section engines'

'Please put your work in hand in connec-tion with the above. Number plates and casings are to be made to drawing S.1755 and fixed to arrangements drawing 13.9225. Numbers are only to be fixed on boilers which are actually fitted or allo-cated to engines. Boilers in shops must not be numbered until they are allocated to engines and a careful record must be kept of the numbers of the engines on which the boilers are placed and also in the case of second hand boilers of the num-bers of the engines from which they were taken. Advices to be sent to the Locomo-tive Drawing Office in all cases of boiler numbering. Numbering will be carried out at Plaistow. Plates and casings should be sent there as early as possible. Casings are not required for the number plates on boilers 10-45' On the order is the note: *'Completed 3 December 1913'*.

These boilers were of five different designs and were henceforth known and recorded as LTS1-5. LTS1 was fitted to the original thirty-six 4-4-2Ts of 1880-92, LTS2 to the eighteen 51 class 4-4-2Ts and fourteen 69 class 0-6-2Ts, whilst the six-teen largest 4-4-2Ts of the rebuilt 37 and 79 classes carried the LTS3 boiler. LTS4 comprised the two boilers on 0-6-0s Nos.49 and 50 and LTS5 were the eight 4-6-4T boilers. No replacements were ever made of these last two types al-though five No.5 boilers were ordered for the Baltics and then cancelled in April 1929.

The majority of replacement boilers made prior to the MR take-over were from outside contractors, but K.H. Leech, who was at Plaistow at the time, has stated that Plaistow built some boilers between 1910 and 1913. The five spare boilers which were given numbers were three No.1 and two No.2. The four not numbered were No.2 boilers and were presumably broken up. Coincidentally, four new No.2 boilers were on order at the time of the take-over and delivered from Vulcan foundry in 1913. These took numbers 4235-4238 in the Midland sequence. Also in 1913, new boilers were ordered at Derby to 0.4326/7 of 3 October 1913 for three No.1A and two No.3 boilers respectively, to cover repairs and renewals at that time. One further order was executed in 1920 for three No.3 boilers, but after Grouping, it was Crewe which built LTS stock boilers, apart from fifteen No.2 and 3 boilers from Derby in 1930-32. Thus some twenty-eight No.1, thirty-four No.2 and thirty-six No.3 boilers came from Crewe up to 1948, after which no more were built.

The last No.1 boilers were C5585-C5589, built in 1929-30 to Crewe Order S40/70510. Building of No.2 boilers ceased as early as August 1934 with the completion of five, Nos.C8797-C8801 to S40/39127, although two more ordered in 1948 were cancelled. The construction of a further thirty-five large 4-4-2Ts by the LMS between 1923 and 1930 produced a continuing requirement for No.3 stock boilers, which remained in production until a final pair, Nos.13151 and 13152, were built to Crewe Order BS7/4653 of 1948.

The last engine to carry a No.1 boiler was No.2073 withdrawn in November 1935 - boiler details unknown. The last No.2 boiler in use was No.C5375, carried by 0-6-2T No.41981 withdrawn as last of class in 1962. The last engine withdrawn with a No.3 boiler was No.41947 (LMS 2129) in December 1960. However, one No.3 boiler survives, No.12750 of Crewe Order BS7 7120 (November 1947) on the preserved 4-4-2T THUNDERSLEY (LTS 80, MR 2177, LMS 2148 and BR 41966) currently resident at Bressingham.

One interesting aspect of these LTSR boilers is that no evidence has come to hand of any proposals to build Belpaire versions of the originals, as was done in

many other instances with pre-grouping round top firebox boilers. In this way, the engines remained characteristically 'different'.

M&GN and S & D Joint Lines

In addition to boilers for their own use, the Midland and LMS provided both standard and non-standard designs for the two great joint lines, the former from its inception in 1893 until 1936 when the LNER assumed control of locomotive matters and the latter from its leasing in 1875 until the LMS absorbed the locomotives in 1930, maintaining them thereafter.

The detail is complex in the extreme in both cases and generally falls outside the scope of this history. But because of the dependency of both Melton Constable and Highbridge on Derby for boilers an outline is appropriate. This section identifies the additional standard boilers made for the joint lines.

Boilers for the M&GN

There was some confusion arising from the Midland boiler class letters and the M&GN engine class letters in some of the early Derby orders for boilers required by the M&GN. For example, the order for the C boilers to rebuild the first four M&GN A class 4-4-0s was written as *'Four A class boilers for rebuilds'* which meant *'Four boilers for A class rebuilds'*. No MR A class boilers were used on the M&GN. 0.2622 states: *'One new D class boiler (This is the same as our H class ...)'* A pencil note adds: *'This should be One new boiler for rebuilding M&GN D class engines. These are the same as our M class standard goods'* and was a B boiler!

A total of fifty-six new engines, forty 4-4-0s and sixteen 0-6-0s were ordered by the M&GN from contractors and delivered between 1894 and 1899. These carried standard Midland B boilers. During the same period four C boilers were

built at Derby for reboilering some M&GN A class 4-4-0s to M&GN requisition. Between 1903 and 1931, some ninety-nine more standard boilers were built at Derby and Melton Constable for reboilering purposes, bringing the total to one hundred and fifty nine.

The majority of the boilers sent from Derby were taken from Midland/LMS stock orders and various notes identify thirty-two, comprising twelve B, four H type and sixteen G7. After that, between 1926 and 1929, six G7 and seven G6 boilers were ordered direct and not taken from stock. Finally, there were the Melton-built boilers - nineteen C and thirty five B. There is no official record for five of the latter but if the engines concerned were *not* reboilered, their original boilers would have had to last between twenty nine and forty years - unlikely for the period.

Boilers for the S&D

So far as the complexities of the Somerset & Dorset are concerned, it may be noted that no boilers were built at Highbridge for reboilering purposes. Derby provided all. Until 1895 the principal motive power designs, the 0-4-4T, 0-6-0 and 4-4-0 were all slightly smaller than the equivalent on the Midland; from the take-over of motive power responsibility in 1875, new boilers were provided as appropriate but were non-standard combinations of A firebox and C barrel and C firebox and A barrel. This had continuing ramifications later on, as these classes were reboilered again and so further non-standard boilers came about - G5 firebox with G6 barrel plus H and G7 with shortened barrels (10ft 0in long instead of 10ft 6in). A number of straight A boilers were also used and G5 boilers replaced some of these.

From 1895, new engines were of similar dimensions to the equivalent current designs on the Midland and so had stand-

Delivered after the MR had taken over the working of the LTSR, No. 2198 of May 1913 (LTS No. 2106) carries the LTS 5 boiler. At St. Albans on 31 January 1934, it was withdrawn the following June. R.G.Jarvis/Mid Rail Photographs.

Johnson C boilers were built at both Derby and Melton Constable to reboiler the A class of the M&GN. No. 28 was rebuilt in 1905 and 1925. Seen here at Spalding on 22 August 1936 it was withdrawn in February 1937. R.G.Jarvis/Mid Rail Photographs.

ard boilers: B on the 0-6-0s and H/H1 on the 4-4-0s. When these were rebuilt G7 boilers replaced them.

Commencing with the celebrated 2-8-0s in 1914, which had G9AS boilers, there came five superheater 4-4-0s in 1914/21, to the same design as the MR 483 class rebuilds, the five 'Armstrong' 0-6-0s of 1922 which were the same as the MR Class 4 0-6-0s, both with G7S boilers and finally in 1929, seven 0-6-0Ts, identical except for details to the LMS standard class, with G5½ boilers.

For boilers built up to 1902, evidence on orders and construction is incomplete but it does not appear that any were taken from MR stock orders. Between then and 1911, some were ordered direct and some were taken from stock orders. If a non-standard requirement, it was adapted to suit.

From 1914 however, all boilers, altered if necessary, were taken from MR/LMS stock, with allocated boiler numbers except those for the 1914 2-8-0s and the Armstrong Class 4 0-6-0s. They acquired boiler numbers in 1930. To muddy the waters a bit more, the boilers for the 1925 built 2-8-0s and the 0-6-0Ts of 1929 were allocated boiler numbers when built, which they assumed after take-over in 1930.

A considered appraisal of the available information shows that the following standard boilers (additional to those ordered by the MR/LMS) were made for the S&D Joint and not allocated boiler numbers in that series at any time:
A69, B5
H 3, H1 2

Two modified G7 boilers (original numbers allocated were 6418 and 7082) were subsequently reconverted to standard after the S&D 4-4-0s which had carried them, Nos.302 and 303, were withdrawn in 1931/32. They were then

given boiler Nos.8313 and 8302 and afterwards were carried variously by MR 2P 4-4-0 No.381 and 3F 0-6-0s Nos.3294, 3652, 3665, 3753 and 3793. The reason for these boiler numbers at the end of the Derby series is obscure. No.8313 may have been in error for 8303, but in any event, as other G7 boilers assumed their originally allocated numbers on return to the LMS, the matter remains a mystery.

One standard G5 boiler also 'returned' for further use. S&D 'Scottie' 0-6-0 (LMS No.2881) was given one in March 1929 and on its withdrawal, the boiler was repaired and subsequently put on MR 0-6-0T No.1844, in October 1939. Later uses for contemporary G5 boilers from other 'Scotties' are not known at the time of writing.

BOILER FITTINGS
This section concerns fittings and associated details which were generally or widely applicable. Other fittings concerning particular classes are considered in the appropriate class chapters.

Live Steam Injectors
Up to about 1860, boiler feed was by means of two motion driven pumps, and from that date one pump and one injector became usual in Kirtley's time. Johnson's practice was to use injectors only, except in the case of engines fitted with condensing apparatus where the pumps plus injector arrangement was retained. This was to cope with warm feed water, for which the standard cold water injector was not suited. Reboilered Kirtley engines were altered but odd cases of the old arrangement are believed to have survived the reboilering for a short period.

Feed clacks were positioned on each side of the boiler barrel, on the middle

ring for goods engines but on the front ring for passenger engines - in order to clear the leading coupled wheels. In the case of B boilers, reboilering sometimes produced a 'passenger' boiler on an 0-6-0, with suitably adapted pipework, but the reverse situation did not of course occur.

Between 1887 and 1890, a progressive change occurred on new engines whereby the clacks were placed on the boiler back; this applied to the majority of boilers built after this date. However, the old layout continued in use on some Johnson pattern boilers and was still to be seen in the 1930s. Those fitted with condensing apparatus and which had pumps continued to have side clacks. In these cases side clacks were retained to the demise of the last examples in 1966.

Exhaust Steam Injectors
Utilising exhaust steam for the operation of boiler injectors promised improved efficiency and in 1911-12 Davies & Metcalfe exhaust steam injectors were authorised for 990 class engines Nos.992, 993 and 995. These were followed in 1913 by two 700 class 4-4-0s, one saturated and the other to be superheated. Tests were carried out in October and December 1912 with Nos.993 and 995 to ascertain the temperature of the steam passing from the blast pipe to the injector whilst working both slow and fast trains between Leeds and Carlisle. Some problems were encountered and no more engines were fitted until 1923, when three more 700 class engines were equipped.

The LMS Locomotive and Electrical Committee received a report on 30 May 1931 stating that: *'Considerable improvements had been made in recent years to exhaust steam injectors. In the latest type operation was automatic and had been found reliable in service and was no more difficult for the fireman to handle than an ordinary live steam injector. There was thus every encouragement for the men to make full use of it. Dynamometer car tests had shown that savings of at least 7% could be obtained. All engines recently constructed were fitted with these injectors and it was now proposed to complete the fitting of all the standard main line tender and tank engines not now equipped, amounting to 1,242 engines. The estimated saving is estimated as £28,500 per annum. The work would be carried out as engines pass shops for repairs and would be spread over 3-4 years.'*

The Midland engines affected were the Class 2 superheater 4-4-0s, the Compounds and the Class 4 0-6-0s. This was undertaken at the various works under instructions of 22 June 1931, later allocated the retrospective Job No.5002. Derby order No.7924 of 25 July 1931 was the first of successive orders to fit various specific series of engines, but there were problems. For example, severe weather caused the freezing up of the class H injectors and on 8 April 1940 authority was given to fit drain cocks below the water strainer. This was done at works and motive power depots.

In November 1933 a halt was called on fitting Class 4 0-6-0s and on 13 April 1937 the CME wrote to all the works involved: *'Due to the introduction of larger types for working the more important passenger and freight traffic, it is considered that the provision of this fitting does not afford the savings previously anticipated and it has been decided that when present stocks have been fitted, no more [of the above classes] are to be dealt with'.* It was reported to the Locomotive & Electrical Committee on 26 October 1938 that 425 engines had been dealt with, leaving a further nine to be done. The various engines fitted are shown under the appropriate chapters in subsequent volumes.

Continuous Blowdown

Water quality and its effect on boilers was a perennial problem. Hard water and dissolved solids could and did have a deleterious effect on the life and work of a boiler, with adverse economic consequences.

The LMS investigated and then implemented the widespread introduction of water softening plants coupled with the fitting of continuous blowdown valves on locomotives. This removed dissolved solids and helped to prevent 'priming', the carry-over of water into the cylinders.

This work was begun in 1931 with the first softening plant coming into operation in May 1932. The CME reported to the Mechanical and Electrical Committee on 26 February 1936 that the average hardness after softening had been reduced from 20 degrees to 7 degrees by May 1933 on the Midland and Western lines. A steady improvement in the condition of boilers was reported as a result. However, pitting of boiler tubes and priming remained a problem and further experimental work was commenced in 1933. The most suitable method of eliminating priming was found to be continuous blowdown, whereby a small volume of water was continuously withdrawn from the boiler whilst the engine was working. In this way the concentration of soluble salts could be kept just below that at which priming would occur. A satisfactory valve was developed by the end of 1934 and a trial on fully softened water was completely successful. Washout mileage increased from 2,500 to 5,000 miles and the condition of boilers showed a marked improvement. Substantial economies would be effected if fully softened water was provided for all engines in England and Wales. It was therefore agreed to provide eighteen additional softening plants and eighty-nine wayside treatment plants (for soft but corrosive waters) and to fit 5,751 engines with continuous blowdown.

The work to fit the locomotives was authorised by the CME on 20 March 1936 on new Works Order 3098 under retrospective Job No.5016. Engines likely to be cut up before January 1939 were excluded. All the MR stock except the Kirtley 0-6-0s were therefore included. The discharge was to the ashpan on tank engines and at the rear of the tender on tender engines – until 1951, when ashpan discharge on these was also required. Seven Derby Orders were issued for fifty each of the Class 2 superheater 4-4-0s, Classes 2, 3 and 4 0-6-0s, Class 1 0-4-4Ts, Class 1 and 3 0-6-0Ts plus the Lickey banker, all on 21 April 1936. Further orders were variously issued up to 1942 at least. Additional detail is shown in the appropriate Class chapters.

Safety Valves

Kirtley used Salter valves on the dome, using an anchor point for the springs on the boiler top, having a 'tuning fork' shape with the springs mounted on each leg, connected to the twin levers from the fulcrum on the dome.

Johnson also used Salter valves on the dome but with twin anchor points and also a direct loaded valve on the firebox,

The M&GN D class of 1896 were similar to the current Johnson MR 'M' class 0-6-0s, but with 2950 gallon tenders. No. 66 was built in March 1899 with a B boiler and withdrawn by the LNER in October 1937. Note the Melton chimney. S Summerson collection.

The M&GN C class 4-4-0s were built with MR 'B' boilers, but seven of the forty engines were given G6 boilers in 1929-31. These are the only G6 boilers to have side washout plugs only. No. 49 was built in July 1894 and rebuilt in February 1931. It was withdrawn in September 1941. R.G.Jarvis/Mid Rail Photographs.

normally set to lift at 5lb/sq.in above boiler pressure. This acted as a back-up to the principal valves and remained a standard feature on all the 4ft 1in diameter boilers of Johnson design.

The first ten 4ft 8in diameter belpaire boilers (classed G) on the 'Belpaire' 4-4-0s of 1900 however, were fitted with a pair of Ramsbottom safety valves, on the firebox. All the subsequent boilers of this diameter – the H type and G7, G8, G8A, G9, G9A series and their superheated equivalents where built, were all given an added lock-up valve adjacent to their principal Ramsbottom valves which was set to lift at five pounds above pressure, like the smaller boilers. To conform with this the ten G boilers on Nos.2606-2610 and 800-804, which became Nos.700-709, had a lock-up valve added within a few years of construction and were reclassified GX. The November 1902 issue of *Locomotives and Railways* notes that work was in progress. When the smaller belpaire boilers G6, G5½ and G5 were introduced from 1917, they received Ramsbottom valves and no lock-up valve.

These arrangements remained standard for the various boilers but in August 1918 comparative tests between Ramsbottom and Ross pop safety valves were undertaken in No.9 shop at Derby, utilising a pair of 3⅛in diameter standard MR valves and a pair of 2½in diameter Ross Pop valves. The results showed that: '*Apparently as far as relieving the boiler goes, the two 2½in valves are quite as efficient as the two 3⅛in valves*'. The Ross valve showed a slight advantage in keeping to the set pressure, but '*the construction of the Ross valves is such that they could not be expected to last anything like as long as the Midland*'. Despite this crushing comment it was decided to fit a 700 class saturated engine; this was

then cancelled and Class 4 0-6-0 No.3877 (with Ross valves) substituted, to ascertain performance under practical conditions. Over a year elapsed before it was done, in November 1919. A report of April 1920 indicated no adverse reports had been made but in the following June, a Toton driver had reported them not blowing off correctly at the working pressure. They were then removed later that month and MR Ramsbottom valves refitted. Clearly there was reluctance to accept Ross pop valves and it was two more years before further experiments were carried out.

Meantime, in September 1919, a trial was carried out '*to ascertain the working of the safety valves under high pressure when running and to note especially whether the lock-up safety valve opened to relieve the boiler pressure when, just after a period of hard steaming, the regulator is shut and the engine and train allowed to coast.*' The engine used was Class 2 superheater 4-4-0 No.489, hauling a goods engine to represent the load on the trip to Trent. Further tests were carried out in November and December and on the latter occasion the lock-up valve was put out of use by cramping it down on its seating. The results showed the percentage rise over the set blowing off pressure in each case and on the final test, the rise in pressure over the rated figure was 7.4% with three valves and 11.25% with the lock-up valve out of use.

On 1 October 1919 the Drawing office issued a statement on 'Safety Valves on Locomotives', recording the proposal to do without the lock-up valve. It also notes the Board of Trade requirement that the area of each safety valve should be '*proportioned to the size of the firegrate according to a set rule and that when tried under full steam and hard firing for at least*

twenty minutes, the pressure in the boiler shall not rise more than 10% over loaded pressure'.Sandham Symes, to whom the reports were sent by Herbert Chambers, the Chief Draughtsman, wrote across the foot of the last memorandum of 10th December 1919: '*Mr Anderson agreed that we still continue to fit the lock-up valves on G9 boilers and reconsider G8 when these required new valves; at present these get the combined fitting.*'

This infers agreement to dispense with the lock-up on the G7 boilers and such photographic evidence as exists confirms this. It also appears that the lock-up valve was dispensed with early in 1920 on the G8AS boilers - photographs of 700 class engines superheated from February 1920 onwards all show boilers without it. The G9AS boilers, however, retained the lock-up valve until replaced with Ross pop valves.

A further test using Ross pop valves was carried out on 10 February 1922, on saturated 700 class engine No.751 using as before, two 2½in valves. This was followed on 15 February by tests on a superheated engine of the same class, No.767 which had the standard 3?in MR Ramsbottom valves (and no lock-up valve). The results showed the amount by which the pressure rose above nominal blowing off point (175lb/sq.in) in each case. With the former valves, pressure rose to 192lb/sq.in and with the latter to 195lb before conditions stabilised. No comments were recorded and No.751 was subsequently refitted with the standard valves. So again, it appears that the results were inconclusive.

No formal decision to adopt Ross pop safety valves has been found, but the batch of twenty LMS Compounds built to 0.6066 of 19 November 1923, Nos.1065-1084, were so fitted and all

The SDJR 0-4-4Ts had a boiler that was basically a 'C' barrel and an 'A' firebox. These were replaced between 1906-10 with a Deeley version having a closed dome and Ramsbottom plus lock up safety valves as on No. 30 rebuilt in September 1906. This photograph taken in the 1923-6 period shows the power class 1P1G on the cabside (see Chapter 3). No. 30 was withdrawn as LMS 1206 in May 1932.

new construction subsequently had Ross pop valves. The twenty Compounds prior to these, ordered on 11 June 1923, retained the earlier arrangement of Ramsbottom valves plus a lock-up valve. The change therefore appears to have been authorised in the second half of 1923. So far as the Midland engines are concerned, Order No.6445 to rebuild ten of the 1900 class tanks with G5½ boilers (issued on 8 May 1925) has a pencil note 'Ross pop valves' and photographs of other engines newly rebuilt with Belpaire boilers suggest that the supply of Ramsbottom valves in stock did not run out until about October 1925. After this Ross pop valves replaced the Ramsbottom valves as they required renewal. The last of them disappeared in the late 1930s, but the restored Compound No.1000 now has a set. Apart from the preserved engines, Nos.158A and 673, the last Salter valves in use were to be found on Class 1 0-6-0T No.41835, rebuilt in September 1961.

Whistles

Warning whistles were a standard provision from the earliest days, but the date of the introduction of a smaller alarm whistle, operated by a cord from the train, is unclear. As early as 1853 a Railway Clearing House meeting considered passenger communication cords and on 6 November 1855 Kirtley reported to the Locomotive Committee 'that by the end of the year he should be prepared to effect the communication between the guard and the driver of all passenger trains.' Unfortunately photographs are not available to show any details. The next reference however, is the specification of February 1865 for the 170 class 2-4-0s which includes an alarm whistle and it

is believed that it then became a standard fitting on all the passenger tender engines. The 0-4-4 passenger tank engines were also fitted, except those with condensing apparatus. The close coupled four wheeled carriages used on the London district workings were not equipped; but an official Gloucester Wagon Co photograph of a Midland four wheeled carriage of 1866 shows the tell-tale eye fittings through which the communication cord passed, along the framing below the doors. Then on 16 March 1869 the Locomotive Committee was advised of the following Board decision: 'Resolved, that the Locomotive Department be requested to fit up with all possible despatch the Company's passenger carriages and vans with the principle of the cord communication between passengers and guard as approved by the Board of Trade'. Note that no reference is made to the engine.

The express goods engines with vacuum brake put into traffic between 1892 and 1902 had the fixings, so that cord communication gear could readily be fitted, enabling them to work passenger trains. However, instead of an alarm whistle, provision was made for a gong to be attached to the weatherboard. The first H boiler 0-6-0s of 1903 briefly carried alarm whistles.

Before this, however, the railway companies had agreed in 1899 that instead of the alarm whistle, in future the communication cord should effect a partial brake application. This took time to implement and the last new passenger engines ordered with alarm whistles were the ten Belpaire 4-4-0s built to 0.2250 of 17 June 1901, Nos.810-819. The final passenger engine to appear so equipped, however, was the last of the first five compounds ordered earlier, No.2635 in No-

vember 1903. The file RAIL 491 876 at the PRO, Kew which contains correspondence received at Sheffield in the period 1900-5 covers the action taken with respect to engines fitted previously. On 6 September 1904, the Divisional Superintendent at Derby, W H Adams, wrote enquiring the extent, if any, that alarm whistles were used and seeking views on dispensing with them. 'If they are only occasionally required a gong might be substituted for the whistle' he suggested. This was followed on 25 October 1904 by instructions to remove them: 'Please remove all the alarm gongs and whistles from your engines and forward to Mr Paget, retaining only six gongs to attach to engines in case they are required when working foreign specials. Do not disturb the sheeting, merely plug up the pipe outside.' Photographic evidence confirms the rapid general removal of the alarm whistles following these instructions.

Details - Fire Irons, Oiling Gear, etc

Various fire irons, shovels, darts, scrapers, oil cans and so on were carried on the locomotives to feed and maintain the fire in a satisfactory condition, to clean the firebars, tube plate, tubes and brick arch as required and to oil the moving parts. This demanded the maintenance of an enormous stock of materials in order to equip each engine. Shovels wore rapidly and other small items were easily lost. In 1904 Deeley decided to reduce the number of fire irons carried on engines and to provide others at strategic positions for common use, as a means of economising on certain items. His instructions were conveyed in a memorandum of 24 April 1904, headed 'Fire Irons carried on Locomotives': 'Mr Deeley has decided that in future the number of fire *irons carried by Midland engines must be reduced from nine to five, viz;*

Firing shovel, clinker shovel, ash pan rake, Dart (which may be slightly bent to suit the particular requirements of the engines) Bar pricker.

By the side of each drop pit or near engine turntables at passenger stations, goods yards etc, a Face Plate scraper, Bent dart and Tube pricker must be kept handy for use. I suggest a special cast iron post should be erected with lamp on top and arms either side from which these fire irons can be suspended.

W H Adams
Divisional Superintendent, Derby'

On 19 September 1904 instructions were issued to remove the tube rods and tube plugs from engines and for other fire irons to be sent to Derby *'as soon as the racks have been provided near drop pits, turntables etc.'*

Portable equipment of this nature remained a problem to the end of steam, through shortage and loss and endless hours were wasted making up sets, especially in the later years, to keep engines running.

Tubes

The most efficacious number of tubes and their dimensions was always a matter of prime concern and in Kirtley's time until 1870 tubes were pretty well universally of two inch diameter. On the later boilers to that date, 168 tubes became the norm. However, during 1871/72 some experimentation took place on both passenger and goods classes. 1½in x 252 tubes were used on seventy 700 class goods and 1½in x 232 tubes on some 800 and 890 class 2-4-0s; twenty-five more boilers on these two classes retained the 2in diameter but with only 148 tubes.

In 1872 a further change to 1¾in tubes was made for one hundred and twenty 700 class goods and fifteen 890 class 2-4-0s with 204 and 190 tubes respectively. The latter change proved successful and on 1 April 1873 the Locomotive Committee decreed that in future, boiler tubes would be 1¾in in place of the previous 2in standard.

Johnson's first boilers duly complied but it was not long before further experimentation took place. The ten 'special' boilers of 1877 for some Kirtley 800 class 2-4-0s were given 1⅝ in tubes, as were the twenty B boilers fitted to the class G 7ft 0in driving wheel 4-4-0s of that year. Otherwise, 1¾in remained standard until towards the close of 1884 when, for the ten 0-4-4Ts Nos.1718-1727 built to 0.538 of 4 October 1884, 1⅝ in tubes were again specified. This diameter was then standard for all new boilers until 1899, when for the first belpaire boilers used on Johnson's 2606 class 4-4-0s (to 0.1869 of 3 February 1899), the diameter reverted to 1¾in and generally remained at that figure for all further construction.

Materials were also a matter of concern. In Kirtley's boilers, brass tubes were usual, but on 6 February 1866 the Locomotive Committee authorised 'two sets of iron tubes to be ordered for trial in locomotive boilers'. No further references are made in the Minutes and it must be assumed that it was not a successful experiment. The specifications issued by Johnson for Contractor-built engines up to 1881 provided for tubes '70 parts Copper and 30 parts Silesian Spelter'. Spelter was Zinc and this alloy therefore was of a similar composition to brass. Pure copper was introduced in the mid 1880s and then remained the standard material. However, the use of steel tubes did eventually become widespread.

Under the conditions of wartime shortages some material was imported from the United States in 1914-18 and as has been noted, some twenty G6 and G7 boilers were fitted with steel inner fireboxes. Steel tubes were also employed but there was trouble with leakage. A representative of Baldwins advised on 1 November 1918 on the best method of fitting steel tubes with or without welding, which had been introduced on many railways around that time. Even so, trouble with leaking steel tubes at Coalville was reported on 28 October 1919, with a request for engines with copper tubes 'as the water at Coalville is not good'. Symes, to whom the memo was addressed, had initialled it and marked it. 'Sir Henry Fowler' so evidently the CME was involved. The affected boilers were rebuilt in normal copper materials as soon as practicable. A number of boilers received steel tubes in the 1930s but a copper shortage arose in the Second World War – the LMS Locomotive Committee considered the problem on 24 July 1941. At that time 997 engines with ex-MR Type boilers were reported as being fitted with copper tubes. These were all saturated engines and comprised the 379 LMS standard 2F and 3F 0-6-0Ts and 2P 0-4-4Ts plus 618 ex-MR 1F and 3F 0-6-0Ts, 0-4-0Ts, 0-4-4Ts, 2-4-0s, 2F and 3F 0-6-0s and the few remaining saturated 2P 4-4-0s.

The CME reported *'that consequent on the improved method of reclaiming steel tube by butt welding, there was no necessity to continue the use of copper tubes, apart from the desirability of ceasing purchases during the war.'* He recommended that steel tubes be fitted to these engines at a net credit of £70,469, having disposed of the copper. It was recognised that the change would take a number of

While some of the 4-4-0s also had non standard boilers, the twenty-eight SDJR 'Scottie' 0-6-0s took a standard 'A' boiler. No. 57 of June 1890, renumbered 2880 in 1930, is here at Derby after withdrawal in December 1932. R.G.Jarvis/Mid Rail Photographs.

The pipe from the base of the smokebox betrays the fitting of an exhaust steam injector in 483 class No. 359, at Hasland in 1934.

years and that sound copper tubes could be made up into sets for further use until the work was completed. It was authorised under Job No.5241 on 6 August 1941, DWO 5864, but was never completed; instructions were issued on 18 June 1949 for it to be discontinued, the copper tube boilers to remain so until broken up.

Heating Surfaces
A word is appropriate about heating surfaces. Midland practice in measuring these varied from generally accepted practice until the Association of Railway Locomotive Engineers agreed a standard calculation in November 1914. Derby

Drawing Office prepared two tables. The first, dated 17 February 1910, shows the differences in calculations between the MR method and 'General Accepted Practice' and its effect on the figures. The second showed 'standard' heating surfaces of the various boilers in 1916. The former list is also of interest in that the various tube arrangements used on individual boiler classes are shown, with the consequent effect on heating surface. These tables indicated how quoted figures changed over the years and help to clarify this complex subject.

Drumhead Tubeplates
On the D, E and F boilers fitted to the 4-2-2 Spinners and the D and E boilers on 4-4-0s, built from 1887 to the close of Johnson's superintendency in 1903, drumhead front tubeplates were fitted. This enabled the smokebox to be flush with the boiler barrel and thus reduced the smokebox diameter by some five inches compared to the conventional raised pattern. Viewed from the front those boilers appeared to be even slimmer than before. The GX, G8 and G8½ boilers used on the first sixty Belpaire and the first five Compounds also had front tubeplates of this pattern but other boilers retained the standard design. The fitting of drumhead tubeplates to the principal passenger engines of the period therefore appears to have been carried out for aesthetic reasons. Ahrons expressed surprise at its introduction as the GWR had just done the reverse. Deeley was not concerned with such niceties and on 15 December 1905, Derby Order 3066 was issued *When any engines having boilers with drumhead tubeplates are in shops for heavy boiler repairs, the boilers must be fitted with new tubeplates of the ordinary type and new smokeboxes.* The D and E boiler 4-4-0s were all rebuilt with H type boilers by 1908, so it is unlikely that many (or any) of their boilers were altered before rebuilding. But the boilers carried by the Spinners and the Belpaire boilers were adapted. The work appears to have been carried out swiftly as hardly any are known in their original state after the 1907 renumbering. Spinner No.668 is one example, photographed at Gloucester with smokebox numberplate on the Johnson door.

BOILER WASHOUT PLUGS

Boiler type	Upper boiler washout plug numbers and positions
G5	2RH and 2LH angle only.
G5½	2RH and 2LH angle only.
G6	2RH and 2LH angle only.
	2RH, 2LH angle plus 3RH and 3LH sides.
	3RH and 3LH sides only (LMS 6400 class orig boilers)
G7 and G7S	2RH and 2LH angle only.
	4RH and 4LH sides only.
	Both as above.
GX, G8 AND G8½	3LH and 2RH sides only.
G8A, G9 AND G9A	3LH and 2RH angles only.
G8AS	3LH and 2RH angles only.
	4LH and 5RH sides only.
	Both as above.
G9AS	3LH and 2RH angles only.
	6LH and 5RH sides only.
	Both as above.
G10S	3LH and 3RH angle only(1)
	6LH and 6RH sides only as rebuilt (1).

BOILER TYPE	FIRST FITTED	ENGINE NO (1907 No)	NO BUILT	LAST ORDER	DATE
A	11/74	1620	525	O.6362	23.12.24
A1	3/95	1845	60	O.3666	3.1.10
B	12/74*	2321	3710	O.6766	12.11.26
C	6/75	1226	545	O.6396	7.2.25
C1	3/95	1381	110	M.6697	18.10.00
P	9/75	91	528	O.2502	15.11.02
D	6/87	600	267	O.2587	20.4.03
E	11/96	670	60	O.2349	3.3.02
F	12/99	685	10	O.1926	25.5.99
H	1/03	3765	427	O.3065	14.12.05
H1	4/07	2000	65	O.3344	2.8.07
HX	4/07	328	115	O.3404	24.12.07
J	8/83	1500	33	O.4188	30.12.12
J1	7/97	1518	13	O.5275	18.12.18
J2	8/07	1528	20	BS 7 7935	1.54
GX	9/00	700	10	O.1869	3.2.99
G8	1/02	710	50	O.2726	6.2.04
G8A	2/05	760	25	O.3999	19.10.11
G8½	1/02	1000	5	O.2109	10.7.00
G9	10/05	1005	43	O.3685	17.2.10
G9A	3/07	999	10	O.3371	10.10.07
G9AS	5/10	998	444	BS 9 56	1948
G7S	10/11	3835	1787	BS 8 10	1956
G8AS	9/13	700	281	BS 7 3568	1958
G7	5/09	338	976	BS 7 7116	4.47
G7X	2/18	3237	10	O.5061	1.6.17
G6X	7/17	2900	10	O.4976	13.12.16
G6	1/18	2918	548	BS 7 6029	8.46
G5½	8/19	1930	927	BS 7 3570	3.58
G5	7/24	1741	157	BS 7 6030	11.45
G10S	12/19	2290	2	O.5738	9.6.22
LTS1	4/80	2110(1)	?	?	?
LTS2	9/00	2158(51)	?	S40 39127	8.34
LTS3	5/09	2176(79)	?	BS 7 4653	1948

* 6 months ending

NOTE 1   2341/87 also rebuilt B 12/74.
     2   331, 425, 3180, 3205 & 3454 also rebuilt HX 4/07.
     3   386 also rebuilt G7 5/09.
     4   3386 & 3680 also rebuilt G7X 2/18.
     5   2932/3/74 also rebuilt G6X 7/17.
    11   First engine numbers shown as 1912 number and LTS No.

Boiler Washout Plugs on Belpaire Boilers

Just as water quality was paramount to boiler condition, so was the efficiency of washing out. It was vital that boiler cleaning was thorough and no corners missed, for retained deposits spelt trouble. In the belpaire boilers therefore, washout plugs were provided at high level on the firebox sides (the only ones visible from the exterior of the locomotive), in addition to the usual tubeplate and lower firebox positions.

The earliest belpaire boilers of 1900-04, the GX and G8 fitted to the 'Belpaire' 4-4-0s which became Nos.700-759 in 1907, as well as the G8½ fitted to the first five Compounds, had upper washout plugs on the firebox sides. These were sited above the handrail, three on the left-hand side and two on the right. They appeared as cylindrical fittings on the cladding. This did not prove to be an entirely satisfactory arrangement to effect the complete cleansing of the top angles and corners of the firebox. Consequently, the next Belpaire boilers, G8A, G9 and G9A of 1905-9, fitted to engines Nos.760-779, 1005-1044 and 990-999 respectively, were given plugs on the top angles of the firebox, three on the left-hand side and two on the right-hand side.

These are usually described as washout doors of the 'hand hold' type. This then became the standard arrangement for all new belpaire boilers fitted to MR engines and LMS built MR designs, until the 1920s. The last known boiler in service with this arrangement was No.6173 which had been fitted new to Class 4 0-6-0 No.4196 at St Rollox in July 1925. It was finally carried by No.44525, the last survivor of the same class when withdrawn in late 1966.

The LYR belpaire boilers and those belpaire boilers fitted to LNWR engines from 1924 however, had upper washout plugs to the firebox sides only and this became the LMS standard for new boilers. These were of the 'plug' type. The Hughes/Fowler 'Crab' 2-6-0s of 1926-32 and the Royal Scots of 1927-30 as built all had boilers with side plugs only, as did the 2-6-4Ts Nos.2300-2424 of 1927-34. These latter engines employed the G8AS boiler as fitted to the superheated 'Belpaire' 4-4-0s in the 700-779 series; from about the end of 1927 new belpaire boilers ordered for ex-MR designs were also made with the new arrangement. Thus the G7, G7S, G8AS and G9AS types incorporated this variation, but the G5 and G5½ boilers, fitted to tank engines, retained the 'angle only' position. This

was due to access problems, arising from the relative height of the side tanks to the boiler.

The last G5 and G5½ boilers built at Derby, to orders issued between 30 May 1928 and 6 November 1929, were given plug (instead of hand hold washout doors) on the boiler angle only, so that thirty G5 and twenty G5½ boilers appeared in this guise, notably the G5s on the Fowler dock tanks Nos.11270-9. Some thirty-nine 1F 0-6-0Ts, six 3F 0-6-0Ts (MR-built) and eighteen 0-4-4Ts are known to have carried these variants at one time or another, and there may have been others. The last in service was a G5½ boiler on 0-4-4T No.58065 (1367) withdrawn in 1959.

No G6 boilers for the LMS appear to have been built with plugs on the firebox sides only, but this is to be expected - after O.6987 of 10 October 1927 no more G6 boilers were ordered until the twelve built to Crewe Order BS7 9064 in 1939, *after* the next general design change. However, when the Stanier 0-4-4Ts Nos.6400-9 were built to O.7861 of 8 June 1932, the second-hand boilers from 2-4-0s and a 2F 0-6-0 were altered from a pair of hand hold washout doors each side (on the angle only) to three 'plug type' on the sides only, to conform with the standard practice of the period. Additionally, the five G6 boilers built for the M&GN to O.7500 of 8 October 1929 were also built to the 'sides only' arrangement. Several boilers from this period survived into the 1960s. Examples were No.C6198, a G7 on engine No.43620 when withdrawn in 1964 and G9AS boiler No.10464 built to BS7 8462 of 1938, which has been preserved on SDJR 2-8-0 No.88.

It became clear once again that the omission of washout plugs on the top angles of the firebox was unsatisfactory and during 1935 a change was made for new Stanier boilers, which henceforth were fitted with two additional plugs on the top angles. From about 1938 this also became standard for parallel boilers. It is possible to identify the four distinct construction periods from the plug positions, as below:

PERIOD	PLUG POSITIONS
1900-4	side only
1905-27	top angle only
1927-c38	side only
c1938-64	top angle and side

Stanier Standard Boilers - A Might-Have-Been

To conclude this survey of Midland boilers it is of interest to refer to the range of tapered boilers schemed out in the 1930s. These would have replaced existing boilers on engine classes that were to be retained.

A drawing was issued on 22 April 1933 headed 'Proposed standardisation of Boilers' showing the outline and principal dimensions of the taper boilers proposed. Three of these were to replace Midland designs. The 4B, it was indicated, should replace the G9AS on the Compounds. This was 12ft 0in between tube plates, 4ft 9in diameter at the front and 5ft 3in at the rear tubeplate with a 28.5sq.ft firegrate 9ft 0in long. The 4E was to replace the G7 and G7S on class 2P 4-4-0s and the 3F and 4F 0-6-0s. It was similar to the 4B but only 10ft 4¾in between tube plates with identical diameters and a firebox of 21.8sq.ft, seven feet long. The third proposal, No.6, was for a replacement of both the G5½ and G6 boilers on the class 3F 0-6-0Ts, standard 0-4-4Ts and class 2F 0-6-0s. This was to be 10ft 10½in between tubeplates, tapered from 4ft 2in to 4ft 9in diameter with a 17.7sq.ft firegrate 5ft 11in long. On the drawing, a note added later says *'where a coned boiler replaces an existing one, a new smokebox and saddle is required as well as new clothing and alteration to pipework and cab front'*.

As is well known, the cost of mass rebuildings and the general financial situation of the railway at that time, coupled with the production of the Stanier designs and downgrading of the work required of his predecessors' engines ensured that these interesting proposals, so far as the ex-Midland designs were concerned, were never implemented.

	LAST WDN	ENGINE	BLR NO	ORDER	DATE	NOTES
A	P9/61	41835	5669	0.5992	4.9.23	
A1	P12/30	1861	1448	M.5356	7.1.98	
B	P6/59	58246	5940	0.6232	6.5.24	NOTE 1
C	P7/56	58071	6376	0.6396	7.2.25	
C1	11/31*	1909	1527	M.5421	17.2.98	
P	P13/27	162	2691	0.2396	20.6.02	
D	P7/28	600	2878	0.2587	20.4.03	
E	P4/28	673	2636	0.2349	3.3.02	
F	7/22	690	1943	0.1926	25.5.99	
H	P3/28	3413	3348	0.3065	14.12.05	NOTE 6
H1	P9/28	3155	3384	0.3187	27.8.06	
HX	P3/28	331	3434	0.3219	11.12.06	NOTE 2
J	P10/55	41516	4147	0.4188	30.12.12	
J1	P2/58	41518	4833	0.5275	18.12.18	
J2	P13/66	41533	5173	0.5528	19.11.20	NOTE 7
GX	2/21	706	1876	0.1869	3.2.99	
G8	P9/25	737	2431	0.2250	17.6.01	
G8A	P13/26	751	2770**	0.2458	8.10.02	
G8½	11/17	1002	2110	0.2109	10.7.00	
G9	P1/28	1022	3793	0.3685	17.2.10	
G9A	1/14***	996	3562	0.3371	10.10.07	
G9AS	P10/64	53807	9118	BS1.5	3.35	NOTE 10
G7S	P10/66	44525	6173	St Rollox	7.25	NOTE 10
G8AS	P9/66	42410	6154	B1.4	8.33	NOTE 10
G7	P2/64	43669	10071	BS 7 9175	8.37	NOTES 3 & 8
G7X	CONVERTED TO STANDARD G7					NOTE 4
G6X	CONVERTED TO STANDARD G6					NOTE 5
G6	P1/64	58182	12374	BS 7 6029	8.46	
G5½	P10/67	47629	14058	BS 7 7933	.54	NOTE 10
G5	P13/66	41708	12038	BS 7 5024	1.44	NOTE 9
G10S	P5/56	58100	5395	0.5738	9.6.22	
LTS1	10/35	2073	?	?	?	NOTE 11
LTS2	P7/62	41981	5375	S.5 10659	2.28	NOTE 11
LTS3	P11/60	41947	12379	BS 7 6027	1.46	NOTE 11

* Several were fitted with C fireboxes not accounted for here.
*** The G9A boilers were all rebuilt with superheaters.
** Boiler 2770 built as G8 and rebuilt to G8A.

NOTE 6   3685 also wdrn P3/28 boiler 3287 0.3038 30.10.05.
    7   41528 also wdrn P13/66 boiler 12600 BS 7 6377 .46.
    8   43620/37 also wdrn P2/64 boiler C.6198 S.40 1339 11.33 and boiler 9262 BS 7 8401 3.36.
    9   41734/63, 41804/35 also wdrn P13/66 blrs 13720, 12341, 10540, 10542.
    10   These last boilers were on LMS built engines.

The alarm whistle on No. 810 is clearly seen above the man standing on the footplating behind the leading coupled wheels. Entering service in October 1902 this whistle was removed within about three years.

MR TYPE BOILERS ON PRESERVED ENGINES
1.   MIDLAND ENGINES

BOILER	BLR NO	ORDER	DATE	ENGINE	NOTES
B	4366	0.4601	9.1.15	158A	
E	2636	0.2349	3.3.02	673	Fitted 12/09
G5	12038	BS 7 5024	1.44	1708	Fitted 15.12.60
G7S	9906	BS 7 8988	12/36-3/37	3924	Fitted 10.1.59
G9AS	12594	BS 7 6381	1.47	1000	NOTE A
					Fitted 3.59
LTS3	12750	BS 7 7120	11.47	LTS80	Fitted 19.1.49

NOTE A The boiler carried by 1000 when withdrawn in P10/51 was 11346. It was removed when the engine was restored in March 1959; subsequently fitted to 13809, it remains with that engine.

2. LMS ENGINES

BOILER	BLR NO	ORDER	DATE	ENGINE	NOTES
G5½	10028	BS 7 8986	2.4.37	7279	Fitted 24.1.56
"	11553	BS1 54	5.42	7298	Fitted 10.11.61
"	14061	BS 7 7933	1954	7324	Fitted 17.5.61
"	14060	BS 7 7933	1954	7327	Fitted 4.10.61
"	10536	BS 7 9062	1.39	7357	Fitted 14.7.61
"	14056	BS 7 7933	1954	7383	Fitted 22.11.61
"	11087	BS 7 9967	1940	7406	Fitted 9.7.59
"	14353	BS 7 3044	1957	7445	Fitted 29.1.60
"	13973	BS 7 7042	4.51	7493	Fitted 29.5.61
"	14383	BS 7 3569	1957	7564	Fitted 16.10.59
G7S	11209	BS1 49	11.41	4027	Fitted 1.7.60
"	14269	BS 7 1576	1955	4123	Fitted 1.9.61
"	14273	BS 7 1576	1955	4422	Fitted 11.9.57
G9AS	10464	BS 7 8462	11.38	13808	Fitted 24.3.62
"	11346	BS 7 3591	1942	13809	Fitted 29.9.61

BS1 Spare boilers intended for use at Crewe
BS7 Spare boilers intended for use at Derby
NOTE Boilers shown are those fitted on withdrawal. Where several are at one site eg Butterley changes are possible.

The position of the upper washout plugs on the belpaire fireboxes gave an indication of the building date of the boiler. No. 3281 of Buxton is visiting Kentish Town in the late 1920s with the MR arrangement of washout doors on the top angles only. S Summerson collection.

All 120 of Johnson's first 0-6-0s, the 1142 class of 1875-6, were built without an engine brake. A hand brake with wooden shoes was fitted to the tender. No. 1245 was built in December 1876, became No. 3013 in June 1907 and was withdrawn in July 1962 as No. 58185.

The fitting of steam brakes to the Kirtley goods engines was not completed until the late 1890s. No. 538 (2483 in 1907) is seen here as rebuilt by Johnson, in 1878 prior to being equipped. S Summerson collection.

Chapter 5 - Brakes

'It complies entirely with all the conditions laid down by the Board of Trade'

Introduction

With low speeds, high frictional values and the light weight of engines and carriages, the means of stopping was not a vital factor in the early development of the railways. However, the increasing power of locomotives and the heavier trains they could haul, together with increasing speeds attained, brought the subject of effective braking into ever-sharper focus.

A simple hand operated brake was introduced by which a wooden block was made to press on the tread of a wheel and so slow the motion of an individual vehicle. A hand brake was fitted only to the tender wheels of tender engines and in order to provide additional brake power, the practice of inserting a 'break van' or vans into the train was instituted, each manned by a guard to operate a brake. When the driver required a brake application he 'whistled for brakes' to a known code and the guard or guards duly screwed down the hand brakes to arrest the progress of the train. This operation, in the days before carriages were coupled tightly together, was fraught with difficulty because of the risk of uneven application by several people. This could result in snatching of the simple couplings which resulted in not infrequent breakages and trains becoming parted, with potentially disastrous consequences. There was therefore a marked reluctance to fit brakes to the driven and coupled wheels of locomotives, because of this perceived fear of excessive stresses and strains being put upon the mechanism. Metallurgy was also in its infancy and this, coupled with the difficulties of designing an effective continuous brake, meant hand brakes and loose couplings remained in use for many years, with all the inevitable accidents and breakages.

It was not until the 1870s, right at the end of Kirtley's years in office, that the subject of improved and continuous brakes was properly addressed. The fact that the Midland Railway, formed in 1844, was nearly 30 years old underlines the lack of progress, common to all railways, that had been made up to that time. The Board of Trade had been calling for continuous brakes since the early 1860s but despite the accident record companies were then, as now, reluctant to spend money on matters which had no direct prospect of a financial return, especially as the costs involved to fit all the passenger locomotives and stock, even then, would have been enormous. This, coupled with as-yet unproved technology, resulted in the lengthy period of inertia.

Kirtley was of course, well aware of the problems. Apart from hand brakes, locomotives could be reversed with steam for additional braking power and this course of action was resorted to if necessary.

Le Chatelier's Brake

On 15 February 1870 the Locomotive Committee received a report on experiments carried out with Le Chatelier's steam brake, held on the Lickey incline on 5 February 1870. The results were regarded as satisfactory and the Committee authorised the fitting of *'the thirty engines now ordered from Messrs. Neilson and Co. and also the engines being built in the Company's workshops'* (i.e. the 800 class 2-4-0s). On 18 April 1871 Kirtley reported that 'it might be further applied with advantage'. Any further application was then referred to the Locomotive Committee. On 2 May 1871 the following Board Minute was read to the Locomotive Committee: *'recommending that the further application of the Le Chatelier brake be referred to the Locomotive Committee and be extended to all passenger engines'*. Nonetheless, no further reference to the brake can be found in the Minutes, or any confirmation that all the 800 class were fitted, though it is likely, for the specification of the subsequent 1070 class 2-4-0s included this brake. On 28 August 1875 a serious accident occurred at Kildwick, when an up Scotch express ran into the rear of an excursion train from Morecambe to Bradford. The evidence revealed that the engine of the express train was fitted with the 'Chatelier Water brake' indicating its use up to that date. In the series of brake trials carried out in 1875, a trial was carried out on the Derby - Castle Donnington and Trent line on 21 September with ordinary hand brakes and it was noted that the 'Le Chatelier tap' on engine No.815 was open, indicating it was not in use. No further references have been noted. It will be observed that the MR minutes of 15 February 1870 referred to a steam brake, but the accident report records a 'water brake'. It was in fact a counter pressure brake, whereby water was injected into the cylinders, confirming the evidence given in regard to the accident. These descriptions illustrate very clearly the problems which can arise occasionally in the interpretation of Company Minutes.

EXPERIMENTAL PERIOD 1873-75

As happens so regularly in our civilised society, improvements in safety often occur only following an accident or accidents. It is no surprise to find therefore, that the slow if inevitable progress towards reliable continuous brake systems on the Midland began with an accident.

The Westinghouse Brake

The Board of Trade had for some years been advocating continuous brakes and following the accident between Dronfield and Dore & Totley on 16 October 1872, Captain Tyler's report was read to the Traffic Committee on 31 December 1872. His remarks on the adoption of continuous brakes were noted and it was re-solved that *'as an experiment, arrangements be made with the Westinghouse Air Brake Co. for several of the Company's trains working upon the Metropolitan line to be fitted up with that system'*.

The Locomotive Committee (M7409) noted the Traffic Committee's views on 14 January 1873 and resolved to fit two trains as an experiment, one to run between Leeds and Bradford and the other to work over the Metropolitan Railway. For the purpose of these trials two 2-4-0s were fitted with Westinghouse non-automatic brakes in February 1873, No.238 of the rebuilt Beyer Peacock 230 class and No.156 of the 156 class. Runs commenced on 21 March 1873 between Melbourne and Trent and the unidentified engines had the brake on the tender only. A second series of tests was carried out between Hendon and St Albans on 12 and 21 May 1873. Locomotive Committee Minutes of 3 June 1873 give a table of results quoting gradient, train speed, time to stop and distance travelled for various combinations of Westinghouse, hand brakes and engine steaming. This clearly showed the effectiveness of the Westinghouse brake. In November 1873 the Westinghouse Brake Co. wrote quoting the terms on which they would be prepared to arrange for the use of that brake on the Midland line. After consideration, the Traffic Committee recommended that this system of continuous brake be adopted but on the same day the General Purposes Committee resolved to fit only one train, to run between Manchester and London, together with the necessary number of engines at a cost of £15 per carriage and £50 per engine.

Whilst all this was in progress, the first of the new American Pullman cars were being assembled at Derby and some special runs were made on 21 February and 17 March 1874 with these vehicles, which were fitted with the Westinghouse brake. This required locomotives fitted with this brake and in February six were so equipped, four 890 class and two 800 class 2-4-0s. A very interesting account of the special run of 17 March 1874 was published in *The English Mechanic* of 27 March, written by 'An Express Driver'. In giving details of the engine (No.906) and the train, the author states that the engine had the steam brake and the cars and tender the new air brake. The first reference is almost certainly to the Le Chatelier brake and not the conventional steam brake which was introduced later. It will be recalled that the Locomotive Committee used similar terminology in 1870. Further experiments with the Westinghouse brake were conducted on 10 April 1874 between London and Bedford.

The regular Pullman car service between Bradford and St Pancras came into operation on 1 June 1874 and five more 800 and 890 class engines were equipped in May. By 3 November 1874, Johnson reported that the cost of fitting 15 engines with the Westinghouse brake amounted to £1,226 5s 0d. This, it is presumed, was the 'necessary number of engines' referred to in November 1873.

Utilising a table quoted in the Locomotive Committee Minutes on 18 March 1879 alongside information contained in Johnson's record of 'Patent Brakes' (RAIL 491/780), it is possible to identify these 1874 fitted engines as follows:

DATE	ENGINE	CLASS
2/74	40	890
2/74	901	890
2/74	902	890
2/74	906	890
2/74	64	800
2/74	66	800
5/74	903	890
5/74	904	890
5/74	809	800
5/74	898	890
5/74	894	890

All these engines, plus the two fitted in 1873, had the original Westinghouse simple air brake controlled by the driver only, which did not operate automatically in the case of the train parting or a pipe being severed. In this system the air pipes remained at atmospheric pressure until the brake was applied.

Early in 1875 the Westinghouse automatic brake was introduced, whereby pressure was maintained in the air pipes to hold the brakes off. The brake was applied by releasing the air. This had the great advantage that by fitting a valve in the guard's compartment, that worthy could apply the brake in an emergency. Moreover, should a coupling break and the train part, severing the air pipes, then the escape of air would apply the brakes and bring the separate sections to a halt. This was a vast step forward and formed the basis of subsequent successful systems.

Trials with the new arrangement were carried out between St Pancras and Luton in April 1875 and further 800, 890 and 1070 class engines were fitted with Westinghouse brakes in the early months of 1875 - No.63 in February, Nos.62, 65 and 905 in March and Nos.895, 900, 907 and 1080 in April, all with brakes on the tender wheels only. It is presumed that all these and subsequent engines were fitted with the automatic arrangement. The next development came with the fitting of 890 class No.134 with brakes to the coupled wheels as well as the tender in June 1875, for use in the Newark brake trials described later. This was the fist engine with a Johnson boiler to be so fitted . Four more of the rebuilt Beyer Peacock 230 class followed, Nos.235, 236, 237 and 239 between August and November 1875, with brakes to the coupled wheels to work the additional Westinghouse fitted trains running between St Pancras and Northampton. No.238 was also provided with engine brakes in the same period.

It is convenient here to bring the Westinghouse story up to 1877. The success of the Westinghouse automatic air brake was demonstrated by the Newark trials and in ordinary service during the latter part of 1875, paving the way for the new Scotch trains to be fitted for work over the Settle and Carlisle line from May 1876. However, in their report to the Locomotive Committee on 15 February 1876, Johnson and Clayton were of the view that, *'pending the issue of the Report of the Royal Commissioners on Railways on the brake experiments at Newark, we think it inadvisable to extend the application of the Westinghouse brake further than can be avoided, yet seeing that we have such a short time to prepare brake power for the express trains on the Settle*

and Carlisle extension, the only way is to fit a sufficient number of engines and carriages with the Westinghouse brake'.

So, with apparent reluctance, thirty one more engines were equipped between March and September 1876. The first of these (they all had Johnson boilers) was No.802, which had engine and tender brakes as on the last of the 1875 engines. The remainder reverted to tender brakes only, such was the continued reluctance to fit brakes to driving/coupled wheels. These engines comprised nine 800 class, two 890 class, all ten of Johnson's new 6ft 2in 2-4-0s and ten of the 1282 class 6ft 6in 2-4-0s, Nos.1302-1311. This brought the total to fifty-seven engines, a figure which remained static for some time. F H Clarke has recorded that the MR had sixty pumps, including one spare and one kept in the carriage and wagon department for testing purposes. In 1877 Johnson specially rebuilt ten Kirtley 800 class engines with a boiler larger than his current standard, and 18in x 26in cylinders in place of Kirtley's 18in x 24in, for working the heaviest passenger trains, including the Scotch expresses. All ten were given Westinghouse brakes taken from 156, 1070, 800 (one each) and 890 class engines. No changes were made for the next few years.

Other Trials And Experiments
Before continuing the main course of developments from 1876, consideration can be given to the use and demise of the less successful systems given a trial.

Wilkins & Clarks' chain brake
The General Purposes Committee had resolved on 4 November 1873 to fit one train with the Westinghouse brake. On the same day they also resolved to fit one train to run between London and Man-

The 1377 class 0-6-0Ts ordered from August 1877 were all fitted with steam brakes when built. No. 1352 (1685 in 1907) has the standard outside pull rod arrangement of the period.

Kirtley 890 class 2-4-0 No. 899 in the late 1890s with standard automatic vacuum brake. This engine had been fitted with Clark's Hydraulic brake in 1875 which was removed by 1879. It was then fitted with a steam brake and was one of the last two steam brake-only passenger engines to remain so equipped, in January 1882. By July 1882 it had been fitted with the automatic vacuum brake for train braking. S Summerson collection.

chester with the latest improvements of Wilkins & Clark's brake, requiring reports on its efficacy in due course.

Experiments with this chain brake were carried out in April 1874 and at the height of the debate on continuous braking systems, the Locomotive Committee, on 20 March 1877, requested Johnson and Clayton to report as to why the use of this brake 'had been suspended' and what they now recommended. An interesting aside asked *how does it work on the LNW Co.'s line?* On 3 April 1877 the Loco Committee heard that 29 carriages had been fitted and that 'after the experiments made by us and the Traffic Department', it was found 'undesirable' to put this train into traffic. Various problems had arisen and several breakaways had occurred. *'We noted that a train worked in this manner would not be safe.'* And that was that.

Ward's brake
In March 1874 a submission was made to the Traffic Committee by a Mr Ward asking for a trial of his continuous brake, though the method of working was not noted. His request was refused 'as the Company are already making trials with continuous brakes.'

Clark's Hydraulic brake
Five engines were equipped with Clark's Hydraulic brake, according to Johnson's records on 'Patent Brakes'. Two were identified as 890 class 2-4-0s Nos.896 and 899, and the total cost was quoted at £917 10s 3d. It is understood that one at least of the others was another 890 class en-

gine, No.136 – see the Newark Brake Trials below .

Very little other information is to hand concerning this brake though Johnson's records show repair costs listed from the half year ended 30 June 1875 to the two months ended 28 February 1879, at which date one engine is shown as still fitted. The half yearly return for 30 June 1880 shows none, indicating the end of these particular trials.

Barker's Hydraulic brake
Two 890 class engines, Nos.132 and 135, were fitted with Barker's Hydraulic brake in 1875 and No.135 was involved in the Newark trials. Further experiments were carried out on the line favoured for testing – that between Chellaston and Castle Donnington, on 26 August 1875, but the engine concerned is not recorded. Barker's brake appears to have enjoyed more success than Clark's, despite the inherent disadvantage of potentially freezing in the winter. The costs of fitting the two engines was £590 3s 1d. Johnson reported on its action to the Locomotive Committee on 3 April 1877 when other systems were also reviewed. The success of No.135 in the Newark brake trials will be noted shortly, and in their report Johnson and Clayton noted that it had worked on the Leeds and Bradford section for nine months during 1875-76. 'For the past seven months', it was recorded 'the two engines have been working between Bradford and London': *'Barker's brake is very powerful, works smoothly and well and has given less trouble than any other*

brake we have had at work; it is however, complicated on the engine and carriages and this forms, so far, as our experience goes, the only objection to it.' Praise indeed!

The two engines continued working in the London district and on 4 January 1881, the Locomotive Committee was advised that the 7.45am Bedford - London and 4.45pm London - Bedford were being worked with Barker's brake. However, by that date, the introduction of Sanders and Bolithos automatic vacuum brake was proceeding apace and these two engines were altered, one in November 1882 and the other in February 1883, concluding an experiment which had lasted in a period of rapid change, for a remarkable seven years.

The Newark Brake Trials
The need for effective braking was common to all the railways and the success of the Westinghouse air brake coupled with the invention of various other types of brake, chain brakes, hydraulic brakes and so on, led to the comprehensive Newark brake trials of 1875, hosted by the Midland. The trials were conducted under the auspices of the Railway Companies Association and under the direction of the Royal Commission on Railway Accidents, with the aim of identifying the most suitable for future use. The 'up' line between Rolleston Junction and Thurgarton was used and for the duration of the trials, between 9 June and 16 June 1875, normal traffic was worked on the 'down' line under single line working rules. The following companies and sys-

tems were represented:-

Company	System
Caledonian	Steel and McInnes Automatic air brake
Great Northern	Smith Vacuum brake
Lancashire & Y'kshire	Fays mechanical brake
LBSCR	Westinghouse Vacuum brake
LNWR	Clark & Webb continuous chain brake
Midland	1 Barkers Hydraulic brake.
	2 Clarks Hydraulic brake.
	3 Westinghouse Automatic air brake.

The following table summarises the results.

Company	Distance run in best stop.ft	Time to stop secs	Speed on brake application mph	Condition of rail	Type of brake
MR	840	18	52	dry	Westinghouse Automatic
MR	1070	21	54½	dry	Clark
LNW	1096	24¾	50¾	dry	Clark & Webb
MR	1116	25	49½	dry	Barker
CR	1132	24	49½	dry	Steel & McInnes
L and Y	1400	28	57½	dry	Fay
GN	1448	29	49½	dry	Smith
LBSC	1728	34½	52	wet	Westinghouse vacuum

The Midland engines involved were a new 890 class 2-4-0 No.134, built in March 1875 with a Johnson P boiler and fitted with the automatic Westinghouse brake in June for the trials. As noted above, this engine was the first to have the brake on the coupled wheels as well as the tender. Radford (*Derby Works and Midland Locomotives*, Ian Allan, 1971) notes that No.135, fitted with Barker's hydraulic brake was also involved in the trials, with a train equipped with that system. A note in *Locomotives and Railways* for November 1901 records the use of Nos.134, 135 and 136 in these trials. It may therefore be deduced that No.136 was the engine fitted with Clark's Hydraulic brake.

All these 890 class engines were new in 1875, having Johnson boilers and rep-resenting the latest practice. The superiority of the Midland train fitted with the Westinghouse automatic air brake is clearly demonstrated. It is interesting to note also that Clark's hydraulic brake on the second Midland train gave the next best performance whilst Barker's hydraulic brake came fourth out of the eight systems in the tables of distances run in the best stop.

DEVELOPMENTS 1876-80
Introduction
In their report to the Locomotive Committee on 15 February 1876 Johnson and Clayton set out the desirability of providing continuous brake power throughout the train and referred to Captain Tyler's report for the year 1875 which agreed that no really suitable system had yet evolved. Hence the reticence over the Westinghouse system expressed at the same meeting, referred to above. Johnson and Clayton's enquiries enabled them to suggest that Smith's vacuum brake was 'most promising.' But, they went on: *'Our present view is that an efficient steam brake can be arranged for engine and tender and this together with the ordinary guards brake power would be found to meet the requirements of ordinary passenger workings'*. Significantly, experiments had only recently been conducted on the Derby - Castle Donnington and Trent line with 890 class 2-4-0 No.892 fitted with steam brake on the engine and tender,

the first engine to be so equipped. These trials took place on 9 February 1876.

Throughout the rest of the year Johnson and Clayton continued to express their reservations on continuous brakes. On 4 July 1876 they reported to the Committee on the cost of fitting Westinghouse, Clark's and Barker's brakes and on the troubles encountered with the automatic Westinghouse equipment. Casualties had been numerous and they were of the opinion that 'it should be worked as an ordinary (i.e. non automatic) Westinghouse brake only.'

On 14 November 1876 came a further report: *'We are still of the opinion that in a continuous brake, intricacy of detail and multiplication of parts are objectionable and from our experience of the continuous brakes we have tried, we do not feel justified in recommending any of them for general use. The addition of a steam brake to the engine and tender as well as the present hand brake on the tender together with two guards van brakes to each train of more than ten vehicles will enable passenger trains to be worked with increased safety'*.

Steam Brakes
Despite Johnson and Clayton's declared preference for steam brakes no immediate authority to proceed with passenger engines was forthcoming, though a start was soon made with new goods engine construction. On 16 January 1877, Locomotive Committee Minute 8917 authorised the building of the first of the 1357 class express goods and the specification, dated 11 January 1877, confirms the fitting of steam brakes. The following 1377 class 0-6-0Ts, ordered from August 1877, were also fitted from new in April and May 1878. From then on steam brakes

Five engines were fitted with Clark's Hydraulic brake introduced in 1875. No. 136 shown here after 1885 was involved in the Newark Trials demonstrating this brake but it did not prevail, and was removed by June 1880.

Following the decision of January 1878 to fit steam brakes to the 'Metropolitan' tanks came the further decision on 15 October 1878 to add the Smiths Simple Vacuum brake. Met type 4-4-0T No. 205 in red livery between 1883 and 1888 is so equipped. Note the two front vacuum hoses required for this two pipe system.

became standard where continuous brakes were not required. Johnson next reported, on 16 April 1878, that 'forty tank engines' running in connection with the Metropolitan trains required fitting up with steam brakes. At this date there were 42 tanks fitted with condensing apparatus, six Metropolitan type 4-4-0Ts, twenty-six Kirtley 0-4-4Ts and ten Johnson 0-4-4Ts. The steep descents to

the Metropolitan widened lines from both Kentish Town and Blackfriars clearly indicated the necessity for something better than hand brakes, though the discrepancy in numbers is not explained. The subsequent provision of steam brakes with vacuum for the train overtook the completion of this work but Kirtley 0-4-4Ts Nos.690, 691, 693, 694, 695, 780, 781, 783, 787, 792, 795, and

Johnson 0-4-4T No.147 are known to have received steam brakes only at first. All these had acquired provision for working vacuum train brakes by the close of 1882.

On 31 December 1878 under the heading 'Additional brake power for engines of West District' Johnson recommended that fifty main line passenger engines should be fitted with steam brakes on engine and tender, at an estimated cost

The last tank engines to be fitted with Smith's brake were Nos. 1718-22 of May/June 1885. This brake was removed from all forty-six tank engines which had been fitted between June 1888 and November 1889. S Summerson collection.

No. 22 of the 3 class variant of the 800 class built in October 1871 was rebuilt by Johnson in March 1876. It was fitted with automatic Westinghouse brake to a replacement Johnson tender which was removed between 1884 and 1893. Note the engine has no brakes.

of £55 each. These fifty engines were identified as
890 class 2-4-0: *12, 40, 43, 46, 49, 68, 90-93, 95, 120-128, 130, 131, 134, 151, 152, 890, 891, 893-896, 898, 899, 908, 909*
800 class 2-4-0: *820-829*
1347 (later 101) class 2-4-0: *1347A-1351A*

Again, the subsequent provision of vacuum equipment for the train brakes overtook the programme, but in addition to No.892 fitted in 1876, the following are known to have received steam brakes only, in the first instance:

890 class 2-4-0: *40, 43, 46, 49, 890, 894-899, 908*
800 class 2-4-0: *815, 820, 824, 826, 827*

Of these, Nos.899 and 908 were the only 'steam brake only' passenger engines on 1 January 1882 and they were altered during the following six month period. It may be noted also that steam brakes on engine and tender were provided where Smith's vacuum brake and Sanders' automatic vacuum brake and its derivatives were fitted for operating the train brakes. On 15 July 1879, in the first of the continuous brake returns made to the Locomotive Committee, Johnson reported that seventy engines were fitted with steam brake only. His own original notes dating from the first half of 1879 show sixty-six engines, as follows:

890 class 2-4-0: *892*
Bogie tanks 0-4-4: *690, 693, 695, 783*
Goods 0-6-0: *1357-76*
Goods tanks 0-6-0T: *1102-1105, 1113, 1115, 1116, 1117, 1126, 1130, 1131, 1377-1396 1347-1356*

It will be noted that eleven of the 1102 class 0-6-0Ts built from 1874 with hand brakes only had also been fitted by this date, and some new passenger engines were also fitted with steam brakes only. These comprised the ten 2-4-0s Nos.1400-1409 turned out to 0.232 of 15 October 1878 in June-November 1879. The same drawing list also shows 0.273/5/9 (Nos.1472-1501) as steam brake fitted but from Johnson's records, it appears probable that all except the first five of these latter engines (together with five to 0.283, Nos.111-115, not included in the lists) were given steam brakes and vacuum for the train from new - see later.

Smith's Simple Vacuum Brake (main line engines)

Despite regarding the general adoption of continuous brakes as undesirable until a sufficiently reliable system was available, on 14 November 1876 Johnson and Clayton recommended to the Locomotive Committee that two trains and engines be equipped for trial with Smith's vacuum brakes, and this was duly approved by the Board.

This was a simple brake (i.e. non-automatic) whereby the creation of a partial vacuum in the train pipes applied the brakes. It had the shortcoming common to all non-automatic brakes, that should a leak occur in the system, or a coupling break, parting the train, then the brakes were not applied, and It was not therefore 'fail safe'. As noted above, it operated in conjunction with a steam brake on the engine and tender, so that all vehicles of the train were braked.

Experiments with this brake took place on 21 March 1877 but the Smiths Vacuum Brake Company published the results without any sanction from the Midland. The latter expressed its disapproval, with Johnson instructed to request 'that no reports in future be printed unless sanctioned by this Committee'.

On 2 May 1877 the Board required monthly reports to be presented to the Locomotive and Traffic Committees on the working of Smith's and Westinghouse brakes on the Manchester and Scotch expresses, to include an account and explanation of any failures, together with repair costs. The Smith's system was cheaper in first cost, and figures of 7 April 1877 show £98 per engine for the Smith's brake against £130 per engine for the Westinghouse. The subsequent failure statistics also showed markedly in favour of the Smith's system.

By August, Johnson and Clayton were able to report that it would be necessary to fit up twenty-four engines and it was ordered that this be done 'with the utmost possible despatch'. Precise dates of the fitting and removal of Smith's brakes do not appear to have survived but Johnson's notes (PRO RAIL 491/780) confirm that a total of thirty-six main line engines were fitted, probably all in 1877. There were twelve at £128.6s.6d each, followed by twenty-four at £116.15s.0d, as follows:

CLASS	BUILT	NOS.	COST/ENGINE
1282 6ft 6in 2-4-0	5-6/76	1282-1290	£128.6.6
1312 6ft 6in 4-4-0	11-12/76	1312-1314	£128.6.6
1282 6ft 6in 2-4-0	6-8/76	1291-1301	£116.15.0
1312 6ft 6in 4-4-0	12/76-2/77	1315-1321	£116.15.0
1327 7ft 0in 4-4-0	6/77	1327-1332	£116.15.0

All ten of the 6ft 2in 1 class and Nos. 1302-11 of the 1282 class were fitted with the Westinghouse automatic brake in 1876. No 1306 (shown as first fitted with brakes to tender wheels only) had this brake removed to 0.1091 of 1 June 1891.

George Westinghouse jealously guarded his patents and was not at all averse to law suits in order to defend them. Thus on 18 September 1877 the Committee was advised that the 'Smith's Vacuum Brake Company will undertake to defend the GN and Midland Companies from any action Mr Westinghouse may take.' This particular set-to was over ejectors.

The appearance of Sanders' automatic brake (see later) led Smith's Vacuum Brake Co. to offer on 19 February 1878 an 'automatic' addition to its ordinary brake. A trial train would be equipped and, if after evaluation it was not retained, no charge would be made. The offer was not pursued.

By early 1879 a number of engines and carriages had been fitted with Sanders' automatic vacuum brake and on 7 May 1879 Mr Allport reported to the Board on *'the great inconvenience in the working of the carriages in consequence of the application of more than one continuous brake to the carriage stock'*. He referred to the recommendations of the Chairmen of the Locomotive and Carriage & Wagon Committees that the thirty-six engines fitted with Smith's brake be altered to automatic vacuum, thus eliminating Smith's brake on the main line. The work of removal began immediately and was completed in November 1880, the non-automatic nature of this brake clearly sealing its fate.

Meantime, the MR Chairman and Deputy Chairman attended the Locomotive Committee meeting of 15 October 1878, when three important matters were considered. The first was a recommendation to the Board to fit the Metro-

politan trains with Smith's vacuum brake and the second a request to the Board to decide the form of brake for the new joint stock for Scotch traffic. Thirdly, it was necessary to remind the Board of its Minute 1628 of 6 February 1878 as to whether *'it was desirable to adopt the principle of automatic action as a necessity in any brake which may be adopted for the general use of this Company.'* The exceptions were those trains running on the Metropolitan Railway. Clearly the Board was still undecided.

Smiths simple vacuum brake (Metropolitan engines)

The decision to fit the Midland's Metropolitan trains with Smith's brake indicates that the Sanders' automatic brake had not yet proved sufficiently satisfactory. Yet the widened lines, with their steep gradients down to Kings Cross and pronounced dip beneath the Ray Street gridiron between Kings Cross and Farringdon Street, were just the sort of situation which required an automatic brake.

The Metropolitan Railway used Smith's brake and that undoubtedly had a bearing on the decision to use this brake on the engines and carriages working over their lines, and in this connection, a letter was received on 5 November 1878 from J. Tomlinson, the Locomotive Superintendent of the Metropolitan Company, 'as to the satisfactory working of the Smith's brake upon that railway'. The Midland Board approved its use on the following day.

The Westinghouse Company, not to be outdone, offered to supply their ordinary non automatic air brake on 14 Novem-

ber 1878 - their offer was declined. Authority was given on 17 December 1878 for fitting thirty engines at £9 per engine and £12 per carriage. The engines were:

Met type 4-4-0T: *204-209*
Kirtley 780 class 0-4-4T: *786-799*
Johnson 6 class 0-4-4T: *6, 15, 18, 137, 140-144, 147*

As before with Smith's brake, the engine was fitted with steam brakes worked in conjunction with vacuum for the train. Subsequent statistics in the Locomotive Committee Minutes show that six more engines other than new construction were also equipped. Kirtley 0-4-4Ts Nos.780, 781, 783 and 785 are confirmed and Johnson's records, by the numbers and dates of conversion to Smith's or Sander's brakes, indicate that Nos.782 and 784 were the others, as all remaining Smith's fitted engines can be accounted for.

Six had been fitted by 31 July 1879 and conversions proceeded apace. Although strictly outside the 1876-80 period, it is convenient to give the remaining history of Smith's brake here. The five new Johnson 0-4-4Ts delivered with condensing apparatus in February-April 1882, Nos.1547-1551, were fitted new (or shortly afterwards) and the other thirty-six were completed in the following November. Five further 0-4-4Ts with condensing apparatus, Nos.1718-1722, were delivered in May and June 1885 and these likewise were fitted new bringing the total to forty-six.

Despite the onward march of the automatic brake on the Midland it was not until 19 January 1888 that the Traffic

Committee requested the Locomotive Committee to fit these Metropolitan engines with the automatic brake in place of Smith's. Smith's brake ceased to be worked after 20 October 1888 and the conversion of the engines was completed in November 1889.

Sanders' Automatic Vacuum Brake

Johnson and Clayton's report of 14 November 1876 had concluded *'When a continuous brake sufficiently satisfactory for general adoption on this Railway can be fixed on, we consider it necessary for the convenience of working that all passenger engines and carriages on the main line and for the Metropolitan trains should be fitted up with it'*. Thus they covered themselves with respect to the views of the Board of Trade.

The first references to Sanders' brake appears on 14 August 1877, when the Midland Board's approval was given for the fitting of a single train with 'Sanders Automatic brake'. This system was operated by maintaining a partial vacuum in the train pipes to hold the brakes off; when a brake application was made, air was admitted to the system, so applying the brakes. Thus, should the system become faulty and admit air or a coupling break and part the train, the result was an automatic application of the brakes. In this way it was 'fail-safe', unlike the Smiths system. In its original form, however, it was far from entirely satisfactory and this will be discussed later. As with the Smith's brake, a steam brake was provided for the engine and tender, worked in conjunction with vacuum brake on the train.

In its original form up to 1881 the large ejector was placed at footplate level beside the smokebox. The steam supply was taken from the boiler side above the handrail down to the ejector and a vertical exhaust pipe led up to a point approximately at the boiler centre line, before passing inside the smokebox. Subsequently, the ejector was mounted on the boiler side, adjacent to the steam manifold with a horizontal pipe to the smokebox.

Authority was given on 14 August 1877 to fit six engines at an estimated cost of £115 each and, as with the early Westinghouse engines, the details were recorded subsequently in the Locomotive Committee minutes. The six engines were Beyer Peacock 170 2-4-0 No.170 (fitted January 1878; Johnson 1327 7ft 4-4-0 Nos.1337-1340 (fitted February 1878) and Johnson 1327 7ft 4-4-0 No.1341 (March 1878).

Operations using Sanders brake commenced on 2 February 1878 and it was added to the monthly statistics of brake failures from March. While the Smith's brake was in use, Sander's brake showed a consistently higher failure rate, but its automatic nature was to prove decisive. Ten more engines were fitted between July and October 1878, as follows:

Class Fitted	Nos.
Johnson 1327 7ft 4-4-0 7/78	1342-1344
Johnson 1347 7ft 2-4-0 8/78	1354A-1356A
Johnson 1347 7ft 2-4-0 9/78	1353A
1327 7ft 4-4-0 9/78	1345, 1346
1347 7ft 2-4-0 10/78	1352A

Decisions

A revealing table on the state of play of the principle continuous systems in use

TABLE 5A - BRAKE FAILURES FOR THE YEAR 1878

	A	B	C	D	E	F Totally	F Partially
West'hse	14	23	14	89	506425	1726	5875
Smiths Vacuum	3	nil	nil	24	295820	nil	nil
Sanders Automatic Vacuum	3	4	10	40	106065	36½	373

A Failed to act when applied
B Failed to act by ceasing to work or by not working at all
C Failed to act by not releasing
D Casualties or failures from sundry causes
E Total miles run with brake operative
F Mileage of brake inoperative through failure

was included in the Minute for 14th January 1879 covering the year ending 31 December 1878:

The Board had decided on 6 November 1878 that any brake to be adopted for general use should have an automatic action but took no decision as to which it should be. However it is significant that on 14 January 1879 approval was given for the payment of £2,000 for a licence to use Sanders and Bolithos patent brake. The following March a report was required giving the date, weight and cost of apparatus when fitted, miles run and

Nos. 1572-81 of the 1562 class were Westinghouse fitted when new in 1883, with pumps taken from earlier 2-4-0s. Fitted on engine and tender, most retained this brake into the 1890s. It was removed from No. 1577, seen here at Bradford c1900, between 1893 and 1895.

No. 1676 at Bedford. The last two engines to be Westinghouse fitted were 1667 class 4-4-0s Nos. 1675/6 when new in 1884. They took the pumps from 890 class 2-4-0s Nos. 904/5, for working the scotch expresses from St Pancras. In this they were unsuccessful and were replaced by Westinghouse fitted 2-4-0s. S Summerson collection.

repair costs for Westinghouse and Sanders brakes. The subject remained under close scrutiny through the summer of 1879 and on 29 September a special meeting was held to agree a report to the Board. This noted that, although Smith's brake was the most reliable, it had to be discounted as it was not automatic. The Committee concluded that the best for adoption was the 'Sanders Improved brake,' as 'its power is fully equal to the Westinghouse and is less liable to get out of order.' Despite this, on 1 October 1879 the Board resolved that it was *'not at present finally prepared to adopt any particular brake for exclusive use on the Midland Railway but that until further orders, Sanders Improved brake should be used on any trains hereafter fitted with automatic brakes'*.

From June 1879 a regular return was submitted to the Locomotive Committee giving the totals of engines fitted with the various brakes and this enables the changes to be followed in detail. Johnson's record of brakes shows twenty new engines fitted with vacuum and steam brakes in the half year ended December 1880. Twenty-five 2-4-0s were built in this period, Nos.1472-1491 and 111-115, so it is presumed that Nos.1472-1476 of 1880 initially had steam brake only and the remainder were the first new engines to have the vacuum brake in addition. For the next six months, to June 1881, thirty-five new engines were recorded as fitted and this accords with Nos.1492-1501 built at Derby and Nos.1502-1526 from Neilson, the latter confirmed in drawing lists.

Both Westinghouse and Sanders' brakes continued to give problems and in 1880 the Board of Trade was pressing the Midland regarding the fitting of con-

tinuous brakes. The response, on 3 August 1880, was that the Company *'have not formally generally adopted a uniform continuous brake ... because of practical difficulties, referring to the present proposals of both Westinghouse and Sanders to further improve their brakes.'* It didn't sound very convincing. Both brake companies submitted 'their latest improvements' in the same month.

The Wennington accident of 11 August 1880 provided the final stimulus. A passenger train not fitted with continuous brakes derailed and struck a bridge abutment; if such brakes had been in operation the train would have been brought to a halt before reaching the abutment. Eight passengers were killed and twenty-three injured. The Board of Trade and the Coroners Inquest Jury severely censured the company and on 1 September 1880 the MR Board resolved that the Locomotive and Carriage & Wagon Committees be instructed to fit a continuous automatic brake *'to the whole of the carriages and other vehicles which run in passenger trains and also to fit the engines with steam brakes, and that the work be proceeded with as fast as practicable'*.

CONSOLIDATION 1880-90
1 Automatic vacuum brakes
Once the decision had been taken to fit automatic vacuum brakes to the passenger stock, the work proceeded apace. On 6 December 1881 it was reported to the Locomotive Committee that, of the 513 engines to be so fitted 349 'were done'; the work was reported as complete by 31 March 1883.

This version of the automatic brake on the carriages was so designed that once the train had been stopped, the

brake gradually leaked off by means of a specially provided hole in the brake cylinder piston, known as a leak hole. This avoided the need for valves to be incorporated, but it had the grave disadvantage in that, should a train be parted on an incline, the brake would initially bring the parts of the train to a stand, but on leaking off could enable a runaway to take place, as in the bad old days. A further disadvantage was that with frequent brake applications such as might occur when running down inclines or approaching termini, the braking effect was reduced.

M. Reynolds published a treatise, *Continuous Railway Brakes* in 1882 and in his summary commented on the Midland system as follows *'We have only to add that the engines and tenders are fitted with powerful steam brakes; and, from a great many drivers, we know that they depend for stopping their trains more on their steam brake than on the automatic vacuum brake. They have told the author repeatedly that they would come daily to grief with the automatic vacuum brake if they had not the steam brake to fall back upon!'*

That Johnson was aware of these shortcomings is evident in his subsequent reports to the Locomotive Committee. On 5 September 1884 he informed the Chairman of the arrangement adopted by the Lancashire & Yorkshire Railway, whereby the leak hole was replaced by a small ball valve. Johnson considered this a great improvement on the MR brake, for it would 'remain on until taken off.' Experiments took place with this arrangement from October 1884, alongside the 'Haigh valve arrangement' (which produced a partial leak off brake) and a 'Perforated piston brake' as devised by Clayton. Johnson reported comprehensively to the Locomotive Committee on 18 March 1886, recommending adoption of the ball valve brake, for the following reasons:

'1st   It complies entirely with all the conditions laid down by the Board of Trade.

'2nd   It is positive and absolute in its action and when applied will remain on as long as it may be desired and until taken off by the driver or the guard.

'3rd   It can be applied as many times as desired in quick succession without materially reducing its power and it can be easily manipulated by the driver.

'4th   The driver, having once created a proper vacuum and started on his journey cannot leave an intermediate station or start again after stopping at a signal without having full brake power.

'5th   It has a great advantage over the leak hole system when required to be used on long and heavy rising or falling gradients as it can be applied with either a moderate or a full amount of brake power and will remain on without practical diminution of power.'

A classic description of the basic essentials of a good brake. The recommendations were accepted and the subsequently recorded statistics show that the Haigh valve and perforated piston arrangements were eliminated by June 1887 and that completion to the ball valve arrangement took place in December 1889. Thus, with the virtual elimination of the Westinghouse brake by that time (see later) the Midland had at last satisfactorily resolved the question of the continuous brake.

Once the fitting of the automatic vacuum brake to the passenger engines had been completed in 1883, attention was turned to some of the goods engines. Johnson reported on 1 June 1883 that in the Whitsun week just passed, forty-nine steam braked goods engines and 136

goods engines fitted with hand brakes only had to be used on special passenger trains. He recommended that fifty express goods engines (i.e. the 1357 class) be fitted with the automatic vacuum brake at a cost of £45 each, 'so as to be available when running passenger trains'. The first engines so fitted were turned out in September 1883.

This process continued over a period of years and individual engines are noted under the classes concerned. The first goods engines to be fitted were in fact the five 1377 class 0-6-0 tanks, built in June 1883 and specially equipped with overall cabs, for working the Keighley and Oxenhope branch. F H Clarke noted 151 Kirtley 0-6-0s as vacuum fitted in 1900 and official MR Drawing Office *Memoranda* issued on 3 March 1911, 31 March 1914 and 6 July 1918 quote the engines fitted at those dates. Thus a picture can be built up of the changes which occurred over the years - these are noted under the class headings.

Westinghouse brakes

This brake had been adopted for the Scotch trains in 1876 and on 19 November 1878 the Board had agreed that new joint stock should be fitted with the Westinghouse Automatic Brake, without prejudice to final decisions. As noted, fifty-seven engines had been fitted by the close of 1876, of which six, 890 class No.134, rebuilt Beyer Peacock 2-4-0s Nos.235, 236, 237 and 239 and 800 class No.802 had brakes on the engine and tender, the remaining having tender brakes only.

Westinghouse then recommended, on 17 August 1880, that driving wheels be fitted with brakes. This advice was accepted and the necessary work was carried out to the other Westinghouse engines over the next few years, though it was not completed until early 1886, when the forty-seven surviving engines are

recorded as so fitted.

It is presumed that the thirteen engines with the original non-automatic arrangement were converted to automatic operation, but as five had this brake removed in 1877 they may not have been altered.

The remaining 230 and 890 class 2-4-0s which were still Westinghouse fitted in 1880, plus those 800 class 2-4-0s not rebuilt and the Johnson 1 class 2-4-0s all had their pumps transferred in the period 1880-84 to rebuilt 800 class engines, two 7ft 0in Johnson 2-4-0s (Nos.101 and 102), the ten new 6ft 9in Johnson 4-4-0s (Nos.1572-1581) and two of the 'Joy' 4-4-0s, Nos 1675 and 1676. This brought the total of engines that had carried Westinghouse pumps at some time or another to eighty-nine. The details are set out in table 5B. F H Clarke recorded that three pumps were smashed in accidents on engines Nos.9, 816 and an unidentified 900 series 2-4-0.

Notwithstanding the standardisation of automatic vacuum brakes, the Westinghouse automatic brake remained in use on those trains so fitted, but from 1882, new 'Scotch stock' was dual fitted. The number of Westinghouse fitted engines required was thus reduced and the gear removed from twelve engines between March and June 1882. The monthly mileage of Westinghouse trains run in the 1883-84 period was around 60,000, rising to an average of over 80,000 during 1886. It declined thereafter but between forty-five and forty-eight engines remained fitted until May 1891, after which it was gradually removed. Very low monthly mileages, usually below 1,000, were operated from the close of 1890 and the last Westinghouse braked train ran in August 1894. The last two locomotives to carry pumps (not identified) had them removed in June 1895. The allocation of Westinghouse engines was generally concentrated at the sheds

2048

No. 106 was built in October 1877 as No. 1352 and was fitted with Sander's Automatic Vacuum brake in October 1878. Note the early arrangement of ejector at the foot of the smokebox and the associated pipework to and from boiler, smokebox and beneath running plate. No. 1352 became 106 in July 1879. S Summerson collection.

TABLE 5B - ENGINES FITTED WITH WESTINGHOUSE BRAKES
1. ENGINES FITTED 1873-75

ENGINE	CLASS	DATE FITTED	ORIGINAL TYPE	ORIGINAL FITTING	REMOVED	NOTES
156	156	2/73	NA	T	1877	Replaced by 800
238	230	2/73	NA	T	1880	
64	800	2/74	NA	T	1881-3	
66	800	2/74	NA	T	***1877	Replaced by 819
40	890	2/74	NA	T	1877	Replaced by 813
901	890	2/74	NA	T	1881-3	
902	890	2/74	NA	T	1881-3	
906	890	2/74	NA	T	1881-3	
809	800	5/74	NA	T	7/1893-6/95	Rebuilt J blr 12/75
894	890	5/74	NA	T	1877	Replaced by 807
898	890	5/74	NA	T	1877	Replaced by 816
903	890	5/74	NA	T	1881-3	
904	890	5/74	NA	T	1881-3	
63	800	2/75	A	T	1884-6/93	Rebuilt J blr 9/82
62	800	3/75	A	T	1881-3	
65	800	3/75	A	T	1881-3	
905	890	3/75	A	T	1881-3	
895	890	4/75	A	T	1877	Replaced by 804
900	890	4/75	A	T	1883	
907	890	4/75	A	T	1881-3	
1080	1070	4/75	A	T	1877	Replaced by 818
134	890	6/75	A	ET	**1878	Replaced by 814
236	230	8/75	A	ET	1880	
237	230	8/75	A	ET	1880	
239	230	8/75	A	ET	1880	
235	230	11/75	A	ET	1880	

NOTES
All engines except 134 fitted with Kirtley boilers. Pumps removed before rebuilding with Johnson boilers except nos 63 and 809.
*** No 66 was refitted in 1882 see section 2.
** There is a certain amount of confusion regarding 134 and 814. Dewhurst shows both fitted by 1876 and pumps removed from 134 in 1878, but Johnson shows 814 replaced 134.

NA	Non Automatic brake
A	Automatic brake
ET	Engine and tender braked
T	Tender only braked

continued overleaf

Steam brakes

The fitting of new goods engines with steam brakes was continued and by 30 June 1883 all except two of the 1102 class 0-6-0Ts had also been fitted. No specific authority has been found for altering existing stock, but commencing with Locomotive Committee Minute 1205 of 3 July 1885, a series of authorisations provided for fitting the remaining engines having handbrakes only, concluding with Minute 2831 of 19 September 1890, which authorised steam brakes for the last of the engine stock, 368 goods engines at £60 each, which was duly sanctioned by the General Purposes Committee on 3 October 1890. The particular engines are not described, but by that date would have comprised the outstanding Kirtley 0-6-0s and miscellaneous engines.

A series of Derby orders, usually for thirty sets of steam brake work for goods engines and tenders was issued for this, the last of the bulk orders being 0.1490 of 16 October 1895. This accounted for some 320 engines and a final order, 0.1840 of 16 November 1898, was for four Kirtley double framed goods, Nos.241, 371, 491 and 500. Of these No.371 had been broken up the previous February and the others may have been the last to be fitted.

The restrictive effect of running with hand brake only, compared with the in-

involved with the Scotch trains. So, at the close of 1880 Leicester had fourteen 800 class for working to London and Normanton, Leeds had six of the same and the two Johnson 101 class 7ft 2-4-0s, whilst Skipton was possessed of three 800 class, three 890 class and one of Johnson's 1282 class. Carlisle ran the other nine 1282 engines and Normanton had five of the 890 class. Kentish Town had only Nos.807 and 809.

The ten 1562 class 4-4-0s built in 1882-83 went to Carlisle where they displaced Nos.1302-10 as the principal passenger engines. They were still there in 1892. The two 1667 class 4-4-0s with Joys valve gear, Nos 1675 and 1676, went next to Kentish Town in 1884, but according to Ahrons were not a success; they were replaced by old 800 class Nos.818 and 819.

No. 1481 built in October 1880 was one of the first passenger engines to be fitted with Sander's Automatic Vacuum brake from new. At Kettering on 9 July 1904, it displays the post-1881 arrangement of large ejector on the boilerside and piping along the right-hand handrail.

TABLE 5B continued - ENGINES FITTED WITH WESTINGHOUSE BRAKES

2. ENGINES FITTED 1876-84

ENGINE	CLASS	DATE FITTED	ORIGINAL TYPEFITTING	ORIGINAL	REMOVED	NOTES
22	800	3/76	A	T	1884-6/93	
60	800	3/76	A	T	6/1891-6/93*	
165	800	3/76	A	T	7/1893-6/95*	
802	800	3/76	A	ET	6/1891-6/93*	
810	800	3/76	A	T	7/1893-6/95	
817	800	3/76	A	T	1884-6/93	
1+	1	3/76	A	T	1883	
9+	1	3/76	A	T	1881-3	
10+	1	3/76	A	T	1881-3	
13+	1	3/76	A	T	1883	
70+	1	3/76	A	T	1883	
71+	1	4/76	A	T	1883	
73+	1	4/76	A	T	1883	
74+	1	4/76	A	T	1883	
96+	1	4/76	A	T	1881-3	
146+	1	4/76	A	T	1883	
41	890	4/76	A	T	1877	Replaced by 805
42	890	4/76	A	T	1877	Replaced by 811
801	800	4/76	A	T	1884-6/93	
806	800	4/76	A	T	1881-3	
808	800	4/76	A	T	1884-6/93*	
1302+	1282	8/76	A	T	1881-3	
1303+	1282	8/76	A	T	6/1891-6/93*	
1304+	1282	8/76	A	T	1884-6/93	
1305+	1282	8/76	A	T	7/1893-6/95	
1306+	1282	8/76	A	T	6/1891-6/93*	
1307+	1282	8/76	A	T	1884-6/93	
1308+	1282	8/76	A	T	6/1891-6/93*	
1309+	1282	8/76	A	T	6/1891-6/93*	
1310+	1282	8/76	A	T	7/1893-6/95	
1311+	1282	8/76	A	T	1884-6/93	
814	800	**	A	T	6/1891-6/93*	Replaced 134
816	800	2/77	A	T	1881-3	Replaced 898
807	800	3/77	A	T	7/1893-6/95	Replaced 894
800	800	4/77	A	T	1884-6/93*	Replaced 156
804	800	5/77	A	T	6/1891-6/93*	Replaced 895
818	800	5/77	A	T	1884-6/93	Replaced 1080
805	800	6/77	A	T	1881-3	Replaced 41
811	800	6/77	A	T	1884-6/93	Replaced 42
813	800	6/77	A	T	1884-6/93	Replaced 40
819	800	7/77	A	T	7/1893-6/95	Replaced 66
101	101	/80	A	?	6/1891-6/93*	
102	101	/80	A	?	6/1891-6/93*	
803	800	/80	A	?	6/1891-6/93*	
815	800	5/80	A	T	1884-6/93	
829	800	12/80	A	ET	6/1891-6/93*	
826	800	4/81	A	ET	7/1893-6/95	
824	800	10/81	A	ET	1884-6/93	
66	800	9/82	A	ET	7/1893-6/95	
812	800	9/82	A	ET	7/1893-6/95	
168	800	10/82	A	ET	6/1891-6/93*	
166	800	11/82	A	ET	6/1891-6/93*	
1572+	1562	/83	A	ET	1884-6/93	
1573+	1562	2/83	A	ET	7/1893-6/95	
1574+	1562	2/83	A	ET	1884-6/93	
1575+	1562	2/83	A	ET	1884-6/93	
1576+	1562	2/83	A	ET	6/1891-6/93*	
1577+	1562	3/83	A	ET	7/1893-6/95	
1578+	1562	3/83	A	ET	7/1893-6/95	
1579+	1562	3/83	A	ET	7/1893-6/95	
1580+	1562	3/83	A	ET	1884-6/93	
1581+	1562	4/83	A	ET	7/1893-6/95	
1675+	1667	9/84	A	ET	7/1893-6/95	Pumps from 904
1676+	1667	10/84	A	ET	7/1893-6/95	Pumps from 905

NOTES

All engines fitted with Johnson boilers

+	Engines fitted when new
*	Pumps removed to 0.1091 of 1.6.91
**	See note ** under section 1
A	Automatic brake
T	Tender only braked
ET	Engine & tender braked

GENERAL NOTES – SOURCES
Dates fitted 1874-6: Johnson's records and Locomotive Committee M 9715 of 18 March 1879
Dates fitted 1877-84: Year – F H Clarke
    Month – Date of building/rebuilding from official registers
Dates removed: Locomotive Committee minutes, F H Clarke records and 0.1091.
Replacement: Johnson's records
Pump Transfers: F H Clarke's records

TABLE 5C RETURN OF ENGINES FITTED WITH WESTINGHOUSE BRAKE

DATES	NUMBER FITTED	SOURCE
End 1876	58	F H CLARKE
End 1877	58	"
End 1878	57	"
3/79-3/82	57	MR LCM
End 4/82	52	"
End 5/82	46	"
6/82-8/82	45	"
End 9/82	46	"
End 10/82	47	"
11/82-5/86	48	"
6/86-2/89	47	"
3/89-12/90	46	"
1/91-5/91	45	"
End 6/91	39	"
End 12/91	33	"
End 12/92	24	"
End 12/93	11	"
End 12/94	3	"
End 6/95	NIL	"

LCM – Locomotive Committee Minutes

TABLE 5D VACUUM AND STEAM BRAKE PROGRAMME FOR GOODS ENGINES 1883-90

LOCOMOTIVE COMMITTEE MINUTE	DATE	VACUUM ADDED TO STEAM	STEAM AND VACUUM	STEAM	ENGINES
M500	1.6.83	50	-	-	EXPRESS GOODS
M903	17.7.84	50	-	-	EXPRESS GOODS
M1205	3.7.85	-	50	100	GOODS ENGINES
M1596	14.10.86	-	-	100	GOODS ENGINES
M1801	1.7.87	21	29	100	GOODS ENGINES
M2201	18.10.88	-	50	100	GOODS ENGINES
M2453	18.7.89	-	75	-	GOODS ENGINES
M2831	19.9.90	-	-	368	GOODS ENGINES

DERBY ORDERS FOR FITTING VACUUM AND STEAM BRAKE TO GOODS ENGINES 1889-98

ORDER	DATE	WORK	NUMBER	NOTES
0.864	8.11.89	Steam & Vacuum	75	
0.914	30.4.90	Steam	20	
0.965	14.10.90	"	30	
0.1003	17.3.91	"	30	
0.1046	21.9.91	"	30	
0.1142	13.4.92	"	30	
0.1176	25.8.92	"	30	
0.1228	6.1.93	"	30	
0.1275	26.6.93	"	30	
0.1323	14.11.93	"	30	
0.1388	1.8.94	"	30	
0.1490	16.10.95	"	30	
0.1840	16.11.98	"	4	Engines 241 371 491 and 500

creased brake power available with a steam brake, is amply demonstrated in the headings quoted in the Working Timetable notice for June 1889 for the two mile Fazakerly North Junction - Alexandra Dock branch in Liverpool, which has a mile long gradient of 1 in 64 up towards the Junction. The double-framed 0-6-0s were allowed only fourteen mineral or twenty goods wagons when not fitted with steam brake, but nineteen mineral or twenty-six goods if fitted. It is a sobering thought that so many engines were still running about, restricted in their haulage capacity with only a handbrake to arrest their progress as late as the 1890s! A table sets out the programme for fitting both vacuum and steam brakes during this period.

Conclusion

From 1898, all goods engines had steam brakes to both engine and tender, with some vacuum fitted too. Whilst 325 goods engines were authorised for vacuum fitting between 1883-89, the majority built after that date were fitted from new. Changes in vacuum fitted engines, tender and tank, subsequently took place as a result of withdrawals and varying needs and the details are shown under individual classes as appropriate. Once the Westinghouse brake was eliminated from 1895, all passenger engines had steam brakes for engine and tender and vacuum for the train.

Having fitted all the passenger engines with Automatic Vacuum brake, a number of goods engines were fitted from 1883. Fifty express goods engines were authorised on 1 June 1883. No. 1375 of this batch shows the vacuum hose at the front end. S Summerson collection.

No. 1563 of September 1882 illustrates the first class to be fitted with carriage warming; Nos. 1566, 1568 and 1569 were authorised in 1887/8 for heating by steam.

A lone member of its class at Manchester No. 820 was the only passenger tender engine included in the first recorded order for fitting hot water carriage warming to existing stock for local trains – 0.1164 of 25 June 1892.

Chapter Six - Carriage Warming Apparatus

*'There appears to be no system which does not involve a
considerable amount of trouble and expense'*

The provision of heating in carriages was regarded as a low priority for very many years. The only facility, in what may now be seen as a minimal comfort for passengers in cold weather, was the provision of individual footwarmers. These were containers pre-heated at principal stations and terminals for individual use and had little practical effect on the temperature of a compartment.

Early Experiments

It was not until the 1880s that consideration began to be given to heating carriages, with either steam or hot water from the engine drawing the train. Ahrons, in his articles *Locomotive and Train Working in the Latter Part of the 19th Century* referred to the fitting of the Kirtley single No.141A of the 136 class with train heating apparatus, when it was rebuilt with new frames and a Johnson C boiler in December 1880. The drawings for this, to provide heating for the Directors' Saloon which this engine was allocated to haul around the system were dated February 1881. It is the earliest recorded date of an attempt to provide adequate carriage heating on the Midland.

Further years were to pass before the Traffic Committee requested the Locomotive Committee (on 15 December 1887) *'to fit up three engines with apparatus for warming carriages by steam at an estimated cost of £91 to work experimentally between Derby and Manchester'*. This was agreed and the work was ordered to be done. The engines were not specified but

drawings dated 14 December 1887 and 8 March 1888 show 4-4-0s Nos.1566, 1568 and 1569 to have been involved. These were Derby engines by 1892 and are likely to be those authorised by these minutes.

The Hot Water System 1890-1902

On 21 November 1890 the Board requested the Locomotive and Carriage Departments to consider and report as to the best mode of heating passenger carriages by steam. This report, by Johnson and Clayton, was presented to the Locomotive Committee on 18 December 1890:

'We beg to report we have spent a considerable time searching the records of the various modes of heating railway carriages in America and elsewhere by steam and other methods. We find that a great variety of systems of heating by steam, hot water and hot air have been tried, upon which some only have been favourably reported on, but even those which have been spoken on in the best terms, we could not recommend the Board either to adopt or come to any conclusion upon any of them without making a trial of one train to enable us to test and ascertain for our own information the practicality of the continuous system of heating. The system of heating by hot water appears to us to be the most practical and effectual method of heating and we therefore recommend that one train of 10 carriages be fitted up which we estimate would be about £60.'

The Board agreed to this the next day and a further report was presented to the Locomotive Committee on 16 July 1891.

The results of trials with this train *'appeared to fully accomplish the purpose intended, it acts well, being convenient, effectual and economical and we believe, from careful observation it will answer the problem of satisfactorily heating carriages...'*

It was then recommended that twelve further trains be fitted *'by next November to test the efficient working of the warming apparatus during the next winter.'* Johnson reported on 5 February 1892 that one train had been so fitted and that it had been working satisfactorily since 30 December 1891. It is clear from the evidence that follows that a general application of hot water carriage warming was then commenced. A series of four Minutes paralleled by Derby Orders can be recorded up to 1895, authorising the fitting of hot water carriage warming apparatus to existing engines.

1. On 3 June 1892 the Traffic Committee requested the fitting of ten engines and fifty carriages for the Manchester South District trains and nine 0-4-4Ts, Nos.1532-1537 and 1648-1650 were fitted along with Kirtley 800 class 2-4-0 No.820, under Derby Order 1164 of 25 June 1892.

2. On 16 February 1893 the Traffic Committee requested that fifteen engines and thirty passenger vehicles be fitted, at a total estimated cost of £637. The area of operation was not recorded but the fifteen engines fitted (to 0.1246 of 21 February 1893) comprised Kirtley 800 class 2-4-0s Nos.168 and 169, 890 class 2-4-0s Nos.130 and 132, Johnson

No. 1745 a 7ft 0in 4-4-0 of January 1886, was fitted with hot water Carriage Warming Apparatus (CWA) in 1893 by now approved for the most important express trains to Scotland. It was converted to steam carriage warming in 1904.

2-4-0s Nos.1505 and 1506, 4-4-0s Nos.1658-1660, 4-2-2s Nos.170, 171, 1864, 1866 and 1870 and 0-4-4T No.1646. Ahron's allocation list for the previous March 1892 showed these engines, with the exception of Nos.170 and 171 which were new, to be scattered widely through the system. No.168 was at Leicester, 169 Wellingborough, 130 and 132 Derby, 1505 and 1506 Leeds, 1658-1660 Manchester, 1864 and 1866 Liverpool, 1870 Nottingham and the 0-4-4T No.1646 at Manningham. Presuming the engines remained at these sheds, this appears to indicate fitting for trial purposes on certain trains between various places. *Appendix 18* of 21 August 1893 duly contains an entry under 'Carriage Warming Apparatus' as follows: *'The carriages of certain trains are fitted with an arrangement for warming the compartments with hot water'*. There then follows instructions for use and connecting up etc.

3. Later that year, on 19 October 1893, the Traffic Committee requested the fitting of Scotch Dining Carriage trains; this was agreed by the General Purposes Committee the same day, authorising ten engines and seven carriages. The ten engines were covered by Derby Order 1325 issued on 20 October 1893. They were: 4-4-0s Nos.1572, 1573, 1738, 1742 and 1745, 4-2-2s Nos.31, 1853 and 1858 and 0-4-4Ts Nos.1538 and 1539.

4. On 8 August 1895 it was agreed to fit seventy-two more engines and 232 carriages for working local services between London and Bedford, Bath, Bristol and Clifton Down; Birmingham, Walsall, Wolverhampton; Kings Norton, Evesham and so on at an estimated cost of £4,152. The order for fitting, 0.1472 was issued on 27 August 1895 but did not specify the engines involved.

Three odd orders issued in 1899 and 1900 covered six Leeds 2-4-0s (3 October 1899), six of the Kentish Town 0-6-0Ts, Nos.1385-1390 on 13 January 1900 and two 0-4-4Ts, Nos.2013 and 2016 on 20 November 1900. Three of the 690 class Kirtley well tanks were also fitted, at an unknown date, to provide a pool with the 0-6-0Ts for working empty stock into St Pancras.

No further specific references were made to the fitting of hot water carriage warming apparatus either in the Minutes or the Order books until 16 January 1902, when 'Twenty heavy goods tank engines on order from Vulcan foundry in order to work the heavier trains which it is proposed to put into the Manchester District Service' were so authorised. Derby Order 2330 of 23 January 1902 covered the provision of parts - usually supplied by Messrs Gresham and Craven - to be sent to Vulcan.

The Minutes, however, do not record the whole story. In respect of new engines, the specification of the twenty 2183 class 7ft 0ins 4-4-0s authorised on 18 June 1891 provided for the fitting of hot water carriage warming apparatus, and so did that for the fifteen 2203 6ft 6in 4-4-0s, authorised on 13 April 1892. The specifications for all subsequent contractor-built passenger tender engines, up to 1901 (except for ten 2581 class 6ft 6in 4-4-0s built in 1900) also included carriage warming apparatus. These latter engines were built to a specification of February 1898 for seven M&GN passenger engines, reissued on 16 March 1900 and amended to ten engines for the Midland. This did not include carriage warming and so they were not fitted when new. New 0-4-4Ts of the same period were also fitted, apart from

Nos.2611-2630 (1411-1430 in 1907) delivered by Dübs in 1900.

Most of the Drawing Schedules for the Derby-built 4-4-0s in the same period show carriage warming, as well as the last thirty-five Singles ordered from March 1892 - these commenced with the 179 class 7ft 6in piston valve design. Subsequent orders for conversion to steam carriage warming support the view that all were fitted. Details are set out in the class Chapters.

The first thirty of the Belpaire 4-4-0s and the first two Compounds were also fitted with hot water carriage warming when new in 1901-02, the last new engine to be equipped being Belpaire No.819, delivered in December 1902.

It is also clear from subsequent orders, issued to convert engines from hot water to steam heating, that further earlier engines were fitted with hot water carriage warming. This appears to be one of those cases where the original authority to carry out alterations was changed so that Committee scrutiny or formal order was not required. Some engines may have been among seventy-two authorised and not listed on 8 August 1895.

In the course of a report to the Locomotive Committee (also referred to later) on 15 May 1902, Johnson reported that 381 engines and 786 vehicles were fitted at that date with the Johnson & Clayton hot water system. From the available information it is possible to account for these as follows:
- Engines fitted from new
- Earlier engines fitted to Derby Orders
- Earlier engines listed in subsequent Derby Orders for conversion from hot water to steam.

These amounted to 368 as set out in Tables 6A and 6B, columns A, C and D.

Ninety 0-4-4Ts were fitted with hot water CWA between 1892 and 1902. No. 1539 was one of the earlier ones to 0.1325 of 20 November 1893. It was converted to steam to 0.2950 of 26 April 1905 but the last order to convert to steam was not issued until 22 May 1913. S Summerson collection.

For heating trains prior to departure from St Pancras six vacuum fitted Kentish Town 0-6-0Ts were equipped with hot water CWA in 1900. The fittings can just be seen on the buffer beam of No. 1387 in this view of 1904. It was replaced by Johnson & Bain steam CWA, to 0.3541 of 10 December 1908. S Summerson collection.

At that date, fifteen engines had been converted from hot water to the PLM steam system, four to Laycock's steam system and probably eleven to the Johnson & Clayton steam system which accounted for 338 with hot water carriage warming, a deficiency of forty-three.

The MR volume *Leading Particulars etc.* (RAIL 491.908) at the Public Record Office lists all engines fitted with carriage warming apparatus at about 1908 and shows a further forty-eight class 1 engines (listed in Table 6B column E) for which there are not specific earlier records. These are believed therefore to have had hot water apparatus. If these forty-eight are added to the calculated figure, the total of 386 is remarkably close to Johnson's figure of 381, bearing in mind that the precise date of this latter figure is not known. The total number of engines fitted with hot water carriage warming, including the thirty-two new engines fitted later in 1902, Table 6A column B, was therefore about 448, the sum of columns A to E in the tables.

EXPERIMENTS WITH STEAM 1899-1902
Laycock's Steam Storage, PLM direct steam and Johnson & Clayton's direct steam systems

The Hot water system proved to be not entirely satisfactory and a 'Heating of Trains Committee' was set up to examine the subject in detail. A record of its proceedings does not appear to have survived but Johnson and Clayton's report of 17 April 1900 was given to the Locomotive Committee two days later. '*In accordance with the Minute of the Heating*

of Trains Committee of 5 January 1900' they declared, '*we sent our Assistants, Mr Henderson of the Locomotive Department and Mr Haigh of the Carriage Department to visit and enquire into the various systems of warming railway carriages on English and Scotch Railways and also on the railways of France, Belgium, Switzerland and Germany. They have been furnished with a great deal of information and have embodied this in a report which together with a summary of the same, we beg to report to the Committee. From their report, it appears that heating by steam is the most general and of steam heating there are two systems, one the direct system and the other with a storage system. The storage system is most general in England, while on the Continent it is not used at all.*

'*With both systems, there is a considerable quantity of condensed water which must be got rid of at the stations. In the storage system, a much greater time is taken in raising the heat of each compartment and a greater amount of condensation is made than in the direct system and it also involves the putting down of stationery boilers at terminal stations or the employment of other engines besides the train engines to heat the carriages before the train starts on its journey.*

'*There appears to be no system which does not involve a considerable amount of trouble and expense. If the Committee desire to have further experiments made, we shall be pleased to take into consideration all the information which has been obtained and to make the best use we can of it.*'

There was no direct outcome of these deliberations but, evidently as a result of an earlier decision of the Heating & Trains Committee, ten engines were ordered to be fitted with 'Laycock steam heating fittings' on 3 October 1899. 0.1988 of that date authorised the fitting of Manchester 1327 class 4-4-0s Nos.1329, 1330, 1331 and 1342, Leeds 2-4-0s Nos.901, 902, 1514, 1515 and 1517 and Derby 2-4-0 No.900. Three Kentish Town 0-6-0Ts, Nos.211, 212 and 1391, were then authorised to 0.2027 of 13 January 1900.

A further report of 1 June 1900 illustrates very clearly the difficulties encountered and the reluctance to extend further the principle of comprehensive heating of passenger carriages. The text runs as follows:

'*1st We agree in recommending that no additions should be made to any system of continuous heating we have at present.*

'*2nd We agree that the continuous heating on both the main line and branch trains already fitted should continue to be used until further investigation enables us to recommend something better.*

'*3rd We agree that we feel ourselves unable to recommend any particular system of heating at present being tried on foreign or home railways, but that Mr Johnson and Mr Clayton should further consider the various systems now in use and they be empowered to fit up experimental trains embodying any improvement of other systems which have been tried.*

'*4th We agree that for the main line expresses and other trains it is necessary that the warming apparatus be inter-*

Top. The fitting of hot water CWA became standard practice on new passenger 4-4-0s commencing with the 2183 class in April 1892.

Middle. The last passenger engines built without CWA were Nos. 2581-90 of 1900, an oddity arising from the fact that they were built to an M & GN specification! All ten were rebuilt with H boilers when only four-five years old and then with steam CWA, becoming Nos. 473-82 in 1907.

Bottom. Belpaire No. 816 was one of the last engines fitted with hot water CWA in 1902, bringing the total having this arrangement to nearly 450 engines. No. 816 became 726 in 1907 and the eventual last survivor of the class in September 1952. S Summerson collection.

changeable with the carriages of other railway companies.

'*5th We agree in recommending that until some decision as regards further continuous heating is arrived at, the use of ordinary footwarmers should be continued and extended in those trains not heated from the engine.*'

The Board accepted the Report on 15 June 1900 enabling Johnson and Clayton to conduct further experiments. Twenty-four more engines were fitted with the Laycock apparatus, to bring the total to thirty-seven; these were 1070 class 2-4-0s Nos.1082 and 1084, 1312 class 4-4-0 No.1312, 1327 class 4-4-0s Nos.1333, 1335, 1343 and 1344, 1562 class 4-4-0s Nos.1661-1664, 1738 class 4-4-0s Nos.1740, 1743, 1744 and 1746, 2203 class 4-4-0s Nos.161-164 and 1853 class 4-2-2s Nos.177, 178, 1863, 1865 and 1872. The apparatus was removed from two of the Singles, Nos.1863 and 1865 under 0.2521 of 16 December 1902 and despatched to Melton Constable for use on the Midland and Great Northern Joint! Nos.161-164 had previously carried hot water carriage warming apparatus.

The No.5 supplement to No.20 Appendix, issued in October 1901, lists the trains heated by 'continuous process', both hot water and Laycock's steam storage system. The expresses heated by hot water were listed plus the following local services: London to Luton and Bedford, Birmingham to Walsall and Wolverhampton, Kings Norton to Redditch, Bath to Bristol and the Manchester South District trains. The Laycock steam system was fitted to five individual trains operating between London and Manchester, Derby and Buxton and Rotherham and Sheffield, together with all trains between Sheffield and Manchester Central.

In 1901 authority was given to fit fifteen 4-4-0s, all previously fitted with hot water carriage warming, with the Paris, Lyons and Mediterranean direct steam system. 0.2292 was issued on 17 September 1901, and covered 2203 class 6ft 6in 4-4-0s Nos.2213 and 2215, 150 class 7ft 0in 4-4-0s Nos.208 and 209 and 60 class 7ft 0in 4-4-0s Nos.64-69, 167-169, 2599 and 2600. This latter pair were then only three months old. Johnson and Clayton also devised a direct steam arrangement incorporating improvements on other systems which had been under scrutiny; by the following year, the way forward was becoming clear.

On 15 May 1902 Johnson read a report '*on the working of train heating apparatus during the past winter.*' In view of its importance, it is quoted in full: '*As explained at the meeting of the Heating of Trains Committee on 20 February, it is intended to carry out experiments with the various systems of train heating taking the steam from a special boiler, so that the actual amount required in each case may be measured. Our recent experience with the various systems has been as follows:*
'*Johnson & Clayton Hot Water system 381 engines and 786 vehicles fitted. There were a good many reports of pipes*

being frozen up during the cold weather, also about some vehicles being not warm enough. There is insufficient heat in the carriages, especially in the new stock with clerestory roofs. Drivers have to shut off hot water when ascending gradients and difficulty is experienced with the rapid consumption of hot water and want of increased tender capacity for increased speeds, heavy loads and long runs.

'Laycock steam system of storage heaters
Thirty seven engines and fifty four vehicles fitted.

None were reported as having been frozen and there were no other complaints. On the other hand it takes a very long time before starting to heat a long train and drivers have to shut off steam on rising gradients. There is also a liability for the couplings to separate and get torn off at cross-roads. [sic].

'Paris, Lyons and Mediterranean steam system
Fourteen engines and eighteen vehicles fitted. [it will be noted that fifteen engines were authorised on 17 September 1901].

A train of eight vehicles was tested in the carriage works yard on 19 February. A considerable amount of steam escaped from each heater along the train and there was difficulty in getting a sufficient supply of steam from the engine until the apparatus had been in use for some time. The system has been in use for two months; there has not been opportunity to test it thoroughly but it is doubtful whether the engines would be able to supply the amount of steam required throughout long journeys. The excessive escape of steam from the condensation pipes is very objectionable.

'Johnson & Clayton steam system
Fourteen engines and sixteen vehicles fitted.

Details were taken on the 2pm express between London and Manchester on 14 February with six vehicles. The outside temperature was 34 degrees Fahrenheit. Steam passed to the rear of the train in about one minute per vehicle It was turned on at 1.42pm. At 3pm the temperature in the carriages was 59 degrees and at the end of the journey 66 degrees, the outside temperature being then 36½ degrees.

'The apparatus was satisfactory, the rear of the train about the same temperature as the front. The 1¾in. pipe as now fitted is a distinct advantage. With this system the time required for the first heating of a train is considerably reduced and engines can without difficulty give an ample supply to carriages throughout the journey.

'As regards the future: with so many systems under trial, considerable difficulty is experienced with the diagramming of engines and more expensive workings are entailed. It is therefore very desirable to decide on a standard system as soon as possible but we think it advisable to let this question stand over until we can make further tests next autumn and winter.

'If however any additional engines or vehicles with heating apparatus will be required for next season, we recommend they be fitted with the Johnson & Clayton steam system.'

Top. One of the original Johnson 7ft 0in 4-4-0s No. 1335 of 1877, was amongst the thirty-seven engines fitted experimentally with Laycock's steam system from 1900-4, when they were converted to the Johnson & Bain steam system. S Summerson collection.

Middle. 'Spinner' No. 1863 in original condition, one of two of the class to receive Laycock's steam CWA briefly from 1900-2, when it was removed and the fittings despatched to Melton Constable for the M & GN to use on trials. S Summerson collection.

Bottom. Further experimental steam CWA was tried in 1901 when fifteen 4-4-0s were authorised to have the PLM steam system fitted. No. 2213, a 6ft 6in 4-4-0 of the 2203 class was one of them, but as with the Laycock system it did not find favour and was removed. S Summerson collection.

The General Purposes Committee accepted this report the next day, 16 May 1902. Evidently a few additional engines with heating apparatus *were* required, for 0.2435 was issued on 28 August 1902 for fourteen 4-4-0s to be fitted with the Johnson & *Bain* system. Eleven of these were conversions from hot water equipment. Bain had succeeded Clayton at the beginning of 1902 and his name thenceforward was given when describing steam carriage warming. Strangely, although Johnson retired at the close of 1903, to be succeeded by Deeley from January 1904, his name continued to be used - so 'Johnson & Bain' became synonymous with steam carriage warming on the Midland. The fourteen engines, all 4-4-0s were 1327 class 7ft 0in engines Nos.1327 and 1328, 2203 class 6ft 6in engines Nos.2206, 2207, 2210, 2214, 2216, 232, 233 and 235, rebuilt 1667 class 7ft 0in No.1667, 150 class 7ft 0in No.207 and 60 class 7ft 0in engines Nos.62 and 63.

It will be noted that the total of engines fitted to this order was the same as the number quoted as fitted with the Johnson & Clayton steam system in Johnson's report of 15 May 1902 and not previously accounted for. It is just possible that it was a retrospective order, confirming work carried out.

The No.6 Supplement to the No.20 Appendix to the Working Timetable, issued in July 1902, duly had instructions regarding operation of the Johnson & Bain steam system added to those on hot water and Laycock's steam system. It was a matter of prestige to demonstrate the effectiveness of the new system and to pre-heat some empty stock prior to attachment of train engines at St Pancras, two of the Kentish Town 1377 class 0-6-0Ts, Nos.211 and 212 (1721 and 1722 in 1907) which had been fitted with Laycock fittings in 1900, were fitted with

Johnson & Bain equipment, under No.0.2522 of 16 December 1902.

As a matter of interest the same order authorised a third tank engine which had received the Laycock fittings, No.1391, to be fitted with MR Hot Water equipment to make it uniform with others of its class at Kentish Town. These engines were also subsequently converted to the Johnson & Bain system, so that No.1391 (1674 in 1907) had the distinction of being the only engine recorded to have been fitted with three different systems of carriage warming.

The Johnson & Bain System 1903

On 3 April 1903, the Locomotive Committee travelled with a train consisting of '10 equals 14' vehicles heated by the Johnson & Bain apparatus 'with a view to considering further the merits of this system.' It was viewed in a favourable light and on 15 May 1903 the Board gave instructions that a 'Heating of Trains Report' and associated diagrams be sent to each Director. A further Board Minute reported to the Locomotive Committee on 3 July 1903 that 'Messrs. Johnson & Bain's arrangement for heating by steam (had been) adopted.' From this time on 'J&B' was the standard MR system. The carriage warming valve reduced the boiler pressure to 30lb/sq.in. which could of course be reduced further or closed in cases of poor steaming. In 1926 the working pressure on class 3 and 4 4-4-0s was raised to 50lb/sq.in. and the valves altered to suit.

Passenger tender engines

With Johnson & Bain apparatus generally authorised, a current order for the tenders of ten Belpaire 4-4-0s Nos.820-829 (in the process of being put into traffic – 820 had appeared in April and 827, 828 in July) was amended on 21 July 1903 to equip them with the new system.

The remaining forty engines of this class were fitted when built, as were the remaining Compounds delivered from July 1903. 0.2633 was also issued on 21 July 1903, to convert fifty-seven main line passenger engines from the MR hot water system to the Johnson & Bain steam system. The engines and shed allocations were:

Leeds: 2-4-0s Nos.813; 4-4-0s Nos.2436, 2437

Manchester: 4-4-0s Nos.205, 206, 1336, 1337, 1657, 1659, 1660, 1668, 1669, 1817, 1822, 2215, 2217

Liverpool: 2-4-0s Nos.1311, 1313, 1315, 1317, 1319; 4-2-2s Nos.1863, 1864, 1866, 1867

Nottingham: 4-4-0s Nos. 2421, 2422, 2423, 2424, 2427, 2430

Sheffield: 4-4-0s Nos.2203, 2204, 2205, 2208, 2211, 2212

Derby: 4-2-2s Nos.20-23

Leicester 4-2-2s No.117, Belpaire 4-4-0s Nos.2781, 2782

London: 4-2-2s Nos.2601, 2603, 2604; belpaire 4-4-0s Nos.2606-2608, 2610, 2783-2787, 2789

This work was anticipated by 0.2630 of 23 May 1903, for three Bradford 0-4-4Ts, Nos.1546, 1833 and 1842 to be altered from MR hot water to J&B steam, along with three Kentish Town Kirtley 690 class 0-4-4Ts Nos.691A, 694A and 695A. This order also covered the conversion of fifteen of the twenty Vulcan 0-6-0Ts delivered only twelve months previously with hot water apparatus, for the Manchester South District trains.

The stage was set for equipping all passenger engines and stock with steam carriage warming, and further orders were issued to convert from hot water. By about 1908, when *Leading Particulars of MR Locomotive Engines* was written out (RAIL 491/908) all the 4-4-0s of class 2 and above were fitted with car-

No. 1674 at Kentish Town in 1922. As No. 1391 pre-1907 this engine was successively fitted with Laycock steam CWA to 0.2027 of 13 January 1900, MR hot water to 0.2522 of 16 December 1902 and Johnson & Bain steam to 0.2775 of 18 April 1904. Note the Deeley cab ventilator fitted to some engines of this class which got double cabs.

Having brought the Johnson & Bain steam system of carriage warming to a state of reliability, it was formally adopted for future use on 3 July 1903, the next batch of Belpaire 4-4-0s Nos. 820-9 (730-9 in 1907) being the first fitted.

riage warming and all except six of the 4-2-2s and some of the 2-4-0s. Such details as are known are set out under the class headings.

Completion orders for the passenger tender engines were issued on 16 March 1908 to cover No.1 class passenger tender engines not previously fitted (2-4-0, 4-4-0 and 4-2-2) and the 56 class 1 engines that required conversion from hot water to J&B steam. The engines were not listed, nor has the completion date been recorded but it is likely that the job was finished within about two years. Instructions on the operation of the hot

water system continued to appear in the *Appendices* up to No.24 of June 1911.

Tank Engines

The forty 0-6-4Ts of 1907/8 were fitted new with steam carriage warming but progress on the 0-4-4Ts and converting those fitted with hot water apparatus was much slower; indeed a few never received carriage warming gear at all.

Various orders were issued up to 13 June 1923, when LMS order 5942 covered the four Brecon and Swansea 0-4-4Ts Nos.1421-1424. These appear to have been the last to be dealt with. All

the remaining Kirtley and Johnson 0-4-4Ts can be accounted for except Nos.1206, 1210, 1215, 1230, 1231, 1362 and 1363; the LMS Drawing Office list of 18 May 1926 in fact confirms these seven as not fitted. The last recorded order for removing hot water apparatus was 0.4271 of 22 May 1913, covering No.1429 which was steam fitted later that year.

Where 0-6-0Ts were working empty stock or branch passenger services, they also received carriage warming apparatus (as well as vacuum brakes) in due course. Apart from the 2761 class 0-6-0Ts

One of the last tank engines to receive carriage warming apparatus in 1923. No. 1421 of August 1900 stands in Derby station on 26 June 1932 with over twenty years service ahead before withdrawal in February 1955. S Summerson collection.

initially fitted for the Manchester South District trains in 1902/3, some of the earlier 0-6-0Ts were also equipped. The Kentish town engines have already been mentioned and the Keighley and Oxenhope branch engines were fitted in 1914. The LMS continued the practice where appropriate and nine Upper Bank class 1 0-6-0Ts were fitted to orders issued in 1924, along with further class 3 0-6-0Ts. Further odd engines were subsequently equipped and these are all dealt with where appropriate.

Goods Engines
Some goods engines were given carriage warming apparatus at various dates. The first application was under 0.3227 of 12 December 1906 for class 2 engines Nos.1464 (3072 in 1907), 2683 (3712 in 1907) and class 3 No.2739 (3768 in 1907). The ability to steam heat goods vehicles found a very practical application in ripening bananas on their journey from the docks to market. With suitably equipped vans available, three more 0-6-0s were fitted, Nos.1950 (3277 in 1907, class 3), 2697 and 2700 (3726, 3729 in 1907, class

2) specifically for working banana traffic. A further order in 1908 covered eight more Bristol and York class 2 and 3 0-6-0s, for the same traffic.

The value of having a few 0-6-0s available with carriage warming gear at various places, able to work local passenger trains and empty stock diagrams when required, soon became apparent and various orders were issued for this purpose. Confined largely to 5ft 3in 0-6-0s of both class 2 and 3, with some class 4s after the Grouping, engines were fitted over a very long period, through the Midland

TABLE 6A HOT WATER CARRIAGE WARMING APPARATUS - NEW ENGINES FITTED WHEN BUILT 1892-1902

Nos.	1907 Nos	A	B	BUILT	NOTES
2183-2202	403-22	20		SHARP STEWART	
156-60	423-7	5		DERBY	
2203-17	428-42	15		SHARP STEWART	
184-99 161-4 230-9	443-72	30		DERBY	
1667-76	483-92	10		DERBY	H
150/3-5 204-9	493-502	10		DERBY	
2421-40	503-22	20		SHARP STEWART	
60-6 93 138/9 67-9) 151/2/65-9 805-9)	523-52	30		DERBY	
2591-2600	553-62	10		NELSON REID	
179-83 75-7/9/80	660-9	10		DERBY	
115-21/3-8/30/1	670-84	15		DERBY	
2601-5 19-23	685-94	10		DERBY	
2606-10 800-4)	700-17	18		DERBY	
2781-8) 2789/90 810-9	718-29		12	DERBY	
2631/2	1000/1	2		DERBY	
2228-32	1381-5	5		DUBS	F
2233-47	1386-1400	15		DUBS	
690-5 780-3	1401-10	10		DERBY	
2761-80	1940-59		20	VULCAN/DERBY	G
TOTAL		235	32		

A = Fitted 1892-1902
B = Fitted May-December 1902
G = Built by Vulcan with fittings supplied by Derby.
F = The specification gives details of fittings but is marked x in pencil and the word 'none' but 0.3541 of 10.12.08 shows conversion from hot water to steam.
H = It is probable that these were given hot water apparatus when renewed as new engines between 1896 and 1901

Thirty-six of the 1377 and 1121 class 0-6-0Ts were fitted with CWA at various dates between 1900 and 1935. No. 1822 of Keighley shows the carriage warming hose beneath the front buffers ex-works at Derby (probably in 1920 as it was fitted to 0.5387 of 29 January 1920). It was withdrawn in December 1932.

TABLE 6B - HOT WATER CARRIAGE WARMING APPARATUS ENGINES BUILT PRIOR TO 1892 AND FITTED 1892-1902

Nos.	1907 Nos.	C	D	E	NOTES
156			1	1	
158/9 110 1601/3/4/53	2 3 12 16-20			8	
168/9 820	26/7 53	3			
806/21-9 93	40 54-62 65			11	
148 132 130	91 109/23	3			
90/2 125/3/7 91 121/31/51/2	90/2/3/6/7				
	104/6/8/10/1			10	
124/6/8/0	120-2 124			4	
146	156	1			
1288-91	163-6			4	
1311	186		1		
1347/8/50	197/8 200			3	
1400/7-9 1505/6	207/14-6/45/6	6			
1403/79/80	210/29/30			3	
1503/4/7-10/8/9	243/4/7-50/8/9		8		
1313/5/7/9	301/3/5/7		4		
1336/7	-, 319		2		
1336 (old 1346)	318			1	
1572/3 1658-60 1738/42/5	338/9/49-51/8/62/5	8			
1575 1657 1747-9	341/8/67-9		5		
1752-4 1817/22	372-4 387/92		5		
31 1853/8/64/6/70	606/8/15/21/3/7	6			
30 1869 97/8	605/26/44/5			4	
170/1	651/2		2		
1860/1/7/8	617/8/24/5		4		
16/7 129/72/3	641/2/8/53/4		5		
691/4/5	1201/4/5		3		
1252/66/9-81 1546	1240/3-56/80			16	
1532-9 1646/8-50	1266-73 1300/2-4	12			
2013/6	1361/4	2			
1729-32/4/5 1823-31	1322-5/7/8/31-9			15	
1325/6 1833-6/8-40/2	1344/5/51-4/6-8/60		10		
1733 1428/9	1326/47/8		3		J
2629 1126	1429 1644	2			K
1385-90	1668-73	6			
TOTAL		51	82	48	

C Engines fitted to Derby Orders.

D Engines converted from hot water to steam to Derby Order with no orders traced for hot water.

E These 48 engines are recorded as CW fitted in 'Leading Particulars etc' at C1908 and are believed, with singles nos 665-9/80 not otherwise recorded as converted, to be most of the fifty-six no 1 class passenger tender engines recorded in 0.3452A of 16.3.08 as still to be converted from hot water to steam. No other orders have been traced for fitting hot water or converting to steam.

J Nos 1326/47/8 were cwa fitted by 1908. All were fitted with steam cwa in 1912/3 and are therefore presumed hot water previously.

K These two were recorded as fitted with cwa at c1908. 0.4271 of 22.5.13 covered the removal of hot water apparatus.

and LMS eras. Carriage warming 0-6-0s were particularly associated with several sheds, notably Gloucester, Bedford and Stratford on Avon, where they were regularly used on passenger trains. Perhaps most remarkable was the fitting of Skipton double framed Kirtley 0-6-0s Nos.2404 and 2504 (to 0.4568 of 19 October 1914), these two having previously been fitted with Johnson 2,200 gallon tenders, vacuum brakes and back weatherboards! How the humble were exalted!

An LMS drawing office list of 18 May 1926 gives all the engines, passenger and goods, which were fitted at that date. It includes ten class 3 0-6-0s for which orders have not been traced.

Banana traffic again came to notice on 23 February 1927, when the LMS Locomotive and Electrical Committee authorised the fitting of thirty No.4 class and four No.2 class 0-6-0s (tender end only) as well as three No.2 class (at both ends). This was followed on 26 March 1930 by a report to the Committee from the Chief Mechanical Engineer: *'In order to meet demands for freight engines to work heavy excursion trains and also for banana specials from Avonmouth, it was recommended that thirty-three Midland Division freight tender engines allocated to Bristol and Gloucester be fitted with carriage warming apparatus at an estimated capital cost of £785.'* This was approved and a further batch of engines adapted.

Wartime led to further class 2 0-6-0s being fitted for steam heating while on loan to the GWR – twenty in 1940 and probably ten more, for which engine history cards have not survived. These would have been dealt with as a Railway Executive Committee or GWR instruction and a further batch was fitted for home use in 1940-41, to Job No.5216.

Remarkably, some further engines were equipped in 1948. In November of that year authority was issued for sixteen class 2 0-6-0s to be fitted at the front end (the tender ends being already equipped) for working at Euston. Only nine were actually done before the order was closed, the last, No.3603 as 58295 in the period ended 12 July 1952. The details for each class so far as they are known are set out under the class headings and a reasonably complete picture emerges, but as not all the LMS history cards have survived, it is possible a few engines may have escaped unchronicled.

The class 3 0-6-0s were familiar motive power on Stratford-on-Avon passenger diagrams and also appeared from time to time at Oxford, from Bedford. No. 43428 was fitted prior to May 1926 and is seen here at Luton on 27 June 1961 in the diesel era, still with CWA hose fitted – just in case! S Summerson.

Interior of one the Steam Motor Carriages showing the pierced bench type wooden seating, not dissimilar to contemporary tram cars. National Railway Museum.

The inadequacies of the small vertical boilers proved the Achilles heel of the railcars. The Walschaerts valve gear and slide valves of the engine unit are here shown to advantage. National Railway Museum.

Chapter 7 - Motor Carriages and Motor Trains

'The Company proposes to run experimental Auto-car services'

MOTOR CARRIAGES: 1
THE STEAM MOTOR CARRIAGES
Introduction

The early years of this century saw a rapid expansion of electric tramways in towns and cities and this had an immediate impact on the local passenger services of the main line railways in many of those areas. To counter the loss of traffic, ways were sought of attracting passengers back to the railway. Frequency of service was paramount while capacity was not critical. At the same time, economy of cost in the operation of lightly used branch lines was also a matter of concern. Out of all this was born the concept of the steam railcar, a self-propelled single passenger carriage.

Construction

The MR Board considered the matter on 19 June 1903 under the heading 'Motor Carriages and Electric Cars'. The Traffic Committee recommended that: *'a small commission be appointed consisting of one representative each from the Traffic, Way & Works and Locomotive departments to examine and report upon what is being done in working motor carriages and electric cars upon and in connection with other Railways and under what conditions they may be of service to the Midland Railway.'* Four subsequent entries relate to this, the last two omitting any reference to electric cars – a matter of some interest in view of subsequent events.

Approval to build two steam motor coaches and one trailer was given under Minute 8813 of 19 February 1904. Anticipating this, Derby Order No.2741 was issued on 8 February 1904 for their construction, the drawings 'to be supplied' and on 18 February 1904 the Locomotive Committee approved a report of three days earlier giving particulars of the vehicles and the cost: for one carriage a sum of £2,023, *'or if two carriages were built at the same time, the cost would be reduced to £1,801 each ... to be constructed at the Company's works at Derby.'* Construction was rapid and the two steam carriages, numbered M1 and M2 (which was not displayed on the vehicles) in the locomotive stock and 2233 and 2234 in the carriage stock, were delivered in June and July 1904 respectively.

The engine compartment contained a vertical boiler, 5ft 0in in diameter with 387 x 1⅛ in tubes and a total heating surface of 498sq.ft. Boiler pressure was 160lb/sq.in. and the grate was 11.3sq.ft. in area. The allocated boiler numbers in the 1912 scheme were 2990 and 2991, but these were never carried, as the boilers had been replaced by that date. The 8ft 0in bogie at the end of the car beneath the boiler had 3ft 7½in wheels which were coupled and driven by 11in x 15in cylinders, with Walschaerts valve gear, at the outer end of the vehicle.

Water capacity was 500 gallons and the small coal bunker carried 12cwt of coal. Steam sanding was provided. The engine compartment was 13ft 0in long and the height to the top of the chimney was 13ft 3in. Adjacent to the engine compartment there was a luggage compartment 6ft 6in long. At the far end was a vestibule 4ft 6in long with driving controls with cable communication from the engine compartment. These cables were carried in a housing above the cantrail on the right hand side. This arrangement enabled the cars to be driven from either end, a matter of great convenience when working an intensive service. However they were not provided on the trailer, so if that was in use, the railcar had to run round at each end of the journey. The 35ft railcar saloon had 55 wooden bench seats, similar to those on contemporary street trams.

Rebuilding

As with other company's steam railcars, the original vertical boilers proved to have insufficient reserve capacity and so on 5 December 1906, 0.2741A was issued: *'Existing boilers of Motor Coaches 1 and 2 to be taken off and replaced by new locomotive type boilers. Boiler of No.2 car to be dealt with before No.1.'* An entry in the Derby *1901 Register - Abstract* for the half year ending December 1907 under the heading 'Boilers reserved' shows Motors Nos.1 and 2 as 'reserved' in July 1907, confirming their removal. In 1909 it was proposed to use the original vertical boiler from No.1 as a replacement of old locomotive No.2063A (A Manning Wardle tank from the Sheepbridge Company) at West India Docks, but this was cancelled in favour of a second electric pump. It was retained and 0.5855 of 22 January 1923 ordered its alteration for use as a stationary boiler No.200.

Table 7A. The 1903 Diagram for the Steam Motor Carriages Nos. 2233 and 2234.

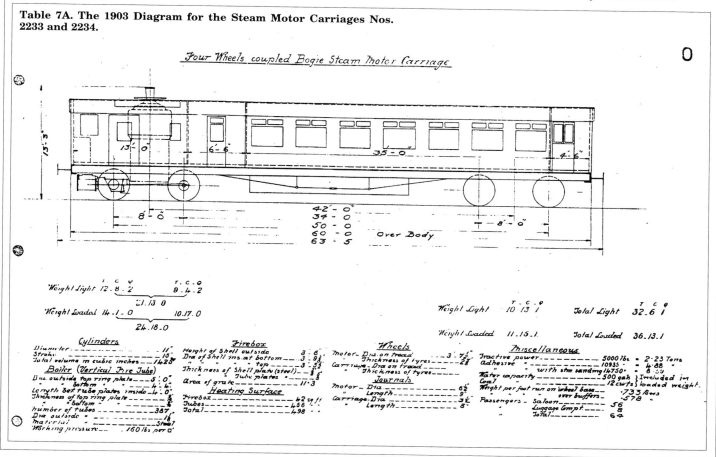

M&GN tank No. 40 as renumbered 10 and painted red by the Midland makes an incongruous sight at Kentish Town shed with Pullman still attached, about 1907.

The new boilers were fitted with the chimney end towards the saloon so that the firebox was over the bogie, as on the original. They were similar to those fitted to the NCC Railcars of 1905 but with a longer firebox. The boiler was 3ft 8in in diameter and was the same as the J1 used on some 0-4-0Ts. The firebox was 3ft 5in long. Boiler pressure was 160lb/sq.in. and the boiler numbers were 3423 and 3424. Coal capacity was increased to 1¼tons by extending the coal box across the whole width of the compartment. It was filled by a chute from an opening in the roof. The chimney, which was now positioned further back consequent on the boiler arrangement, was reduced by 4in to give an overall height above rail of 12ft 11in. Weight in working order was increased by 4 tons 15cwt on No.2233, to 41 tons 8cwt.

Alterations to No.2233

As the new boiler took up the space previously occupied by the engine compartment *and* the luggage vestibule, it was necessary to provide a new, smaller luggage compartment, 4ft 6in long. This was achieved by removing one seating bay and reducing the large side windows from seven to six on this vehicle. The alterations were carried out to Drawings S.918 on Diagram 479 and were completed about July 1907. It then continued in service but with a reduced seating capacity of forty-eight. No.2233 was not further altered and was eventually broken up on 2 January 1926. The Erecting Shop list recording this incorrectly shows 'Motor Coach 2234'. There is, however, ample evidence of that coach not being cut up - as will be seen.

Alterations to No.2234

No.2234 was taken out of ordinary service on reboilering and converted into a self-propelled saloon for the General Superintendent, Cecil Paget - appointed to the post on 5 April 1907. It is well known that he spent much of the following summer at Masborough, observing the coal traffic prior to the introduction of his famous Train Control scheme, during which time he inhabited an 'Inspection Coach'. This was No.2234 and Paget had wasted no time in having the coach converted for his use. The MR *Carriage Register* at the National Railway Museum lists drawing No.2794 of 20 April 1907 as 'Alteration of Steam Motor Car for Mr Paget's use' The Traffic Committee resolved on 7 June 1907 that Motor Carriage No.2234 be altered at an estimated cost of £206 which was accepted by the Carriage & Wagon and General Purposes Committee on 20 June 1907. It was clearly urgent, for it was read first and second time at the same General Purposes Meeting. It was completed about July 1907.

This conversion, apart from the new boiler which was identical with that on No.2233, involved alteration of the original passenger saloon. This was divided into an office and bed-sitting room and, at the inner end, a small bathroom and a WC compartment obliquely on one side. The remaining space probably contained primitive kitchen facilities.

As it was not necessary to provide a replacement luggage compartment, the saloon retained its original length and seven large windows on one side. This fact has given rise to the erroneous suggestion that the car was not reboilered. The other side was altered to accommodate the new layout and had five win-

---

Table 7B Internal arrangements of Steam Motor Carriages.

Internal Arrangements of Midland Railway
Steam Motor Carriages Nos *2233 & 2234*

B	S		L	O E	*2233/2234* as built 1904
B	S		L	O E	*2233* as rebuilt 1907
B	O	Li	Ba W / K	O E	*2234* rebuilt 1907
B	O	Li	Ba W / K	D	B — *2234* as rebuilt 1917

B Brake compartment
S Saloon
L Luggage space
E Engine compartment
O Office

Li Living sleeping room
Ba Bathroom
W WC
K Kitchen
D Dining compartment

← Existing → ← New part →

M&GN 4-4-0T No. 8 with Pullman car No. 10, formerly 'Apollo' and Derby destination board. Note the mechanical control cables from cab to carriage.

dows, and a small one for the WC. The end driving brake compartment was retained.

The alterations to this carriage were to Diagram 480, and it remained in this condition for some ten years before it was subject to a further rebuild. Meanwhile, in March 1909, the Drawing and Sketch Registers record details ('Alteration to steam motor coach') for fitting water pick-up; this is presumed to refer to No.2234 as clearly this fitting would not be necessary on No.2233. In the same year, F.H. Clarke shows it as allocated to Toton, presumably selected as a convenient local base for the General Superintendent. Drawing No.4517 of 11 January 1917, titled *'Alteration to General Superintendent's Service Car No.2234 (Engine room replaced by Salon compartment)'* shows that it was converted from a self-propelled inspection saloon to a hauled one.

The boiler was removed and a brake compartment 4ft 6in long (similar to that at the other end), a 10ft 6in dining saloon and an enlarged kitchen all provided, in the space formerly occupied by the engine compartment.

This drawing shows the detail of the original conversion and has a pencil note: *'finishing to be similar to that in living compartment and office.'* It is clear also that the work was to be entirely new and not an adaptation of the engine room as the drawing is also marked *'Existing part'* and *'New part to be spliced on'*. This drawing and the wording of the alterations gives further confirmation to the fitting of the larger boiler in 1907, for if it had not been done, there is no reference to the fate of the original luggage compartment. Furthermore, it seems most unlikely that the original boiler would have been suitable for the much longer con-

tinuous runs involved in Paget's travels around the system.

The driving apparatus of the carriage was also overhauled (to Derby Order No.0.5001 of 9 January 1917) for it to work specifically with the original Johnson Spinner 4-2-2 No.600, fitted with vacuum controlled regulator gear under the same order, so that the ensemble could work in either direction without being turned. No.600 had the VCR gear removed around 1927 but it is not known how long the saloon continued as an inspection vehicle into the LMS period.

It subsequent history may be conveniently covered here. Renumbered 45010 in the 1933 scheme, it was transferred to the Signal and Telegraph Engineer at Crewe, at an unknown date. It was eventually withdrawn in July 1968 and purchased by the late George Dow. He refurbished it and in 1977 it was accepted

The pioneer 4-2-2 with vacuum control regulator gear (from 0-4-4T No.1252) and ex-steam motor carriage No. 2234. This was after its second major rebuild in 1917, to operate as a hauled vehicle.

by the National Railway Museum for preservation as a unique survivor of a distinctive episode in the development of railway passenger service. There it remains, pending a decision on any further restoration.

Allocation

The first of the two cars, No.2233 arrived at Morecambe on 3 July 1904 and began a regular service from there to Heysham on 11 July 1904. It was followed by No.2234 at the end of the month. The *Weekly Notice* for the week ending 16 July 1904 contains the following entry: '*Motor Carriages are being run between Morecambe station and Heysham Harbour as required for experimental purposes.*' A further note states that they are not suitable for being shunted or worked with ordinary stock and must be dealt with specially. A halt was opened at Middleton Road to serve Higher Heysham. Most unusually, their workings were not shown in the *Working Timetables* and the only record in the Public Timetables is a footnote to the Lancaster - Morecambe table for March 1905 which reads. '*A local service by rail is given at convenient intervals between Heysham and Morecambe.*' This, read in conjunction with the 'as required' note, in the *Weekly Notice* referred to above, clearly indicates the operation of an untimetabled 'on demand' service and accounts for no times being shown in the WTT.

The steam railcars however, were taken off about the end of June 1905, the WTT for July showing a timetabled passenger service being run - *Clinkers Register* shows Middleton Road Halt as closed in June 1905 and the cessation of railcar working is confirmed by a Traffic Committee Minute of 6 April 1906. A memorial had been received from local residents requesting its reopening and in refusing this request, the minutes confirm its opening on the introduction of the motor service and subsequent closure when this was '*taken off and ordinary trains run, it not being suitable for dealing with ordinary trains*'. The WTT Notice for May 1908 records the introduction of electric services on 13 April in place of 'engines and carriages', further confirming the alteration. There is no evidence that the railcars worked in passenger service between Lancaster and Morecambe or that they worked to Heysham until electrification as stated by some earlier authors, though their maintenance was Lancaster shed's responsibility.

The cars were photographed together back at Derby in 1905. As early as March of that year other possible uses were under consideration and on 26 March 1905 a trial was conducted on the Harpenden to Hemel Hempstead branch, described in the local press as 'successful'. Doubtless as a result of this, it was then decided to operate a service on the Harpenden to Hemel Hempstead branch and three new halts were constructed. The service began on 9 August 1905 and special arrangements for providing water at Harpenden and Hemel Hempstead, together with washing out facilities at Harpenden, were provided to 0.3003/4 of 17 July 1905. The branch service was then operated '*part ordinary trains and part motor carriages*' and all the motor carriage workings were shown in the WTT. Which of the two railcars were involved or indeed if both were used is not known, but the severe gradients of the branch, including a mile at 1 in 39 out of Hemel Hempstead, would have severely tested the steaming capacity of the boilers.

On 24 October 1905 one failed half a mile up this bank and further local references, glowing or otherwise, are conspicuous by their absence. One of the cars was used to inaugurate motor carriage workings from 1 March 1906 on the Derby - Wirksworth, Derby - Melbourne and Derby - Ripley branches, but was taken off after two weeks. In contrast to the instructions about not working with ordinary stock when at Morecambe, the March 1906 WTT Notice instructs '*the 8.45am and 1.55pm Derby - Wirksworth coupled to Derby - Sheffield trains to Duffield.*' That this actually took place is confirmed by a contemporary newspaper account, the car travelling 'on its own' up the branch.

It was replaced by an M&GN 4-4-0T and Pullman Car (discussed later), an identical pairing commencing work on the Hemel Hempstead branch on 2 April 1906. As these were also described as 'motor carriages' it is not possible to be certain whether a steam railcar continued to work on the Hemel Hempstead branch during the period to 1912, when the M&GN tanks returned to their native heath, but it seems unlikely. In any event, both were out of service for reboilering in 1907, with No.2234 appropriated to the General Superintendent in that year.

Locomotive Drawing office correspondence indicates that No.1 Motor Car (i.e. No.2233) was working the Ilkeston Town branch in July 1911. The car, having fouled the crossing gate stops at Ilkeston town, was in need of repairs and was examined at Toton on 18 July 1911: '*The motor car had passed over the crossing in question with safety on three occasions on that day before fouling and it is believed the primary cause was that the crossing gate stops were not put properly down by the signalman*'. The WTT, however, does not record any motor carriage workings for that date. The WTT for the Harpenden - Hemel Hempstead branch continued to show motor carriage workings from 1912-1916 and the edition dated 1 October 1915 shows the empty motor carriage working from St Albans - Harpenden in the list of light engine

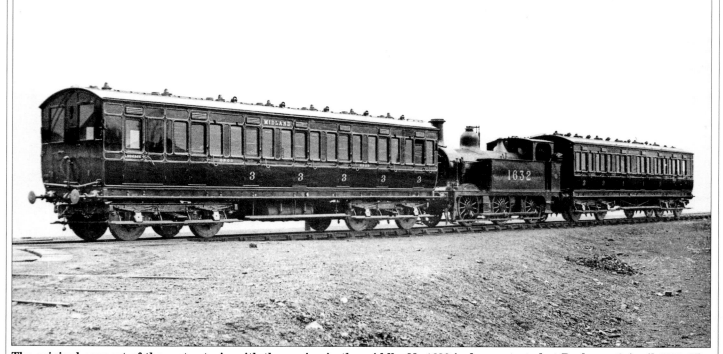

The original concept of the motor train with the engine in the middle. No.1632 is demonstrated at Derby on 6 April 1908. The gear subsequently went to 0-4-4T No.1254. S. Summerson collection.

One of the four 0-4-4Ts fitted with VCR gear in 1923-4 by the LMS utilising the apparatus previously used in 1909-17. No 1340 gave thirty years further service having acquired a G5½ belpaire boiler in February 1928. In September of that year it was running trials at Blackpool!

workings leaving St Albans shed. Presuming the WTT details are correct, the fact that No.2233 was the only 'Motor Carriage' at the time indicates that it returned to the Hemel Hempstead branch for that period, but the local press is silent on the subject and no photographs from this period have come to light.

The initial service on the Hemel branch in 1905 gave six return trips with three ordinary trains as well, and from

October 1905 some trips on the main line were run in addition. Initially, an early morning run was put on from Radlett to St Albans, altered to 8.30am from Elstree in March 1906. From October 1914 until cessation (with the wartime cuts of 1917) only four return branch trips were shown in the WTT as 'motor carriage'. In the absence of any subsequent recorded motor carriage workings, No.2233 is then presumed to have spent lengthy periods out of use. On 23 March 1922 0.5709 was

issued: *'Motor Coach No.2233 to be loaned to M&GN line. All work of examination and repairs to be charged to this order'.* This was followed by 0.5977 of 3 August 1923: *'Put work in hand with overhauling the engine belonging to the steam motor coach in order to put into traffic again. At present in the Carriage & Wagon Department.'* Its stay on the M&GN was apparently very brief in 1922, working on the Mundesley line from Cromer where it was at least photographed. What service

No. 1322 with shortened cab to increase bunker capacity. Note the 'spider' on the front of the cab roof. This was a tube inclined from front to back through which the whistle wire passed via a pulley wheel just in front from the whistle to the driving position in the leading carriage. This was prior to the introduction of bell communication in 1935, though 'spiders' often remained in position for many years afterwards. S Summerson collection.

TABLE 7C 4-4-0Ts LOANED BY M&GN
Dimensions in Original Condition

	2	10	1 and 5
Cyls	14" x 20"	15" x 20"	15" x 20"
Water Capacity	750 galls	750 galls	800 galls
Coal Capacity	17 cwt	17 cwt	25 cwt
Weight (WO)	32t 10 cwt	33t 10 cwt	34 tons
Wheels Driving	4' 6"		
Bogie	2' 4"		
Wheelbase	4' 10" + 5' 10½" + 6' 9"		
Length over buffers	28' 1½"		
Height	11' 6½"		
Max axle load 13 tons 16 cwt (as reboilered)			

TABLE 7D M&GN ENGINES LOANED TO MR 1906-12

ENGINES			PULLMAN CARS		
M&GN No	MR No	NAME	BUILT	No#	RPC
8*	2	Juno	28.4.76	2	1894
40*	10	Apollo	19.1.77	10	1894
10	5	Minerva	28.7.77	5	1894
19	1	Saturn	10.9.75	1	+

RPC = Year rebuilt to Picnic Car
+According to Lacy and Dow this was still a Parlour Car *circa*1895.
*At first the engines retained their M & GN numbers; 8 was attached to Pullman no.10 and 40 Pullman no.2. These were changed over by October 1906 and all the engines renumbered to accord with their attached Pullmans.
The numbers were allocated by March 1888.

TABLE 7E INTRODUCTION OF MOTOR TRAIN WORKING

Line	First shown in WTT	Notes	
Bedford-Northampton/Hitchin	1.7.08	A see also 12.9.32	
Sheffield-Doncaster	1.7.08	A	
Wakefield-Sandal & Walton	1.7.08	A	
Sutton Jc-Sutton Town	7.7.30	B	
Burton-Tutbury	7.7.30	B	
Skipton-Earby-Barnoldswick/Colne	20.7.31	B	
Southwell-Rolleston Jc	20.7.31	B	F
Mansfield-Pye Bridge-Ambergate	20.7.31	C	
Wellingborough-Higham Ferrers	20.7.31	B	E
Keighley-Oxenhope	18.7.32	B	
Keighley-Bradford	18.7.32		
Pye Bridge-Chesterfield	18.7.32		
Stonehouse-Stroud/Nailsworth	18.7.32	B	
Redditch-Ashchurch	18.7.32	C	
Ashchurch-Tewkesbury	12.9.32		
Cudworth-Barnsley	12.9.32	B	C
Ilkeston-Nottingham/Trent	12.9.32	B branch only	
Elmton & Cresswell-Mansfield-Nottingham	12.9.32	B	
Bedford-Hitchin/Northampton	12.9.32	B	C
Millhouses-Sheffield-Barnsley	7.7.33		
Buxton-Millers Dale	7.7.33	B	
Wellingborough-Kettering/Northampton	30.4.34		
Sheffield-Hope	9.7.34		
Nottingham-Newark	9.7.34		
Mansfield-Kirkby	9.7.34	B	
Romford-Upminster-Tilbury	1.10.34	B	D
Leicester-Nuneaton-Coventry	8.7.35		
Leicester-Ashby/Rugby	8.7.35		

NOTES
A Discontinued from 1917.
B Lines still operating motor trains WTT 2.10.44.
C Authority given by L & E Committee on 16.12.31 to fit engines to operate motor trains on these lines.
D Authority given by M & E Committee on 20.12.33.
E Trains office diary shows working commenced on 5.1.31.
F Last service to be operated by MR engine.

OTHER LINES WHICH MR 0-4-4T OPERATED MOTOR TRAINS ON A REGULAR BASIS FOR A NUMBER OF YEARS

LINE	DATES
Walsall-Wolverhampton	c1928-31
Bedford-Bletchley	c1928-50
Manchester-Wilmslow via Styal	c1930-9
Burnham-Glastonbury- Wells	c1928-51

it saw from 1923 until being broken up in 1926 is not known, a somewhat sad conclusion to a very interesting venture in locomotive and train working.

MOTOR CARRIAGES: 2
THE M & GN 4-4-0T AND PULLMAN CAR
Introduction
This account is included here because it forms an integral part of the development of motor carriage and motor train working. At the same time it is useful to consider a unique loan of locomotives, unusual for its protracted length.

The 4-4-0T and Pullman car, introduced in 1906, had a mechanical control mechanism between the engine and carriage. This brought the arrangement into the definition of a vehicle with a non-detachable engine and it was therefore regarded as 'a motor carriage'. As seen above, this leads to some difficulty in determining whether a steam motor carriage or one of these units was operating on the Hemel Hempstead branch at one period.

Origins
When the steam railcar service was inaugurated on the Harpenden - Hemel Hempstead branch in 1905, the service comprised nine return trips, three of which were by ordinary train. The *Hemel Hempstead Gazette* of 19 August 1905 comments: '*So that the ordinary trains can also stop at the Halts, a Pullman Car is attached to the engine instead of the customary coaches which made the train too long for the platforms at the Halts.*'

It seems quite probable, therefore, that the idea of using a Pullman carriage and a small tank engine permanently coupled as a more satisfactory arrangement than the steam motor car arose from this circumstance.

The MR was responsible for locomotive matters on the M&GN and this is reflected in the sequence of events which followed. On 14 December 1905 the Traffic Committee resolved that four old Pullman cars be altered for running in motor service and four engines also, at an estimated cost of £262. On 21 December 1905 the Derby Order book contains an entry relating to '*Combined tank engines and carriages as Motor Cars*', indicating the novelty of the concept. '*Please note it has been agreed to fit up four tank engines for this work and arrangements are being made for four M&GN tank engines to be provided for the purpose.*' On the following day the MR representatives at the M&GN Officers' conference stated that '*the Company proposes to run experimental auto-car services and for this purpose is desirous of obtaining temporarily the use of four of the Committee's small tank engines, which are suitable for this class of work*'.

It was recommended that four locomotives be transferred to the Midland, for a period of twelve months in exchange for three MR tank engines; 'the capital values were approximately equal', which explains the discrepancy in numbers. The MR engines were Johnson 0-4-4Ts and the arrangement was agreed by the M&GN Board on 9 January 1906.

The Locomotives
Four of the seven Hudswell Clarke 4-4-0Ts built in 1878-81 for the Lynn & Fakenham and Yarmouth & North Norfolk Railways (inherited by the M&GN on its formation in 1893) were sent. They were diminutive engines of slightly varying details.

All had been rebuilt between 1894 and 1903 with boilers built at Derby to Order Nos.1313 of 20 October 1893 and 1441 of 23 April 1895. These were described as 'B class boilers for rebuilds' but should, to avoid misunderstanding with MR boilers, have been described as 'Boilers for B class rebuilds'! These were 3ft 9in diameter having 822sq.ft. heating surface, 190 x 1⅝ in tubes 11.3sq.ft. grate area and 140lb pressure. They carried the distinctive Johnson boiler mountings and so harmonised with their new surroundings.

The MR Locomotive Committee had approved the costs of fitting communication from the engines to the driving position at the far end of the Pullman Cars on 5 January 1906, at a total cost of £80. The cable passed from the

E.R.O. 46483.
OP. 2.

London Midland and Scottish Railway
Company.

INSTRUCTIONS

RESPECTING THE WORKING OF

RAIL MOTORS

AND

MOTOR TRAINS

Euston Station,
LONDON,
October, 1935.

By Order.

11

SECTIONS OF THE LINE AUTHORISED TO BE WORKED OVER BY RAIL MOTORS AND MOTOR TRAINS.

Notes.—On sections marked (P) working in accordance with instruction 4 is authorised.
* Winter only.
† Certain of the stations on this section are halts and are only provided with rail-level platforms. Vehicles must be equipped with collapsible steps, or suitable ladders if required.

Section.	To work engine leading to.	Whether any halts.
Midland Division		
Skipton and Barnoldswick	Barnoldswick	No.
(P) Earby and Barnoldswick	Barnoldswick	No.
Earby and Colne	Colne	No.
(P) Keighley and Oxenhope	Oxenhope	No.
(P) Keighley and Bradford (Sundays)	Bradford	No.
(P) Cudworth and Barnsley		No.
(P) Millhouses, Sheffield and Barnsley (via Chapeltown)	Barnsley	No.
(P) Sheffield and Hope	Sheffield	No.
(P) Buxton and Miller's Dale	Buxton	No.
Sutton Junc. and Sutton-in-Ashfield	Sutton Junction	No.
Southwell and Rolleston Junction	Rolleston Junction	No.
(P) Nottingham and Newark	Newark	No.
Nottingham and Ilkeston	Ilkeston	No.
Trent and Ilkeston	Ilkeston	No.
Ilkeston and Langley Mill	Ilkeston	No.
(P) Mansfield and Ambergate	Mansfield	No.
(P) Ambergate and Pye Bridge	Pye Bridge	No.
(P) Pye Bridge and Chesterfield	Pye Bridge	No.
Mansfield and Trent	Mansfield	No.
(P) Trent, Nottingham and Langley Mill	Nottingham	No.
(P) Mansfield and Nottingham	Mansfield	No.
Mansfield and Kirkby	Mansfield	No.
(P) Mansfield and Elmton & Creswell	Elmton	No.
(P) Leicester, Nuneaton and Coventry		No.
(P) Leicester and Ashby		No.
Leicester and Kettering		No.
(P) Leicester and Peterboro'		No.
(P) Leicester and Rugby		No.
Wellingboro' and Kettering	Wellingboro'	No.
(P) Burton and Tutbury	Tutbury	No.
(P) Redditch and Ashchurch	Redditch	No.
(P) Ashchurch and Tewkesbury	Tewkesbury	No.
(P) Gloucester, Stonehouse, Stroud and Nailsworth	Nailsworth	No.
(P) Gloucester and Coaley Junction		No.
Wells, Glastonbury and Burnham	Wells	No.
(P) Wellingboro' and Higham Ferrers	Higham Ferrers	No.
Walsall and Sutton Park		No.
(P) Walsall and Burton		No.
(P) Bedford and Hitchin	Hitchin	No.
(P) Bedford and Northampton	Bedford	No.
(P) Northampton (C.) and Wellingboro'		No.
(P) Tilbury and Upminster	Tilbury	No.
Upminster and Romford	Upminster	No.

These official instructions show the lines which were actually authorised for motor train working at October 1935 and the engine disposition to be adopted. Reference in the heading notes to instruction 4 relates to lines which may be worked without a guard under certain circumstances provided there were not more than three vehicles. The situation remained substantially the same in the January 1946 issue of instructions with some local variations, principally in the Leicester/Nottingham areas. Additional lines authorised were Evercreech Jc-Glastonbury and the Bridgewater branch on the SDJR plus Bath-Mangotsfield and Bristol-Coaley Jc on the south-west main line. Authorisation of course, did not necessarily imply that motor train working was in force; some operations were shortlived.

engine cab over the top of the car in much the same way as on the steam railcars.

Numbering and Livery

The engines loaned were M&GN Nos.8, 10, 19 and 40 which after one change, were coupled to Pullman cars Nos.2, 5, 1 and 10 respectively. These, built in 1875-77 had once rejoiced in the names, JUNO, MINERVA, SATURN and APOLLO but had acquired their numbers by 1888. At first the engines retained their numbers and No.8 was attached to Pullman car No.10 with No.40 attached to car No.2 but these were changed over by October 1906 and the engines were then renumbered to display the same number as their attached Pullmans.

The M&GN lined yellow livery was retained at first, with the oval number plates fitted beneath the cab windows. The numbers remained painted on the front buffer beams but despite the engines being only 'on loan' the M&GN initials were removed and the early MR crest placed centrally on the tank side instead, a distinction not normally accorded the MR tank engines. When renumbered, individual brass numerals were placed on the tank side, where the crest had been, and the MR initials appeared on the front buffer beam. To complete the transformation they were painted red.

No.1302, at Bedford on 10 August 1935, was fitted with vacuum control regulator in 1932. On withdrawal in 1946, the gear was transferred to No. 1367 which became the last in active service in 1959 as No.58065. The Transport Treasury.

Rebuilding, fittings and details

Two of the four engines, MR Nos.2 and 10, were reboilered at Derby to 0.3442 of 3 February 1908. Vacuum brakes had been fitted when the class was first rebuilt and 0.3053 of 27 September 1906 for fitting carriage warming to engines and Pullmans was cancelled early in October 1906. Foot warmers reigned if available! The re-railing jacks carried on the footplates were soon removed.

Some other details were changed to a Midland pattern. Nos.10 and 19 are confirmed as having Deeley smokebox doors and the former also acquired a parallel chimney, but it is not known if either of the others were altered.

Allocation

The Traffic Committee considered proposed timetables on 18 January 1906, *'showing services which it is proposed to run by auto and motor cars'* on the following branches:-

> Derby-Melbourne and Ashby
> Derby and Wirksworth
> Derby and Ripley
> Wakefield branch
> Mansfield and Sutton Town
> Newark, Rolleston and Farnsfield'

In view of what actually transpired, this is interesting, particularly because there is no mention of the Harpenden - Hemel Hempstead branch. Up to that time, it was operated by steam railcars and a change of plan must have occurred shortly after the decision above, as photographs show M&GN No.19 with cabside plate at Harpenden - that is, before the renumbering of 1906.

The WTT Notice for March 1906 records the commencement of Rail motor services on the branches from Derby recorded above but not the others.

After operations commenced with the steam railcars, the 4-4-0T and Pullman coach ensemble is believed to have commenced later in the month running as far as Melbourne on the Ashby line and from 2 April 1906 on the Hemel Hempstead branch. So far as can be seen, two units were based at Derby and two at St Albans. F.H. Clarke recorded Nos.1 and 10 at St Albans in 1909. Both were photographed in the area, the former as M&GN No.19 at Harpenden and the latter at Kentish Town. As for the other two, Nos.2 and 5 (M&GN 8 and 10), the former was recorded as M&GN 8 at Derby and the latter as M&GN 10, at Wirksworth.

The WTTs record the motor carriage services on these branches up to October 1910, but the July 1911 issue shows only the Melbourne and Hemel Hempstead workings and by October 1911 only Hemel Hempstead.

The Hemel Hempstead motor carriage was intensively used. In July 1911 for example the service comprised 8.00am St Albans - Luton, 8.25am Luton - St Albans, 9.00am St Albans - Harpenden and then five return branch trips. The day was ended as the 7.30pm empty carriage to Luton and 8.10pm Luton - St Albans. The small engine and large Pullman carriage must have presented an entertaining spectacle on the four track main line.

In view of the fact that the steam railcar No.2233 possibly continued to work on the Hemel branch for a while, it seems unlikely that the M&GN tanks worked after the summer of 1911 before returning home in the following year - this after twelve months loan was agreed in 1906!

Some earlier authors have suggested they worked on the Higham Ferrers branch but diligent searches in the official sources referred to above have not revealed any evidence.

Withdrawal

The subsequent history of the loaned engines may be briefly summarised. All were sold by the M&GN to the War Department in May 1917, becoming WD Nos.51-54. Two were sold subsequently to industrial concerns while No.10 (MR No.5 and WD No.51) achieved notoriety in becoming Longmoor No.1 KINGSLEY which was retained ultimately for re-railing practice and was not broken up until 1953.

MOTOR TRAINS
Definitions and Services

From the concept of a motor carriage it was but a short step to a motor train. The subsequent LMS definition sums it up neatly: *'A Motor Train means a train consisting of detachable engine with specially fitted coaches capable of being driven from either end of the train.'*

Carriages could be attached at one or both ends of the engine. An early photograph at Hitchin shows an engine with two carriages each side but later practice was generally to have the carriages at one end only.

With motor carriage workings well established, the General Manager submitted a report to the Traffic Committee on 20 July 1907 on various trials which had been made with motor traction, recommending *'the extension of experiments'*. It was resolved *'that the necessary alterations be made to seven tank engines and fourteen carriages at an estimated cost of £900 to make them suitable for working in autocar services between the following places -*
Bedford - Hitchin and Northampton
Sheffield and Doncaster etc.
Wakefield and Sandal & Walton etc.
and that the matter be referred to the Locomotive and Carriage & Wagon Committees'.

The process of fitting engines with gear from withdrawn examples continued into the British Railways era and No. 58077 (LMS 1397) was the last of six to be equipped in 1948/9. It was renumbered in September 1949, and is seen here in lined livery. Gresley Society/K R Pirt.

A total of sixty-eight MR 0-4-4Ts carried VCR gear at one time or another with about forty fitted at any one time in the late 1930s and 1940s. Four engines were given general repairs as late as 1954 of which No. 58085 (in plain black livery) was one, finishing its life on the Southwell-Rolleston Jc branch in 1959. S Summerson collection.

It will be noted that the terms auto car and motor car are used in Minute and Order books when referring to both motor carriages and motor trains which tends to confuse, but the Working Timetables are consistent when showing 'motor carriage' and 'motor train' in the column headings. These latter terms are used here except where quotations are given.

Motor trains were introduced on 1 July 1908 on the lines proposed in the previous year between Sheffield, Rotherham and Doncaster, Wakefield, Sandal and Cudworth and the branches from Bedford to Hitchin and Northampton. Instructions for the working of empty motor trains from Sheffield passenger station to Grimesthorpe and Millhouses engine sheds and at Northampton were shown in the No.1 Supplement to Appendix No.23, dated 23 October 1908. These arrangements continued until the wartime service cuts of 1917 when all the motor trains were withdrawn and were not resumed under Midland Railway authority. Apparently a trial was carried out on the LTS line. J.F. Gairns, writing in *The Railway Magazine* of October 1918 noted, when referring to the presence of MR 0-4-4T on the line that *'one was employed for a time working with two Midland bogie coaches as an 'auto train' on the Grays-Upminster-Romford services'*, thereby anticipating subsequent events. F.H. Clarke recorded the allocation of the 'Autos' in 1909, without indicating whether they were steam railcar, M&GN tank and Pullman, or Motor Train, as follows:

Derby 1	Wakefield 1
Bedford 2	Millhouses 2
St Albans 1	Mansfield 1

From the available information, it seems clear that Derby and St Albans autos referred to the M&GN tank and Pullman, the Bedford, Wakefield and Millhouses autos to motor trains, but was the Mansfield auto No.2233?

Locomotives

Derby Order No.3425 was issued on 8 January 1908 to cover the necessary work to adapt the engines required - 'seven engines to be fitted up as special autocars'. Whereas on the motor carriages, control arrangements from the non driving end were mechanical, a new system of vacuum controlled regulator was introduced for the operation of motor trains.

The system was operated in conjunction with the vacuum brake and engines and carriages carried two vacuum pipes, one for the brake as normal and the other for the regulator vacuum pipe. This was connected to the brake vacuum system via a choke to provide the vacuum source. A supplementary regulator valve was fitted in an external housing on the left hand side of the smokebox and this valve operated according to the presence or absence of vacuum in the pipe. The main regulator was maintained in the open position at all times when running, control of the supplementary valve being effected by the operation of a valve fitted in both the engine cab and driving compartment of the end coach. The engine whistle was operated from the coach end by means of a wire passing through a conduit over the roofs of the carriages.

The seven engines originally fitted for motor train operation were 0-6-0Ts Nos.1632-1638 of the 1102 class built in 1874, but within a year or so the gear was removed and fitted to 0-4-4Ts Nos.1242, 1252, 1254, 1255, 1257, 1258 and 1261 of the 1252 class. When Motor train working ceased in 1917, these engines had the fittings removed; in true thrifty Midland practice these were stored for possible future use. As the engines were members of a principal MR class, details are given in the appropriate class Chapter.

In 1923/4 four 0-4-4Ts were fitted with vacuum controlled regulator gear (VCR) utilising old material where possible, but no further ex-MR engines were equipped until after the LMS Locomotive and Electrical Committee had considered the various methods of operating push-pull

trains inherited from the constituent companies, and determined the adoption of a standard method.

On 24 November 1926 the Chief General Superintendent, Chief Mechanical Engineer and Carriage & Wagon Superintendent submitted a joint report:

'Present methods of operating a push-pull train and operating the regulator from the opposite end are
1 By rodding underneath the bodies of coaches.
2 By means of compressed air.
3 By means of vacuum control.

In future, vacuum control should be adopted as the most satisfactory and economical.'

Authority was given for fitting twenty tank engines and forty coaches at a total estimated cost of £4,200. It was, however, competition from road traffic and the generally depressed economic situation of the country which prompted a considerable expansion of motor train working in the early 1930s and the consequent fitting of further engines as a result. As can be seen, some twenty-five groups of services were in operation by 1935, falling in the war period to fourteen by 1944. To work these services thirty-nine 0-4-4Ts were equipped with VCR between 1927 and 1935 and others were subsequently fitted with gear from withdrawn engines. Around forty fitted engines were maintained, until 1949 when withdrawals began to reduce the numbers. Branch line closures, the introduction of motor fitted Ivatt 2-6-2Ts from 1950 and withdrawal of the 0-4-4Ts brought to an end the operation of motor train working by Midland engines.

The last branch to be worked by a motor fitted Midland engine was that from Southwell to Rolleston Junction, which closed on 15 June 1959. No.58065 (MR 1365) worked until the closure, assisted in the last months by a non fitted engine when necessary. The last MR VCR fitted engine to be withdrawn was No.58086 (MR 1423) in 1960. Again full details of the engines fitted are shown in the class Chapter.

Straight framed Kirtley goods No. 478 (2385 in 1907) has hand sanding to the front of the leading wheels only. The operating rod from the cab is clearly seen running to the sandbox on the footplating adjacent to the smokebox. When running in reverse of course it was completely ineffective. S Summerson collection.

The later Johnson arrangement of hand sanding, on No. 3141 of 1885 with delivery each side of the centre wheels and sandboxes below the platform. No. 3141 is at Derby, in March 1938. S Summerson collection.

Chapter 8 - Fittings and Details

'All passenger and goods tank engines are to be fitted with additional steps and handrails'

FITTINGS

A number of important fittings and details were common to all or large numbers of classes. Their development, range and application are now considered.

1 Bogie brakes

In order to provide additional brake power, bogie brakes were fitted to three classes of engines. The first application was to some of the Deeley 0-6-4Ts in 1908-11, to enable them to take heavier goods trains. The Working Timetable for October 1910 recorded three engines so fitted, and authorised to convey the same load as No.3 class goods tender engines (unfitted engines were limited to class 2 loadings). Six more of the 0-6-4Ts had been fitted by June 1911, but there is no evidence that any more were equipped.

The 483 Class superheated rebuilds of Johnson's 4-4-0s, introduced in 1912, and the Belpaire 4-4-0s when superheated from 1913 were fitted with bogie brakes, but the larger 990 class and the Compounds were not. Pencil notes were included in the 1908 *Register* to the effect that *'Engines 328-562 are bogie braked when supd'* and there is a similar note for engines 700-779. There is also a note against the class 4 4-4-0s: *'990s and Compounds are NOT bogie braked'* but no official statement of reasons has come to light. The LMS clearly saw virtue in the provision of bogie brakes and some of the earlier stand-

ard class 2 4-4-0s and 2-6-4Ts, plus all the Fowler 2-6-2T (among others) had them when new.

By 1933 it had become clear that bogie brakes were a source of trouble and expense and were found to be unnecessary; on 7 March 1933 instructions were given for their removal. The CME reported to the Mechanical and Electrical Committee on 21 February 1934 on his decision and advised that the work, carried out as the engines went through shops, would be completed in about four years. And it was.

2 Sanding

The problem of maintaining adhesion between wheel and rail is one which has exercised railway engineers from the beginning. It was specially sensitive in engines with only one pair of driving wheels – that is, those which did not have any coupled wheels, usually referred to as 'singles'. The principal passenger engines of the Midland were of this type until the 1860s and at an early date the principle of placing sand on the rails in front of the driving wheels was adopted for use in poor adhesion conditions.

Sandboxes filled with dried sand were fitted on or under the running plate and a pipe, containing a valve at the base of the sandbox operated by rod control from the cab, discharged the sand close to the rail in advance of the driving wheel. In early applications the discharge point was up to a foot away from the contact

point of the wheel and there wasn't a corresponding sanding arrangement behind the driving wheels for running in reverse. This was not too significant for passenger engines, which were unlikely to perform much train haulage running in reverse, but where 0-6-0 goods engines had a sanding pipe in front of the leading wheels only, problems occurred. The distance from discharge to wheel was also a handicap in high winds, for sand blew off the rail before the wheel reached it. Modifications and improvements were undertaken. Radford (*Derby Works and Midland Locomotives*, Ian Allan, 1971) records the alterations carried out to a Kirtley single at Leicester in the mid-1880s whereby the discharge pipes were brought as near as practicable to the rail/wheel contact point, with great success.

The next development was the introduction of a compressed air system to blow the sand to the desired spot, a much more reliable arrangement than hitherto. This system was invented by Francis Holt, Works Manager at Derby in 1886, and was doubtless inspired by the presence of a compressed air source on a number of engines with Westinghouse brake compressors. 1282 Class 2-4-0 No.1309 thus equipped, had the coupling rods temporarily removed and was fitted up with the new system. Operating on the Settle and Carlisle line with its notorious weather, it proved entirely successful and so paved the way for further applications. The

The single discharge point for steam sanding as first provided did not prove satisfactory on the Spinners and by about 1893 those so fitted had had a second sandbox and feed added behind the driving wheels, with a horizontal discharge as on No. 610 at Kentish Town on 7 August 1920. Note also the Furness lubricator (for cylinder lubrication when coasting) at the base of the smokebox.

Westinghouse Brake Company, ever protective of its systems, took strong exception to these liberties, so Holt then hit upon the idea of using boiler steam instead. This was most successful; once again the Midland had pioneered a significant advance in engine working, which was widely adopted by other Companies.

The success of steam sanding is said to have been a principal factor in Johnson's decision to introduce his famous 4-2-2 Spinners, the first of which was ordered in July 1886 and successful they were too, the first appearing in June 1887. The famous 7ft 0in 4-4-0 No.1757 BEATRICE (the last engine built to 0.615) built in December 1886, was fitted with steam sanding unlike the earlier engines of this series, and drawing 87-2526 of 25 February 1887 shows the horizontal steam sanding valve for this engine. All subsequent 4-4-0s and Singles had steam sanding. New 0-4-4 passenger tanks from 1889 were also equipped but there was no attempt to equip earlier engines of any class respectively, then or later, except where the 4-4-0s were substantially rebuilt. New 0-6-0s from 1890 were fitted, but 0-6-0 tank engines, having regard to their more sedentary duties, continued to be fitted with gravity sanding. An exception was the first thirty 2441 Class 0-6-0Ts; these had condensing apparatus and were provided with steam sanding to work over the Metropolitan widened lines, which provided difficult gradients and adhesion conditions in tunnels. The retention on many engines of gravity, or 'hand sanding' as it was described in official papers, was to have repercussions in later years. It was believed that the excess sand left on the rails by hand sanding was a cause of 'wrong side' (that is, false) clear indica-

tions of track circuits. It was however largely a localised problem before the widespread introduction of track circuiting in the 1930s. The first reference to de-sanding apparatus is found in Sketch No.227 of 21 April 1922, for a proposed de-sander using a wire brush, for trial on 0-6-0T No.1839. This was evidently unsatisfactory having regard to subsequent events and further sketches were issued, dated 22 January 1923 for 0-6-0Ts Nos.1940-1959 and 17 December 1923 for certain Kirtley and Johnson 0-4-4Ts in the London area.

0.6115 was issued on 11 February 1924 to fit seven Kirtley and four Johnson 0-4-4Ts with 'water de-sanding gear' for working over track circuited lines in the London area. The engines were Nos.1214, 1217-1222, 1294, 1312, 1320 and 1321 of Kentish Town and Cricklewood sheds. In 1932 a Joint Committee consisting of the CMEs, Signal Engineers and Locomotive Running Superintendents of the various railway companies investigated the problem generally, recommending that all engines equipped with hand sanding apparatus and liable to work over track circuited areas should be fitted with hot water de-sanding gear. This was reported to the LMS Mechanical and Electrical Committee on 28 June 1933 and it was recommended that 4,300 engines be so fitted, at an approximate cost of £15 each. The Minister of Transport agreed to approve £50,000 under the scheme for the Remission of Government Passenger Duty, subject to conditions.

So far as Derby was concerned, some 500 engines were involved, and sheet 4 of 0.8495 dated 31 January 1934 details the number range of the Midland engines involved: 0-4-4Ts up to No.1330, class 1 and 3 0-6-0Ts (including, erroneously, Nos.1900-1929), LTS 4-4-2Ts and

0-6-2Ts and class 2 0-6-0s Nos.2900-3199. These engines were to be fitted unless likely to be broken up before the end of 1935. The work was under the authority of New Work Order (NWO) 3138. This was one of those projects of wide application which was allocated a Job number retrospectively, in this case No.5003. It will be noted that no surviving Kirtley engines were included, nor any 2-4-0s.

Due to the rapid withdrawal of many older engines, the Derby list was reduced to 408 by 23 November 1936. Successive orders were given for these engines to be equipped and the last, 0.286, was issued on 5 November 1937, for the remaining twenty-four class 2 0-6-0s. It is presumed that all were fitted. None of the LTS class 1 4-4-2Ts were equipped. The total number of class 2 0-6-0s to be fitted in the 1936 amendment was 147 but as some 168 engines survived to 1939 and beyond, some uncertainty remains.

3 Condensing Apparatus

The tunnels of the Metropolitan widened lines, together with that under Snow Hill leading up to Blackfriars in London, provided one of the worst environments in the country for engine crews to endure. The steep descent at 1 in 60 from St Pauls Road Passenger Junction to Kings Cross, the sharp dip under the Ray Street grid-iron below the Circle line, with a rise at 1 in 40 to Farringdon Street, not to mention the sharp climb up Snow Hill bank, together made for extremely difficult working conditions until the demise of steam.

With hard working steam engines in tunnel conditions on a frequent passenger service interspersed with freight traffic, the atmosphere was at all times foul. Apart from that, the main problem

At Gloucester on 2 June 1923 this 2-4-0 (No. 164) shows the four studs on the cabside betraying the presence of the hydrostatic cylinder lubricator attached inside. The feed pipe runs inside the handrail and down just behind the smokebox. **The Transport Treasury.**

Kirtley back tank No.1211 with condensing apparatus ex-works after its last service repair on 2 May 1933. Note the London district lamp brackets, curved levers to the Salter valves and rear sandbox on the firebox. The trip cock lever can be seen behind the brake rodding, between the coupled and bogie wheels. R.G. Jarvis/Mid Rail Photographs.

was lack of visibility in the tunnels for signal sighting, especially in winter when the London air itself would be foggy and smoke ridden. To minimise the difficulties so far as was practicable, engines had to be fitted with condensing apparatus. With this in use the exhaust steam was diverted from the blast pipe by a valve into twin pipes which emerged, one each side of the smokebox, to pass into the back tanks of the Kirtley 0-4-4Ts and the side tanks of the other engines which were fitted. Discharge was into the feed water. In order to prevent water vapour escaping from the tank filling hole, the lids were made watertight and vertical ventilation pipes provided on top of the tanks so that the driver's vision would not be impeded. Condensing the exhaust steam of course raised the feedwater temperature, with the attendant risk of the standard cold water injectors failing to work. The engines were therefore equipped with one or two feed pumps and one injector, perpetuating the later Kirtley practice. A rapid discharge valve was fitted to the water tanks, so that if boiler feed problems arose the warm water could be disposed of quickly and a fresh fill of cold water taken. Facilities for this – a water column and drainage pit – were specially provided at Moorgate.

An interesting feature of the later tank engines was the provision of ventilated side tanks; an additional outer sheet was provided with a one inch gap to the tank and slit openings in the ends 'for air to circulate', as the specification describes it. Presumably this was a device for cooling the water but it appears to the writer of the 1990s to have been of doubtful benefit.

Whilst the condensing apparatus was in use, the draught on the fire was maintained by the blower, but of course this was not so effective as the steam exhausting up the chimney. At tunnel entrances there were large boards bearing the commanding notice 'ENGINES MUST CONDENSE'. Clearly drivers would only use the condensers when they had to, and one suspects that if the engine was not steaming well, then ordinary working was resumed. They were not going to stall in the tunnel if it could be avoided, not on those gradients!

Which leads to the question of the sound made by an engine when condensing. Because ordinary working was resumed on emerging into the open air it was not a sight and sound observed by many and the author has not seen any comments in earlier works. One suspects it must have sounded somewhat like the modern day cafeteria apparatus which passes steam into cold milk to heat it and therefore was a muffled, regular, crackling, bubbling sound! Perhaps a retired driver or fireman will recall.

A total of one hundred and twenty-four Midland tank engines were fitted with condensing apparatus, beginning with ten 2-4-0Ts, Nos.230-239, specially designed for the initial service to Moorgate Street from 13 July 1868. The condensing tanks concluded with eleven of the 2441 Class 0-6-0Ts fitted in 1925-28, by then LMS class 3 and numbered 1940-1949 and 1951. Details of all these engines are shown in the various class chapters. As a matter of interest, the last two Midland engines to be withdrawn, in December 1966, were two ex-condensing tanks, Nos.47201 and 47202. The

gear had been removed from No.47201 (which had left London many years before) but the latter still retained its condensing pipes. It had left the capital in 1962, by which time the apparatus would have already been long out of use. One suspects that in the last years of steam, condensing was favoured more in the breach than observance...

4 Cab Signalling Systems
a) MR Experiments

The safety of trains has been of prime concern since the beginning of railways. Semaphore signalling systems were devised and constantly improved; the Absolute Block system and the introduction of track circuiting, together with continuing improvements to locking systems to prevent errors, produced a very sophisticated and reliable method of regulating trains. This in turn has largely been displaced by modern electrically and electronically controlled systems and colour light signals. Despite the best regulation, the problem of drivers passing signals at danger, in fog or as a result of momentary lapses of concentration or illness, with potentially disastrous consequences, has regularly engaged the attention of signal engineers. The GWR began trials of an automatic warning system utilising a ramp between the rails and apparatus on the engine in 1906, which was the forerunner of the Automatic Train Control (ATC) system, widely applied on the Great Western. The Midland followed suit with 0.3312 of 4 June 1907, which provided for two 0-4-4Ts, Nos.1428 and 1429, to be fitted with fog signalling apparatus, 'GW type'. Trials were conducted on the Wirksworth branch commencing on 3

The Hudd Automatic Train Control was developed as the British Railways Automatic Warning System. Nine MR 0-6-0s were ordered to be fitted with Hudd ATC in 1935/8. No. 58197 (3045) was fitted after transfer to the LTS in April 1955 and is seen at Tilbury on 2 August 1955. S. Summerson collection.

February 1908, the Notice stating that: *'As many of the booked trips over the branch as possible will be worked by tank engine No.1428 and autocar No.5, which are fitted with the special apparatus'.* Autocar No.5 was one of the M&GN 4-4-0Ts and Pullman Car units, working on the branch at that time, so that the notice infers that this, and not No.1429 was fitted. It seems improbable that No.1428 ran with the Pullman car.

In the same period, Vincent Raven on the North Eastern Railway devised an Automatic Cab Signalling apparatus. This likewise gave visual and audible indications to the driver, the latter by a bell activated by a brush consisting of a bundle of steel wires fitted in a frame beneath the engine, making contact with a series of ramps laid between the rails at and near the distant and home signals. Midland officers made a visit to Darlington on 2 December 1910, to study the system and in the same period No.1428 was fitted with a new pattern cab signalling instrument, which was tested on the engine from 21 November 1910 to 4 February 1911.

On 3 March 1915 a Drawing Office memorandum records (in a related matter) details of 'Biddle's Mechanical Train Stop Apparatus', setting out objections to its use and noting that *'The whole arrangement must be very carefully protected from weather, or it may freeze up'.*

These investigations and experiments were not pursued and a further fifteen years or so were to pass before the LMS focused attention on the subject, in the 1930s.

b) LMS developments - the Hudd system

A.E. Hudd was engaged as a consultant in the early 1930s to develop a practical system of Automatic Train Control on the intensively used London Tilbury and Southend lines. In the Hudd system a permanent magnet and an electro-magnet were placed on the track between the rails, fifteen yards apart and adjacent to a distant signal. With the signal at caution, the permanent magnet opened a horn valve and began a brake application on the locomotive passing over, which was fitted with a receiver. When the signal was clear, the electromagnet was energised, cancelling the brake application. The apparatus was set on the engine to give a clearance of four inches above the magnets so no physical contact was involved. Considerable difficulties were encountered in the all-important search for reliability, but urgency does not appear to have been a prime consideration. The introduction of Hudd Automatic Train control on the LTS was accordingly a very protracted affair. Initial experiments had been carried out at Ashwood Dale on the Buxton branch, in 1932, with MR 0-4-4T No.1247 fitted with the receiving apparatus.

On 22 February 1933 the Traffic and Works Committees authorised, on an experimental basis, the fitting up of six locomotives and six signals. An interim report of July 1934 indicated that further experiments were desirable to determine if the apparatus was suitable for adoption. On 29 May 1935 a report to the Mechanical & Electrical Commit-

tee from the Chief Operating Manager, Signal & Telegraph Engineer and the CME, indicated that success had been achieved and that the Ministry of Transport had given provisional sanction to a comprehensive installation, as an experiment for a period of not less than six months. The total anticipated cost of £28,500, which included the fitting of 275 locomotives, was then approved. A batch of Derby orders was issued on 3 July 1935 covering all engines allocated to the LTS line, plus those at London area sheds likely to work over the line. These included MR 0-4-4Ts, 0-6-0Ts, class 2, 3 and 4 0-6-0s and several 2P 4-4-0s, in addition to the native LTS 4-4-2Ts and 0-6-2Ts. These will be covered in the class chapters.

All was not well however and on 23 July 1937 a further report had shown that 'certain fundamental alterations' were necessary in the design of the receiver on the engines and that a definite design – the No.2 type – had been decided upon. Six sets which had been brought into service had given 'excellent results, sufficient to warrant a more extended trial'. Authority was sought and given for further expenditure of £13,925. It was also approved that *'Mr A.E. Hudd's agreement as consultant at a fee of five hundred guineas per annum which expires on 30 June 1937, be extended for a further period of twelve months'.* The report also noted that 250 engines had been fitted. A further series of orders for fitting the No.2 receiver followed on 30 June 1938. The War then intervened and hampered progress. Unconditional approval of the Minister of Transport was given on 23 January 1941 but on 28 May 1942 further failures were reported and it was decided that 'trials throughout another winter' would be necessary, in order to test proposed modifications before being finally adopted: *'as the engine situation of the Southend line was by no means stable, owing to war conditions, it was recommended that the remaining sixty-eight fitted engines at present running on the LTS be modified at an estimated cost of £1080'.* Mr Hudds' appointment was terminated on 31 December 1940. The figure of sixty-eight engines would imply that the apparatus had been removed from a considerable number.

Finally, on 20 February 1946, the M&E Committee was advised *'that the Hudd ATC system had now reached a state of reliability and efficiency as to justify its being brought into use next winter. This would involve the fitting of a further fifty six engines before next winter and a further thirty eight for the summer of 1947'.* Various problems further delayed its introduction but it was finally brought into use on 1 December 1947, with, officially 183 engines fitted.

The receiver on the engine was centrally fixed just above rail level. In those cases where it was fitted behind the front buffer beam it was found necessary to fit a protector plate behind the coupling to prevent it swinging back and causing damage. This is clearly visible on photographs of the engines so fitted. As allocations changed, so engines were altered to suit; this makes it difficult to produce a definitive list from incomplete records, but the broad picture is clear.

5 Oil Burning

The railways were completely dependent on adequate supplies of suitable coal and whenever a threat of major interruption occurred, there was considerable alarm and a rapid concentration of minds to find ways round the difficulty. On four main occasions a serious threat was posed, in 1912, 1921, 1926 and 1947 and each time, an essay into oil burning was undertaken. Some Midland engines were converted to oil firing in each of the first three episodes but by the last, the survivors were not of sufficient importance to be considered.

The miners' strike of February to April 1912 prompted the Midland to undertake some experiments with three Belpaire 4-4-0s over a period of five weeks from 6 April to 11 May of that year. These trials used oil gas tar, though a small amount of coal was burned on the grate. The oil burners were inserted through the firehole door and both Holden Great Eastern type and 'Best' type burners were tried. The former produced a deafening noise and steaming problems but the latter was more successful. The costs of using coal and oil were over twice the cost of coal alone, a report of 23 May 1912 showing 0.0124 pence per ton mile for oil and coal compared to 0.0065 pence per ton mile for coal. The resolution of the strike saw the end of these experiments, but each engine had run an average of 5,896 miles during the tests. Further details concerning the operation of the 'Best' apparatus were obtained in September 1920 from Mr J.F. Durnford, Works Manager of the Argentine Great Southern Railway, concerning experience with this

burner. Doubtless this was because another miners' strike threatened at the time – in fact it materialised the next month. The information proved useful again in the following year, the strike of April 1921 lasting longer and prompting the conversion of some forty-one engines. Derby Order No.5593 of 2 May 1921 covered the bulk of the work and was initially for twenty engines: *'These engines are urgently required and you are requested to make arrangements to carry out your part of the work as expeditiously as possible even if necessary at the sacrifice of the rebuilding programme. Every effort is to be made to have eight engines ready for traffic by Monday 16th instant, and the remaining twelve by Monday 23rd instant'.*

Various additions and amendments were made up to 4 June 1921 so that sixteen superheated class 2 4-4-0s and twenty-three class 3 4-4-0s were covered. A solitary 0-6-0T, No.1888, was added on 7 June and the Lickey banker in July 1921. On the tender engine, the oil was carried in two 450 gallon cylindrical tanks fitted in the coal space, 8ft long and 3ft 7⅛in diameter on the majority of engines, though one or two exceptions to this arrangement are known. The burner was inserted in the firehole and lighting up was in the conventional manner with wood and coal until the steam pressure was 30-40lb, sufficient to use the burner. The firebars were covered with broken firebrick to prevent excess air entering the firebox.

Twenty tenders were to be fitted up for transporting fuel oil to the sheds and twenty more for storage at the sheds housing the oil burners. Pipelines for fill-

0-4-4T No. 1375 of September 1893 built with condensing apparatus as rebuilt with a G5½ boiler in January 1927. Note the condensing pipe from the smokebox and the control rodding beneath, also the tank vent pipe above the L in LMS. No 1375 is ex works at Derby.
S Summerson collection.

ing purposes were installed at Derby, Bedford, Kentish Town, Bristol, Gloucester, Leeds and Leicester, covering operations on the principal main lines. Again, resolution of the strike saw the oil burning engines quickly revert to coal, but details of the removal of apparatus were not recorded.

Only five years later came the General strike of May 1926, though the miners' dispute continued until the following November. This lengthy stoppage again brought serious disruption to coal supplies and once again prompted a limited conversion to oil firing. The first two MR engines to be adapted were class 2 4-4-0 No.527 and class 3 4-4-0 No.765, to Order 6664 of 27 May 1926. In the interests of economy, it was commanded, 'materials from stock should be used wherever possible', so some material must have been retained from the 1921 episode. Thirty-three further class 2 4-4-0s were fitted and commencing with 0.6671 of 29 May 1926 forty Compounds, ten of which were original Midland engines, were also adapted. Twenty-five more were authorised under 0.6682 of 23 June 1926 but there is no evidence of any more Midland-built Compounds altered to this order. Twenty-eight class 2s were given 8ft long 450 gallon cylindrical tanks, as were six of the MR Compounds. No.1041 had a flat sided tank 8ft long and the remainder had 9ft flat sided tanks, carrying 500 gallons of oil. Of the remaining class 2 4-4-0s, one had an 8ft flat sided tank and four flat sided 9ft tanks.

Again, tenders were fitted up for transporting the oil, with pipework installed at the sheds. On the ending of the strike in November, 0.6789 was issued on 6 December 1926, for stripping the apparatus off the engines: '*All material to be boiled, listed and sent to the Loco Stores with credit notes (except oil cylinders)*'. So with an eye to possible future trouble the 1926 oil burning operation came to an end; as it turned out this was the last occasion requiring the adaptation of any ex-Midland Railway engines.

6 Lubricators

Cylinders on saturated engines were lubricated by a Roscoe hydrostatic displacement lubricator; this was fitted on the left hand side of the smokebox on the boiler centre line on the Kirtley engines and the arrangement was continued by Johnson. From 1888, however, these were placed in the cab. They were fixed to the left hand side cab sheet adjacent to the cut out where practicable and on the spectacle plate where not. Piping was led behind the boiler cladding in the first applications but subsequently ran adjacent to the left side hand rail and down, adjacent to the rear of the smokebox. The presence of the lubricator on the cab side was indicated by the four nut heads visible on the outside of the upper cab side sheet. The last new engines to have the earlier arrangement were the first of the Johnson Singles, built in June 1887 and the final members of the 1698 Class of 0-6-0s,

Top. Class 2 superheated 4-4-0 No. 396 on the centre road between platforms 5 and 6 at Birmingham New Street in January 1931. It was fitted with bogie brakes when rebuilt in May 1923. Note also the cylinder bye pass valve under the footplate, above the bogie.

Middle. Superheated Belpaire 4-4-0 No. 769 was one of twenty-three members of the class to be fitted for oil burning in 1921. A Derby engine, it is seen here at Kentish Town showing cylindrical oil tanks mounted on the tender. S Summerson collection

Bottom. Class 3F No. 3644 at Peterborough on 29 August 1936. Note the wide smokebox seating ring and replacement block style number plate. The Transport Treasury.

Top. **Class 4 0-6-0 No. 3953 showing the mechanical lubricators for cylinders and axleboxes outside Kirkby shed where it was based between 1936 and 1939. It was the last of the MR series to remain in service and was withdrawn in November 1965. S. Summerson collection.**

Middle. **The restricted bore of Glenfield tunnel is very apparent as 0-6-0 No. 3229 emerges on 12 April 1948. It wasn't until 1960 that a trial demonstrated that a Deeley cab would just clear at eaves level. S Summerson collection.**

Bottom. **The Johnson smokebox door and smokebox with a one piece chimney, as on No. 595 (at Lancaster on 12 August 1902) had a very neat appearance. Note the rodding to the leading sandboxes passes through the handrail and down adjacent to the smokebox front, necessitating a separate handrail round the smokebox.**

completed in January 1888. When examining photographs for this feature it is noticeable how few left hand side pictures are available in comparison with right hand side views; it is therefore not possible to be wholly clear as to the last engines of these two batches. The Johnson 0-4-0STs retained the hydrostatic lubricator on the smokebox until withdrawn.

Photographic evidence suggests a rapid change to the new arrangement on all the surviving earlier engines and only a few of the externally fitted lubricators were still in place by the time the tender and tankside MR initials became standard, from 1892. One example known is 0-6-0T No.1389, photographed in St Pancras after being vacuum fitted, around 1893.

Between April and October 1910 tests were carried out on the sight feed lubricators, resulting in modifications to the old pattern and the introduction of new style lubricators, which gave a similar efficiency to the Wakefield mechanical lubricators. For keeping the cylinders fed while coasting, Furness lubricators were fitted, one each side of the smokebox, low down above the running plate and these remained a standard fitting until the 1920s on the saturated engines. Some experimentation was undertaken in 1916-18 by removing those lubricators from selected Derby engines and studying the effect. On 26 April 1917 a report was submitted on class 3 0-6-0s Nos.3613 and 3401 carrying H boilers. The former had the Furness lubricator removed on 12 June 1916. The report did not indicate any adverse effects, but the driver had reported that the engines were not so free in working their usual train loads. They continued to run without them. Similar trials were carried out with saturated Belpaire 4-4-0s. No.767 had these lubricators taken off on 27 December 1916 and in a report of 7 June 1917 it had been reported as 'running sluggish and groaning when starting from stations and burning more coal than usual'. The experiment was to continue, but on 2 May 1918, Herbert Chambers reported that the experiment on engines running without the Furness equipment had been stopped. Further trials were conducted later and a Drawing Office record of 22 February 1922 noted that the question as to the effect of removing Furness lubricators had been raised at Millhouses and Grimesthorpe sheds, Sheffield. All concerned reported no detrimental effect at all as a result of removal, a verdict which agreed with examinations made at Derby works.

Nevertheless, general removal of the Furness lubricators did not apparently commence until 1924. Class 2 0-6-0s rebuilt with Belpaire boilers in that year still retained them, but engines so rebuilt in 1925 did not. Removal after that however was quite rapid and very few engines are known to have retained them after the livery change of 1928. No.3566 was still fitted when photographed on 20 May 1931, but had the earlier livery style, indicating that some time had passed since a major works overhaul.

The superheated engines were all fitted with mechanical lubricators for cylinders, which displaced the earlier methods. Mechanical lubrication was also introduced for axleboxes on the class 4 0-6-0s from 1920 and was fitted subsequently on the earlier members of the class, a process complete by 1925. These were fixed on the left-hand footplating adjacent to the cylinder lubricator. Mechanical axlebox lubricators were also fitted to some of the Compounds. The Chief Mechanical and Electrical Engineer recommended on 27 April 1944 that with a view to reducing the number of hot boxes, the forty-five 4-4-0 Compounds, originally built with trimming feed oil boxes, should be fitted with mechanical lubrication. In this case the equipment was fitted on the right-hand footplating, but the difficulties of wartime and the subsequent withdrawal of the class meant that, so far as can be judged, not all were in fact fitted.

7 Piston and Bye-pass Valves
a) Piston Valves
The Schmidt piston valve used on the superheated engines from 1910, having a single wide ring, was prone to steam leakage as it wore in service, thus reducing the efficiency of the engine and increasing the coal consumption. This shortcoming was most critical of course on the principal express engines (it was later to cause considerable concern on the Royal Scot 4-6-0s of 1927) but it obviously also affected a large number of pre-grouping engines, principally from the Caledonian, LNW and Midland. At Derby, a new design of 10 inch piston valve with narrow rings was prepared for use on Compounds, the Lickey banker and the ex-SDJR 2-8-0s; instructions for fitting, which also required new liners, were issued on 24 June 1930.

The pursuit of improved efficiency went on unabated. On 20 May 1931 for instance, the same day as the decision taken to fit 1,242 engines with exhaust steam injectors, the CME reported to the Mechanical and Electrical Engineering Committee (Minute No.1184) on the savings obtained (11½% in coal) following the fitting of new piston valves to the Royal Scots and Claughtons.

Authority was sought and given, to fit 1,657 further engines, comprising the more important main line types which included all the 2P superheater rebuilds of the 483 Class, the sixty-two surviving 'Belpaire' class 3 4-4-0s and the 192 4F 0-6-0s, giving an estimated annual cost saving of £47,600 on the assumption of a 6% saving in coal. Again the work was to be spread over three to four years, with the engines fitted as they went through the shops for repairs. By 25 July 1934 the CME reported to the Committee that, in view of the results obtained, all piston valve engines should be similarly equipped which, *inter alia*, included the Compounds. This increased the number to be dealt with to 2,496 and was agreed for recommendation to the Board. Subsequent correspondence showed the correct figure to be 2,442.

The work was of sufficient importance to be allocated a retrospective Job number, No.5004. At Derby, specific Orders were issued for the work (with the exception of the Compounds), the last order being 0.267 of 8 October 1937, for class 2 4-4-0s.

b) Bye-pass Valves
When an engine with slide valves is coasting, the valves fall free of their seats and compressive forces are not built up in the cylinders. As a result, slide valve engines will coast very freely. When piston valves are employed, a pumping action is set up when coasting which, if not relieved, will cause products of combustion from the smokebox to enter the cylinders, with a potential for damage. To prevent this and to reduce the pumping action, relief valves were fitted, which assisted in the free running of the engine when steam was shut off. Under the direction of J.E. Anderson, a bye-pass valve was designed at Derby which had the effect, with steam shut off, of creating a bye-pass between the ends of the cylinder. This further improved the free running characteristics with steam off.

The byepass valves were fitted to all the superheated piston valve simple 4-4-0s, Compounds and 0-6-0s after a series of trials carried out on 990 Class 4-4-0 No.998 in August/September 1911, which clearly demonstrated the benefits in reduced cylinder compression with the valves in operation. Some further tests were carried out in December 1920 on Compounds, with and without byepass valves to the low pressure steam chest, which showed no detectable differences in the running of the engines. The low pressure cylinders had slide valves which undoubtedly had a bearing on the results. At the M&E Committee meeting of 25 July 1934 referred to above, the CME also reported that '...*in view of the improvements to the design of valves and valve gear, it is considered that the fitting of bye pass valves is no longer necessary*' and he recommended that they be removed from 2,114 engines as they passed through the shops. At Derby, general instructions had been issued in connection with this work on the previous 8 May(!) the costing to be charged to the individual engines, without specific orders.

Whilst the result of the piston valve alterations was universally welcome, the removal of the bye-pass valves was not, for engines did not then run as freely with steam shut off.

The final design of Johnson smokebox door was convex with central locking wheel and long straps from the hinge closing onto a narrow seating ring. Three securing 'dogs' have been added to the base in this 1905 view of No. 823 (733 in 1907) at Leeds Wellington, a forerunner of things to come.

Rebuilt Kirtley 890 Class No. 115 at Bedford on 15 September 1934. It was one of the few of this class to receive new deeper frames after 1890. R.G. Jarvis/Mid Rail Photographs.

8 Ejectors and Blowers

Up to 1905 in the case of passenger engines and 1907 for goods engines fitted with vacuum brakes, separate large and small ejectors were fitted, with the blower combined with the small ejector. The last thirty Compounds, the ten 990 Class 4-4-0s, the rebuilt 4-4-0s with G7 and G7S boilers, the 0-6-4Ts and 0-6-0s from No.3815 upwards were all fitted with combined ejectors and independent blowers. The original separate ejector arrangement was retained on some earlier boiler designs and was subsequently fitted to examples of the smaller replcement belpaire boilers. Several of these lasted into the 1950s.

Attention was turned to fitting earlier engines with independent blowers, a process which took many years to carry out. On 3 January 1906, 0.3072 was issued to cover the fitting of all engines stationed in London and on 1 March 1909 the Belpaire 4-4-0s were ordered to be fitted as they passed through shops for repairs. Thirteen 0-6-0Ts were covered later the same year and consideration was being given to fitting 0-4-4Ts Nos.1381-1385 in January 1912.

Problems of noise form the discharge of the ejectors arose when engines were converted to independent blowers, as the exhaust was then turned directly up the chimney. Accordingly, blast pipe caps with a double ring of holes were designed (drawings dated 7 February 1911) which proved satisfactory as a silencer. Some sixteen engines had been equipped by August 1912. By that date about sixty-seven of the Belpaires had acquired independent blowers but otherwise progress was slow – some fifty-eight other passenger engines and sixty-three 0-4-4Ts. It is probable that the conversion programme was never completed.

9 Rerailing Jacks

Until the early years of the century, engines always carried screw jacks for rerailing purposes and in this connection it is interesting to note that drawing 75-425 was for 'Screw Jack - Great Eastern pattern', reflecting Johnson's previous appointment. However, on 2 November 1903 instructions were given for their removal from passenger engines, for it was then not deemed necessary to carry them. As a memorandum of 21 February 1905, from Derby to Sheffield locomotive department indicates, they were very soon not required on goods engines either: *'It does not appear worthwhile to retain the jacks on goods engines. Be good enough to remove jacks and jackbars from goods and shunting engines. If you think that any exceptions should be made, please inform me of the engines you consider jacks should be retained and state reasons'*. Jacks were duly taken off, and seem to have been retained only in a few cases where localised trackwork was so bad as to result in repeated derailments.

DETAILS

As with fittings, many details were common in their application to various, and in some classes to all classes of engines at any given period. In themselves, they changed in accordance with the ideas of successive Locomotive Engineers and draughtsmen and in so doing, provide an interesting study, which is often of assistance in the dating of photographs.

1 Loading Gauge

A prime consideration was for each engine design to come within the loading gauge of the lines over which it had to work and this overall constraint had its effect on the design of some details, particularly chimney length and cab. The loading gauge was recorded in the Working Timetables under three main dimensions within the overall profile; width, height in centre and height at side. The general MR loading gauge was 9ft 0in width, 13ft 9in height at centre and 10ft 9in height at side.

Two sections of line were particularly restricted, firstly the Metropolitan Railway widened lines, over which Midland trains and engines ran from Kings Cross to Moorgate Street and secondly the celebrated Glenfield Tunnel on the Leicester West Bridge branch, once the main line of the pioneer Leicester and Swannington Railway. In the former case, whilst width remained at 9ft 0in, the height at centre was only 12ft 8in and at the side 10ft 0in, later raised to 10ft 6in. On the West Bridge line, the maximum width was 7ft 7in, height 12ft 10in and height at side 10ft 9in. In the former case engines were designed to suit but in the latter the dimensions did not produce problems until engines got larger and this is discussed further under cabs. Other individual restrictions need not be considered here. Various other details can now be considered.

2 Smokeboxes

Smokeboxes suffered the abrasive and corrosive effects of the exhaust gases from the fire and as occasion required, were renewed in the same way as other parts and charged to repairs. However, in one instance a wholsale renewal was the subject of a formal order and noted in Chapter 4 in connection with the replacement of drumhead tubeplates. 0.3066 of 15 December 1905 provided for new smokeboxes as a consequence of fitting a standard design front tubeplates on the engines concerned.

2a Smokebox Doors

Kirtley engines had two flat rectangular smokebox doors, each hinged on its outer side on a frame standing proud of the front plate. These were secured by a single 'clock hand' on the left hand door without a locking handle, which enabled the doors to be screwed up tight to maintain the smokebox vacuum. One cannot help thinking they must have been prone to leak air and so produce steaming difficulties, but such photographs that are available of Kirtley engines in the early Johnson period, where Johnson chimneys have been fitted to Kirtley boilers, all appear to show the original smokebox doors still in situ. They certainly survived into the 1880s, as a photograph of 0-6-0 No.1054, taken beside No.484A (rebuilt with a Johnson blower in September 1880) still retained original doors. It could therefore be possible that replacement generally came with the provision of Johnson boilers, when new smokeboxes were also provided.

The Johnson smokebox doors by contrast, were circular, as became standard thereafter, closed flush to the smokebox front and concave dished from the centre. They were secured by two 'clock hands' to an internal dart and presented a very sleek look, appearing on many Kirtley engines as they were rebuilt. This pattern remained standard on all the 4ft 1in diameter boilers until Johnson's retirement, but an entirely new design was produced for the majority of the 'Belpaire' class 4-4-0s and the first Compounds. The first ten 'Belpaire' engines had standard Johnson doors, but the next fifty and the first five Compound 4-4-0s had convex doors closing onto a narrow seating ring secured by a small central hand wheel. These engines entered traffic between January 1902

and January 1905. This pattern of door was also used on the first forty 0-6-0s built with H boilers in 1903-4 and also on all 4-4-0s and 0-6-0s rebuilt with H boilers from 1903 until about November 1905, after which a further major change took place.

Before that, the last twenty 'Belpaire' 4-4-0s which had entered traffic between February and September 1905 were given the first Deeley pattern door. Slightly dished and secured with six dogs around the perimeter, this formed the basic smokebox door pattern for all boilers until the Stanier era of the 1930s. A few rebuilt 4-4-0s, including Nos.232 and 2590, were also given this door but a revised, flat version, appeared on Deeley's first Compound 4-4-0s in October 1905. This became the standard for the large boilers for the next few years. Flat smokebox doors appeared on rebuilt 4-4-0s from January 1906, but before that, on 14 November 1905, instructions were issued to fit a similar smokebox door to the small boilered engines ('as per drawing 05-6454'). This covered all A, A1, B, C, C1, D, E, F and P class boilers which were to be fitted with new smokeboxes, to be charged to 0.3071 issued in December. This therefore included all the engines with small diameter boilers which did not have drumhead tubeplates covered by 0.3066 noted above. The American 2-6-0s are not mentioned, but limited photographic evidence shows that they were also part of this programme.

So, with the exception of the Johnson 0-4-0STs, all the small boilered engines were involved. The large doors were 4ft 1¼in diameter and the small doors were 3ft 6½in diameter. The work was pushed ahead rapidly, so that very few photographs are known of engines carrying

1907 numbers with other than the new standard doors. Several Johnson smokeboxes also got them. The introduction of this door pattern coincided more or less with the livery change whereby the engine number was displayed on the smokebox door and tender. The Compounds, from October 1905, were the first to have the smokebox door numberplate.

Clearly the flat design of door secured by six or seven dogs on a narrow seating ring was not entirely satisfactory; the smokebox vacuum tended to pull the centre in and so cause air leaks around the perimeter, inhibiting steaming. The design of the retaining ring (with the dogs partly attached to the smokebox front plate and partly to the ring) was therefore changed to a wider ring, with the retaining dogs on the ring and a slightly dished door. These alterations appeared in 1909-10 and engines with the earlier arrangement were subsequently altered. The new pattern was to remain an LMS standard until the Stanier regime. Midland engines continued to carry the 1910 style until the last was withdrawn in 1966. On all these doors where continuous hand rails were retained a small vertical grab handle was fitted adjacent to the rim opposite the hinge.

3 Chimneys

It is remarkable how the shape, length and diameter of a chimney influences an engine's overall appearance. Kirtley chimneys, throughout his tenure of office, retained the early 'bell mouth' top with parallel sides and this, with the double frames on the majority of his designs, made for a distinctly antiquated appearance by the early 1870s. A low pitch to the boilers resulted in chimneys

The special London district lamp irons with rear extension brackets for destination boards or discs are seen to good effect on 0-4-4T No. 1376 about 1930. Note the hinged bracket to the centre buffer beam iron in the down position to avoid fouling the smokebox door when opened. S Summerson collection.

An up local for St.Pancras slows for the Elstree stop. The London district bunker and brackets show how the top lamp had to be fitted at the bunker top to allow room to attach a board or disc to the centre bracket below.

4ft long, adding to the effect. They gave the impression of being rather frail and this view is reinforced by the fact that a number of Kirtley engines were photographed in original condition but with Johnson chimneys in the 1870s, before any other alterations to cabs, boilers and the rest had been made. Johnson chimneys, on the other hand, had a much sturdier appearance and the design has received much favourable comment over the years. It tapered outwards from the top to the base and the initial design was built up from three sections, which are clearly apparent in photographs. An internal liner was fitted, tapering the opposite way to provide the correct exhaust arrangements. For the 1853 Class 4-2-2s, the first of which appeared in February 1889, a one piece casting was produced of more pleasing appearance; subsequent chimneys (up to December 1902) were of this pattern. Johnson's eye for detail and proportion resulted in different chimney length for various classes. The design was varied by increments (generally 3in) from the longest at 3ft 10½in on the first 0-6-0s of 1875 down to 2ft 5in on the Compounds.

Then came a complete and remarkable change. A new 'flowerpot' design appeared on the 2736 Class 0-6-0s (which also saw the introduction of the new 4ft 8in diameter H boiler) in January 1903. This new pattern appeared only on a hundred new engines, the fifty 2736 and 245 class 0-6-0s (Nos.2736-2740 and 240-284) and fifty Belpaire 4-4-0s Nos.820-869, all of which were built in 1903-7. During this period many of the earlier 4-4-0s and 0-6-0s were being rebuilt with H boilers and a larger number of these also received the new 'flowerpot' chimneys.

Several other engines, of various classes, got replacement flowerpot chimneys during this period, including a small Kirtley well tank, an 'American' 2-6-0, a Spinner, an unrebuilt 4-4-0 and a few 0-6-0s. Why is not clear, but it is very apparent that these chimneys were rapidly removed from all classes during the next few years, only a handful of engines surviving to carry them with their new 1907 numbers. They were therefore very far from being life-expired. The flower pot design must have been approved by Johnson but it has generally drawn unfavourable comment from observers, when comparing it to the previous attractive shape. An ink note on the drawing list for the new 0-6-0s says: *'made without liner - 15.9.02 - first time thus'* indicating the impact of the change in the Drawing Office.

The first of the thirty Deeley Compounds, Nos.1000-1029, appeared in October 1905, with a new design of chimney, having only a slight outward taper from the bottom. This chimney had a capuchon, a feature which had been introduced on the first five Johnson Compounds of 1902. Rebuilding of the earlier 4-4-0s and 0-6-0s was continuing apace; this new chimney began to appear from about February 1906 on the 4-4-0s and was used for about a year. Photographic coverage for this period is far from comprehensive but No.2185, rebuilt February 1906 and No.1671, rebuilt February 1907, had this style. Meanwhile No.2209, rebuilt in April 1906, had a flowerpot. Later that same year a further change introduced the parallel sided chimney with capuchon, setting the standard for tender engines until the Stanier era. 4-4-0s rebuilt from November 1906 carried this style of

chimney, which appeared in various lengths for the different classes. The flowerpot was not quite finished though. 4-4-0 No.1743, rebuilt in February 1907, carried a short flowerpot; new 0-6-0s (Nos.275-284 of January 1906-January 1907) carried them whilst No.3758 (rebuilt in November 1907) had one, all of which implies it remained the standard for rebuilt goods engines up to about that time. From January 1908 new goods engines had the parallel chimney with capuchon. By contrast, tank engines, commencing with the forty 0-6-4Ts built in 1907, were given parallel chimneys *without* capuchon, for which no official explanation has been noted.

Early in Stanier's regime, new chimneys were designed to replace the Deeley/Fowler pattern generally and these had no capuchon. The top rim, however, was to the same height as the capuchon on the earlier chimneys; this made the body of the chimney slightly longer and again various lengths were fashioned to suit particular classes. The earlier pattern became generally extinct on Midland built engines in the 1940s.

A particular note is required in respect of the Midland designs which became part of the LMS standard range – that is, the Compounds, class 2 4-4-0s and class 4 0-6-0s. The formation of the LMS in 1923 and the adoption of a composite loading gauge resulted in *most* new engines of Midland design having shorter chimneys but to the same general pattern, and lower domes also. This was to cause complications later on. Despite the lower LMS general loading gauge, new Stanier chimneys to the Midland gauge were also produced in due course, so instead of gradually conforming to the new standard, the MR built engines began to display both long and short chimneys. This situation did not remain stable, however, and new chimneys for these classes were 2ft 0in and 1ft 7in (nominal).

Further complication lay with the domes, in particular those on the G7S boilers of the class 2 4-4-0s and class 4 0-6-0s. Until 1924 these had high domes with covers 2ft 1¼in height, but the new boilers had low domes with covers 1ft 9½in. Boiler changes therefore brought a continuous succession of loading gauge restriction changes, and four combinations of chimney and dome -

1 Short chimney and low dome
2 Short chimney and high dome
3 Long chimney and low dome
4 Long chimney and high dome

This clearly produced difficulties when considering engines for the Northern Division, with its lower height limit. To readily identify engines prohibited from the Northern Division, Job No.5174 was issued on 3 August 1939, requiring a 3½in diameter blue disc to be stencilled 5in above the engine number on each cabside of the engines with high chimneys or domes. The colour was Azure Blue, BS colour No.4 and the work was to be carried out at the sheds as well as on engines in works. This instruction also required the fitting of short chimneys to all engines with long chimneys and low domes as engines passed through workshops for any class of repair. This involved a total of 504 engines.

There were, however, 168 engines still running which had boilers with high domes, as well as seven spare boilers of this type. A month later, on 4 September 1939, a further instruction was issued to alter the fifty-one LMS-built engines with short chimneys and high domes in this group with long chimneys. This would then leave only matching chimneys and domes, whether long or short, on any particular boiler. With the onset of war, it was decided (on 27 September 1939) to curtail expenditure as far as possible by fitting short chimneys to those with low domes only as renewals were required. This effectively scuppered the scheme, for some boilers with high domes also remained in service and so long as these were fitted to other engines, those with 'blue spots' would constantly change.

The economy instructions had a list of engines with the various combinations of long chimney/high dome but none had short chimneys and high domes at that date – though several were known at other times. The list also gave the boiler numbers of the high dome engines. It did not of course show which still had chimneys with capuchon and which had Stanier long chimneys. The Midland engines are listed below and it will be seen that, by deduction, only eight of them conformed to the composite gauge, with short chimneys and low domes. These were class 2 4-4-0s Nos.433, 434, 436 and 463, as well as class 4 0-6-0s Nos.4007, 4008, 4009 and 4016.

Top. 0-6-0 No.1589 illustrates the pre-1902 standard lamp iron positions – top of smokebox, smokebox door, two over left buffer and one over right buffer.

Middle. 2-4-0 No. 227 shows the post-1902 lamp irons on the smaller boilers. On the larger boilers the top bracket was placed on the smokebox door and the handrail fitted <u>below</u> the top hinge, though exceptions did occur.

Bottom. The well coaled bunker of 0-4-4T No. 1409 shows the mid-position of the top lamp iron, so placed to allow a standard height driver of 5ft 6in to reach it from track level.

The gradual process of changing to short/low fittings continued through the war but long Stanier chimneys were still in use into the BR period and of course, high dome covers could conceal low domes beneath. Comment is made in the individual class chapters. Through all this, the little 0-4-0Ts displayed several generations of stovepipe chimneys – just to add interest to the historian's task!

Chimney/Dome status August 1939
Long chimneys and low domes
Class 2 4-4-0
332, 337, 351, 353, 356, 359, 362, 394, 395, 397, 400, 401, 404, 405, 407, 408-416, 419, 420, 422, 423, 425, 426, 427, 432, 438, 439, 443, 446, 447, 450, 452, 453, 455, 458, 461, 464, 468, 470, 472, 477, 478, 482, 487, 490-493, 496, 497, 498, 500, 501, 505-513, 516, 519, 521, 523, 524, 526, 528-537, 539, 540, 541, 543, 545, 546, 547, 548, 551, 553, 554, 557, 560, 561, 562
(100 out of 157 engines)

Class 4 4-4-0 Compound
1000-1006, 1009-1015, 1017-1034, 1036-1041, 1043, 1044
(40 out of 45 engines)

Class 4 0-6-0
3835-3845, 3847-3851, 3853-3874, 3877, 3879-3886, 3888-3893, 3895, 3897, 3899, 3901-3909, 3911- 3913, 3916-3921, 3923-3925, 3927-3929, 3931-3942, 3945-3960, 3963, 3965-3976, 3978, 3979, 3980, 3983-3988, 3990-3992, 3994-3999, 4000-4003, 4005, 4006, 4010, 4011, 4013, 4014, 4017, 4021, 4022, 4025, 4026
(154 out of 192 engines)

Long chimneys and high domes
Class 2 4-4-0
364, 370, 377, 396, 402, 403, 406, 417, 418, 421, 424, 430, 437, 444, 448, 454, 456, 459, 462, 466, 471, 479, 480, 483, 484, 485, 486, 488, 489, 494, 495, 499, 502, 503, 504, 514, 515, 517, 518, 520, 522, 525, 527, 538, 542, 544, 549, 550, 552, 555, 556, 558, 559
(53 out of 157 engines)

Class 4 4-4-0 Compound
1007, 1008, 1016, 1035, 1042
(5 out of 45 engines)

Class 4 0-6-0
3846, 3853, 3875, 3876, 3878, 3887, 3894, 3896, 3898, 3900, 3910, 3914, 3915, 3922, 3926, 3930, 3943, 3944, 3961, 3962, 3964, 3977, 3981, 3982, 3989, 3993, 4004, 4012, 4015, 4018, 4019, 4020, 4023, 4024
(34 out of 192 engines)

4 Domes
The majority of the Kirtley engines had tall parallel sided domes surmounted by Salter valves and were of somewhat plain aspect; the Johnson domes (which also had Salter valves) were much more shapely and attractive. His early design (to drawing 74-193) had a pronounced bell mouth and this pattern was fitted to the 6 and 1252 Class 0-4-4Ts, 1102 Class 0-6-0Ts, the early 2-4-0s and the 1312 and 1327 Class 4-4-0s, all turned

Top. No. 437 with block style front number plate and exhaust steam injector exemplifies one of the hybrids with a tall Stanier chimney and low dome. S. Summerson collection.

Middle. The bogie splash plates on Compound No. 1044 were secured to the buffer beam and the guard irons. Kentish Town 19 May 1923.

Bottom. 483 class No. 501 at Kentish Town in the late 1930s retains the parallel Fowler chimney with capuchon and tall dome cover, as originally fitted. S Summerson collection.

out between 1874 and 1877. A neater pattern then appeared, to drawing 78-990 and this, with minor variations, remained the standard for boilers with Salter safety valves. The levers on these valves, from the fulcrum to the top of the spring, were usually straight but with his typical eye for proportion and symmetry, Johnson prepared a version with a reverse curve, downwards to shorter springs. This was used on the condensing 0-4-4Ts built from 1882 and on passenger tender engines (with shorter chimneys, up to 3ft 1in) from 1896. The later 4-2-2 Spinners of the 115 and 2601 series were thus similarly fitted. The entry on the drawing list for the 115 Class uses the less decorous word 'bent' to describe the safety valve levers, the niceties of description presumably being lost on the drawing office staff. This detail was also introduced in the 2421 series of the 150 Class 4-4-0s of 1899, and on the following 60 class, as well as the 2441 Class 0-6-0Ts.

Closed domes were introduced with the adoption of Ramsbottom safety valves in 1900; these were similar to the Johnson pattern, but of course there was no opening for the Salter valve. This was used on all new boilers until February 1906, when a new design, narrower 10½in radius curve and a small flat top with securing nut was introduced on 4-4-0s rebuilt with H boilers. This then became standard on the H, G7 and G7S boilers on the various class 2 4-4-0s and class 4 0-6-0s only, all other boilers and classes retaining the more shapely earlier pattern. These new domes were 2ft 1¼in high but, as indicated above, in connection with the LMS composite loading gauge a lower version was produced with a cover 1ft 9½in in height. This had a broad flat top with no secur-

ing nut and sharply radiused top corners. A number of high dome covers subsequently served as replacements for the earlier pattern on other classes, notably the Belpaire 4-4-0s. From 1917, Belpaire versions of Johnson A, B and C boilers were introduced and these all had closed domes. Again, the Johnson pattern was repeated and though flat topped dome covers appeared on the four 2441 Class 0-6-0Ts rebuilt before grouping, this does not seem to have been perpetuated for subsequent rebuilds of this class.

Although no official references have been found, it seems highly probable that, with a typical MR eye for economy, the standard routine was to re-use the Johnson dome covers on the new Belpaire boilers, fitted with a top closure plate or patch. Certainly when 0-6-0T No.1708 was being restored, its dome was found to be of copper with a top patch. A number of 2-4-0s and 0-6-0s were transferred to the LNW section by the LMS and, remarkably, a few of these acquired LNW Webb dome covers whilst 'away'. This must have been carried out at sheds as they were not normally shopped at Crewe. These dome covers had slightly tapering sides and a sharper radius at the base.

5 Boiler Hand Rails

In order to give a reasonably consistent height above the running plate the position of the hand rails varied with the pitch and diameter of the boiler. Thus the rails on the 1322A Class 0-4-0STs which were mounted on the saddle tank were in line with the top of the boiler; at the other end of the scale, on the Compounds, the rails were set just above the centre line of the boiler. This generally

maintained the rail at a convenient position, 3ft 6in to 4ft above the running plate. In the Kirtley period, engines had separate side rails and a horizontal rail across the upper part of the smokebox front above the doors, but with Johnson's adoption of circular smokebox doors a continuous rail was fitted instead. This passed round the smokebox front above the door in line with the boiler contour, and remained the standard for new engines until 1905. The last to receive this pattern were the first ten Deeley compounds built between October and December 1905. The Kirtley 0-6-0s and 0-6-0 well tanks were an exception, however; when rebuilt with Johnson boilers they got separate hand rails round the smokebox, though the ten 'Poplar' tanks had the standard pattern.

The rails round the top of the smokebox on the larger boilers were rather high to reach, as were the top lamp brackets, but in this case Deeley acted quickly and from early 1906 separate rails were fitted, with a straight rail across the smokebox door below the top hinge strap. All new engines from Compound No.1010 (old number) onwards were so fitted. In the first few months some rebuilt 4-4-0s still received the continuous rail but the new pattern was quickly applied to the large boiler engines.

The 4-2-2 Spinners when fitted with new smokeboxes, plus a small number of Kirtley double framed goods engines rebuilt with D or E boilers, all had straight hand rails. By contrast the smaller engines with A, B, C and P class boilers (as well as the 0-4-0STs with J or J1 boilers) retained the continuous hand rail and the B boilered Kirtley double framed goods engines their separate curved smokebox rails. This state of af-

483 class No. 454 has a replacement tall Stanier chimney and also the blue disc above the engine number, indicating its prohibition from the Northern Division. Note also the additional rain gutter just above the cab cut out which is absent on engine No. 501 in the previous photograph. S Summerson collection

fairs was reviewed in 1918 and a Drawing Office statement of 11 July 1918 summarised the position, with changes to be made. Engines with A, B, C and P boilers, but not the 0-4-0STs, were to have the continuous rails removed and straight smokebox rails fitted instead. Drawings for the necessary alterations were issued on 12 March 1917. These new rails were usually fitted above the top hinge strap, but occasionally below it. Exceptions are noted in the class chapters.

As the Kirtley goods had low pitched boilers and hand rails 15 inches above the boiler centre line, they were to retain their old curved hand rail round the smokebox door. Photographic evidence nonetheless suggests that straight hand rails were subsequently fitted, so that all except the small Johnson shunters then carried the standard arrangement.

6 Cabs
General
Cabs to protect the engine crew from the elements did not form part of the standard layout on locomotives generally for very many years and it was the 1870s before Kirtley fitted any Midland engines with a cab. The first passenger engines to be fitted were the 890 Class, his penultimate 2-4-0s which first appeared in July 1871. Contractor-built goods engines nevertheless continued to appear without cabs until 1873, though Derby had begun fitting cabs to new and earlier goods engines late in the previous year.

The new cabs took two forms. On the first batch of 2-4-0s and on the earlier straight framed 0-6-0s the rectangular side sheets were at first retained and a cab section simply added, but on the new 0-6-0s the previously universal side sheets were dispensed with and a new 'one piece' cab fitted. This then became the standard arrangement on all the Kirtley 0-6-0s and the later Derby-built 890s. Subsequent Kirtley and Johnson passenger engines followed suit. However, when the Kirtley 170 and 800 Class 2-4-0s received cabs, the earlier form was used, retaining the side sheets. This panel-plus-cab layout was revived much later, on the 2606 (Belpaire) 4-4-0s of 1900 and the first five Compounds; Johnson also used the form on all his 0-6-0s and it was continued by Deeley for new goods engines until 1906. By contrast the many other 4-4-0 classes had the 'one piece' cab sides, integrated with the rear coupled splashers. The two Kirtley 0-6-0 well tank classes were never fitted with cabs and contrived to retain their simple weatherboards with short rear extension until withdrawn. Thus the primitive arrangements provided in the early days remained to be seen until the last well tank was withdrawn in 1928!

In contrast, the first Johnson shunting tanks of 1874 were given overall cabs (double cabs in Midland parlance) but their successors, built in batches from 1878 to 1892, had 'single' cabs only (often referred to as half cabs today). Double cabs were used thereafter and had

been provided on the 0-4-4 passenger tanks since 1875 except in the case of engines fitted with condensing apparatus for working over the Metropolitan widened lines. The successive batches of these engines had front weatherboards only up to 1885 and when it was decided to fit several more of the 1885-built engines with condensing apparatus (to 0.757 of April 1888) the previously fitted overall cabs were taken off and weatherboards substituted! The reason for this and the rule of 'no cabs on condensers' is unclear but may have been related to perceived visibility problems, or the use of the Smiths simple vacuum brake on these trains. The rule remained until the early 1890s; Kirtley 0-4-4T No.692 was rebuilt with a Johnson boiler in December 1890 and turned out with a new weatherboard, but subsequent condensing engines built from 1893 had conventional double cabs, and all the earlier ones were fitted in the 1890s.

The Spartan Kirtley cab and the Johnson version after it, gave very little protection, though it remained the standard until Johnson's retirement. It fell to Deeley to provide something better. The first 4-4-0s rebuilt with H boilers in 1904-5 got new one piece cabs with short roofs and rounded eaves which did not extend back as far as the side sheets. These were really no improvement on what had gone before. Rebuilt 0-6-0s merely had longer and deeper side sheets with the old cab adapted and refitted. However, No.657 (2451 in 1907), the first of the Kirtley double framed goods engines given an H boiler, in July 1905, had a new cab design with a much longer roof, extending beyond the rear of the side sheets and supported by hand rails behind the semi-circular cut-outs. This was then adopted for future rebuilding of both passenger and goods engines, except that on the former a reversion was soon made to a cab cut-out with two radii, as before.

Later, in October 1905, the first Deeley Compounds appeared and these had a modified version of this cab, with a piece cut out on each side at the rear behind the hand rail, above the access to the footplate between engine and tender. This gave greater headroom at eaves level for the crew getting on and off and this modified cab was subsequently adopted as standard by Fowler. It was used on all new MR-type construction up to the last of the 4F 0-6-0s, in 1941.

The original long roof pattern appeared briefly on rebuilt 4-4-0s but was quickly superseded by the modified version. No.2211 (436 in 1907) rebuilt in November 1905 had the earlier pattern but No.2185 (408 in 1907) rebuilt in February 1906 had the new type. As with other detail changes the cut off point was not clear cut and several engines received the earlier style in March and April 1906. On the goods engines by contrast, the original long cab design was retained on all the subsequent rebuilds with H boilers up to 1915.

The last twenty H boilered 0-6-0s built in 1908 had 'one piece' cabs with

the rear splasher combined, as on the 4-4-0s. The class 4 0-6-0s which followed from 1911 had similar cabs but separate rear splashers. This completed the evolution of Midland cab design but several related matters must now be considered.

7 Cab Ventilators
The Midland maintained a distinctly equivocal attitude to cab roof ventilation. None of the short cabs of Johnson and Deeley design was fitted, reasonably enough, though all the double cab tank engines had ventilators. The first of these, the 1102 Class 0-6-0Ts, had a circular hinged flap which closed flush to the roof, but subsequent goods and passenger tanks (from 0.289 of 8 April 1880 at least) had double rectangular sliding vents set across the cab roof. A new type was introduced on the 0-6-4Ts and Deeley 0-4-0Ts of 1907. This comprised a raised moveable rectangular 'lid' supported on hinged arms at each corner, overhanging a rim onto which the lid closed. It could be raised at an angle forward or back, or horizontally as desired. It was then used as standard on long roof cabs of tender engines and this is where the anomalies become apparent.

The first tender engines with long roofs to have ventilators were the last twenty H boiler 0-6-0s Nos.3815-3834 of 1908. No official documentation has come to light on the subject but the evidence shows that ventilators were only fitted thereafter to new engines or engines which were fitted with new cabs, usually in the course of rebuilding. Thus, when G7 boilers were fitted to class 2 4-4-0s in the period 1909-11, only the rebuilt 1808 Class Nos.378-393 along with Nos.460 and 465 which had new cabs acquired ventilators – likewise the Belpaire 4-4-0s (700-779 in 1907) and first five Compounds (1000-1004 in 1907) when superheated, received new cabs with ventilators. So did the 483 Class rebuilds, but not the 990 Class or the remaining Compounds. The Compounds later became part of an LMS standard class and subsequently acquired cab vents; the dates are not recorded but they were clearly fitted from the 1930s. It was a similar story on the smaller 0-6-0s. Those rebuilt with G7 boilers had new cabs with ventilators, as did the 1357 Class (3020-3129 in 1907) when given G6 boilers, whilst the 1142 Class (2900-3019 in 1907) were given second-hand Deeley cabs modified with a ventilator from H boiler rebuilds. On the other hand, when some of the 1798 Class (3190-3764 in 1907) were rebuilt with G6 boilers (replacing H or B boilers) by the LMS from 1925 the long cabs, where fitted, remained without ventilators.

The 2441 Class 0-6-0Ts (1900-59) when rebuilt with G5½ boilers had new cabs with raised ventilators. On all classes, these were frequently to be seen in the open position, demonstrating their usefulness; the reason for not adapting earlier cabs therefore, remains obscure. The fact that the vents stood proud of the roof even when closed, enables easy identification of the engines so fitted.

8 Driver's name and station tablets

The agreeable practice of indicating the driver's name and his depot on the cabside was introduced in 1909. 0.3577 was issued on 10 May that year to cover the fixing of small brackets to the cabside of 'no 2 and 3 class passenger engines Nos.328-562, 700-79, 990-9 and 1000-44'. It is of interest to note that the latter two classes had not then been upgraded to class 4. The order was extended on 18 June 1913 to cover the class 1 passenger engines, 2-4-0s, some 4-4-0s and the 4-2-2 Spinners, Nos.1-281, 300-27 and 600-94, the items 'to be fixed at outstations'.

Strangely, very few photographs show the name plates in position. Clearly they would be retained in the driver's possession when not on the engine, which would account for their absence on shed photographs of solo engines. That they were used is not in question – V.R. Webster recorded them at Leicester in 1920 and the brackets remained long after the practice fell into disuse, as the engine went down the social scale, so to speak.

9 Rain Gutters

On both the short and long Deeley cabs and their successors which had rounded eaves, the rain strip was positioned some distance up the roof. The roof below it was painted as the cabside and on the standard long roof the rain strip passed just above the rear cut-out section. This layout meant that rain falling on the lower roof went straight on to the enginemen if their heads were outside the cab. Eventually the problem was addressed by the LMS in the Stanier era, but only in respect of engines regarded as LMS standards – the Midland class

2 superheater and Compound 4-4-0s and the class 4 0-6-0s. The work of fitting eave rain strips was covered by Job No.4957, issued on 22 October 1936. Successive Derby orders for a hundred engines then appeared, commencing with 0.9885 of 9 December 1936 to cover those engines maintained at Derby. All Compounds were shown as maintained at Horwich on the Job number instructions and the Derby Orders do not refer to them! One assumes the paperwork was regularised later.

The standard class 3 0-6-0Ts were dealt with later and this also involved the rebuilt MR 2441 Class, Nos.1900-1959 (by then Nos.7200-7259). Job No.5330 was issued on 10 March 1943 for the work, with the following note - 'With the view of eliminating the discomfort caused to enginemen during inclement weather it has been decided to weld rain gutters to the cabs of the above engines'. As the work was charged to maintenance, detailed records are not available; while all *should* have been fitted, odd engines escaped, No.43854 for example, recorded in 1963. So far as the tank engines are concerned, a circular letter dated 9 July 1957 noted the work as complete and Job 5330 closed, some fourteen years after its instigation.

10 Canvas Screens

In the 1914-18 War there was perceived to be a danger of glare from open firehole doors at night, giving away a train's position to enemy Zeppelins. In November 1915 a series of sketches was issued to show an arrangement for canvas screens between various tenders and cabs. The fitting of 1,845 tender engines was authorised on 15 February 1916, but only two weeks later the instruction was al-

tered, to apply only to engines stationed in the London district and on the LTS line. The fitting of screens was discontinued after 19 June 1917 but those screens already fitted were ordered 'to be kept in repair'. The number of engines equipped is not known but several were photographed showing part of the screen in the short period covering this exercise.

11 Tank Engine Details - Footsteps and Hand Rails

To facilitate access to the footplate of tank engines, a general order was issued on 28 March 1903: 'All passenger and goods tank engines are to be fitted with additional steps and hand rails as they came into shops for repairs. The distance of the lower step from rail level made to correspond with the step at the trailing end'. The new steps were fitted behind the footplate valence just in front of the side tanks, where long hand rails were fitted on the front of the tank. New passenger tender engines were given front steps from 1902 and goods engines followed suit from 1908. The steps were flat, but the risk of boots slipping off resulted in the LMS period in the outer corners, or in some cases the whole of the side edges, being angled up as a safety measure.

12 Tank Engine Details - Coal Rails

At about the same time as the general introduction of coal rails on tenders an order of 23 March 1892 was issued to fit 'railings round the bunkers of all goods and passenger tank engines (which are not fitted already) as they came into shops'. This increased the bunker capacity but also increased the likelihood of damage to back cab windows, especially when coaling the bunkers.

The wartime anti-glare canvas screens authorised in 1916 as applied to a 2-4-0. Note the cabside brackets to hold the driver's name plate.

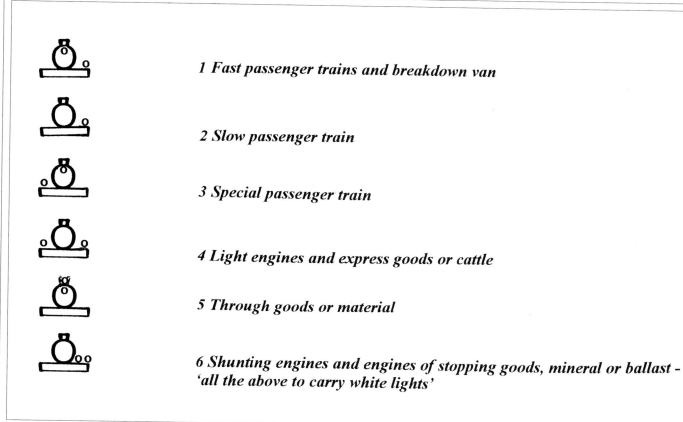

1 Fast passenger trains and breakdown van

2 Slow passenger train

3 Special passenger train

4 Light engines and express goods or cattle

5 Through goods or material

6 Shunting engines and engines of stopping goods, mineral or ballast - 'all the above to carry white lights'

13 Tank Engine Details - Cab Windows

Window glass in the rear spectacle plates of double cab four and six wheel tank engines was easily broken during coaling, a nuisance largely resolved following the fitting of wrought iron bars to protect the glass, from August 1905. The work was carried out at the sheds as well as on engines in the shops and was quickly executed. It is perhaps surprising that it was not done earlier.

14 Lamp Irons

The practice of displaying a headlamp and therefore the provision of a bracket or brackets to carry them dates back to the early days of railways. The earliest mention of lamps for a specific purpose on the Midland is in the Working Timetable for December 1868, in which lamp or disc positions are specified to show the *destination* of goods trains working over the newly opened widened lines to depots south of the Thames. These trains were to carry lights and discs:

'To and from Herne Hill, by day – one square white board with diagonal black cross and by night, two purple lights on buffer beam

'To Battersea by day – one square plain white board and by night, two purple lights, one on the smokebox and one on the buffer beam'.

Thus one smokebox and two buffer beam brackets were required on the condenser fitted tank engines working this traffic from the outset. Up to January 1872 the position of the white board on the Battersea goods trains was not specified but in the WTT for March 1872 this is shown as 'centre of buffer beam' so that by this early date four bracket positions were in use on the engines work-ing over the Metropolitan line.

The general use of lamps to indicate the *class* of train, however, dates from later in 1872 and the September 1872 WTT contains the following prosaic statement: *'In order that Station Masters, Pointsmen, Platelayers and Porters and all other servants of the Company may be able in the night to distinguish the type of train that is approaching by the headlights on the engine, it has been decided to adopt the following arrangement of headlights and on and from September 2nd, engines will carry headlights as in the diagrams above:*

Separate instructions for the Derby-Manchester line followed, along with a note that this 'did not interfere with instructions on lights and discs for engines when running over other Company's lines'.

A bracket was also provided at the foot of the chimney as well as on the smokebox door and two over the left-hand buffer. There was no centre bracket on the buffer beam as on the London district tanks. Passenger engines carried only one bracket over the left buffer as they were not normally used for class 6 duties and not all of them carried a smokebox door bracket as well as that at the foot of the chimney, which was required for class 5 duties. A table of 'Discs and Headlamps to be carried by engines' in Appendix No.11 of 18 April 1878 records for the first time a bracket position at the foot of the chimney, for engines working to London district destinations. Thus the London tank engines then carried the same number of brackets as other engines except that the buffer beam positions differed – one in the centre and one over the left-hand buffer, instead of two in the latter position. The No.9 Appendix of 1 October 1876 instructed that *'Engine headlights must always be carried in their proper positions, whether lighted or not.'*

While the subject of headlamp codes is beyond the realm of this volume, this initial set is shown for its intrinsic interest and primarily because it shows the lamp iron positions which remained standard for the next thirty years. (As an aside, it may be noted that despite subsequent changes and standardisation of codes the Somerset and Dorset passenger train headcode remained unaltered from this original MR code until final closure in 1966!) To provide a satisfactory arrangement for carrying discs or boards on the London district tank engines additional tall brackets (except at the chimney foot) were provided just behind the lamp brackets to carry the boards/discs; when not required they were merely turned round to face the engine. The central bracket on the front buffer was hinged so it could fall sideways. This was to avoid fouling the smokebox door when opened for servicing.

These 'London District' brackets were carried by all the condensing engines as well as the various batches of 0-6-0Ts built for working to Poplar. They also appeared on other tank engines allocated to Kentish Town or Cricklewood, principally class 1 0-6-0Ts used for trip working over the Dudding Hill and Acton route, to the south from Cricklewood. The tall brackets also carried the destination boards displayed by London district local passenger trains. These are first referred to in the No.12 Appendix of 1 December 1879: *'Midland Passenger trains running between St Pancras and Earls Court must carry the prescribed destination board and lighted headlamps and tail lights by day and night'*. This service had commenced on 1 May 1878 and ceased in 1880. The Appendices make no further reference to destination boards until December 1888:

Destination boards on Midland City and suburban passenger trains
'Engines must carry a Board in front to indicate for the information of passengers the destination of the trains.'

A drawing of March 1887 shows 'Destination Boards (Metropolitan Railway)' for this purpose. These boards continued in use until the 1930s and the latest confirmed date known by the author is 24 August 1938. The onset of war clearly put an end to the practice which latterly, in any case, appeared to be very intermittent.

The relatively minor matter of lamp bracket dimensions was pronounced upon by the Railway Clearing House in 1899, when standard dimensions were adopted to resolve difficulties over lamps not fitting. In 1903, in the interests of uniformity, a fundamental change of headcodes took place under the direction of the Railway Clearing House. On the Midland this involved dispensing with the smokebox door bracket and one of the left hand buffer brackets and the provision of a bracket in the centre of the buffer beam. The new codes were set out in No.7 Supplement to Appendix 20 of 12 June 1903. Prior to this, a Derby Order of 2 February 1902 had been issued, to cover the provision of the additional lamp irons.

This change in lamp bracket positions is a useful date marker for photographs. The introduction of 4ft 8in diameter boilers from 1900 increased the height of the lamp bracket on top of the smokebox and so made for difficulties of reach to attach lamps, the bracket in many cases being over 6ft from the running plate. Around 1907-9 a number of piston valve H boiler 4-4-0s had a footstep positioned on the right-hand side of the smokebox front, level with the bottom of the door, as well as a hand hold on the same side near the bracket, to ease the changing of these top lamps.

Class 2 4-4-0 No.381, rebuilt with a G7 belpaire boiler in August 1910, was one of the last to have the bracket on top of the smokebox but thereafter, on engines with the large boilers and on the 'Princess' 4-2-2s, it was repositioned on the smokebox door above the top hinge strap. On the bunker end of tank engines, the top lamp was always placed in a mid-position on the bunker back so it could be reached form track level. Engines fitted with London district brackets were an exception, with the top bracket fitted centrally at the top of the bunker. This gave sufficient space below to allow placing and removal of the middle board/disc on its bracket. This in turn was just above the lamp bracket in the centre of the buffer beam. There were no more changes to lamp brackets, but a further headcode alteration took place in May 1918 – this provides a further date marker in respect of some non-passenger trains.

15 Lamps

According to Ahrons, by the early 1880s headlamps carried the driver's name and shed, but from 1902 the lamps displayed instead the locomotive number and district. The practice became increasingly difficult to maintain and eventually fell into disuse. Until the early years of the century, rape oil was used in the lamps but 0.2809 of 17 June 1904 covered the alterations necessary for all lamps to burn petroleum oil, marking an interesting and long lasting change in practice.

16 Footplate and Buffer Height

On the later Kirtley classes, until 1869, the standard footplate height was generally 4ft 2¾in from rail level, but with the introduction of the final design of double framed 0-6-0 which first appeared in August 1869 this was changed to 4ft 0¾in. It is immediately apparent when compared to earlier 0-6-0s, as it resulted in more pronounced 'humps' over the wheel centre in the running plate of the new engines. On these and subsequent classes, the buffers were positioned almost centrally top to bottom, on the buffer beam but on the earlier designs, the buffers, to maintain the same height, were nearer the lower edge of the beam. It is thus easy to identify other classes with the lower footplate.

Johnson continued the 4ft 0¾in footplate on all his tank engine designs except the 0-4-0STs (they were non standard, after all) but reverted to the old standard of 4ft 2¾in from mid-1877 for the tender engines. Thus the 1 and 1282 Class 2-4-0s, 1312 class 4-4-0s and 1142 Class 0-6-0s had the lower footplate and the remainder, 4ft 2¾in. The effect of this could be seen when comparing the 1142 Class 0-6-0s with the 1698 Class of 1885, both having 4ft 11in wheels. The latter clearly have smaller splashers arising from the higher footplate. Deeley continued the same standard but the 483 Class 4-4-0 superheater rebuilds, 700 Class 4-4-0s and the Compounds, had 4ft 8in running plates and a drop panel above the buffer beam.

A Locomotive Drawing Office statement dated 9 February 1910 has particulars of engine and tender buffers, giving the height from rail with 3in tyres for all classes. The figure varied from 3ft 4⅛in

No. 1505, a 1400 class 2-4-0 with 6ft 8½in driving wheels, about 1906. Note the brass 1 power class on the cabside, running plate 4ft 2¾in above rail and the one-piece final design of Johnson chimney.

0-4-4T No. 1298 near Wincanton in 1947 shows the sliding cab vent open on the Johnson double cab. Note also the 'wrought iron grids' to drawing 05.6354 'to protect glasses from coal' on the rear spectacle plate.

on the 0-4-4Ts Nos.1266-1430 to 3ft 5¾in on the 4-2-2s Nos.608, 609 and 620-684. Then comes the following note: '*The standard was at first 3ft 4in for all engines except goods tanks which were 3ft 4½in the tyres being 2 ⅛ in thick. It was altered about 1877 to 3ft 5in for passenger and goods engines with 2¾in tyres, the tanks remaining as before, viz Bogie 3ft 4¼in and Goods 3ft 4¾in except the latest lot of goods tanks (1900-59) which were made the same as standard 3ft 5in, all with 2¾in tyres. The present standard for new engines is 3ft 5in with 3in tyres. Centre to centre of buffers 5ft 8in for all engines and diameter of buffer heads 1ft 1in except for 2000 Class 0-6-4T and saddle tanks.*'

17 Wheel Splashers

Kirtley driving wheel splashers were open or slotted, in an attractive manner. These were replaced by closed in splashers when these engines were given Johnson boilers – though sometimes they had been replaced even before that. The work was carried out in the 1880s, and an article on the Kirtley singles by E.L. Ahrons in *Locomotives and Railways* for March 1901 declared that '*the old open splashers were retained on all these engines until about 1887*'.

Johnson's 2-4-0s and 4-4-0s all had closed splashers. On the earlier engines, the coupled wheel splashers with their brass beading were shaped with a short flattened section, where the splasher line dipped close to the running plate between the coupled wheels. From 1881-83, the line of the splasher top became a sweeping curve of considerably more attractive form and the earlier

engines were then provided with splashers to the new configuration, illustrating Johnson's constant attention to detail and appearance.

18 Bogie Splash Plates

When an engine took water from troughs, there was frequently an overflow from the filled tank. Where this occurred with the leading engine of a double headed train, it was found to cause some problems with water affecting the bogie bearings of the train engine. Two rectangular plates were therefore fitted below the front buffer beams of the principal class 2, 3 and 4 4-4-0s to shield the bogie axleboxes from the

water. The plates were produced to sketch No.1455 of 30 September 1909, termed 'screens for bogie axleboxes'. It was noted that class 3 4-4-0 No.769 and Compound No.1044 were already fitted. The screens were removed, so far as can be judged from photographic evidence, in the 1920s.

Perhaps the last word in this chapter can be left to E.S. Cox writing in *Chronicles of Steam* (Ian Allan 1967): '*Although Midland engine designs as a whole did not appear to be very progressive, their mechanical integrity was superb for their day, and detail design was far ahead in quality over that of any of the other constituents of the LMS*'.

4-2-2 No. 685 'Princess of Wales' in store at Kentish Town in 1920 showing the wartime canvas screen arrangement applied to a number of Kentish Town engines. Note also the brackets on the cabside for the driver's name and station tablet. The removal of two of the tender springs shows the fixing brackets to the frame.

Straight framed Kirtley 0-6-0 No. 450 was built by Fairbairn in September 1860 with a 1,400 gallon tender. It is seen here after rebuilding in June 1874 with Johnson chimney and cab and 5ft 6in firebox Kirtley boiler.

The tender on No. 2632 of the Kirtley 700 class (at Hasland on 9 May 1932) has a Johnson pattern 2,000 gallon tank fitted to the original frames. The standard Johnson tender front can be seen and also the modified coping pattern and vertical hand hold on the tender side. These readily distinguished the rebuilds. S Summerson collection.

The greater tank depth of the rebuilt 2,200 gallon Kirtley tenders is readily apparent in this view of No. 2858, at Derby in the late 1920s. Having the Johnson tank layout, they also had the 1902-8 style front toolbox flared down to the tender sides. Note also the long vertical hand hold.
S Summerson collection.

Chapter 9 - Tenders
'Where the old horseshoe tanks are worn out they are to be replaced with new 2,000 gallon tanks'

KIRTLEY TENDERS
General Survey

Official records of Kirtley tenders are very thin on the ground, especially concerning the early classes and previous authors have offered little comment, doubtless for this reason. The Locomotive Committee minutes authorising the purchase of engines from contractors rarely quoted the tender capacity, though in the case of the ten 232 Class 0-6-0s authorised on 17 December 1850 the tenders were specified at 1,000 gallons. Earlier Jenny Lind 2-2-2s of 1847 are known to have had 800 gallon tenders. On 18 March 1851 the Locomotive Committee resolved *that the offer of Hawthorns to supply four tenders to hold 1,400 gallons be accepted*. These were for 240 Class 0-6-0s, ordered in August 1850. This pointed the way ahead and the following 260 Class 0-6-0s for which a specification survives, were required to have a tender with *'tank to hold not less than 1500 gallons'*.

A short list of tenders broken up, where the capacity is shown, is contained in *Costs of engines, repairs, train mileage, machinery, stores, running expenses etc.* (PRO Rail 491 879). This is dated July 1883 and lists tenders from seven various passenger and goods classes built in the 1850s, all of them shown at 1,400 gallons capacity.

F.H. Clarke's records show that, generally, the straight framed 0-6-0s had 1,400 gallon tenders but his list of c.1900 is, of course, too late to show many of the earlier tenders, which had either been broken up with their engines or replaced with later examples. It may therefore reasonably be inferred that 1,400 gallon tenders were the norm throughout the 1850s, though an increase in capacity to 1,600 gallons was effected in the early 1860s. The 80 Class 2-4-0s of 1862 and the first 480 Class 0-6-0s which appeared from Stephensons in September 1863 were given 1,600 gallon tenders. Radford, additionally, records that the 150 Class 2-4-0s of 1859 also had tenders of this size. On the other hand, some of the 30 Class 2-2-2s of 1863-64 were paired with 1,400 gallon tenders. However, the 1,600 gallon version remained standard. The final increase in size during the Kirtley period came in 1869, when 2,000 gallon tenders were introduced on 0-6-0s and subsequently for 2-4-0s, including those engines ordered but not delivered until after Johnson's arrival in 1873.

As to the number of tenders built, it is not possible to be precise, but from available information and on the basis that one tender was built for each engine, some round figures can be deduced. This gives about 368 tenders of 1,400 gallons and 313 of 1,600 gallons built between 1850 and 1869. There were ten 2,000 gallon tenders for the rebuilt 230 Class tank engines, and some 453 more built between 1869 and 1874.

Details

Details varied considerably, especially among the 1,400 and 1,600 gallon tenders. A basic distinction which remained throughout, however, was wheel size, for goods and passenger tenders. The former were 3ft 6ins, diameter, the latter six inches bigger at 4ft. These sizes increased as thicker tyres were used, increasing eventually to 3ft 9in and 4ft 3in. These differences were very useful for identification purposes where tenders were subsequently changed.

The wheelbase of the 1,600 and 2,000 gallon tenders was 6ft 0in + 6ft 0in but was less on the 1,400 gallon size. The 1910 tender diagram shows the 1,600 gallon tender sides to be 3ft 11½in high to the top of the coping and 17ft long, while the 2,000 gallon tender sides were 4ft 4in high and 18ft long. Coal capacity was 2½ tons in each case. All the 1,400 gallon and some of the earlier 1,600 gallon tenders had tie-bars between the horns but the later 1,600 and 2,000 gallon ones had solid slotted outside frames. On the tie-bar tenders the shape of the framing varied considerably in the various batches. The tenders on Stephensons 130 Class 2-2-2s of 1852 had outside frames which formed a shallow gothic arch between the wheels. Others formed a continuous curve of varying radius, in many different shapes. An attractive feature of many of the earlier pattern frames was a small oval slot in the framing above the axle boxes but this was not present on some tie-bar 1,600 gallon or on any of the slotted tender frames. Springs were above the footplate, outside the tank. The later Kirtley engines, from 1869, both passenger and goods, had footplates at 4ft 0¾in, some 1¾in lower than the previous 4ft 2½in standard. The 2,000 gallon tenders were made to match and this resulted in minor variations in the shape of the cutout slot. These later passenger tenders were immediately recognisable as the slots were significantly shallower, with a relatively longer horizontal top section, in line with the top of the axle box frame opening. On all other tenders the top of the slot was above the axlebox frame opening. This feature is particularly helpful in tracing the subsequent transfers of these tenders to goods engines.

Tank construction varied even among tenders of the same capacity, revealed by the pattern of rivets visible on the sides. They divided into two principal forms. The first had two parallel vertical rows of rivet heads close together centrally on the tank side with short horizontal rows at intervals along the centre line of the tank, resembling the mathematical 'equals' sign. The second variation showed two sets of parallel vertical rivets dividing the tender into three 'panels' On other 2,000 gallon tenders a continuous double row of rivets was present along the horizontal centre line. The flared coping (the top edge) on all these

tenders was slightly tapered, rising from front to rear. Two tool boxes were normally provided at the rear until Board of Trade requirements had them transferred them to the tender front from 1904. The shape of the tank on all of these tenders was always referred to in official papers as 'horseshoe'. Whilst this clearly conveys an idea of the tank configuration a more accurate description would be 'U' shaped but such wording is clumsy and awkward so 'horseshoe' they were!

As built, the rear buffer beam on all these tenders was unlike the later conventional flat beam, but was crescent shaped with upper and lower horizontal plates, having vertical struts between. The draw hook was positioned centrally at the apex of the curve. Conventional buffer beams were subsequently fitted to the later tenders but photographs confirm that the old arrangement was still extant around the turn of the century. In some cases where new buffer beams were fitted the rear framing was shortened by nine inches, close to the rear of the tank.

The American Pullman Cars introduced in 1874 had the Miller automatic coupling, some six inches below the British drawhook. As this was incompatible with British couplings, modified buffer and draw arrangements had to be fitted to the tenders of 800 and 890 Class 2-4-0s allocated to the Pullman trains. Various coupling problems arose and the fittings were removed in 1879 and standard couplings provided.

Rebuilding

Replacement tanks to the original pattern were provided when required, but in 1898 a new drawing ('98-4498') was issued for a Johnson tank layout, of 2,000 gallons capacity. These were readily distinguishable from the originals by having flush sides, parallel coping flares with a simplified curve to the vertical at the front and a short vertical hand hold at the front end. (The originals had a horizontal hand hold).

Dimensionally they were similar to the Kirtley 2,000 gallon tanks and a note on the 1910 tender diagram for a subsequent variation reveals *'about 100 tanks made to outline drawing 98-4498'*. It is clear that they replaced both 1,600 and earlier 2,000 gallon tanks. F.H. Clarke noted 'about 454' 2,000 gallon tenders about 1900; that is, a few less than originally built. Fifty went to Italy with their engines in 1906 but the MR tender list of 30 September 1918 shows a total stock of 451, which can only be explained by the rebuilding of some 1,600 gallon tenders. Derby Order No.3714 was issued on 29 April 1910: *'Double framed goods tenders: Where the old horseshoe tanks on any of these tenders are worn out and there are no second-hand tanks of the same type available, they are to be replaced with new 2,000 gallon tanks, to outline drawing 98-4498 with tank draw-*

ing 10-8080'. These tanks had a rectangular tool box across the tender front and high front plate, in accordance with current practice. On the order was a note: *'five completed – tender shop 18 October 1920 all for DF* [Double Frame] *goods'.* With engine withdrawals and spare tenders becoming available there was no need for more rebuilds.

There was another version of rebuilt 2,000 gallon tender for which no information has been located. Whereas the two previously described were dimensionally similar to the originals, this third type had sides about four inches lower and easily recognisable. Only four engines have been noted with these tenders – No.2300, broken up in February 1921, Nos.2814 and 2829 withdrawn at the end of 1932 and No.2818, which acquired one about that time. There may have been others. The one on No.2818, remarkably, survived until 1947.

From 1907, in connection with the rebuilding of double framed ('DF') goods 0-6-0s with D or E boilers, some thirty tenders were rebuilt in similar style to the rebuilt 2,000 gallon tenders but with 2,200 gallon tanks without a well. These tenders held three tons of coal compared to 2½ tons on the 1,600 and 2,000 gallon tenders. They were readily distinguishable, with a height of 5ft 11in to the top of the coping (1ft 5in taller than the rebuilt 2,000 gallon tank) and long vertical hand holds.

Later History
Many of the earlier engines outlived their original tenders, by a considerable period. Johnson built some 235 tenders between 1874 and 1896 in addition to those required for new engines, as replacements for many of the Kirtley tenders. In particular new tenders were attached to all the larger 2-4-0s and many of the smaller ones, which initiated a complex cascade of tenders to the earlier 0-6-0s (in the main) so that the 1,400 gallon tenders were the first to be eliminated.

The records of F.H. Clarke indicate that all of these had been taken out of service by about 1900. Withdrawals and the availability of Johnson tenders meant the 1,600 gallon tenders declined until by 1918 only four remained in stock. Examples of 2,000 and 2,200 original and rebuilt tenders remained with surviving engines. All except one of the 2,000 gallon tenders had been withdrawn by 1936 and the last rebuilt 2,200 gallon tender was withdrawn in 1951. The surviving original pattern 2,000 gallon tender has been preserved with 2-4-0 No.158A. The detailed history of the tenders will be covered in the relevant class chapters.

JOHNSON TENDERS
As the size of locomotives increased, so the capacity of tenders grew to match. Consequently Johnson built tenders from 2,200 gallons to 4,500 gallons capacity between 1874 and 1902, as shown in Table 9B. The history is complex and information incomplete, but an overall picture of Johnson tender development can be divided into three principal periods.

Above. **From 1879 outside tender springs were adopted. Johnson 2-4-0 No. 179 at Bedford on 15 September 1934, with one of the few 2,950 gallon tenders to be rebuilt with the 1917 pattern high front plates. R.G. Jarvis/Mid Rail Photographs.**

Top. **When the 1698 class 0-6-0s were built in 1885-8, they received second-hand tenders from passenger engines, which in turn received new ones. No. 1767 has an inside spring 2,950 gallon tender from 2-4-0 No. 102, built in June 1877.**

1 The Early Years 1874-78
a) New Engines
The earliest 0-6-0s of the 1142 Class (120 engines) and the first twenty engines of the subsequent 1357 Class ordered between 1874 and 1877 had 2,350 gallon tenders, while the first fifty 2-4-0s and the first ten 4-4-0s ordered up to March 1876 had tenders of 2,750, 2,760 or 2,800 gallons. From September 1876 2,950 gallon tenders became standard for all passenger engines, remaining so until 1883.

b) Replacement Tenders
A recurring theme as the years passed was the need to replace older tenders and an initial series of orders was issued for tenders, additional to those required for new engines. The first was 0.2 for six 2,350 gallon tenders, followed by 0.76 of about December 1874 for twelve more. In the MR file *'Order numbers which concern the Loco. Drawing Office'*, this latter dozen are shown as 'No 2 class goods tenders'. This, having regard to locomotive classification discussed in Chapter 3, must refer to replacement tenders for Kirtley goods. The capacity is not given, but subsequent orders and the total shown in the 1918 'Distribution of Tenders' table suggests that they were 2,200

gallons capacity. The next order for additional tenders, 0.166 of 16 August 1876, was for ten 2,200 gallon tenders, for rebuilds. Three more orders followed up to 1 June 1878, one for ten 2,350 gallon tenders, one for ten at 2,200 gallons and one for ten capacity unknown, but believed to be 2,200 gallons, for rebuilds. No more 'additional' tenders of these capacities were built, further old Kirtley tenders being replaced by later examples, which themselves were displaced by larger Johnson tenders – as will be seen.

One further batch of ten additional tenders appeared in this period, to 0.174 of 6 September 1876. These were the first 2,950 gallon examples and were for the Kirtley 800 Class 2-4-0s, rebuilt with the ten larger Johnson boilers (with 6ft 2in fireboxes) for principal express work.

c) Design Details
The 2,200 gallon tenders had narrow tanks and outside springs above the platform, but all the others had wide tanks, with springs below the platform concealed behind the outside framing, as was the current fashion on a number of railways. This arrangement clearly made the inspection of springs difficult, and the early detection of faults. As a result, all

The 3,250 gallon tenders as on Spinner No.662 were by far the most numerous type. When the 4-2-2s were withdrawn in the 1920s the tenders were retained for further service.

TABLE 9A - TENDERS BUILT 1850-1923						
GALLS.	A	B	C	D	E	F	Notes
1000	29	-	29	-	-	-	1
1400	368	-	368	-	-		1
1600	313	?	?	2	-		1
2000	463	-30	433	433	217		1
2050	-	+1	1	1	1		2
2200T	-	+30	30	30	21		3
2200B	232	-	232	229	218		3
2330	70	-	70	70	66		
2350	156	-20	136	156	56)		4.5
2750	60	-	60	60	53)	154	4
2950	267	-	267	266	184)		4
3250	747	-	747	747	739)		4
3500	359	+82	436	292	436		6
4000	20	-20	-	-	-		6
4100	20	-20	-	-	-		6
4500	25	-25	-	-	-		6

A = total built
B = changes brought about by rebuilding
C = final total
D = total at 31/12/19
E = total at 31/12/37
F = frames to LMS tenders

1. Kirtley tenders (1000-2000 gallons) – the totals are calculated from the engine stock. A number of 1,600 gallon tenders are believed to have received 2000 gallon replacement tanks.

2. 2,050 gallon tender - this tender was rebuilt from a 2350 gallon tender to 0.4553 of 20.8.14 for No.2290. There is therefore a disparity of one in the 2,350 gallon total for 31/12/19 as 156 tenders are shown in stock in addition to this one. All the remaining Johnson tenders with springs below the platform were still in stock except for one 2,950 gallon tender. This might have been altered to 0.3709, which referred to 2,750 gallon frames, as all the 2750 gallon tenders were still in stock.

3. 2,200 gallon tenders - of the 239 tenders of this capacity surviving at 31/12/27, twenty-one are known to be 2,200T class, ie rebuilt Kirtley tenders. It is possible that there were more and if so the number of 2,200B class tenders would be reduced by the same amount. 0.3330 of 27.7.07 as amended provided for rebuilding twenty tenders having 2,000 gallon tanks with new 2,200 gallon tanks. As the 1919 list shows thirty T class 2,200 gallon tenders, it is presumed that ten more were rebuilt without the benefit of a formal order.

4. Second-hand tender frames for LMS engines - 154 tender frames were used with new tanks for 164 LMS built engines from a total of 176 tenders withdrawn by 31/12/27. Ten were used twice as ten of these tenders originally with Compounds were transferred to class 4 0-6-0s.

5. 2350 gallon tenders - 0.3709 of 28/4/10 as amended provided for five 2,350 gallon tanks to frames previously carrying 2,750 gallon tanks. The 1919 tender totals suggest that only one was fitted to a 2,950 gallon frame.

6. 3500 gallon tenders - the total built includes the three built to 0.3486 for exchange with bogie tenders but only sixty-two rebuilt from bogie tenders. The three unrebuilt were put to other uses.

subsequent tenders from 1879 were made with inside frames only, with the springs exposed in what then became the standard layout.

d) Summary

The situation by mid-1878 can be conveniently summarised. A total of 256 wide tenders with concealed (inside) springs were in service, comprising 156 2,350 gallon, sixty 2,750-2,800 gallon and the forty 2,950 gallon tenders made to that date. To these must be added the narrow 2,200 gallon tenders believed to number forty-two. No more 2,350 or 2,750/2,800 gallon tenders were built after this.

2 Middle Years 1879-88
a) Passenger Engines

The first of a new design of wide 2,950 gallon tender, with outside springs below the platform, were built to Order No.0.233 of 16 October 1878, appearing with 2-4-0s Nos.1400-1409 in June-November 1879. These tenders set the standard for most future construction and were fitted to the majority of new passenger engines up to the second batch of 1808 Class 6ft 6in 4-4-0s, Nos.1818-1822, ordered in January 1888. Between 1881 and 1884, eight orders were issued for a total of forty-two 2,950 gallon tenders additional to those required for new engines. Many replaced the original tenders on the Kirtley 800 Class 2-4-0s. The allocation was not a straightforward exercise and in some cases the tenders were intended for new engines. Fortunately details of some of the original tender allocations have survived in PRO RAIL 491 879 at the Public Record Office, *Costs of Engines etc*. Further comment is made in the relevant chapter.

A further advance in capacity, to 3,250 gallons, came with the 7ft 0in express passenger 4-4-0s Nos.1738-1757, ordered from January 1885. Apart from Nos.1818-1822 noted above, subsequent passenger engines in this period were given these new larger tenders.

b) Goods Engines

With the goods engines, the situation was more complex. It will be recalled that the first twenty of the 1357 Class 0-6-0s of 1878 had 2,350 gallon tenders. A change was then made for the subsequent ninety engines, the last of which was delivered in March 1884. These had 2,250 or 2,200 gallon tenders, similar to those built earlier for the Kirtley rebuilds.

The next series of goods engines, the 1698 Class, had 4ft 11in wheels and appeared in 1885. With these sixty engines, thirty 2,950 gallon tenders and thirty 3,250 gallon tenders were ordered. These were followed in 1888 by the first ten of the 1798 Class 0-6-0s which reverted to 5ft 2½in wheels and with these, 2,950 gallon tenders were ordered. In the event, however, all these goods engines were given second-hand 2,750 and 2,950 gallon inside spring tenders displaced from earlier 2-4-0s and 4-4-0s. Fifty-one of the new tenders went direct to the passenger engines whose tenders had been appropriated. An incidental result of this was thirty-two engines being upgraded from 2,750 to 2,950 gallons and several 2-4-0s acquiring 3,250 gallon tenders for the first time – Nos.104, 105, 108 and 110. The remainder went to various engines, involving further tender changes. A final batch of ten 2,950 gallon passenger tenders for replacements were ordered in 1888, bringing the total built of this capacity to 267.

3 Later Years 1889-1903
a) Passenger Engines
For passenger engines, 3,250 gallon tenders remained the standard until 1895 when the 115 class 4-2-2s were provided with 3,500 gallon tenders. The size specified in subsequent orders depended on the class of engine and duties required. Thus the 60 Class 4-4-0s ordered in 1897 had 3,500 gallon tenders; the last to receive 3,250 gallon tenders were the ten 6ft 6in 4-4-0s Nos.2581-2590, ordered in 1899 and virtually identical to the earlier 1808 Class of 1888.

Larger engines and heavier trains by the close of the century demanded a further increase in capacity in the absence of water troughs. As a consequence, the ten 4-2-2s of the 'Princess' class and the first ten of the 'Belpaire' 4-4-0s both ordered in 1899, were given a new design of 4,000 gallon tender mounted on bogies. These were followed by even larger versions of 4,500 gallons for the first five Compound 4-4-0s and further 'Belpaires' while the last twenty 'Belpaires' ordered by Johnson in October 1902 and April 1903 had 4,100 gallon tenders. This gave a total of 65 bogie tenders.

b) Goods Engines
Between 1889 and 1900 a further 565 0-6-0s were ordered. These were of the basic 1798 Class with minor detail changes and entered traffic between 1890 and 1902. The first ten, it will be recalled, had received second hand 2,750 gallon tenders, but then a reversion was made to 2,200 gallons for the next hundred, followed by seventy with 2,330 gallons. All these latter examples had outside springs above the platforms. After that however, all the remainder (395 engines) commencing with No.2093 (3370 in 1907) built by Sharp Stewart in August 1892, were given standard 3,250 gallon tenders. No.2735 (3764 in 1907) was the last new engine to receive a 3,250 gallon tender, in August 1902. Johnson's final 0-6-0s with the larger H boiler ordered in 1902-3 were given 3,500 gallon tenders; this became, and remained the standard, for all subsequent new goods tenders.

c) Replacement Tenders
A further series of ten orders for a total of 102 tenders additional to those required for new engines was commenced with 0.821 of 29 March 1889, concluding with 0.1588 of 13 October 1896. These 3,250 gallon tenders were specified as 4ft 1in platform height from rail level, that is, to match the

Top. **Only seventy 2,330 gallon tenders were built, for 5ft 2in 0-6-0s Nos. 2023-2092 (3300-3369 in 1907). Most were transferred to other engines, No. 2912 (at Barrow) running with this one until 1934.**

Above. **For the last of the 4-2-2s and the first 'Belpaire' 4-4-0s a large ungainly 4000 gallon bogie tender was produced, with single inverted springs to each bogie and standard Johnson tender front. No. 2608 was built in October 1900 and in this view has yet to be lined and lettered. S Summerson collection.**

TABLE 9B - PRINCIPAL TENDER DIMENSIONS

Capacity Water galls	Coal tons	Tender side length	Tank width	Tank height	Notes
Kirtley tenders					
1600	2½	17ft 0in	5ft 11½in	3ft 5½in	
2000	2½	18 0	5 11½	3 8½	
2000R	3	18 4	5 11½	3 6	to 0.3714
2200R	3	18 5½	5 11½	4 0	to 0.3330
Johnson tenders					
2200	3	18 8¾	5 11½	3 2¾	
2330	3	18 8¾	5 11½	3 6	
2350	3½	18 8¾	6 4	3 2¾	
2750	3½	18 11¾	6 6	3 6¾	
2950	3½	19 1¾	6 7	3 7¾	A
3250	4	19 3¼	7 1	3 11	
3250	4	18 0	7 11	4 3½	B
3500	4	19 3¼	7 1	4 2	C
4000	5	23 9¹/₁₆	7 1	4 4	0.1927
4000	5	22 7⁷/₈	7 5	4 4	0.1870
4100	5	23 6³/₁₆	7 8	4 2	
4500	5	23 6³/₁₆	7 8	4 2	
Deeley Tenders					
3500	7	21 0½	7 5	3 11½	
3500R		21 0½	7 5	4 4	to 0.3454
3500R		21 0½	7 8	4 2	to 0.3454A
3500R		21 0½	7 1	4 4	to 0.3698

R = rebuilt tenders
B = Baldwin tenders
A = Those originally built with inside springs were 2in shorter
C = Tenders to 0.1475, 1636, 1660 and 1835 have tank height 4ft 0in

tenders were built new to facilitate this work so three were not rebuilt. The ten 4,000 gallon tenders on the last ten 4-2-2 followed suit, to 0.3698 of 15 March 1910, and the job was completed in 1915.

b) Six Wheel Tenders

Coming now to the smaller tenders, one rather odd order was issued in 1910 to provide new tanks on 2,750 gallon tender frames. 0.3709 of 15 April 1910 provided for five 2,950 gallon tanks to replace the 2750 gallon variety. Two weeks later, on 28 April 1910, this was cancelled and replaced by five 2,350 gallon tanks instead. There are no further references to this episode, but the 'Redistribution of Tenders' table which gives the situation as at 30 September 1918 shows the 2,950 gallon tender total down by one and the 2,350 gallon total up by one, while the 2,750 gallon total was unchanged. This could infer that one 2,350 gallon tank was fitted, but to a 2,950 gallon frame to this order (0.3709).

The table does however show another interesting proposal. Rebuilding 0-6-0s in the 3190-3764 number range with G7 boilers was in full swing and many of these had tenders of less than 3,250 gallons capacity. As the ultimate intention at that time was to rebuild all these engines, the question of adequate tender capacity had to be addressed. The table suggested changes based on the rebuilding of 157 (that is, all) 2,350 gallon tenders with new tanks of 3,250 gallons capacity and the provision of twenty-one new 3,250 gallon tenders. Subsequent events caused this proposal to be abandoned, but a limited rebuilding of 2,350 gallon tender frames with *3,500 gallon* tanks did take place.

Four orders for a total of thirty-five rebuilds were issued, commencing with 0.5330 of 30 August 1919 and concluding with 0.5998 of 6 September 1923. The tanks were similar to those for contemporaneous new class 4 goods, but slight alterations were required as the 2,350 gallon frames were 2in shorter at the back end and the frame height also varied from standard. They were easily distinguished from the class 4 tenders, having large frame slots with the spring hangars clipped round the slot, whereas the class 4 tenders had the small slots, of the current standard. One order for five

---

Kirtley 890 and 1070 Class 2-4-0s to which they were principally attached. This in turn released their 2,000 gallon Kirtley tenders for further use on the older double framed 0-6-0s.

No more 'additional' tenders are recorded and the total of 227 known from the records set in progress various 'cascades' of earlier tenders, which ultimately involved the withdrawal of the oldest Kirtley examples.

d) Modifications

The problems of maintenance arising with the concealed (inside) spring tenders were eventually addressed in the 1890s when all were altered to the standard arrangement. It is not known exactly when this work commenced but a series of orders for the 'alteration of B class tenders from inside to outside bearing springs' (usually ten at a time) appeared, commencing with 0.1419 of 12 December 1894 and concluding with 0.2037 of 26 January 1900 for the final two tenders, noted 'completed' on 21 June 1900. The total accounted for by these orders was 212 tenders, so it may be that the work was commenced before a decision was taken to cover it by formal orders.

Summary

By the close of this period, some 747 3,250 gallon tenders had been produced; the number of 2,200 gallon examples had risen to 232 and 2,330 gallon tenders to seventy. No more in any of these three sizes were made. The 3,500 gallon tenders had reached seventy-five by December 1903 and to these must be added the series of sixty-five bogie tenders completed in February 1904.

Rebuilding

Apart from the routine repair and replacement of tender tanks, rather more extensive work was undertaken in a number of cases.

a) Bogie Tenders

Following the introduction of water troughs and pickup gear on tenders from 1904, there was no need to retain tenders of such large capacity. They were said to ride badly and their length, over 27ft for the largest, made for difficulties in turning engine and tender – in the case of the Johnson Compound the combined length was 60ft 10in.

These factors were behind the issue of 0.3454 and 0.3454A of 19 March and 22 June 1908 to 'rebuild' the 4-4-0 bogie tenders into 3,500 gallon six wheel tenders on new frames similar to current production for new Compounds. Three

was cancelled but it appears from the official 1927 tender number list that only twenty conversions were actually carried out, the last in January 1924. They were attached to G7 0-6-0 rebuilds and although equipped to take pick up gear, were not actually fitted.

c) Six Wheel Tenders for LMS Engines

When the old Kirtley 1,400 gallon tender tanks required replacement in the later years of the last century, the most suitable solution, larger tanks, was not possible due to limitations of frame length. So, new Johnson tenders were built and attached to later Kirtley engines, with a resultant cascade of displaced 1,600 and 2,000 gallon tanks used to replace the 1,400 gallon variety on older engines. By contrast, in the case of the Johnson tenders, larger new tanks were a practicality, as noted above.

The LMS took full advantage of this by fitting frames from withdrawn tenders with new tanks for some of the new class 4 0-6-0s and Compound 4-4-0s built in the 1920s. Some 176 tenders, of which 168 were 2,350, 2,750 and 2,950 gallon capacity were withdrawn between 1924 and 1927 so making frames available for new tanks. Thus twenty-nine Compounds, followed by 135 class 4 0-6-0s ordered in this period were to have tenders with new standard tanks on second-hand MR frames. These were readily identifiable by their larger frame slots. The engines involved were Compounds Nos.1056-1074 and 1105-1114, while the class 4 0-6-0s were Nos.4047-4056, 4207-4301 and 4407-4436. Ten tenders were used twice, firstly on Compounds which were subsequently given newly released tenders from withdrawn Belpaire and 990 Class 4-4-0s, and then on new 0-6-0s, so that only 154 sets of frames were required. Five of these originally intended for 0-6-0s in the 4407-4436 group were sent to Horwich and used with new standard tanks on the first five Horwich Moguls, Nos.13000-4.

In some cases, drawing schedules and tender history cards quote the origin of the frames, while the tender history cards of the new engines give a date which refers to the building date of the engine from which the tender frame was taken. Thus the origin of the tender frames can be deduced. They came from two principal groups of engines: withdrawn Johnson 4-2-2s, 0-6-0s class 1 4-4-0s and Kirtley 2-4-0s, and a considerable number from Johnson 2-4-0s and a few 0-6-0s still in service. None of the engines involved ran with 2,350 gallon tenders and although details of the consequential tender changes are not now available, some points in this connection may be noted. Between 1922 and 1926 orders were issued for breaking up forty-three 2,350 gallon tanks (but not the frames) so confirming that these frames were available. Similarly, there were thirty-three 2,950 gallon tanks in stock on 31 December 1927. Large numbers of Kirtley 0-6-0s were withdrawn in this period, so some spare 2,000 gallon tenders were available to replace Johnson 2,200 gallon tenders on engines not withdrawn, these latter going to Johnson class 2 0-6-0s whose 2,950/3,250 gallon tenders were available for the 2-4-0s whose tender frames had been appropriated. It may be noted also that the 2,950 gallon tenders which originally had inside springs were two inches shorter than the later standard tenders and this had a bearing on which of them was selected for donating frames, in order to minimise the cost of adaptation. The complexities were considerable!

Remarkably, one of these tenders has survived into preservation. The pioneer Horwich Mogul No.13000, now LMS 2700 and usually to be seen at the NRM York, retained its original tender until withdrawn. The history card for this tender, No.3826, shows it as *'Derby, April 1899 rebuilt April 1926'*, which indicates that the frames came from a tender attached to an engine built in April 1899. The only engine of this date was 4-2-2 No.683 (1907 number) which had a 2,950 gallon tender when withdrawn. The frames of this tender have a circular slot in front of the leading tender wheels which betrays it as a Neilson-built example. It is therefore possible to confirm its date of construction as 1881, as the only tenders to this description were those attached to a batch of MR 2-4-0s built in that year.

Deeley and Fowler Tenders

Deeley and subsequent tenders were all of 3,500 gallons and four to seven tons coal capacity but varied considerably in themselves. New 3,500 gallon tenders for the class 3 and 145 of the class 4 0-6-0s retained the general Johnson pattern and had a four ton coal capacity. The design of these, built up to 1922, was basically a larger version of the 2,350 gallon tenders of 1875 with a frame two inches longer! The last thirty of the 'Belpaire' 4-4-0s were also similar in appearance to standard Johnson tenders but had a 4ft 8in running plate to match the engines. For the Compounds built from 1905, however, an entirely new design was produced, having high side sheets with scalloped ends and an enhanced 5½ to 7 ton coal capacity. Ten more were made for the 990 class of 1907, and three were built to 0.3486 of 2 June 1908 'to interchange with bogie tenders whilst the latter are rebuilt'. One more for the Paget locomotive produced a total of fifty-four to this design. These had 7ft 5in wide tanks and had side panels 5ft 9¾in in height.

In addition, sixty-two tenders were rebuilt from the Johnson bogie tenders – as noted above. These rebuilt tenders showed detail differences according to the dimensions of the originals. The tank widths remained the same as before, varying from 7ft 1in to 7ft 8in, and while the height of the side panels on the rebuilds was uniform at 5ft 11½in, the position of the top horizontal bead differed, again depending on the material from the originals. The 1910 diagrams show the vertical dividing bead as off centre, which presumes the use of original side panels but this bead was in fact central on the tenders. The 4100/4500 gallon tender tanks had coved bottom angles unlike the

4,000 gallon tanks and these differences were retained in the rebuilt tenders. A further variation was to be seen in the tender frame slots as their construction spanned the change from large to small slots, discussed later. From 1929 replacement tanks began to be required for all these tenders.

Standard Fowler tanks were used, carrying 3,500 gallons and these were some nine inches shorter than the Deeley tanks, with 5 tons of coal compared to 7 tons on the majority of the Deeley/rebuilt Deeley variety. This left a nine inch platform at the tender rear on those so altered. A succession of orders for this work was issued commencing with 0.7478 of 11 September 1929; five more followed up to 0.8682 of 5 March 1934, covering a total of thirty tenders. Rebuilding continued until after the Second World War and a total of some forty-nine tenders rebuilt in this way have been identified. This figure is not definitive and it is possible there were others. These again varied in detail. Three main varieties were to be seen:-

1 Flush riveted tank, rebuilt 1930-c1932
2 Visible riveted tank, rebuilt c1932-c1945
3 Unbeaded tank, post war rebuilds.

The details of these variations are noted in the appropriate class chapters. In summary, 354 tenders were built with 3,500 gallon tanks; fifteen for 4-2-2s, 123 for 4-4-0s, one for the Paget locomotive and 215 for 0-6-0s. Additionally sixty-two were rebuilt from bogie tenders and twenty from 2,350 gallon tenders, a grand total of 436.

Classification of Tenders

Tenders were generally described by their water capacity, but when the early Johnson tenders of 2,350, 2,750 and 2,950 gallons having concealed springs below the platform were rebuilt with outside springs, the orders, issued from 1894 referred to 'alteration of B class tenders'. The letter is thought to refer to the general arrangement of the tenders, but confirmation is lacking. F.H. Clarke, in an allocation list of 1908, notes the types of tenders in use, indicating official letter descriptions for Kirtley 2,000 gallon tenders as T and *all* the Johnson tenders as B. This limited use of letters is confirmed in official tabulations of 1918/20. These show 2,200T and 2,200B to distinguish the rebuilt Kirtley tenders from the Johnson tenders of the same capacity. The Johnson pattern 3,500 gallon tenders are shown as 3,500B to distinguish them from the 3,500 Belpaire and Compound tenders but the remainder have no suffix shown. Various Derby Orders up to 1927 also refer to B class tenders of 3,250 and 3,500 gallons. The system is therefore confirmed but its precise function remains obscure.

Dimensions

Fortunately the 1910 *Tender Diagram* book has survived, giving side and rear elevations of the principal tender types. A few general observations on the main

0-6-0 No. 43200 has one of twenty tenders rebuilt with 3,500 gallon tanks on 2,350 gallon tender frames between 1919 and 1924. These were similar to new tenders on Class 4 0-6-0s but were distinguishable by their large frame slots. P H Groom.

TABLE 9C - DEELEY AND REBUILT BOGIE TENDERS
DETAIL DIFFERENCES
1. NEW TENDERS

ENGINES	TOP BEAD	FOOTPLATE TYPE	VALENCE	FRAME SLOTS	PILLARS	TENDER WIDTH	NOTES
1005-14	A	Continuous	Flat	Large	In line	7ft 5in	1
1015-34	A	Steps only	"	"	"	"	
1035-44	A	"	"	Small	"	"	
990-9	A	"	"	Large	"	"	
2299)	A	"	"	"	"	"	
1055)	A	"	"	"	Commode	"	2

2. TENDERS REBUILT FROM DOUBLE BOGIE TYPE

ENGINES	TOP BEAD	FOOTPLATE TYPE	VALENCE	FRAME SLOTS	PILLARS	TENDER WIDTH	ORIGINAL CAPACITY	NOTES
685-94	B	Steps only	Flat	Small	In line	7ft1in	4000	
1045-54	B	"	"	"	Commode	7ft1in	"	3
700-9	B	"	"	Large/ Small	In line	7ft5in	"	4
710-49	C	"	Coved	"	"	7ft8in	4100/ 4500	5, 6
1000-4	C	"	"	Small	"	7ft8in	4500	6

RELATIVE POSITION OF TOP BEAD TO TANK HEIGHT,
A-C ABOVE ARE AS FOLLOWS:

		HEIGHT OF TENDER SIDE		
		BASE TO BEAD	BEAD TO TOP	TOTAL
A	Shallow top panel. Bead meets flare	4ft 0in	1ft 9¾in	5ft 9¾in
B	Deep top panel. Bead just below flare	4ft 0in	1ft 11½in	5ft 11½in
C	Deeper top panel. Bead well below flare	3ft 10in	2ft 1½in	5ft 11½in

NOTES
1 = Continuous narrow footplate with steps at each end.
2 = Tender from the Paget locomotive No2299 as modified for No.1055 to 0.5967 of 24/7/23.
3 = Tenders from Nos.685-94 as modified for nos 1045-54 to 0.5940 of 11/6/23.
4 = After rebuilding, the tenders with small frame slots were attached to nos 700/2/7/14 and 1002. The tenders with large slots were attached to nos 701/4/8/9/45.
5 = Only the tenders on Nos.717 and 728 confirmed as having large frame slots.
6 = The MR 1919 tender list shows 115 3,500 gallon tenders for these classes. As three new tenders were built for exchange whilst the bogie tenders were being rebuilt and attached to Nos.720-2, it is clear that only forty-two tenders, taken from Nos.710-49 and 1000-4, were rebuilt. These were subsequently attached to nos 703/5/6/10-3/5-9 723-44/6-9 and 1000/1/3/4. Later tender changes are recorded under individual classes.

TABLE 9D - TENDERS FITTED WITH PICK UP GEAR

Number of tenders fitted			Engines	Number range	Tender cap.	Notes
1908	1917/9	1924			1924 only	
23	51	59	Class 1 2-4-0	between 1-281	2950	
2		10	Class 1 4-4-0	between 300-27	2950	
193	250	195	Class 2 4-4-0	328-522	3250	
40		40	Class 2 4-4-0	523-62	3500	
37		15	Class 1 4-2-2	between 600-69	3250	
10	72	12	Class 1 4-2-2	between 670-84	3500	
-		10	Class 2 4-2-2	685-94	3500	A C
68	80	80	Class 3 4-4-0	700-79	3500	A
1	10	10	Class 4 4-4-0	990-9	3500	
35	45	45	Class 4 4-4-0	1000-44	3500	
1	1	-	Class 3 0-6-4T	2015	-	
20		-	Class 2 0-6-0	between 3326-3764	-	
3		11	Class 3 0-6-0	between 3326-3764	3250	
60	96	70	Class 3 0-6-0	3765-3834	3500	
		2	Class 4 0-6-0	3835/6	3500	
		50	Class 4 0-6-0	3937-86	3500	B
493	605	609				

A Pick up gear not fitted to the 4000 gallon bogie tenders on 4-2-2 nos 685-94 and 4-4-0 nos 700-9.
B The number of existing tenders to be fitted was approaching completion in 1908. Nine 990 class, ten Compounds and fifty-two class 4 0-6-0s were subsequently built and fitted.
C The ten tenders from nos 685-94 were spare in 1924 pending allocation to new Compounds.

Until 1905 MR tender sides had a flared coping with (latterly) coal rails, but for his new Compounds Deeley introduced the high flat sided tender, with a vertical flare at each end and a top bead between the bases of the flare. This is tender No. 2851 with No. 41040 on 30 September 1951. It remained in original condition until withdrawn with the engine in April/May 1952. S Summerson collection.

dimensions are, however, appropriate. All tenders from the Kirtley 1,600 gallon to the Johnson 2,330 gallon which had outside springs above the platform were 5ft 11½in width. Those with springs below the platform varied from 6ft 4in on the 2,350 gallon tenders to 7ft 8in on the 4,100 and 4,500 gallon bogie tenders. The bogie tenders on the Baldwin 2-6-0s were even wider at 7ft 11in. These and the bogie tenders of 4,000/4,100 gallons did not have a well between the frames, common to all the other wide tenders, and neither did the Kirtley tenders. These latter had a 6ft 0in+6ft 0in wheelbase and all the Johnson tenders 6ft 6in+6ft 6in, but the high sided Deeley tenders and those produced by rebuilding the bogie tenders had a 7ft 0in+6ft 9in wheelbase. The 3,500 gallon tenders for the class 4 goods reverted to the 6ft 6in+6ft 6in wheelbase and 7ft 1in width, which was to become an LMS standard for all new tenders in the Fowler period. The

2,350 gallon tenders had 4ft 0½in wheels but all subsequent tenders were fitted with 4ft 2½in , later increased to 4ft 3in wheels. Table 9B shows the principal dimensions.

Water Troughs
The problems of insufficient water capacity for the longer non-stop runs finally prompted investigations into the provision of water troughs and associated pick up gear on the engines. The first suggestion, reported to the Locomotive Committee on 19 December 1901, was to construct troughs at Finedon, north of Wellingborough. The MR solicitors advised the Engineer against taking water from the adjacent River Ise so a survey was authorised to find a suitable site for a well. This proved difficult and on 20 March 1902 it was suggested that as an alternative, troughs be constructed three quarters of a mile north of Oakley station. It must then have been realised that

more comprehensive arrangements were required if the full benefits of water troughs were to be achieved. Before smaller tenders with pick up gear could be generally instituted, a proper system of troughs, spread about the system, would be needed. Accordingly, a comprehensive plan was submitted to the Locomotive Committee on 16 October 1902 for ten sets of water troughs, at various locations. The total estimated cost was £73,440 for the Engineer's work. The sites were as follows:-

Site	No of troughs	Line
Hawes Junction	2	Settle-Carlisle
Methley	2	Leeds-Normanton
Woodhouse Mill	4	Old road' south of Rotherham
Hathersage	2	Sheffield-Manchester
Matlock Bridge	2	Derby-Manchester
Loughborough	4	Derby-Leicester
Melton Mowbray	2	Nottingham-Kettering
Kingsbury	2	Derby-Birmingham west of Tamworth
Bredon	2	Birmingham - Bristol north of Ashchurch
Oakley	4	Kettering-London

The stock of engines at June 1902 was quoted as 2,928, of which 2,307 were tender engines. At £25 per engine the cost to fit them all would have been £57,675. The Traffic Committee then considered the matter on 7 November 1902 and, daunted, requested troughs at Oakley, Melton and Loughborough only. This was approved by the General Purposes Committee on 18 December 1902 and work put in hand to a series of Orders beginning in January 1903. The new troughs and the dates brought into use were as follows:

Oakley	5 February 1904
Loughborough	18 April 1904
Melton	3 May 1905

A major consequence was to obviate the need for very larger tenders and a reversion to 3,500 gallons took place for all new engines, passenger and goods, from 1904. This in turn prompted a re-examination of trough provision at other sites and two further sets were subsequently laid. The main line north of Leeds was of the greatest concern. In a report to the Locomotive Committee on 19 July 1906 (this followed earlier consideration of troughs between Hellifield and Settle Junction, to serve both the Morecambe and Carlisle lines) the case was made for troughs at Hawes Junction, which would *'enable the Company to utilise the new compound engines on the Leeds-Carlisle section where they are now unable to work owing to the water they carry being insufficient'*. The point being made here of course was that non-stop runs were not practical with the new 3,500 gallon tenders. Provision was agreed at £5,550, subject to the usual General Purposes Committee approval. The severe weather conditions which often prevail at that lofty location prompted the further decision on 5 April *1907 'to provide heating apparatus for warming the water in the troughs in frosty weather'*. These troughs were duly brought into use on 22 October 1907 and despite the 'heat-

TABLE 9E - STOCK TENDERS, 4th December 1917
(Chief Mechanical Engineer's Office)

No	Capacity Gallons	Remarks
old 2904	2350	Fitted with back weatherboards
old 2997	2350	Fitted with back weatherboards
old 2638	2000	
old 2536	2000	New Tank 0/3714 required from stock
old 2384	2000	New Front Ends 0/3641A, required
old 2746	2000	New Front Ends 0/3641A, required
old 2650	2000	Tank rivetted to foot plate, heavy repairs to tank
old 2436	2000	Tank scrap, frames badly damaged (air raid)
old 323A	1600	Frames suitable for Boiler Truck
old 117A	2000	Tank scrap, Frames suitable for Boiler Truck
old 2463	3250	Experimental Water Pick-up
old 2202	3250	Baldwin type fitted with Double Buffers
old 2200	3250	Baldwin type, (Engineer's Dept), fitted with Double Buffers
old 2502	1600	On Loan to Engineer's Dept
old 2550	1600	On Loan to Engineer's Dept
old 2415	2000	Working old 330 engine for Stationary boiler work
old 2206	3250	Baldwin type. Nottingham
old 2210	3250	Baldwin type. Nottingham
old 2211	3250	Baldwin type. Nottingham
old 2213	3250	Baldwin type. Nottingham
old 2214	3250	Baldwin type. Nottingham
old 2216	3250	Baldwin type. Nottingham
old 2218	3250	Baldwin type. Nottingham
old 2223	3250	Baldwin type. Nottingham
old 2224	3250	Baldwin type. Nottingham

Engine Frames on Ground awaiting orders, which may require Tenders

88	Engine Frames on Ground	Tender used up
91	Engine Frames on Ground	Tender used up
2343	Engine Frames on Ground	Tender used up
2367	Engine to be broken up?	Tender used up
2418	Engine Frames on Ground	Tender used up
321	Engine Frames on Ground	Tender on Park
601	Engine Frames on Ground	Tender used up
2379	Engine Frames on Ground	Tender used up
2857	Engine Frames on Ground	Tender used up
2313	Engine Frames on Ground	Tender used up
2712	Engine Frames on Ground	Tender used up

Number of Engines which may require Tenders - 4
(Nos 88, 91, 2343 and 2418)
Number of Tenders suitable for changing - 7
(Off Engs 2904, 2997, 2638, 2536, 2384, 2746 and 2650)

ing apparatus' were destined to prove a headache every winter. The final set of troughs to be approved were those at Tamworth, sometimes referred to as Wigginton, after the nearby village. The Traffic Committee requested their provision on 2 August 1907 but the Way and Works Committee encountered various difficulties, including land purchase, and it was April 1909 before they were brought into use.

Pick up Gear

As soon as authority to proceed with the installation of troughs had been given in December 1902 orders were issued to fit some passenger and goods engine tenders with pick up apparatus. 0.2482 of 15 January 1903 covered an initial hundred main line engine tenders; a later note includes the fitting of tenders for new 0-6-0s Nos.245-284, yet to be ordered. A supplementary order, 2482A of 1 August 1903, covered the last three original Compounds Nos.2633-2635 and twenty 'Belpaire' 4-4-0s Nos.820-839, all in the process of delivery. From then on all new passenger engine tenders had pick up apparatus. Drawing 04.5879 of 7 September 1904 detailed a 3,250 gallon tender, No.2680, to be fitted with an 'Observation Tube' to monitor pick up experimentally. All the new H boiler goods engines built from 1903 were also equipped

but only fifty of the subsequent class 4 0-6-0s had the gear. Of the earlier tenders, no Kirtley examples were fitted and the smaller Johnson tenders of 2,200, 2,330, 2,350 or 2,750 gallons were not usually eligible, though an order, 0.3000, of 2 August 1905 records that 'It has been decided to fit all 2,200 and 2,330 gallon tenders with water pick up apparatus'. This order listed eleven Burton and Wigston engines to have early attention and nine of these were recorded as fitted in 1908, though the tender type is not shown. Only two photographs have come to notice with 2,200 gallon tenders indicating pick up gear – on Nos.3099 and 3566 in the 1920s. It therefore seems likely, in the absence of other evidence, that 0.3000 was rescinded at an early date and fitting confined to the larger 2,950, 3,250 and 3,500 gallon tenders.

To quickly release the air displaced by the rapid pick up of water on the move, two vents with protective caps were provided, one each side of the tender, protruding through the coal space. On some later tenders the vents were sited behind the coal space, to reduce the risk of coal particles entering the tank and clogging the filters. This feature usually identified those tenders with pick up gear. It was not infallible, however, as a batch of 3,500 gallon tenders for class 4 0-6-0s emerged new with vents, to facilitate the fitting of pick up gear at a later date – in the event this was not carried out. There were a number of cases moreover, where tenders, once fitted on passenger engines, were subsequently transferred to goods engines and the pick up gear, but not necessarily the vents, removed. It is highly likely, too, that as engines went down the social scale with the passing of years, that the equipment just fell into disuse. Photographs have to be interpreted!

A fitting which assisted the engine crew in timing the raising of the scoop after taking water, to prevent overfilling and wastage, was the water level indicator. 0.2682 of 27 November 1903 covered the fitting of an initial 120 tenders with this standard fitting. The volume *Leading Particulars of MR Locomotive Engines* (RAIL 491.908 at the PRO, Kew) which was compiled about 1908, shows

the engines fitted with pick-up gear at that time. All the large boiler 4-4-0s having 2,950 or 3,250 gallon tenders with a few exceptions had been equipped plus a few class 1 2-4-0s and 4-4-0s. The majority of the 4-2-2 Spinners were fitted by that time but none of the 4,000 gallon bogie tenders on Nos.685-694 and 4-4-0s Nos.700-709. It is believed that these were not fitted until subsequently rebuilt as 3,500 gallon six wheeled tenders. The three 0-6-0s rebuilt with 6ft wheels had been equipped together with some twenty other class 2 0-6-0s of the 1798 series of 5ft 3in 0-6-0s, which were engaged in express goods working. Only one tank engine, 0-6-4T No.2015 was equipped and this was to remain the only example.

A series of water pick up experiments and trials were then conducted on Loughborough troughs (presumably chosen because they were nearest to Derby) during October 1909. A revised design of scoop was then produced to improve pick up and a report made in April 1911, comparing water lifted with old and new pattern scoops.

The total number of tenders with pick up gear can probably not now be accurately determined, but the Mechanical Engineer's Office Derby issued a *Return of Large Passenger and Goods Engines* as at 14 February 1917 and also on 14 January 1919. These were followed by a statement of the empty weights of Midland Division engines and tenders on 8 January 1924 giving the position at 31 December 1923. All of these gave the numbers of tenders in each category which had the pick-up gear. This is valuable because it provides comparisons before any new LMS engines had been delivered and shows the final Midland Railway situation of over 600 engines fitted. Table 9D compares the situation in 1908, 1917/9 (the same) and 1924.

The working of the heavy mineral traffic to London was always a problem and in an effort to speed it up, it was decided in the summer of 1929 to discontinue the water stop between Wellingborough and London for up mineral trains. At this date only three Garratts were in service and the burden of moving this traffic still fell on various combinations of 0-6-0s. Accordingly, instructions were issued on 3 September 1929 for a whole series of transfers of engines with water scoops to Toton and Wellingborough, thirty class 3 0-6-0s and forty-two class 4 0-6-0s with an equal number of each type displaced. There was also the added benefit that in most cases 3,500 gallon displaced 3,250 gallon tenders. How successful this was is not recorded, but it did not entirely eliminate the Luton water stop.

DETAILS
1 Back weatherboards and storm sheets

The fitting of back weatherboards is less than well documented. They were provided for tender first running where conditions were particularly adverse – on snowplough engines for instance. The earliest reference comes in the *Derby Drawing Register* in 1880. This makes

The back weatherboard arrangement to engines with short cabs and 2,200 gallon tenders, Derby 16 November 1910. Note the coal rails round the rear of the tender on No. 3096.

reference to 'Tender weatherboards for 10, 13 and 1302 class', dated 25 November 1880. No photographs of these have so far come to notice to confirm that they were ever made. Then came drawing 86.2438 for 'Weatherboard, mineral engine tenders for snowplough' along with drawings for the plough. It is known that the Hellifield snowplough engines were fitted and among these were Nos.1373 of the 1357 class and 2073 and 2074 of the 1798 class photographed at Hellifield, the former prior to 1892. In that year No.1229 was at Carlisle and this was also recorded with a back weatherboard about this time.

Later, between 1906 and 1914, formal Derby Orders were issued, which had not previously been the case, for a total of 170 engines to be equipped. There was also a corresponding new series of drawings, for 2,200, 2,350, 2,950 and 3,250 gallon tenders. The engines included ten Kirtley goods with 2,200 gallon Johnson tenders and thirty-one H boiler class 3 0-6-0s. There were more of the latter, as one Order merely specified class 2 and 3 engines, but the vast majority were class 2 Johnson 0-6-0s of all the various varieties. In most cases, the allocation of the engine concerned was noted on the orders – Buxton, Leeds, Manchester, Sheffield and Burton being prominent, but two orders for a total of seventy-four engines showed neither engines nor depots. Such details of these as are known are noted in the class chapters. During this same period a number of the single cab 0-6-0Ts were provided with double cabs for similar reasons – those at Liverpool and Kentish Town may be noted.

No Kirtley tenders are known to be fitted and the majority of the weatherboards were to tenders of engines with the standard Johnson cab. They took the general form of an engine cab with spectacles in reverse, mounted on the tender front, hence the unofficial name 'tender cab'. They varied in detail according to the tender to which they were attached, but all were higher than the Johnson engine cabs, a feature readily apparent in photographs. The shape of the weath-

erboard must have created an appalling draught when working in a forward direction, playing on the enginemen's backs. A much neater design was produced for those engines in class 3 which had long cabs. The weatherboard was the same height as the engine cab with a protruding vertical front plate.

All except the pre-1906 fitted tenders were also provided with rear footsteps and long commode handles attached to the rear end of the tender sides. Photographs show two Kirtley 890 Class 2-4-0s, Nos.130 and 138 running with back weatherboards on their tenders in late Midland days, the latter recorded on 7 October 1922. These are not mentioned in the order books and it is not known if others were fitted. When photographed again in November 1923, No.138 was running without a weatherboard.

After the 1914-18 war, ways were sought of minimising the cost of providing protection for tender-first running, so on 11 October 1919 0.5344 was issued for two sets of 'Tarpaulin protection sheets for enginemen (for trial) in lieu of back weatherboards'. One was for a 'No 2 class goods engine with short cab and new tender toolbox' and the other for a 'No 2 class goods engine G6 rebuild with 2,200 gallon tender.' A note on the order reads: 'engines 83 and 3068 fitted in lieu of these'. Then in March 1920, a further order for five was issued to be fitted to two Kirtley and two Johnson 2-4-0s Nos.34, 41, 154 and 217, plus a Kirtley goods engine No.2851. These sheets, for which a series of sketches was prepared showing the various cab/tender combinations, were deemed successful and a succession of orders for 'storm sheets' as they came to be known was issued, commencing with 0.5670 of 9 January 1922 for twenty. Having become a standard LMS fitting, formal orders ceased to be issued after 0.7571 of 7 January 1930, which covered fifty engines.

Back weatherboards appear generally to have been removed fairly quickly once the storm sheets had been brought into use, judging by the paucity of photographs of them in the LMS period. Of these, class

2F 0-6-0s Nos.3197 of Cricklewood and 3350 of Leeds are confirmed in the post-1928 LMS livery and No.3552 was noted at Cricklewood on 14 May 1931. All these were withdrawn by 1936.

The weather on the Settle-Carlisle line does not change and storm sheets are clearly ineffective to deal with snow conditions. It was therefore decided in 1928 that back weatherboards should be fitted to a number of class 4F 0-6-0s and 0.7283 of 4 December 1928 specified Nos.4000 and 4009 'urgently required for working snowploughs in the Carlisle district'. Four more Hellifield and Carlisle engines were equipped in 1934, whilst four years later a pair of Buxton class 4Fs, No.3842 and LMS-built 4382, were equipped for the same purpose.

In 1940 new snowploughs were built at Derby and Crewe and as a result a number of additional 3,500 gallon tenders were ordered to be fitted with back weatherboards. Four of these were on MR-built class 4F 0-6-0s and the others on LMS-built engines having standard tenders. Some ex-LNWR 0-8-0s were also involved. The MR engines were Nos.3877, 3955, 3960 and 4024. These were based at Kingmoor, Rowsley, Skipton and Derby for work in these same mountainous districts. Finally and surprisingly, in October 1946 Ivatt decided to fit back weatherboards to the tenders of five class 2F 0-6-0s 'at present in use in the banking arrangements at Rowsley and Peak Forest.' Job No.5467 was accordingly raised on 15 October 1946. It was extended to cover three more engines on 15 April 1948, but in the event only five were fitted and the Job was formally closed on 16 February 1951. The engines were all of the rebuilt 1357 Class and the details are noted in the relevant chapter.

2 Toolboxes

In the Kirtley and early Johnson eras, a toolbox, or more usually two, were fitted at the rear of the tender. To reach them meant climbing over the tender which was not an easy task with coal on board. The Kirtley tender with its horseshoe shape was perhaps not such a problem for the enginemen as the Johnson tender with a full width tank and front plate to surmount. The first tenders to have a toolbox at the front were those attached to the earliest of the 4-2-2 Spinners of 1887. On these it was positioned on the right hand side behind the driver.

The number of accidents to enginemen caused by climbing over tenders on the move and being struck by overbridges, eventually led to legislation to compel railway companies to fit toolboxes at the front. This legal requirement was embodied in the Railway Employment (Prevention of Accidents) Act 1900 which gave added powers to the Board of Trade to improve safety in this particular sphere. The Board of Trade of course was regarded as 'Authority' and the Midland Mandarins with their fair share of the failings of human nature were rather inclined to the view 'that if Authority requires something which costs money with no return, then there must be ways of resisting or not doing it' despite the clear benefits to the safety of staff.

However, matters came to a head with Derby Order No.2709, issued on 22 June 1904 for the work of 'altering the position of toolboxes on passenger and goods engines to meet Board of Trade requirements'. Further detail is contained in a letter of instruction issued at Derby on 25 June 1904: *'To comply with Board of Trade Regulations. Tool boxes on tenders must be arranged so that enginemen may be able to reach the contents without exposing themselves to unnecessary danger'*. Modern tenders with built in toolboxes across the front, tenders of the Singles and the Baldwin 2-6-0s, it was noted, did not require alteration. *'The standard tender on a number of goods engines will require to be altered but instead of an additional box on the tender a standard toolbox must be fitted over the left trailing splasher'*. As a result of all this, the number and position of the rectangular toolboxes on the older tenders varied; one or two placed parallel with the sides or at right angles to the tender side. Where two boxes were fitted it was often the case that one was parallel and the other at right angles. A further letter dated 7 July 1904 was received at Sheffield: *'The matter is urgent – have you sufficient smiths and how many could you turn out each week to complete the work by August 8th? Under the circumstances, all fixed toolboxes on the backs of tenders must be put out of use before August 8th 1904'*. The oracle had spoken. The point was taken and from 1902 all new tenders had toolboxes built in across the front. The new design had scalloped ends to the tender sides and was fitted to the low sided tenders on all belpaire 4-4-0s (except the first ten), Compounds Nos.2631-2635 and the first fifty new H boiler 0-6-0s which became Nos.3765-3814 in 1907. The Kirtley tenders rebuilt with 2,200 gallon tanks also had this arrangement.

From 1908 a new arrangement for the low sided tenders was produced. This incorporated a high front plate to which the tender coal rails were attached, with

the tool box or boxes built in above the access hole over the shovelling plate. This allowed better management of the coal and reduced the problem of it falling onto the footplate. The first with this layout were the 3,500 gallon tenders attached to 0-6-0s Nos.3815-34, built in January-May 1908.

The situation with the older tenders was again considered in December 1912, in respect of placing the toolboxes across the front on 2,750, 2,950, 3,250 and 3,500 gallon tenders, as in the 1908 arrangement. Yet it was 1917 before further progress was made. Second-hand 3,250 gallon tenders were used for forty-five new class 4 0-6-0s in 1917-20 and these were all rebuilt with high front plates and built in toolboxes. The work also involved altering the feed gear, from a plug cock type to a drop valve type. This was followed by a decision to modernise the 3,250 and 3,500 gallon tenders used with the G7 passenger and goods rebuilds, to the same standard as those running with the class 4 0-6-0s. 0.5293 of 17 March 1919 was the first of a series of orders issued at intervals, up to 0-7450 of 26 July 1929 which covered some 480 tenders. This last order was suspended on 6 November 1930 and the job never finished, the two types continuing in use until the last unrebuilt tender was withdrawn with No.43658 in 1963. These toolboxes were all to pattern C. Five tenders were ordered to have pattern A toolboxes and five more to pattern B were ordered in February 1918 but very few tenders other than the 3,250 gallon ones noted above have been recorded. It is believed that these ten were the only examples altered to patterns A and B. Such details as are known are referred to in the appropriate class chapters.

3 Extended Sides and Coal Plates
Towards the close of 1922 an attempt was made to further improve the front end details of the 3,250 and earlier 3,500 gallon tenders of the Johnson pattern, to bring them in line with the latest 3,500 gallon tenders on the class 4 0-6-0s. 0.5800 was duly issued on 19 October

1922, covering an initial ten engines. The work included fitting cast iron columns for brake and water pick-up and the tender sides extended forward with commode handles fitted instead of pillars. The built up platform on the tender was to be of steel instead of wood, and the work applied to tenders fitted or being fitted with built-in toolboxes. Several tenders altered in this way were put with newly rebuilt 483 Class 4-4-0s. Two more orders were issued in 1924, one for thirty tenders on G7 rebuild goods engines and a second for twenty including the 3,500 gallon tenders taken from Singles for new class 4 0-6-0s. This second order has a note indicating 'ten tenders fitted', and this is confirmed as being for the class 4s. Both orders were closed on 26 July 1926. The work was not completed with the expense, presumably, deemed not worthwhile, given the number of eligible tenders.

All went quiet until 29 July 1943 when the Mechanical and Electrical Committee considered the matter. Fairburn then issued instructions which commenced with some understatement: *'There are a number of tenders, which have not yet been altered to have extended side plates [!] and consequently there is an opening near the hand rails through which small coal falls from the footplate onto the track'*. The instructions, dated 13 September 1943, provided for spillage plates to be fitted. They continue: *'It should be clearly understood that when new tank side plates are required, these should be of the extended type to the 1922 drawing and that when these are fitted, spillage plates are not required'*. Again, there is no evidence to show that this latter course of action was in fact taken. The spillage plates consisted of small metal sheets angled at the top, fitted to the base of the tender side sheet outside the hand rail pillars. Whilst records of the tenders needing this alteration are incomplete, it was estimated that 425 3,500 gallon tenders and 713 3,250 gallon tenders required adapting. Forty-seven were still outstanding on the London Midland Region on 23 November 1953 and the Job was closed on 13 March 1958 with tender No.2558 'possibly outstanding'. It had in fact been fitted more than ten years previously!

4 Coal Rails
Fitting coal rails (or 'fenders' in official parlance) to tenders and bunkers in order to increase coal capacity was not undertaken until the 1890s. The first new tender engines to be equipped were the L class 4-4-0s Nos.2183-2202 which appeared in April 1892. Drawing 91.3561 shows rails on a 2,200 gallon tender but the first goods tenders to carry them were the 2,330 gallon examples on Nos.2023-2092 from Kitsons, which appeared in October 1891. Contemporary tank engines were also fitted and 0.1128 of 23 March 1892 required the provision of 'railings' round the bunkers of all goods and passenger tank engines (which were not fitted already) as they came into shops for repair. In this way earlier Johnson tenders were also retrospec-

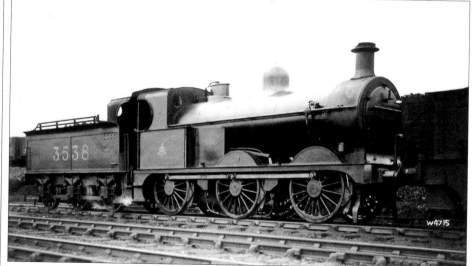

0-6-0 No. 3538 shows the weatherboard fitted to engines with long cabs i.e., the Deeley pattern. Both engine cab and weatherboard have shallow vertical flat plates, the function of which appears to have been to prevent accidental binding on curves or when in reverse. Note also the rear tender steps and handrail.

tively fitted. Two rails, flared at each end, was the usual arrangement on each tender side but there were a number of cases where the rails were taken right round the rear of the tender. Tank engines likewise usually had two rails all around the bunker but on a number of 0-4-4Ts three rails were fitted, while a few had four. These variations are discussed in the class chapters. Some of the early rails were specified as 'half-round' in section but flat bars became the standard application to all the Johnson style tenders. The Kirtley tenders were never fitted, nor the high-sided Deeley 3,500 gallon tenders in their original form. Some of those rebuilt with standard Fowler tanks from the 1930s, however, were fitted with coal rails following approval of the Mechanical and Electrical Committee on 29 January 1936. Work was suspended on the outbreak of war in 1939.

5 Frame details and hand rails

From the late Kirtley tenders onwards, tender frames had slots of various shapes and sizes cut in between the axle openings,. The standard Johnson tenders with springs below the platform had large slots with the spring hangers fitted round the opening, but from about 1908 general tender frame design was changed to provide smaller slots – spring hangers could then be attached to the frame in a position of greater strength than before.

The Deeley and rebuilt Deeley tenders of 7ft 5in width and over had the front end hand rails in line with the tender side but the 7ft 1in wide rebuilds and the final 3,500 gallon tenders built for the class 4 0-6-0s had commode handles fitted on the side. The twenty 3,500 gallon tenders rebuilt from 2,350 gallon versions also had commode handles. Johnson tenders had short pillars, the outer of which stood outside the tender width.

6 Rear hand rails and Lamp Irons

From about 1881 a horizontal hand rail was fitted on the upper half of tender backs. Drawing schedules included this item until 1897, but not after then – it is apparent from the limited photographic coverage of the rear of tenders that its provision was discontinued about that time.

Until 1902, tenders generally carried only one lamp iron for a tail lamp. It was therefore not possible to display the appropriate headcode if running tender first. The situation was resolved following the Railway Clearing House standardisation of headlamp codes in 1902. From that period, tenders were made capable of displaying codes, and 0.2818 of 24 June 1904 covered any work required: 'Lamp irons to be fitted at the back of tenders requiring them as they pass through Derby shops in accordance with photo print S.292'. This involved three irons across the buffer beam and a centrally placed upper bracket so that the appropriate codes could be displayed. The positioning of the latter bracket was the cause of some difficulty and resulted in some circulars and correspondence. This is a note from W.H. Adams, Divisional Superintendent at Derby to Pegler of

TABLE 9G - 1927   TENDER NUMBERS

CAPACITY	TENDER NUMBERS	TOTAL	ADJUSTMENTS (see below)	TENDER NUMBERS	FINAL TOTAL	NOTES
2000	83-299	217			217	
2050	343	1			1	
2200	395-634	240	-1	629	239	B
2330	692-759	68	-2	738/55	66	B
2350	763-819	57	-1	793	56	B, C
2750	1173-1227	55	-2	1202/25	53	B
2950	1385-1568	184	-1+1	1548/69	184	A, B
3250	1884-2606	723	+16		739	A, B
3500	*	436			436	

*3500 GALLON TENDER NUMBERS

2691-2861/4/6-72
2876-3004/6-3115/26-35
3176-80
3346/7/50

Tender Nos 2731/5, 2803/8 were in stock on 31.12.27, having been allocated to engines nos 700/5, 801/7 withdrawn in 1927.

1927 TENDER NUMBERS ADJUSTMENTS

A. ADDITIONAL UNALLOCATED TENDERS IN STOCK ON 31.12.27

No.	EX-ENGINE	SUBSEQUENT ALLOCATION	CAPACITY
1569	184	-	2950 GALLS
2607	352	2958	3250 GALLS
2608	354	3124	"
2609	429	2920	"
2610	431	2979	"
2611	441	3058	"
2612	467	84	"
2613	3542	3347	"
2614	3694	3346	"
2615	3732	2981	"

B. 3250 GALLON TENDERS INCORRECTLY NUMBERED IN OTHER SERIES

No.	RE-NUMBERED	DATE	ENGINES	NOTES
1548	2616	18.12.29	3161	NOTE 1
755	2617	10.1.30	3423	NOTE 2
1202	2618	10.1.30	237	"
629	-		3477	NOTE 3
738	-		3018	"
793	-		2964	"
1225	-		3527	"

NOTE 1: THIS TENDER DID NOT APPARENTLY CARRY THE NUMBER 1548 ORIGINALLY ALLOCATED IN ERROR.
NOTE 2: THE RENUMBERING DATE IS THAT OF INSTRUCTION TO RENUMBER. THE ORIGINAL TENDERS HAD BEEN BROKEN UP AND 3250 GALLON TENDERS TOOK THE NUMBERS 755 AND 1202 INITIALLY
NOTE 3: THESE TENDERS WERE NOT RENUMBERED AS NOS 2619 UPWARDS COMMENCED A NORTHERN DIVISION SERIES.

C. TENDERS REBUILT AFTER 1927 RETAINING ORIGINAL NUMBER

No.	CAPACITY	REBUILT	DATE	NOTES
808	2350GALLS	2950G	17.2.32	Vacuum fitted 27.2.32

(808 is shown as Neilson 6/76 as it was with 2997 of that date in 1927)

Millhouses in November and December 1904: *'As complaints have been made that lamps cannot be placed on the upper lamp iron on the back of tenders without climbing on top of the tenders, it has been decided to lower these so they can be reached by a man 5ft 6in (the minimum height for enginemen when standing on a bare sleeper). Be good enough to alter all the upper lamp irons to be 1ft 7in above the lamp iron resting on the buffer beam. The upper and centre bottom irons to be shortened to 6½in, the latter as there is scarcely sufficient space to lift the bottom lamp without it coming in contact with the top lamp iron'.* There were some additional reach problems with the hollow back (i.e.

Kirtley) tenders as the buffer beams projected so far out from the back of the tender, but it was eventually decided that they should conform to the standard for the sake of uniformity except where irons had already been fitted 8½in from the lower side of the coping. The toolbox saga and the Board of Trade were clearly in mind, while all this was sorted out!

7 Capacity and Number Plates

A plate carrying the company name and the number of the engine was introduced in 1874 with Johnson's new designs. Early plates carried both Old English and Serif lettering but the style was changed in 1887, to a plainer form using Sans Serif letters. A water capacity plate was not introduced until later. Drawing Schedules and so on remained blank, but drawing 92.3709 of 12 March 1892 shows a 3,250 gallon plate which was subsequently included in specification and drawing schedules, indicating its introduction in that year.

Dow (*Midland Style*, HMRS) records the size of these oval plates as 10½in x 6in. The plate which displayed the engine number showed 'MIDLAND RY. CO. DERBY' above with the appropriate date below the number. The latter displayed the words 'WATER CAPACITY' above and 'GALLONS' below the capacity figure, which was in larger type in the centre of the plate. Unfortunately, very few pre-1907 photographs show the tender rear. These oval plates became well known, but a photograph of 0-6-0 No.1930 (built December 1890) taken after 1892, clearly shows plates which are much more nearly circular. This therefore suggests some latitude in relation to contractor-built engines of the period. The two plates were fitted one above the other, centrally on the tender rear. The practice of fitting number plates continued after 1905 when the MR began painting the engine number on the tender. This in theory rendered the plates unnecessary but some are known to have been fitted with a post-1907 number. Whether all contemporary tenders had new plates made after this renumbering is not known nor when the practice was discontinued. Essery (*An Illustrated History of Midland Locomotives*) suggests it was around the time of World War I, but again photographs are lacking of the tender ends of engines in the late Midland and early LMS period.

While the practice of swopping tenders between engines was not very frequent and the tender carried the engine number there was no particular problem. The decision of the LMS to alter the position of the insignia and numbers as from late 1927, whereby the engine number was displayed on the cabside and the Company initials on the tender brought the matter into focus. Some of the pre-group companies had given tenders a separate identifying number and it was not necessary to alter them, but for those which had not and for the engines built from 1923, a tender numbering scheme was introduced.

The Chief Mechanical Engineer's Department at Derby produced a list (dated 24 January 1928) which gave a number range of 1 to 6270 in ascending order of capacity, with blanks to allow for future additions, particularly in the 3,500 gallon range. The tenders of the individual companies were slotted in to the list according to their capacity. With regard to the 3,500 gallon tenders, numbers were allocated on a Divisional basis. The majority of the Midland tenders were therefore numbered together in the Midland division series, but because a number from the 700 and 990 Class 4-4-0s had been transferred to Compounds on the Western Division by 1928, their tenders were numbered in that series. At the time the numbers were allo-

cated, nine 3,250 gallon tenders were spare. These were allocated Nos.2607-2615 when placed with fresh engines. Due to uncertainty as to the type of tender fitted in several other cases, it was subsequently found that incorrect numbers were given to seven 3,250 gallon tenders. Three of these were renumbered 2616-2618 in 1929/30 but it was not possible to renumber the other four, as No.2619 commenced a Northern Division group of higher capacity – they retained their incorrect numbers to the end. One 2,350 gallon tender, No.808, was fitted with a 2,950 gallon tank in 1932 and this also retained its number. These LMS tender number plates were rectangular, 8in x 5¾in, and showed 'LMS, No.X and date' in three lines of letters and numerals in descending order of size. They were mounted centrally on the tender back above the top lamp bracket and capacity plate.

Miscellaneous Uses

Tenders no longer required for their original purpose come into that category familiar in every sphere of human activity – 'something useful which might come in handy, so don't throw it out.' The retention and subsequent use of tender frames with new tanks has already been mentioned. Another opportunity to use spare frames arose in 1908, a consequence of the programme to replace the bogie tenders with standard six wheeled tenders. 0.3499 was issued on 26 June 1908 to utilise four bogie tender underframes from among those attached to Nos.700-709 as the basis for the large independent Hellifield ploughs. Over many years old tender frames served as trucks to move boilers around, particularly at Derby. 0.5382 of 29 January 1920 for example, covered the conversion of six Kirtley tender frames into trucks for conveying boilers between the shops at Derby. Nos.2323, 2325, 2327, 2330, 2536 and 2645 were identified. An earlier conversion using a set of early Kirtley tender frames, *circa* 1880, had been a riding van, for use with the Hellifield snowplough train. As three new tenders had been built 'for exchange' while the bogie tenders were rebuilt, the last three of the latter were available for other uses at the end of the programme. Thus the tanks from the bogie tenders attached to Nos.724, 735 and 748, were adapted for petroleum storage, under 0.5071 of 3 July 1917. Other tenders had been adapted for 'petrol' carrying the previous year, with tenders from Nos.608, 2411, 3024, 3070 and 3246 specified in an Order of 17 February 1916. The list of stock tenders at 4 December 1917 is of interest, as much for the tenders 'on hand' as for their status. From this list, shown at Table 9E, items of particular interest are three surviving Kirtley 1,600 gallon tenders and the number of Baldwin tenders retained after withdrawal of the engines. More predictable perhaps, was the use of tenders as water carriers, where difficulties in supply were experienced. This was a perennial problem at Highbridge on the S&DJR, for example, where sea water could contaminate the locomotive

water supply. When this occurred the engines suffered boiler problems so the Highbridge 'water train' was formed, of old tenders filled from a sound supply and conveyed down the branch for use when required. A succession of Kirtley and Johnson tenders were put to this use, the subject even coming before the Mechanical & Electrical Committee of the LMS on 26 June 1935. The conversion of eight more tenders, including Nos.2266 and 2599 (3,250 gallons from class 2F 0-6-0 No.3407 withdrawn in 1933 and class 4 No.3874 replaced by a Fowler tender in 1929) was authorised to replace ten previously in use.

Water softening plants built by the LMS in the 1930s needed a means of containing and conveying the resultant sludge and a wide range of pre-grouping tenders were used for this purpose. Of these, one of the ex-990 class 3,500 gallon tenders, Tender No.2809 ex-engine No.998 was noted being converted to a sludge tender at Crewe under Derby authority of 9 October 1942, for use at Eccles. It was at Bedford by November 1948.

This account of other uses does not pretend to be exhaustive, but is at least an indication of the wide range involved. Doubtless other tenders were utilised before finally being broken up, the records of which are now lost to us.

Major allocation changes and withdrawals

This general review of tenders is concluded by an outline of the main allocation changes and the tenders' eventual demise. Swopping tenders became increasingly a routine procedure and is covered in the class chapters, but more significant changes also occurred, which may be conveniently mentioned here.

The construction in the 1890s of an additional 102 3,250 gallon tenders for Kirtley 2-4-0s has already been referred to, with its resultant cascade and withdrawal of earlier Kirtley tenders. There then followed major exchanges in 1903-7 to provide, in the majority of cases, 3,250 gallon tenders for 0-6-0s rebuilt with H boilers where they had previously run with 2,200, 2,330, 2,750 or 2,950 gallon tenders. This involved over a hundred of the 1798 Class engines alone. Full details of the consequential changes appear not to have survived but the subject is further considered in the class chapters. An attempt was made in 1913 to rationalise the tender allocations on the passenger engines and an official manuscript dated December 1913, *'Tender Classification – changes required to make groups more uniform'* showed the few changes still required to complete the scheme. The main rationalisation involved the class 1 and class 2 engines up to No.522. Thus all the class 2 4-4-0 engines Nos.328-522 now had 3,250 gallon tenders, the class 1 4-4-0s 2,950 gallons and of the 2-4-0s, the Kirtley double framed engines Nos.1-22 had fifteen 2,750 gallon and seven 2,950 gallon tenders. The remaining 2-4-0s had 181 2,950 gallon and seventy-eight 3,250 gallon tenders. The principal outstanding changes required was for No.22 to swap tenders with 0-6-0 No.2928, losing a 2,350 gallon and gaining a 2,950 gallon one (with carriage warming apparatus transferred); 4-4-0 No.323 exchanged its 3,250 gallon tender with 4-2-2 No.608 to provide the 4-4-0 with a 2,950 gallon tender. This stability did not last long. Although the report notes 'The goods engines can be dealt with separately' it is clear from the 'Redistribution of Tenders' list of 16 October 1918 that the 2-4-0s had more of their 3,250 gallon tenders poached to provide tenders for the then new class 4 0-6-0s. The figures then showed thirty-two 2,750 gallon, 209 2,950 gallon and only thirty-one 3,250 gallon tenders on the 2-4-0s, reflecting their declining status.

More detail has fortunately been retained on the provision of second-hand tenders for the forty-five new class 4 0-6-0s in 1917-19. The CME's office issued a table of 'changes and probable changes to suit engines, 0.4991 and 0.5064', i.e. Nos.3837-3861, on 4 December 1917. Sources were threefold – other engines, which involved consequential changes in some cases, stock tenders and the five petroleum carrying tenders referred to above. As an example of the first category No.3852 was to receive a 3,250 gallon tender from 2-4-0 No.118, which was to have a 2,750 gallon tender from 0-6-0 No.3186. This in turn was to receive a 2,200 gallon tender from Kirtley 0-6-0 No.2541 which was to have a 2,000 gallon tender from similar engine No.2529, which would be broken up! It was not all as complex as that, but there are some fascinating trails to follow – note also the word 'probable' in the title. The known use of the Schenectady tenders does not entirely agree with the table! It was originally intended to provide fifty tenders and sources were identified, but as noted above, only forty-five 3,250 gallon tenders were taken.

When the first seventy 4-2-2 Spinners were withdrawn in the 1920s their 3,250 gallon tenders were retained and this enabled a further major cascade of older tenders. (This exercise was in part responsible for a subsequent major replacement of tenders on the same class 4 0-6-0s in the late 1940s and after, due to a combination of their age and the availability of second-hand Fowler 3,500 gallon tenders only twenty years old from

withdrawn 0-8-0s.) The availability of tender allocations for 31 December 1923 and 31 December 1927 from the *Rating of Railways* list and the 1927 *Tender Number List* respectively, clearly shows the major changes of the 1920s. During that period (1924-27) some sixty-seven 4-2-2s and 4-4-0s with 3,250 gallon tenders were withdrawn. Availability of the latter continued the 'cascade' of tenders already begun, whereby the principal effect at this time was the withdrawal of 2,350 gallon tenders from the 1142 Class, then numbered 2900-3019. These received a variety of 2,200, 2,330 and 2,950 gallon tenders from other engines which received the 3,250 gallon tenders in exchange. The 2,200 and 2,330 gallon types also declined in this period, from 229 to 218 and seventy-two to sixty-six respectively.

The withdrawal of Kirtley 0-6-0 engines and tenders reduced the 2,000 gallon total by a hundred but on the remaining Kirtley engines the 2,200/2,330 total increased by eighteen, displaced from later Johnson 0-6-0s. As noted above, over 150 frames from various withdrawn tenders were utilised for new LMS engines. Ten years on, by December 1937, the majority of the Kirtley 0-6-0s and Kirtley/Johnson 2-4-0s had been withdrawn, together with more 4-4-0s and Johnson 0-6-0s. Thus by this time, with further cascading of 3,250 gallon tenders, only one 2,000 gallon tender remained and the 2,200, 2,330, 2,350 and 2,750 gallon tenders were all reduced to very small numbers. However, examples of all except the 2,350 gallon variety survived the war.

The last three 2,200 gallon Johnson tenders stayed with the surviving Kirtley 480 Class double framed 0-6-0s Nos.22567, 22579 and 22589 until their demise in 1946, while No.22834 of the 700 Class retained its 2,000 gallon tender until the following year – it was subsequently preserved. The last 2,750 gallon tender ran with 2-4-0 No.20002 also until 1947. A study of the surviving engine and tender history cards shows that by the close of the LMS period on 31 December 1947, some 1,063 MR tenders were still in stock, of which 1,019 were of 3,250 or 3,500 gallons.

The last 2,200 rebuilt Kirtley tender remained in use until 1951, coupled with No.22630/58110, and the final 2,330 gallon tender was with Johnson 0-6-0

No.3011/58183 until December 1952. It is not possible at the time of writing to be certain about the last Deeley tender to retain an original tank but available evidence suggests that tender No.2867, removed from LMS Compound No.41062 in January 1953, was probably the last. Although reduced to thirty-five examples by the close of 1947, the last 2,950 gallon tender remained with No.22967/58148 until withdrawn in December 1963 and the last 3,250 gallon tenders accompanied the final class 3 0-6-0s until withdrawn in February 1964.

Preservation

Only three Midland and one S&DJR tenders have been preserved. The 2,000 gallon tender still retaining its horseshoe tank which was with 0-6-0 No.22834 was attached to 2-4-0 No.20002 after they were withdrawn in 1947, and remains with the latter as 158A at Butterley. A 2,950 gallon tender is with the preserved Single No.673 and a Deeley tender with a Fowler tank is with S&DJR 2-8-0 No.13808 on the West Somerset Railway. Conversely, a Deeley tender built for the S&DJR, retaining its original tank, is with the Compound No.1000 at the NRM. Further details of these tenders are given in the appropriate class chapters.

Finally, an interesting episode of temporarily borrowed tenders may be mentioned. In May 1938 several photographs were taken of various tenders attached to Stanier Jubilees Nos.5590 and 5626, for reasons which are at present unknown. On 9 May 1938, No.5590 was photographed with MR 3,250 gallon tender No.2215 from 3F No.3340, MR 3,500 gallon tender No.2752 from belpaire No.722 (this was of the low sided pattern originally fitted to 770-779) and LMS standard 3,500 gallon tender No.3907, originally on Royal Scot No.6111. Three days later, on 12 May 1938, No.5626 was photographed with three tenders, identified as 'MR early 3,500 gallon', 'Old LMS standard' and 'MR 3,250 gallon'. These are clearly the same tenders used with No.5590. After this they were returned to their rightful owners; the Tender History Card for T.2215, incidentally, does not show any changes from 1927 to the withdrawal of 43340 in late 1960. A further oddity is the note on the Engine History Card for MR 4F No.3927 which indicates 'alteration to 3,500 gallon tender to suit 5X engines' on 10 July 1937. This tender, No.3016, did not figure in the photographic episode above and a search in the Negative Register for 1937-38 does not reveal any 5x locomotives with this tender. It remained with No.3927 until that engine was withdrawn in October 1957.

No.755 at Bedford on 11 May 1935 has one of the first Deeley tenders to be rebuilt with a shorter Fowler tank. It shows the original rear steps and buffer beam retained on the first five rebuilds. This tender originally had bogies and was rebuilt with six wheels in 1909. It was transferred from engine No. 709 to 755 in September 1928 and Compound No. 1064 in 1947. It was taken out of service ten years later in 1957.

TABLE 9F - DISTRIBUTION OF TENDERS 1919, 1923, 1927, 1947

1. PASSENGER TENDERS 2750-3250 galls

ENGINES	Cl	2750				2950				3250			
		1919	1923	1927	1947	1919	1923	1927	1947	1919	1923	1927	1947
1-281	1	33	33	33		207	206	124	1	27	5	21	2
300-327	1					21	16	5				4	
328-562	2												
600-684	1									195	195	158	122
STOCK								2		69	31	1	
TOTAL		33	33	33		228	222	131	1	291	231	184	124

2. PASSENGER TENDERS 3500 galls

ENGINES	Cl	3500B				BELPAIRE				COMPOUND				NOTES
		1919	1923	1927	1947	1919	1923	1927	1947	1919	1923	1927	1947	
1-281	1			1										
328-562	2	40	40	39	38									
600-684	1	15	12											
685-694	2													A
700-779	3			1						9				
990-999	4					30	30	30	8	50	50	39	14	
1000-1044	4									10	10	6		
2299	-									45	45	45	45	
LMS Comp.										1				
STOCK												22	32	
TOTAL		55	52	41	38	30	30	30	8	1 116	11 116	4 116	91	

3. GOODS TENDERS 1600-2200 galls

ENGINES	Cl	1600				2000				2200T				NOTES
		1919	1923	1927	1947	1919	1923	1927	1947	1919	1923	1927	1947	
2300-2867	1	2				413	317	211		15	15	6		
2300-2867	2					9		6		15	15	15	4	B
STOCK						11			1					
TOTAL		2				433	317	217	1	30	30	21	4	C

4. GOODS TENDERS 2200-2750 galls

ENGINES	Cl	2200B				2330				2350				2750				NOTES
		1919	1923	1927	1947	1919	1923	1927	1947	1919	1923	1927	1947	1919	1923	1927	1947	
2290										1	1	1	1					
2300-2867	1	36	79	88		3	29	31		8	2							D
2300-2867	2		5			1	1	3		1		1			1	2		
2900-3019	2		6	29			4	12	1	120	110	48		1				
3020-3129	2	89	88	70		1	3	3		20	19	5				2		
3130-3189	2	21	9	6		5	4	4		6	4	1						
3130-3189	3													7	7	8		
3190-3764	2	82	46	20										12	8			
3190-3764	3													1	4	4		
STOCK						1	1			1	3			6	4			E
TOTAL		229	229	218		70	72	66	1	157	139	57	1	27	27	16		C

5. GOODS TENDERS 2950-3500 galls

ENGINES	Cl	2950				3250				3500B				NOTES
		1919	1923	1927	1947	1919	1923	1927	1947	1919	1923	1927	1947	
2300-2867	1													
2300-2867	2	5	5	2										
2900-3019	2		21	28			2	44						
3020-3129	2		4	4			7	38						
3130-3189	2	4	5	9		12	16	21			1			
3130-3189	3	5	2	1		5	7	7		4	4	4		
3190-3764	2	2	15	15	1	58	74	138	65		1			
3190-3764	3	15	11			352	373	331	299					
3765-3834	3									15	16	16		
3835-4026	4	2				44	45	45	43	70	70	70	63	
STOCK		5	6	1		1	2	9		21	147	147	146	F
LMS 0-6-0	4													
S&D 0-6-0								2		10	10			
TOTAL		38	44	53	33	455	511	555	519	91	236	249	239	C

NUMBER OF TENDERS BUILT

Capacity	Number
1600	313
2000	463
2200T	30 (rebuilds)
2200B	232
2330	70
2350	156
2750	60
2950	267
3250	747
3500B	290
3500Belpaire	30
3500Compound	116

TOTAL IN STOCK

Date	Number
1919	2285
1923	2289
1927	1991
1947	1063

A   <u>Nos 670-84</u>
1923-47
Fifteen 3500 gallon tenders. Two transferred to class 4 0-6-0 in 1922, ten to LMS class 4 and three to 2-4-0 no 276, 0-6-0s nos 3133 and 3642 by 1927.

B   <u>Nos 2300-2867</u>
1919
Two additional 1,600 gallon tenders nos 2502/50 not included in the totals, were in use as service vehicles.
1923
Division between class 1 and class 2 not available.
1927
2200T class tenders. Thirty were rebuilt from 2000 gallons. Twenty-one are known in the 1927 list. It is possible there were more and if so, the 2200B total would be reduced by the same amount.

C   <u>TOTALS</u>
2000 Gallons
The figure given represents the number made new. Additional 2000 gallon tenders were made by placing new 2000 gallon tanks on 1600 gallon frames – the precise number is not known.
2330 gallons
The 1923 figure of 72 is two more than the number built – possibly due to error in 'Rating of Railways' list.
1947 totals
Tender capacity of tenders on nos 22969 23016 and 3050 uncertain.

D   <u>No 2290</u>
1919
This tender was 2050 gallons rebuilt from a 2350 gallon tender. As the 2350 gallon total exceeds the number built (by one) and 2290 was built 12/19, it is possible the 1919 Table had not been adjusted.

E   <u>Stock tenders</u>
1947
Number and types not known but one 2750 gallon tender from 20002 withdrawn 1947 remained in stock until 1951. The 2000 gallon tender which was preserved with 20002 (as 158A) was shown as stock at 31.12.47.

F   <u>Nos 3835-4026</u>
1947
Three engines were running with LMS built 3500 gallon tenders, nos 3874/7, 4019.

<u>Sources</u>
1919   Derby Drawing Office table of 4 March 1920 'Distribution of Tenders on December 31st 1919'
1923   Derby Mechanical Engineers Office table of 8 January 1924 under 'Rating of Railways' showing empty weights of Engines and Tenders at 31st December 1923
1927   Derby Mechanical Engineers Department table of 24 January 1928 'Distinctive Numbers of Tenders'
1947   Calculated from Engine and Tender History Cards

<u>Glossary</u>
2200B   Johnson 2200 gallon tenders
2200T   Rebuilt Kirtley tenders
3500B   Low sided 3500 gallon tenders
Belpaire   Low sided 3500 gallon tenders built with engine nos.840-869 (750-779 in 1907)
Compound   3500 gallon tenders including those on nos.990-999, 2299 and rebuilt bogie tenders

Single No. 1868 at St. Pancras in Standard Johnson lined red livery; company initials on tender and, from 1885, crest on the driving splasher. S. Summerson collection.

A number of engines, particularly tank engines not repainted, were given 1907 numbers in Johnson brass numerals. No.1723 became 1316 in November 1907.

No. 3914 at Kentish Town about 1920. It has the insignia layout standard from 1905; crest on cab side, numerals on tender and company initials on front buffer beam. The Class 4 0-6-0s appearing after the edict of 1910 were always black. S. Summerson collection.

Chapter 10 - Livery and Insignia

'All Midland locomotive engines are to be painted with oxide of iron'

Livery

From the beginning in 1844, Kirtley adopted a dark Brunswick green livery for the engine stock and this was retained throughout his tenure of office. Two passenger specifications have survived, those for the 170 and 1070 class 2-4-0s of 1867/73. Both confirm 'Brunswick green' for these engines.

Johnson continued this colour until 1876-77, then changed to a lighter green which remained the standard until 1883. Smokeboxes were black and buffer beams were vermilion on both Kirtley and (apart from a brief early use of *green*) on Johnson engines as well. The specification for the first fifty Johnson B Class 0-6-0s and the D Class 0-4-4Ts of 1874/5 provided for green buffer planks and the contemporary C Class 0-4-4Ts built at Derby were probably painted similarly, but no evidence to confirm this has survived. This was a short-lived experiment, doubtless based on Johnson's Great Eastern experience, and vermilion then remained the standard. The shade varied slightly from one works to another, that applied by Bow works in the later days of the LMS is recalled as a particularly bright shade.

Lining varied considerably, from none at all on the earlier Kirtley engine to some very elaborate schemes on certain London district passenger engines towards the close of the 1890s. The lineaments of individual designs dictated to a degree the possibilities of lining variations and this is a subject in itself which has been explored in some depth by George Dow in *Midland Style*, HMRS 1975, and Essery and Jenkinson in *Mid-land Locomotives* Wild Swan 1984 et seq. and will therefore not be considered at great length here.

Until 1883 then, the principal engine livery was green, but before that it is clear that concern was being expressed on the cost of engine painting. On 6 September 1881, the General Purposes Committee received a report from the Chairman of the Locomotive Committee, advising that *'ten engines had been painted red and not the usual green colour in consequence of the former being less expensive to maintain'*. It was resolved not to paint any more red for the present and that the Locomotive Committee report the relative cost and maintenance of the two colours. The identity of the ten engines was not given, but Hamilton Ellis in *The Midland Railway* (Ian Allan, 1953), states that *'No.1500 is reputed to have been the first Midland engine to be painted red, a dark shade, like that of the Furness.'* Johnson reported the Locomotive Committee again on 1 November 1881: *'Mr Johnson explained that the cost of painting engines red and green is about the same. It is estimated that the oxide of iron paint – not being such a fugitive colour as green, will stand better and much longer, say at least double the time before requiring repainting'*.

The cost of engine painting for the year 1880 was £5,176 and it was estimated that if the engines should last twice as long before repainting, the probable saving after all were painted 'oxide of iron' would be £2,000-£2,500 per annum. No decision was taken, but Johnson was ordered to report further in March 1882. It was however, 18 October 1883 before the matter was considered again: *'Mr Johnson reported that the trial of engines painted with oxide of iron and green had resulted in proving the durability of the oxide of iron paint as being much greater than green. The estimated annual saving is £2,000'*. This was reported to the General Purposes Committee on the same day, whose classic Minute 4002 *'approved the recommendation of the Locomotive Committee that in future all Midland locomotive engines be painted with oxide of iron instead of green'*. This red livery, with differing ingredients as technology advanced, lasted into the final years of steam on some LMS Duchess Pacifics.

The lining style was similar to that used with the green livery but a certain degree of latitude was permitted during the late 1890s, particularly in regard to the express engines based at Kentish Town and, to a lesser extent, at Bristol and the other outstation shops. The additional embellishment and lining, coupled with the magnificent standards of maintenance and cleanliness of Kentish Town have been frequently commented on, contemporary photographs confirming the splendid appearance of these engines.

The standards of that time provided a pinnacle of locomotive appearance which was never subsequently matched and having regard to the essentially dirt producing environment of steam engine operation is still something to be marvelled at. Deeley took the view that a simpler form of lining was more appropriate in the new century – and less expensive to apply and maintain – and this was effected on new engines in the third quar-

The 0-4-4Ts and goods tank engines did not carry the crest (with the odd exception) but the large passenger 0-6-4Ts and LTS 4-6-4Ts had them, as on No. 2011 at St. Albans. The Transport Treasury.

ter of 1904. Tender lining was confined to the edge beading instead of on the panelling, Belpaire 4-4-0 No.840 of June 1904 having the Johnson style and No.843 of September 1904 the new version. Subsequently boiler lining was reduced.

A circular under Deeley's hand was sent to the outstation shops as early as 7 January 1904 and was reinforced by a letter from W.H. Adams (Divisional Locomotive Superintendent Derby) on 21 December 1904: *'Reference Mr Deeley's circular of Jan. 7th, engines and tenders recently turned out of the shops are lined in a somewhat different way from those previously turned out. It is Mr Deeley's wish that this standard be kept to and that no alteration either as regards colour, thickness of lines etc. should be made in any way'.* Thus the outstations were brought into line, the previous latitude firmly at an end. Two other economies were tried from 1904 on goods engines. Some Kirtley 0-6-0s were repainted unlined red and a number of goods engines with the steam brake only were painted a dark brown with boiler bands and splasher beading in black. These variations were discontinued after 1905 and the standard lined red livery resumed for all engines.

The first reference to black livery is a note by F.H. Clarke on 8 August 1906, to the effect that Beyer Peacock 4-4-0T No.204A was painted black. It has also been suggested that some goods engines were turned out in black about that time. The general adoption of plain black for goods engines however, resulted from one of Fowler's first actions following his appointment on 1 January 1910. In a report to the Locomotive Committee on 4 February 1910, he stated that, *'the goods engines at the present time are painted engine lake about every two years at a cost of £11 each'.* He recommended *'that in future they be painted black instead, once every four years at a cost of £13 each, which would effect an annual estimated saving of about £3,700'.* In the simple language of the time it was ordered that *'the same be agreed to'.* Thus, after twenty seven years, the 'all red' policy was at an end.

Midland ascendancy at the Grouping of 1923 meant that initial LMS policy was to retain the status quo for the inherited Midland engines, and this lasted for some five years. The Rolling Stock Committee considered the question of liveries on 31 May 1923 and after consideration, it was ordered *'that in future, the passenger engines be painted in the crimson lake colour and that the freight engines be painted black without the lining which has hitherto been adopted'.* This last proviso reflects the fact that the committee was a continuation of the LNWR Rolling Stock Committee. The LMS Board divided it into the Locomotive & Electrical and Carriage & Wagon Committees from March 1924.

In 1927, however, it was decreed that only the principal passenger engines should retain the red livery. So far as the Midland engines were concerned, only the Compounds came into this category, retaining their red livery until the aus-

terities of World War Two resulted in the application of plain black. The remaining class 1, 2 and 3 2-4-0s and 4-4-0s, along with the 0-4-4 and 0-6-4 passenger tank engines were favoured with the so called 'Intermediate' passenger livery of black with red lining. Contemporary photographic emulsions did not always record the red lining, so it is difficult to be certain in many cases if in fact the engines *were* lined. Goods engines remained plain black.

The wartime 'plain black for everything' became BR black in 1948, and after some experimentation, the LNWR style of lining, red cream and grey, was put on mixed traffic and secondary passenger classes. This was applied to the Compounds, class 2 and 3 4-4-0s and the 0-4-4Ts and, despite its origin, proved not unattractive. This lining was discontinued at Derby in March 1952, all surviving MR engines being repainted plain black at subsequent repairs, apart from No.40513, specially lined out in 1955. The three preserved passenger engines, the Kirtley 2-4-0 No.158A, the Johnson single No.673 and Compound No.1000, however, proudly carry the red livery which so marked out the Midland as 'different' in its heyday.

Insignia
In Kirtley's time the engines bore no indication of ownership and the earliest Johnson engines of 1874-75 followed suit. From 1876 however, commencing with the 6ft 6in 4-4-0s of the 1312 Class (authorised on 1 February 1876) the initials MR were carried in san serif letters 6in high on front and rear buffer beams, and this was continued until 1898. The specification for the Class R 4-4-0s, dated January 1898, however, indicated that the MR initials were to be placed on the rear of the tender tank, instead of on the buffer beam as hitherto. This practice was extended to all new and repainted engines from that year and continued in use until about 1906; after that the rear tender panels and buffer beams remained plain. The 'Princess' singles, the first of which appeared in December 1899, displayed the MR initials on the front buffer beam in slightly larger 6½in serif characters and this form was applied to the Belpaire 4-4-0s and the first Compounds when new. The sans serif version was then resumed, but serif initials reappeared in 1909-11 on some passenger engines and again in 1920-22, this time mostly on 0-6-0s – doubtless to use up existing stocks of transfers.

Displaying the company initials on tender and tank sides in serif character started with the class L 4-4-0s, authorised on 18 June 1891. They began to enter traffic in 1892 and all classes were subsequently made to conform. The practice continued until the major changes of 1905 whereby the engine number was displayed on the tender. Belpaire 4-4-0 No.859 of April 1905 was the last new engine in the 1892 style. Prior to all this, it was decided that the company's armorial device, introduced in the 1880s, should be applied to the driving wheel splashers of passenger tender engines

and it is believed that 4-4-0 No.1757 'Beatrice' of December 1886 was the first engine to carry it. This then became standard for all the passenger tender engines except the several Kirtley double framed 2-4-0 classes – on their splashers, there was insufficient space.

The change of style introduced by Deeley in 1905 involved the placing of the armorial device on the cab side sheets instead of the coupled wheel splasher and this was extended to the goods engines as adequate space was now available. The exceptions continued to be the Kirtley 2-4-0s and now the Kirtley 0-6-0s with Johnson boilers too, which could have accommodated the arms, but did not! Tank engines, with odd exceptions, were not included. This particular position was in use for just a year, from July 1905 to June 1906. A new and perhaps more familiar arms appeared in that year, Compound No.1017 being one of the first to carry it. Tank engines and Kirtley engines as before were not favoured, but when the 2000 Class tanks were introduced in April 1907 they were; the arms were carried on the bunker side. When the LTSR engines were taken into stock in 1912 the large 4-6-4Ts, but not the 4-4-2Ts, carried the arms on the cabside.

Derby continued in the LMS era belligerently turning out new engines with full MR insignia, until August 1923, the final examples being LTSR type 4-4-2Ts Nos.2110-2117 which also, unusually, carried the crest on the cabside. A few repaired engines appeared without any ownership markings during this year, pending decisions on these matters by the new company.

From about August 1923, to sketch No.S.4034 of 20 July that year, company ownership was displayed on repainted engines, both red and black, by the initials LMS in Serif characters approximately 4½in high on cab or bunker sides, widely spaced at about 18in centres. Front buffer beams were now unlettered and remained so through all subsequent livery variations. This style was short-lived and in use for about twelve months only, into mid-1924. While it is not possible to give a complete list of engines so painted, a total of fifty-six Midland engines have been identified, as noted below, and there may have been others. Engines known to have received small LMS insignia 1923-24 include:

Class	Numbers
Kirtley 2-4-0	7, 82
Johnson 2-4-0	147, 155, 201, 223,
Class 2 4-4-0 sat.	329, 335, 367, 476
Class 2 4-4-0 sup.	332, 416, 439, 482, 487, 489, 490, 497, 507, 520, 525, 530, 549, 551
Class 1 4-2-2	665
Class 3 4-4-0	723, 724
Class 4 4-4-0	1012
0-4-4T	1293, 1402
0-4-0ST	1514
Class 1 0-6-0T	1673, 1701, 1861, 1864, 1869
0-6-4T	2019, 2031
Kirtley 0-6-0	2388, 2472, 2477, 2563, 2592, 2626
Johnson class 2 0-6-0	2946, 2968, 2969, 3086, 3124, 3303, 3518, 3537
Johnson/Deeley Cl3 0-6-0	3226 3562 3805
LTS 4-4-2T	2118

That this style was an interim meas-

ure appears to be borne out by a decision at the end of 1923 to replace the insignia by the company coat of arms, 14in diameter, on the red engines and to replace the individual letters on black engines by a panel with concave corners. This was 2ft 9in long by 1ft high with a vermilion background on which the LMS initials were placed in serif characters 6in high (sketch No.S.4053 of 10 November 1923). A variation of the panel, with rounded corners, was produced at the end of 1926 to S.4178 of 4 February 1926. This was far less numerous than the first version, for another, more marked variation, was introduced at the close of 1927.

From that time, the company initials were placed on the tender or tank sides in 14in characters, (drawings dated 30 September 1927) in what became the longest-lasting style in the twenty-five years of the LMS to 1947. An interesting variation was produced in early 1936, whereby the position was retained but a new block style appeared, of shaded letters ten inches high. This was introduced at Derby on repainted MR engines in July 1936. It did not find favour and a reversion to the previous serif style was made from late 1937. A study of available History Cards for engines known to have received the 1936 pattern and the dates of their general repairs suggests that its use was discontinued from October 1937. However, the records of a number of engines known to have carried this style show no visits to Derby, or only minor repairs in the relevant period. In these cases, heavy repairs are known in October-December 1938 and December 1939-July 1940 which suggests, but cannot prove of course, that some old stocks of transfers were used up at these later dates. At all events, odd examples survived as late as 1950. Seventy-six engines have been identified as having been treated in this way and of course, there may have been others. The table below sets them out. Engines known to have received 1936 insignia include:

Class	Numbers
Class 2 sup. 4-4-0	370, 404, 407, 419, 424, 425, 454, 455, 468, 471, 525, 534, 535, 537, 549
Class 3 4-4-0	707, 725, 729, 739, 740, 741, 743, 749, 757, 759
Class 1 0-4-4T	1273, 1389, 1428, 1429
Class 1 0-6-0T	1700, 1712, 1726, 1754, 1779, 1810, 1889
Class 3 0-6-0T	7200, 7201, 7209, 7214, 7252, 7258
Kirtley class 2 0-6-0	22567, 22589, 22863
Johnson class 2 0-6-0	22901, 22904, 22924, 22965, 22982, 2990, 2994, 2995, 3049, 3130, 3150, 3156, 3173, 3343, 3543, 3554, 3691, 3726
Class 3 0-6-0	3207, 3226, 3251, 3256, 3317, 3371, 3587, 3675, 3728, 3760, 3763
Class 4 0-6-0	3932, 3947

It might be thought that the nationalisation of the railways in 1948 would have lessened the need to display ownership on the locomotives but instead of the initials BR, the full legend BRITISH RAILWAYS was displayed on tender and tanksides. For some eight months until August 1948, the lettering was applied in an unattractive block style but was

Top. 2-4-0 No. 82 in 1923, displaying the new company initials in place of the Midland crest on the cabside. Note also that the Midland practice of lettering the lamps was continued (although briefly), No. 82's right-hand lamp showing 'LMS 82 Sheffield'.

Middle. Compound 4-4-0 No. 1043 still in saturated condition at Kentish Town in 1924/5 with LMS crest on the cabside. The headlamps are now unlettered.

Bottom. A 'Liverpool' tank No. 1736, with overall cab and as rebuilt with a G5 belpaire boiler and Ross pop safety valve's in April 1927. It shows the 1926 style LMS panel with rounded corners on the bunker with LMS 'rebuilt' plate beneath. S Summerson collection

then changed to Gill Sans type of an altogether more pleasing appearance. This in turn was in use for only some twelve months and was replaced in August 1949 by the first BR lion and wheel emblem. Its application was begun by Derby Works in the week ending 20 August 1949, and Class 2 4-4-0 No.40548 was the first Midland engine to be so attired. This emblem remained in use until 1957 when it was superseded by a new design, but a couple of examples lasted on 0-4-0T No.41533 and 0-6-0T No.41804 until 1966. Derby works commenced using the new emblem in late March 1957 and this version lasted until the end of steam. By 1957 of course, Midland engines were more likely to be withdrawn than repaired, but nevertheless examples of various goods tanks and tender engines, plus some Class 2 4-4-0s, of which No.40557 was the first, received this style in their last years.

Two versions of the first emblem were produced, a left facing and right facing lion, so that it always faced forward on the engine/tender. When the second emblem was produced, it was also in two versions and was so applied up to late 1958. But from then on, only the left facing emblem was produced. The right-hand facing lion on the right-hand side of engines is heraldically incorrect, and following representations from the College of Heralds, was discontinued. Therefore preserved engines carrying BR livery with this emblem all have rear facing lions on their right-hand sides.

Numerals
Throughout the Kirtley period, numbers were generally displayed in individual brass numerals affixed to the cladding on the centre line of the boiler, below the dome. There were some variations however, particularly in the early 1870s. The Derby-built 890 Class of 1872-74 had their numerals on the leading coupled splashers and photographs of the Neilson batch of 1871, taken after Johnson chimneys had been fitted, show numerals on the cab panels. Generally, this position was not used until engines were rebuilt with Johnson boilers, though it is just possible that they were turned out new with this position, anticipating subsequent developments.

Likewise, there were variations on the 0-4-4Ts of 1869-70, discussed in greater detail in the class chapter. Engine numbers were painted on the rear tender panels. Coming from various manufacturers, the brass numerals displayed slight variations; those on some 30 Class 2-2-2s built at Derby in the 1860s were noticeably different and of slightly larger dimensions than was usual. Photographs of the Kirtley period are of course relatively sparse, so it is only practical to present a general picture and difficult to find photographs which have not previously been published.

Johnson continued the practice of using individual brass numbers but to ensure uniformity they were manufactured at Derby and supplied to outside manufacturers as required. *'Brass numbers to*

be supplied by MR and fitted by contractor' runs the specification. They were of similar size to the Kirtley version, 6½in high and on new engines were fitted on the cab side sheets or rear coupled wheel splashers. This was adopted as the standard position but the surviving Kirtley engines were not generally altered to suit until rebuilt with Johnson boilers, a process which took until 1891 to complete on the tender engines. It is however likely that there were exceptions and in any event, the 800 Class 2-4-0s retained their boilerside numbers until the major changes of 1905-7. Initially, the numbers on new passenger engines were set on a curve to match that of the rear splashers and this applied to both 2-4-0s and 4-4-0s, from the 1070 Class 2-4-0s of 1874 to the first 1400 class 2-4-0s of 1879. Thereafter the numerals were set in a straight line and the earlier engines altered to conform. Johnson dispensed with the practice of painting numbers on the rear of tenders. From 1897, the flat topped 3 was replaced by a round topped figure to render it more readily distinct from a 5, but from July 1905 a radical change was introduced whereby the engine number was displayed in painted numerals on the tender and subsequently the tankside of tank engines. Two sizes of numeral were used, 18in as standard and 14in where space was limited on the smaller engines. The last ten 'Belpaire' 4-4-0s, Nos.860-869 of July-September 1905 were the first new engines with the new style, but there was no external identity on the engine itself. This was quickly remedied by the provision of cast iron number plates fitted to the centre of the new type smokebox doors, then being introduced. These carried on the Johnson tradition by utilising the same design of numeral, now 4¼in high, on plates of various lengths to suit the number of digits. The first Deeley Compounds built from October 1905 carried the new plates, which were rapidly multiplied as engines were repainted in the new style.

The LMS did not alter this practice of tender numerals for some five years after 1923. During that time the differing maintenance regimes of the other constituent company works in regard to tender changing, as well as the need to change tenders independently of engine repairs produced the ridiculous spectacle from time to time (even on the Midland) of engines and tenders bearing different numbers. The problem was resolved from late 1927 by a decision to revert to the Johnson layout of engine number on cabside and company insignia on the tenders or tank sides In the case of Midland engines and new standard designs the smokebox door numberplates were retained as before. At first the cabside numerals were to be 10in high to drawings dated 30 November 1927 and a number of engines were repainted so. No change was made to the classification. Further drawings dated 2 April 1928 were produced showing three sizes of numeral, 10in, 12in and 14in, and it was quickly decided to use the largest size which would conveniently fit the

engine. While the need to make the numerals large enough for signalmen and others to read on passing trains is appreciated, the aesthetic effect in some cases was less than pleasing. With this change, the power classification was amended (to S.4344 also dated 2 April 1928) to include the suffix letters P or F. These and the associated painted numeral, where no classification had previously been displayed, were in 2in characters.

This standard arrangement persisted until 1947, interrupted only by the interlude of the 1936 livery style. In this case numerals were always 10in high. Coincident with this livery, a new plain style of numeral was introduced for the smokebox numberplates of new engines and for those cases where replacements were required on other engines, and this was used up to 1947. As noted earlier, the 1936 style was only applied for a short period. Some repainted engines also acquired new smokebox plates, but not all, so it is not clear whether there was an initial intention to replace these plates as a matter of course on all repainted engines or not. Be that as it may, it is clear that many engines in standard livery acquired them in due course.

BR cabside numerals were in a block style on repainted engines from January to August 1948 as with the BRITISH RAILWAYS legend, but from then on, the Gill Sans type was used in 8in high numerals. There were of course odd exceptions, particularly on class 4 0-6-0s repainted at Scottish works, where a 10in size was used. BR front numberplates on the MR engines carried plain numerals of a similar but not identical style whereby the 6 and 9 had curved-over heads/tails and the 2 was noticeably different. The design was subsequently replaced on LMS standard classes by Gill Sans numerals.

Engines not requiring a repaint at works visits (usually where intermediate or minor repairs were carried out) were generally given their new BR numbers in LMS style figures. These were a drab shade of yellow, in 10in, 12in or 14in numerals with repainted LMS initials on the tender or tankside! Clearly this style did not last long, as complete repaints were undertaken at the next General Repair or the engine was withdrawn. This practice continued until about the close of 1951, by which time engines last given 'generals' by the LMS were becoming scarce, but it did ensure survival of the company initials until late 1955, more than seven years after nationalisation.

During this period, several classes became extinct and where the last survivor still retained the LMS insignia on withdrawal, this was painted out on one side of the engine only and BR numerals and emblem were applied for official photographs. Class 3P 4-4-0 No.40726 and 0-4-0ST No.41516 were examples of this practice. For a brief period at the end of 1948, most engines in for classified repairs were given new style numerals and the 'BRITISH RAILWAYS' legend, whether repainted or not, but this new-

Top. Class 3F 0-6-0 No. 3446 with standard 1928 style10in numerals and 14in LMS letters in the early 1930s, at Carnforth, still with Ramsbottom safety valves. S Summerson collection.

Middle. At Derby up to about the end of 1951, when full repainting was not necessary at a particular repair (generally at Intermediates - termed 'Service' until January 1949 - or at Casuals) the BR number was applied even though 'LMS' on the tank or bunker might be retained. This is well illustrated by 0-6-0T No. 41713 which received a service repair in July/August 1948. Note also the home-daubed smokebox number. S Summerson collection.

Bottom. Class 2P 4-4-0 No. 40443 of Stafford shed sports the lined out livery afforded this class from 1948-52. Note the 2P painted above the number, a practice adopted at this period. S Summerson collection.

found enthusiasm of the BR era soon gave way to practical economics and the previous practice was resumed. Bow works at this period also contrived to add variety and used a distinctive handpainted style of numbering, instantly recognisable from the pointed tops to the figure 4.

NUMBERING AND RENUMBERING
The numbering of Midland engines was a complex and changing affair and it is appropriate to consider an outline of the policies adopted. During the Kirtley period, in particular, there was a considerable amount of renumbering consequent, in part, on the relatively short lives of some of the earlier engines.

1. The Kirtley Period
In May 1844, with a few odd exceptions, the engines from the three constituent companies were numbered by wheel arrangement, commencing with the passenger engines. A few gaps were left in the sequence so that, for example, the Sheffield & Rotherham engines could be included. Thus 2-2-2s commenced at 1, 0-4-2s at 60, 2-4-0s at 70, 0-6-0s at 74, 0-4-0s at 79 and 2-2-0s at 100.

This basic concept ruled for some twenty years, until the 1860s. Its drawback was that insufficient gaps were left between the various wheel arrangements to allow for future construction, further absorbed engines and changes of wheel arrangement by rebuilding, which occurred in a number of instances. This necessarily resulted in various renumberings and confusion of groupings. With hindsight, this was inevitable but at the time, the complexities which were to unfold could not be anticipated. A major renumbering took place in February 1847 to accommodate the Bristol & Birmingham Railway engines and to allow new 2-2-2 passenger engines to occupy the low numbers below 100, followed by 2-4-0s and then the 0-6-0s, from No.167. The absorbed stock then took numbers in the 230-301 range.

Five years later, in June 1852, the Locomotive Committee ordered *that a new classification of the Company's' engines be arranged by 1st July next*. Despite its wording, this is thought to be a reference to the renumbering scheme of June 1852, continuing but revising the previous numbering (classification) by type of the engine stock. The 2-2-2s were then included within the number range 1-149, the absorbed passenger engines from the 'little' North Western Railway became Nos.151-159, and 0-6-0s continued from No.165. The celebrated double framed 0-6-0s built from 1850 commenced at No.232, but the complexities were considerable.

A further, lesser, renumbering took place in May 1866 which removed the remaining low numbered 0-6-0s from the 167 series to the 530-539 group, and the NWR engines from No.151-159 to 200 onwards. Miscellaneous tank engines at that date were renumbered into the 200-239 series. This naturally brought some consequential alterations in its wake.

In the year prior to this partial renumbering scheme, engines regarded as duplicate stock began to be renumbered into the 600 series, that is to say at the end of the latest goods engines. This commenced in September 1865 but the further construction of 0-6-0s necessitated another renumbering so that surviving engines in this series at December 1866 were renumbered into the 700 series and fresh additions to duplicate stock were added to this number block.

Only seven engines received 600 series numbers, Nos.625, 632, 637, 656, 657, 659 and 699. Four became 725, 732, 737 and 757 and thirty-seven other engines were renumbered into this latter series. This short-sighted attitude to necessary renumbering continued in evidence and in September 1868, engines on the duplicate list were renumbered from 1000 to make way for further Capital stock 0-6-0s. Additions to this list brought the series up to No.1054 by April 1870. The acquisition of two Manning Wardle tanks and the Sheepbridge 0-6-0WT in November/December 1870 concluded the group at Nos.1061-1065. Again, the capital stock caught up and this time, in an effort to stay clear, the duplicate stock (commencing in January 1872) was renumbered from 2000. One further Manning Wardle H class 0-4-0ST was added as No.2066 in 1873, completing this series.

Reverting to the capital stock passenger engines, the 2-2-2s had continued to occupy the lowest numbers and from the early 1860s, new 2-4-0s were commenced, from No.50. New engines of the latter type were successively numbered up to 199, the last thirty of which, Nos.170-199, comprised the 6ft 2in 2-4-0s built in 1867 by Beyer Peacock Ltd. At this juncture, Kirtley appears to have abandoned the principle, maintained with variations since 1844, of numerical groupings by wheel arrangement, with passenger engines taking the lowest numbers and goods engines to the highest. The recurring need for renumbering, consequent on not using a sufficiently wide range of numbers, must have finally induced a change in the system, plus the fact that in 1869, the first of a series of 0-4-4Ts were turned out with condensing apparatus for the London district. Until that date, very few tank engines were in stock and of these a number were on the duplicate list. The 0-4-4T numbering therefore posed a problem.

From that date, therefore, new capital stock engines were merely numbered in sequence as they were built, whatever wheel arrangements they possessed, passenger or goods. These first six 0-4-4Ts were therefore Nos.690-695, followed by 0-6-0s Nos.696-779, 0-4-4Ts Nos.780-799, 2-4-0s Nos.800-829 and so on, so that it became completely impossible to identify wheel arrangements solely by engine numbers.

Within the general framework, renumbering was not solely confined to the major revisions referred to above. Inevitably, some engines received a whole series of numbers in Kirtley's time and more after that in some cases, whilst

changes in wheel arrangement could also provoke a renumbering. As an example, the case of 6ft 2-2-2 No.4 of February 1855 may be quoted. It was renumbered 39 in January 1862 so that No.1 class 6ft 8in 2-2-2, No.54, could be renumbered 4. Rebuilding to a 2-4-0 in December 1863 required renumbering to 163 and then from 1868 transfer to the duplicate list produced numbers 743 in June 1868, 1017 in July 1869 and 2017 in May 1873. By contrast, three of the 6ft 6in 2-2-2s Nos.67-69 built in 1848/49 contrived to retain their original numbers until broken up in 1872/73.

2. The Johnson Period

Johnson continued the later Kirtley practice of numbering new capital stock successively whatever its type or duty, and this remained his numbering policy until retirement in December 1903. Thus the last two series of capital stock engines were Nos.2751-2780, heavy 0-6-0T shunting engines and Nos.2781-2790, belpaire 4-4-0 express passenger engines all delivered in 1902. A departure was made however, with the numbering of duplicate stock. From 1874, engines placed on the duplicate list had a suffix letter 'A' added to the number. The first affected were two surviving members of the 41 class 5ft 6in 2-2-2s which had been rebuilt as 2-4-0s in 1859-61. These were renumbered 42A and 48A in December 1874 and were broken up shortly afterwards. Four of the 120 class 2-2-2s, Nos.120, 124, 126 and 128 also received an 'A' suffix at the same time. One oddity occurred in 1892. The first ten Johnson 0-4-0STs were placed on the duplicate list in February-March 1892 but three of the duplicate numbers were already occupied by 'absorbed' tank engines. These were accordingly tacked on to the end of the final Kirtley duplicate series and given an 'A' suffix for good measure. Thus Nos.1428A, 1429A and 1697A became Nos.2067A-2069A and the last survivor of these, ex-Fox Walker 0-6-0ST No.2067A, was not broken up until March 1906!

The building of new Johnson passenger engines to Revenue account resulted in many of the older surviving Kirtley passenger engines being duplicated around the turn of the century.

3. The Deeley and Fowler Period

Of the reduced output of new engines under Deeley, most were built to Revenue account, the passenger engines taking numbers in the 800-1000 series. Instead of adding the 'A' suffix to Kirtley 0-6-0s numbered in this series where necessary, the affected engines were renumbered into blanks amongst lower numbers created by the withdrawal of older engines. This further complicated the system and so a complete renumbering was undertaken. In this, Deeley reverted to Kirtley's early system of grouping classes by wheel arrangement, passenger engines first, commencing with the oldest and concluding with the goods engines with the tank engines in between. The whole operation was completed between March and December 1907. No of-

ficial list of this renumbering with dates is available, but F.H. Clarke's records entirely agree with information in the *Classification of Passenger Engines* given in the *Loading Tables* for July and October 1907 and so are accepted as authentic for all dates. The number range was as follows:

Passenger Tender Engines

2-4-0 Class 1	1-281
4-4-0 classes 1 and 2	300-562
4-2-2 classes 1 and 2	600-94
4-4-0 class 3	700-79,
	990-1034*

* subsequently class 4

Passenger Tank Engines

4-4-0T	1198-9
0-4-4T	1200-1430

Goods Tank Engines

0-4-0ST	1500-27
0-6-0T	1600-1959

Goods Tender Engines

2-6-0 class 2	2200-39
0-6-0 class 1 and 2	2300-3764
0-6-0 class 3	3765-3814

This renumbering was more successful and long-lasting than earlier schemes, for two reasons. Firstly, it was more generously laid out than any of Kirtley's schemes and so could accommodate some additional new engines without involving further renumbering and secondly, it was undertaken at a time when new construction had fallen and remained at a low level. Most new construction concerned 0-6-0s, added at the end. It was therefore not subject to quite the same pressure of the Johnson and Kirtley eras, but even so problems arose.

It may perhaps be noted that, in 1907, rebuilding of many of the Johnson 0-6-0s from class 2 to class 3 was in full swing and the opportunity could have been taken to segregate them into separate number series. This would have simplified the historians' task, but it must be remembered that rebuilding most of the class 1 4-4-0 passenger engine classes to class 2 was also in progress at this time and the intention was, with Orders already issued, to rebuild all the later 4-4-0s and 0-6-0s, so that at the end uniformity would again prevail. In the event of course, the chosen 4-4-0s were all rebuilt, but the 0-6-0s were not, which resulted in class 2 and 3 goods engines becoming and remaining numerically intermixed for many years.

Strangely, the 0-6-4Ts when built in 1907, were numbered with the goods tanks, becoming Nos.2000-2039. That this was not an error is evident from the Working Timetable Notice for August 1907 which, under the heading 'Loads for goods engines' gives *'Goods tank engines of 2000 class will convey the same loading as No.2 class goods tender engines.'* When the LTSR engines were added to stock in 1912, the passenger engines were numbered in the 2100-2179 range and the 0-6-2 goods tanks followed as Nos.2180-2193. Thus the passenger and goods tank engines became inter-mixed because there was insufficient space available after the 0-4-4T numbers. The two 0-6-0s were slotted in between the Kirtley and Johnson 0-6-0s as Nos.2898 and 2899.

The celebrity engine No. 41835, the only example of a Johnson boilered engine to survive long enough to receive the later BR emblem and, moreover, the front facing version on its right-hand side. Here it pauses when shunting at Rotherham on 15 May 1959. P H Groom

4. The LMS Period

LMS policy resulted in the Midland engines generally retaining their numbers. A few Kirtley straight framed 0-6-0s and well tanks however, were renumbered in late 1923/early 1924 to blanks in their own number series, in order to accommodate some ex-North Staffordshire engines which were assimilated into the Midland series. The LMS thus perpetuated the principles of the Midland system.

Following Stanier's arrival in 1932, it was decided that all LMS 'standard' engines were to be numbered below 10,000. Any such engines above this were therefore to be renumbered and this affected some Fowler and Stanier designs. A partial renumbering scheme was therefore drawn up in 1934 which affected some Midland and LNWR classes. This involved adding 20,000 to the existing numbers of certain engines which had the merit of retaining their earlier identity. All surviving MR 2-4-0s, Kirtley double framed 0-6-0s and Johnson 0-6-0s Nos.2900-2984 were affected, with some ninety-seven engines actually renumbered into the 20,000 series between 1934 and 1937. Two orders were issued, O.8696 covering the 2-4-0s on 15 March 1934 and then O.9341 on 14 November 1935: *'In connection with the renumbering of engines, please put work in hand for the provision of 167 smokebox door plates'*. For some reason only MR engine No.22968, renumbered previously in May 1934, was ever given a standard Johnson style smokebox numberplate (so far as is known), whilst 2-4-0 No.20002 (now preserved) and 0-6-0 No.22846 subsequently received block style numberplates. The other engines renumbered in this series thus ran without plates and frequently had handpainted numbers provided in a very untidy fashion at sheds, so they could be identified round the turntable like the others.

This scheme was extended in 1945 to make space for new post-war construction, with engines to be renumbered when necessary. The following MR engines were included – 0-4-0T Nos.1516, 1518, 1523 and 1528-1537, remaining 0-6-0Ts between 1660 and 1895 and 0-10-0 No.2290, plus remaining 2F and 3F 0-6-0s between 2985 and 3834. In addition, the ex-LTSR tanks were to be completely renumbered to Nos.1910-1978 and 1980-1993. The only engines of this group to actually be renumbered by the LMS were the sixteen class 2F 0-6-0s between 3000 and 3018, the LTSR 0-6-2Ts Nos.2180-2193 and the Lickey banker No.2290. This resulted from the construction of the new Ivatt class 4F 2-6-0s and further Fairburn 2-6-4Ts. The LTSR 4-4-2Ts were subsequently given their proposed numbers, as amended by the BR series described below.

5. The British Railways Period

In the first three or four months of the new regime, before the renumbering scheme had been finalised, repainted engines continued to carry their old numbers, with BRITISH RAILWAYS in full on the tank or tender side, plus a regional prefix letter. LMS engines were prefixed 'M' and sixteen Midland engines were so adorned in this period.

Engines which received the M prefix

Class		Numbers
2P 4-4-0		436, 536
3P 4-4-0		741
4P 4-4-0		1000
1P 0-4-4T	1365	
1F 0-6-0T	1708	
3F 0-6-0		3186, 3776
4F 0-6-0		4010, 4014, 4023
3F 0-6-0T	7203, 7205, 7226, 7238, 7242	

In the BR renumbering scheme which came into operation in March 1948, the LMS engines (with the exception of those already in the 20000 series) had 40,000 added to their numbers. The first of Ivatt's new class 2 2-6-2Ts appeared in late 1947, numbered from 1200. As it was anticipated that they would be built in quantity, their numbers potentially conflicted with the remaining MR 0-4-4Ts. The 20000 series, along with the 0-4-4Ts, were therefore allocated numbers in the 58000 series, after the Scottish pregrouping engines; this avoided any conflict with numbers allocated to the LNER engines. The opportunity was also taken to separate the MR class 2 and 3 0-6-0s by renumbering all the remaining class 2 engines into this series. As the spread of available numbers was limited, it was not possible to place engines in such a way as to readily identify their former numbers. None of the remaining 2-4-0s lasted long enough to be renumbered, but were allocated 58020-58022. The 0-4-4Ts were given the 58030-58091 series and the Lickey banker became 58100. The class 2 0-6-0s then followed in the 58110-58310 group. These numbers were then retained until the engines' final demise. All, including the ex-20000 series engines, received smokebox number plates, except for a few early withdrawals.

TABLE 11
SHED CODES

SHED NAME	1898	1911	1923	1935	1950	LATER	DATE	CLOSED	NOTES
DERBY	1	1	M1	17A	17A	16C	9.9.63	6.3.67	
Wirksworth								pre 1911	
BURTON	2	2	M2	17B	17B	16F	9.9.63	1.8.66	
Overseal		2a						1.8.64	
SALTLEY	3	3	M3	21A	21A	2E	9.9.63	6.3.67	
Bournville		3a		21B				15.2.60	
Walsall		3b						2.9.25	
Redditch		3c						1.6.64	1
Aldridge								25.4.32	
WORCESTER	4	4	M4					12.12.32	2
Bromsgrove		4a		21C	21C	85F	1.2.58	26.9.64	3
						85D	1.1.61		
Malvern		4b						14.9.31	
BRECON	5	5	M5		89B			31.12.62	4
Hereford								10.12.24	
UPPER BANK	6	6	M6	4C				4.2.63	5
Gurnos		6a						2.4.62	5
GLOUCESTER	7	7	M7	22B	22B	85E	1.2.58	10.5.64	
						85C	1.1.61		
Tewkesbury		7a						7.9.62	
Evesham		7b						14.9.31	
Dursley		7c						10.9.62	
Nailsworth								by 11.1895	
Stroud								pre 1911	
Ashchurch									
BRISTOL	8	8	M8	22A	22A	82E	1.2.58	4.10.65	
Bath		8a		22C	71G	82F	1.2.58	7.3.66	
Thornbury		8b						19.6.44	
PETERBOROUGH	9	9	M9	16B	16B	35C	13.8.50	31.1.60	
						31F	1.2.58		
LEICESTER	10	10	M10	15C	15C	15A	9.9.63	13.6.66	
Stockingford		10a						7.11.32	
Coalville		10b		17C	17C	15D	20.4.58	4.10.65	
						15E	9.9.63		
West Bridge								28.6.26	
Coventry								1904	
Rugby								2.4.09	
WIGSTON	11	11	M11					5.11.34	6
KETTERING	12	12	M12	15B	15B	15C	9.9.63	14.6.65	
WELLINGBRO'	13	13	M13	15A	15A	15B	9.9.63	13.6.66	
Northampton		13a						1.10.24	
BEDFORD	14	14	M14	15D	15D	14E	20.4.58	10.8.63	
						14C	9.9.63		
Hitchin		14a						1911-23	
Olney								1928	
CRICKLEWOOD	15	15	M15	14A	14A			14.12.64	
Hendon								1882	
St Albans				14C	14C			11.1.60	
Hemel Hempstead								pre 1911	7
KENTISH TOWN	16	16	M16	14B	14B			c.11.62	
Poplar		16a						1911-23	
TOTON	17	17	M17	18A	18A	16A	9.9.63	c.10.65	
NOTTINGHAM	18	18	M18	16A	16A	16D	9.9.63	4.4.65	
Mansfield		18a		16D	16D	16C	8.10.55	11.4.60	
Kirkby		18b		16C	16C	16B	8.10.55	3.10.66	
						16E	9.9.63		
Lincoln		18c						5.1.59	8
Southwell		18d						8.1.55	9
Newark								14.9.31	
LIVERPOOL (Brunswick)	19	19	M19					2.29	
BUXTON	20	20	M20					19.8.35	10
Rowsley		20a		17D	17D	17C	20.4.58		11
						16J	9.9.63	4.5.64	
MANCHESTER (BELLE VUE)	21	21	M21	19E	13B	26G	22.5.50	16.4.56	
						26F	8.10.55		
WESTHOUSES	22	22	M22	18B	18B	16G	9.9.63	3.10.66	
HASLAND	23	23	M23	18C	18C	16H	9.9.63	7.9.64	
STAVELEY	24	24	M24	18D	18D	41E	1.2.58	3.10.65	
Sheepbridge		24a						3.10.65	
SHEFFIELD	25	25	M25	19A	19A	41B	1.2.58	11.9.61	
Millhouses		25a		19B	19B	41C	1.2.58	1.1.62	
Canklow		25b		19C	19C	41D	1.2.58	5.65	
NORMANTON	26	26	M26	20D	20D	55E	1.1.57	2.10.67	
YORK	27	27	M27	19F				9.39	12
LEEDS	28	28	M28	20A	20A	55A	1.1.57	2.10.67	
Stourton		28a		20B	20B	55B	1.1.57	12.66	
MANNINGHAM	29	29	M29	20E	20E	55F	1.1.57	30.4.67	
Keighley		29a						18.6.62	13
Ilkley		29b						5.1.59	
SKIPTON	30	30	M30	20F	23A	20F	9.51	3.4.67	
						24G	4.3.57		
						10G	9.9.63		
Hellifield		30a		20G	23B	20G	9.51	17.6.63	
						24H	4.3.57		
Colne		30b						28.9.36	
Barnoldswick		30c						7.11	
Ingleton								12.4.54	
CARNFORTH	31	31	M31					17.12.44	
LANCASTER	32	32	M32	11C	23C	11E	9.51	17.4.66	14
						24J	4.3.57		
						10J	9.9.63		
CARLISLE	33	33	M33	12C				15.2.36	15
Appleby		33a						1911-23	
LTSR SHEDS									
PLAISTOW			M34	13A	33A			18.6.62	16
TILBURY			M35	13C	33B			18.6.62	
UPMINSTER			M36	13E				17.9.56	17
SHOEBURYNESS			M37	13D	33C			18.6.62	

Chapter 11 - Engine Shed Codes and Plates

'Derby is 17A, but in Midland days it was 1'

Introduction

Shed plates and codes were for long a vital means for staff to identify the allocation of engines. The changes and developments across the years provide much of interest and are among the many aspects of a locomotive which aid the dating of photographs. In the early days the small number of engines in stock, and their relatively restricted travels, posed no problem in knowing the allocation of each one working in or out of any given depot. There was, therefore, no need to provide any external indication on the engines. Even with the rapid expansion of the fleet, the fact that long through runs were relatively uncommon on the Midland, allied to the long-standing practice of allocating blocks of numbers to particular sheds, with infrequent transfers, meant that in the ordinary way problems did not very often arise. In addition, by the early 1880s engine headlamps had the driver's name and shed painted on them, so that difficulties were rare.

Nonetheless, there were periodic requirements for additional or special workings and the motive power to work them. It was always tempting to use somebody else's engine rather than one's own in such circumstances, to prevent shortages later on and this sort of activity was, and is! fundamental to railway operation. It was this situation which lay behind Ahron's classic tale about a Kentish Town engine in the early 1880s. Kirtley 2-4-0 No.805 was sent to Northampton on a special train when it was purloined by that depot for another spe-cial to Wigston, minus its own lamps removed by the Kentish Town driver to take home. This process was repeated by other sheds until eventually No.805 arrived at Gloucester. There it was put into a siding, its ownership not known, awaiting enquiries. Eventually of course, Kentish Town began to wonder where it was and enquiries were made to establish its whereabouts. In Ahron's picturesque description *'A circular letter to all the locomotive depots on the line resulted in the eventual discovery of No.805, grazing peacefully in the Gloucester siding.'* It was doubtless situations like this which eventually resulted in the decision to introduce an identification system for the principal sheds and means of displaying the allocation on each engine.

MR Codes

In the system introduced in 1898, the principal District sheds were numbered 1 to 33 as shown in Table 11. Oval tablets 5¼in x 3in were produced with raised sans serif numerals 1¾in high. Initially, these were fixed inside the cab on the spectacle plate. Clearly, the allocation of an engine was primarily a matter for shed staff and the inside of the cab was an appropriate place which would not affect the all important external appearance. However, a number of cases are known subsequently where the plate was fixed elsewhere. 4-4-0 No.2587 displayed a shed plate on its front buffer beam after rebuilding in 1905 and about that time 2-4-0 No.1504 and Compound No.2632 had their shed number 28 painted on the front buffer beam. About 1906, several Nottingham and Sheffield engines had the shed name painted on the front buffer beam and eight have been identified, 1907 numbers in brackets:

4-4-0s	153, 155 (494, 496), 161 (459), 1670 (486), 2424 (506)
4-2-2	2605 (689)
0-6-0s	1606 (3104), 2104 (3381)

A further variation was to position the shed plate on the outside of the spectacle plate. Examples of this were 4-2-2 No.119 (674) and 2-4-0 No.1500 (280) and after 1907, 4-2-2 No.672 and 0-6-0 No.3608. These departures from the usual arrangement are known from photographic evidence and there may well have been others. It will be noted that the majority occur in the pre-1907 period. Displaying the plate externally was clearly an advantage and from about 1909, roughly coincident with the introduction of the dished Deeley smokebox door, the plates were fitted centrally on the lower part of the smokebox door. This was to remain standard until the end of steam. An interesting oddity about 1910 was 4-2-2 No.672, which had a 3 plate on the external cab spectacle and a 10 plate on the smokebox door! Internal cab photographs are rare but a view of 0-4-0ST No.1508 clearly shows a 1 shed plate attached to the spectacle plate as late as June 1924. An official Midland list of locomotive depots dated 26 June 1911 shows the principal sheds with their numbers and also the smaller depots of each district, giving the majority an iden-

continued from opposite page

SHED NAME	1898	1911	1923	1935	1950	LATER	DATE	CLOSED	NOTES
CLC SHEDS									
BRUNSWICK	19	19	M19		13E	8E	22.5.50	11.9.61	
						27F	20.4.58		
Walton		19a		23F	13F	27E	22.5.50	15.12.63	
						8R	9.9.63		
Widnes									
(Tanhouse Lane)		19c						16.4.56	
TRAFFORD PARK		21a		19G	13A	9E	22.5.50	4.3.68	
						17F	1.1.57		
						9E	20.4.58		
Heaton Mersey		21b		19D	13C	9F	22.5.50	6.5.68	
						17E	1.1.57		
						9F	20.4.58		
Northwich		21c			13D	9G	22.5.50	4.3.68	
						8E	20.4.58		
LMS-built									
ROYSTON				20C	20C	55D	1.1.57	5.11.67	18

NOTES
1   Redditch was made a sub shed of Bromsgrove 85F on 1 February 1958.
2   On closure, Worcester engines were transferred to Bromsgrove.
3   Bromsgrove became a sub shed of Saltley on closure of Worcester.
4   Brecon became a sub shed of Upper Bank in 1935.
5   Upper Bank and Gurnos became sub sheds of Swansea W33 in 1928 and again in 1950 (as 87K).
6   Wigston - on closure its engines were transferred to Leicester. It was reopened in 1944 while Leicester was being rebuilt and finally closed on 18 April 1955.
7   Hemel Hempstead was still in use in 1897. It remained standing in 1913.
8   Lincoln MR was made a sub shed of Lincoln GN (40A) on 17 May 1953.
9   Southwell - on closure, engines transferred to Newark GN (sub to Ratford 36E). When it closed on 5 January 1959, the engines moved to Lincoln GN (40A) as Lincoln MR had closed the same day.
10   Buxton. From 2 January 1928, the LNW shed was transferred to the Midland division under Buxton MR (M20). The whole allocation was transferred to Buxton LNW in August 1934 which became in 9D in 1935. Buxton MR was then closed.
11   Rowsley. When Buxton MR closed, the engines sub shedded at Rowsley remained there and this shed became 17D under Derby.
12   York. No LMS engines were allocated after the outbreak of war in September 1939.
13   Keighley was made a sub shed of Skipton from 1932 when push-pull working was introduced on the Oxenhope branch. It reverted to a sub shed of Manningham in May 1957 consequent on boundary changes between London Midland and North Eastern regions.
14   Lancaster became 20H in 1936.
15   Carlisle Durran Hill was reopened as a servicing point in 1943 and finally closed on 2 November 1959.
16   The LTS sheds were not allocated a code until 1930; Plaistow was made a sub shed of Tilbury on 2 November 1959.
17   Upminster was made a sub shed of Plaistow in 1950.
18   M26A was allocated when the shed opened in 1932.

Class 2 4-4-0 No. 486 carrying one of the short lived plates showing a suffix in the 1920s. '21B' was Heaton Mersey.

tifying letter suffix. Thus for example, Bedford was 14 and Hitchin 14A. So far as is known no plates were made by the Midland carrying these suffix letters.

The LTSR was absorbed into the Midland system in 1912 but strangely the four sheds, Plaistow, Tilbury, Shoeburyness and Upminster, were not given identifying numbers. The MR 1914 list does not show any allocation against the LTS engines. Subsequently, Midland period transfers of MR engines to or from that line merely showed 'LTS'.

Stabling on other Company lines

The Midland stabled engines at a few sheds belonging to other companies. In a couple of cases shed numbers were allo-

cated, as at Brecon (Brecon & Merthyr) shed 5 and York (NER) shed 27. On the Cheshire Lines Committee system, the situation was more complex. Shed numbers 19 and 21 were allocated to Liverpool and Manchester respectively. At the former, the MR had its own shed at Brunswick and stabled some engines at Walton. These all carried 19 plates along with any at the MR/GC joint shed at Widnes. The MR shed at Brunswick was closed in February 1929 and the engines transferred to the GC shed while Walton, briefly 23F, was given up by the LMS from 28 September 1936. The MR engines at Trafford Park, Heaton Mersey and Northwich carried the 21 plates of Belle Vue. Some MR engines stabled at

Cornbrook, until it closed upon the opening of Trafford Park in 1895. In the 1935 scheme, Trafford Park and Heaton Mersey were given their own codes.

The MR made use of one or two other 'foreign' sheds at times and the 1911 list allocated a sub shed number to some of them. All carried the parent shed plates. These were Stoke (NSR) 2B, Cambridge (GE) 12A, Doncaster (GN) 25C, Wakefield (GC) 26A, as well as Kings Lynn (GE), Starbeck (NE), Bourne (M&GN) Sandhills (L&Y), Lower Darwen (L&Y) and Newton Heath (L&Y).

LMS Codes

On the formation of the LMS, the newly formed English 'Divisions' generally re-

Compare the shape of Midland Plate 17 (Toton) on Kirtley goods No.2692 with the 1935 style 9D plate on 4-4-0 No.448 on page 154. S. Summerson collection.

Stockingford shed, sub to Leicester, was closed in 1932 and its allocation transferred to Nuneaton LNW. Class 2F 0-6-0 No. 3726 stands outside its new shed about 1933 showing the distinctive white enamel LNW-style plate with black numeral 4 (Nuneaton). S. Summerson collection.

tained the appropriate pre-grouping shed numbering. For record purposes only, a prefix letter was used for identification – M, W, and so on but the plates remained as before. During the 1920s/early 1930s, plates were made for three Midland sheds carrying the appropriate suffix letter as shown in the MR 1911 shed list, plus the new shed at Carlton (or Royston as it was known after 1940). These were:

21B Heaton Mersey
25B Canklow
26A Carlton (Royston)
28A Stourton

G.H. Daventry recorded 0-6-0T No.1859 and Kirtley 0-6-0s Nos.2472, 2509 and 2682 as carrying 28A plates on 9 September 1926. Other examples known are a 21B plates on 4-4-0 No.486 and a 25B plate on 0-6-0T No.1863. These plates appeared to be of standard size except that on No.1863, which was rectangular with concave corners. The reason for making these few plates is unknown. They probably represent unofficial enthusiasm and initiative at one or more of the outstation repair shops such as Sheffield, Leeds or Saltley.

The transfer of a few Midland engines onto the Western Division in the late 1920s and early 1930s resulted in the engines involved, naturally enough, carrying LNW style plates. These enamel plates had black numerals on a white background as compared to the Midland pattern, which were cast iron and painted black, with raised numerals painted white. The Midland shed at Walsall closed in 1925, engines being maintained thereafter at the LNW premises. Here things were done in proper LNW fashion and 0-6-0T No.1690 was fitted with a

Western division 9 plate on the rear of the cab roof! It was photographed on 18 October 1931 so adorned but by 1934, still at Walsall, the plate was in the usual place on the smokebox door.

Carnforth LNW became W36 on 1 March 1926 and from that date, the Midland shed came under its control, the engines then carrying LNW style 36 plates in place of their Midland 31 plates. Control of the Midland engines at Brecon, Upper Bank and Gurnos passed to the Western A division in 1928 and they then carried Swansea LNW, Western 33 plates.

From 1930, several more major changes were effected. Hitherto, the ex-LNW and L&Y lines formed Western A and Western B divisions but from that year the 'L&Y division' became the Central Division. New enamel shed plates were made bearing the prefix C to distinguish them from the Western division plates. A sole Midland engine, 0-4-4T No.1343 was at Wakefield in 1933 and is therefore likely to have carried a C6 plate.

Control of the SDJR motive power was assumed by the LMS from 1 January 1930, following which the depots at Highbridge and Templecombe were allocated numbers 5 and 6 in the Midland series. In 1930 also, it was finally decided to allocate numbers to the LTS line sheds but even then, it was not straightforward. A March 1930 allocation list showed P, T, S or H as appropriate but the numbers 34-36, following the MR series were then allocated to Plaistow, Shoeburyness and Tilbury respectively. By June a number of Plaistow and Shoeburyness 4-4-2Ts were noted with their new plates. Second thoughts then prevailed to include Upminster, but instead of adding it to

the end, it was given number 36; Tilbury then became 35 and Shoeburyness 37. The new plates were in use by November 1930. When Stockingford closed on 7 November 1932 its engines were transferred to Nuneaton LNW and so exchanged their Midland 10 plates (having been a sub shed of Leicester) for the LNW 4 plates.

The use of these shed numbers between 1898 and 1934, for what were regarded as the principal sheds, resulted in a number of large depots not receiving an identifying number, their engines carrying that of the principal shed. In the allocation sections of the class chapters it is thus not possible to demonstrate this detail and this must be borne in mind. The sheds mainly involved (they all had significant numbers of engines) were Kirkby, Mansfield, Millhouses, Canklow and Stourton.

A major reorganisation of the servicing and maintenance arrangements at all LMS sheds was implemented in the 1930s under the 'Motive Power Area Locomotive Supply, Repair, Concentration and Garage Scheme' of 1933. The principal sheds of each district were provided with more extensive and sophisticated arrangements than the smaller or 'garage' sheds for carrying out routine maintenance and repair work not requiring a visit to one of the main works. As a consequence, a more complex shed number scheme was devised, whereby the principal shed was given a number and suffix letter A, the garage sheds of that district having the same number with successive letter suffixes. Thus, for example, Wellingborough became 15A, Kettering 15B, Leicester 15C and Bedford 15D. The minor sheds did not carry a separate identity. This scheme also had the merit of avoiding any possibility of

The Western Division clearly interpreted the new plates in traditional style, initially; this view of No. 448 at Shrewsbury in March 1936 shows a '9D' Buxton plate with black figures on a white background. S Summerson collection.

misunderstanding, which could have arisen before. The Western Division sheds commenced at 1A, the Midland were numbered 13A Plaistow through to 22C Bath, with the SDJR sheds at 22D and 22E. There were a few adjustments; Coalville and Rowsley became garage sheds of Derby, the former previously sub to Leicester and the latter to Buxton whilst Lancaster was given 11C in the Western Division, though it returned as 20H in 1936.

All this of course required the production of new shed plates. To accommodate the number above the letter, the shape of the plate had to be changed from the Midland design, the new version retaining the raised rim and characters in a larger oval, now 7¼in x 4⅝in. The numerals were 2in high and the suffix letters positioned underneath were 1½in height. An amusing story may be told relating to this. When the restored Midland compound No.1000 was about to be released from the paint shop in its pristine glory in 1959, the late Vic Forster was privileged to be invited to view it. Going carefully round the engine with approving nods, he came to the front to see a gleaming 17A plate upon the smokebox door. 'Get it off' was his stern demand to the astonished paint shop foreman. 'But Derby is 17A' says he. 'So it is' says Vic 'but in Midland days it was 1'. Needless to say it was 'got off' in double quick time and a 1 plate made and fitted before the engine was released. This new plate was LMS shape and therefore still not quite correct. The matter was finally resolved when a genuine MR plate was located, made

available and fitted to the engine, which carries it to this day.

BR Codes
British Railways adopted the LMS system of shed identification in its 1950 scheme, the majority of the LMS sheds initially retaining their previous identity. Regional reorganisations and the rundown of steam power subsequently produced a variety of code changes. All these are set out in Table 11. The nature of some of them, where the suffix letters became changed within a district or where sheds were absorbed into an adjoining district, mean that care is needed in the interpretation of some photographs of the BR period in the absence of a date.

Conclusion
The closure dates of several minor sheds have proved elusive and only a tentative period can be given. At the end of steam, several sheds remained open for a few months to service visiting engines after the allocation had been withdrawn or sent away. The last Midland sheds to close were Leeds and Normanton on 2 October 1967, together with Westhouses which had been specially retained for twelve months to maintain and service four tank engines loaned to Williamthorpe Colliery until that date. The LMS-built Royston shed closed one month later, on 5 November 1967.

British Railways continued the LMS system of shed coding. 0-4-4T No. 58086 is at Highbridge SDJR which was coded '71J' from February 1950 to February 1958 when, on transfer to the Western Region, it became a sub shed of Bath. S Summerson collection